Wedding of the Waters
by
Craig Carrozzi

To Mary,
I hope you enjoy this
adventure.
Best wishes
Craig Carrozzi
1/13/88

Southern Trails Publishing Co.
P.O. Box 34 - 7009
San Francisco, CA 94134

Published by:
Southern Trails Publishing Company
San Francisco, California

Copyright © 1988 by Craig Carrozzi
All rights reserved
1st Printing - 1988
2nd Printing - 1988

Library of Congress Catalog Number: 88-60526
ISBN: 0-9620286-0-6
Printed in the United States of America

Cover art: Richard F. Brown

A special thanks to Fortune Zuckerman, Fernando Arévalo, and my mother, Alice, without whose help and encouragement this book would have been much more difficult to create.

"Amazonas"

CHAPTER I

LETICIA

I awoke at daybreak to the customary gray dankness of downtown Bogotá. Without a thought I rolled out of bed and threw on my clothes. Gathering my travel gear, which consisted of one soft leather bag, I padded from my room and onto the street. A passerby gave me a funny look. And good morning to you, I thought. Slinging my bag over my shoulder, I took a last look at the Pensión Alemana; a venerable, red brick building frequented by many Peace Corps volunteers and other such poor travelers. I thought of the quixotic old lady who managed the Alemana who — as several colleagues had informed me — was a real bitch. Funny, I've never had a problem with her. In fact, she's gone out of her way to help me on more than one occasion. I wonder why? . . . Maybe I'm quixotic. Well, time to get moving.

I stepped over a particularly large chunk of buckled pavement and stood at the corner. The morning chill, with its promise of rain, sent a shiver down my spine. Good riddance to this weather. I stuck out an arm and almost immediately a creaky 1950's Chevy screeched to a stop. For a moment I hesitated, the cab looked as though it would be lucky to make it around the block. The driver reached across the seat and opened the door. His leathery wizened face smiled kindly to me. Reassured, I climbed into the front seat.

"Where to?" he asked.

"To the El Dorado Airport. I'm going to Leticia."

His eyebrows shot up and he said, "To the jungle, then!"

"To a different kind of jungle."

"Ha, ha. I know what you mean. Driving this taxi is no easy thing."

"For sure. By the way, how much are you going to charge me today?"

The driver cackled and pointed to the taxi meter. "Whatever this machine decides when we arrive at the airport. How's that?"

1

"Fine," I said, surprised and pleased. Amazing, I thought, he's charging me according to the meter without the usual pain-in-the-ass haggling. A good omen for sure. This was the first time — and also the only time — that a Bogotá cabbie charged me according to the meter without fabricating some additional charges.

For a time we fell silent, I leaned back against the worn upholstery and, as we clattered and bounced toward the airport, pondered on the myth of El Dorado; the golden land of Indian and Spanish lore. What an appropriate memorial to the brave conquistadores, who had risked such great dangers and endured much suffering in their futile quest for El Dorado, to give Bogotá's airport this name. Who would have believed that in the year 1979 more wealth (in cocaine) was passing through this airport than could have been imagined in the wildest dreams of Cortez and Pizarro. They missed the promised land. What's gold compared to a renewable resource like coke?

When we reached the airport the taxi driver kept his word. A short while later I received another pleasant surprise — my flight left right on schedule. What's going on? I thought. First the cabbie charging me a fair price and now this. Things are definitely looking good.

My companion during the three hour flight was an elderly, well-heeled Parisian woman who contradicted my accepted stereotype of French people by speaking decent English. A stereotype nurtured in me by my mother's French parents who managed to live in San Francisco for almost forty years without learning to speak even functional English. I used to communicate with them by grunting a lot and pretending I knew sign language; acquired skills that served me well when I first arrived in Colombia. Anyway, this Parisian woman seemed a nice lady. We had a pleasant conversation over our lunch of poached salmon and trimmings. A bottle of good white wine helped our discussion along.

"Yes," she expounded, as I opened a second bottle of wine, "I have wanted to see the Amazon my whole life. I shall go on a tour arranged by the Hotel Amazonas and really see the wonders of the river and the jungle. It should be exciting, no?"

"I suppose. But it sounds like a Club Med thing to me."

"You disapprove of my plan?"

"No, not at all. For you it should be fine."

"And you? What do you want to do?"

"I want to strike out on my own and have some adventures. I want to get on a boat and head deep into Brazil."

She laughed goodnaturedly. "When I was young and poor I

2

dreamed of such adventures. But now that I'm old and comfortable I prefer to see the wonders of this earth with a bottle of champagne by my side."

I nodded diplomatically and turned to look out of the window. What she says sounds good, I thought. But I wonder if champagne distorts the sight as much as beer or cane alcohol, and what kind of adventures did she have in her youth?

Actually, save for the lunch break, I spoke at sporadic intervals with the woman. My attention was diverted from her by the spectacular scenery passing below my window.

Geographically Colombia is a diverse and gorgeous country. I watched entranced as a spectrum of topographies flowed past. Shortly after takeoff we eased through a layer of clouds and the savannah of Bogotá lay spread below us, the huge city' and the cultivated fields beyond filling the bowl of the green clad mountains and brimming onto the upper slopes. . . . Minutes later the Andes dominated my eyes, etched against a dappled blue sky, arching sculpted spires towards the rising sun, a crazy quilt of towns clinging to its slopes and valleys like condor's nests. Magnificent . . . . As we continued on the clouds dissipated. The mountains fell away to what is known in Colombia as *los llanos* (the plains) — a seemingly limitless expanse of grasslands. For more than an hour the terrain swept monotonously past in shimmering humps; the sameness relieved only by an occasional village or by an oases of jungly growth that sprouts forth near any permanent water source. *Los llanos* — a deceptive land of drought and deluge; six months of bone bleaching sun; six months of soil leaching rain. Its boundless space offers the promise of bountiful production; its extreme climate provides scant yield. A land of madness for many a treasure seeker . . . . Finally the *llanos* acquired a darker, scruffier face, shooting leafy arms skyward to mesh and tangle until the earth is covered by a sea of forest green. The Amazon Jungle. A trackless mass of vegetation broken only by silvery watercourses — the veins and pathways of the immense labyrinth. . . . It won't be long now, I thought.

As the plane banked to begin its gradual descent my stomach quivered. I won't have the comfort and security of this plane much longer. Time to think about business in Leticia. I guess I should go by the Brazilian Consulate first and see about a visa. And then . . . What the hell!

"What could that be?" I asked, nudging the Frenchwoman and pointing out of the window to an immense body of water. "It looks like a lake — or an inland sea."

"Why . . . I don't know. But it might very well be the Amazon River."

"That? Nah, it's too wide to be a river. Isn't it?"

She shrugged. "It must be the Amazon. What else could it be?"

"A lake."

A moment later the pilot announced over the P.A. that we were circling over the Amazon River. I was caught with my size eleven in my mouth. Before I could say something to the woman to save face the same announcement was repeated in French and English.

"You were right," I said.

The woman smiled and said, "*C'est la vie, mon cher*," which I interpreted to mean, "Don't open your mouth unless you know what the hell you are talking about."

"I still can't believe how wide it is," I said. "Nothing I've ever read prepared me for this sight."

"*C'est magnifique!*"

"Yeah."

I turned to the window and studied the terrain below us. Evidence of civilization began to appear; charred gaps, indicative of slash-and-burn agriculture, pockmarked the jungle landscape. Other clearings, the work of lumberjacks, were left with broken stumps sitting forlornly amidst fallen timber like the bristly stubs of a five o'clock shadow. So much for my virgin rainforest, I thought.

Shortly the airport appeared. A functional, no-frill complex with all the charm of a military installation. As the plane banked slowly over one of the runways we noticed that the black top was quite cracked and weathered. The Parisian woman gasped and paled a shade more.

"My God," she said, "I don't like how the runway looks."

"You haven't flown much in Colombia?"

"This is my first trip on a Colombian plane."

"Don't worry," I said, patting her hand. "This is nothing for them. Avianca may have some of the best commercial pilots in the world."

"Yes?"

"Yeah, they have to be. . . . Listen, I've seen them land under some of the worst conditions imaginable — on top of plateaus, in narrow mountain valleys, during severe tropical lightning storms. . . . Don't worry, they're good."

"Oh, I pray you are right," she said, rubbing her hands anxiously.

"Sure, this is a piece of cake. You know, after some French company, Avianca is the oldest passenger airline in the world. And they've only lost one passenger flight in their history."

4

"Is that so? How do you know this?"

"It says so in the travel brochure."

"Oh."

"Yeah, but they're far from perfect. I hear they lose a lot of cargo planes. And the main problem I have with them is that flights are always getting delayed or cancelled."

"Yes, that would be vexing."

"Well, it used to be. Then I got used to the culture and I learned not to be concerned with trivial matters like arriving on time. Besides, I've met some very nice people while sitting around the airport waiting for a flight. You know, some drink and talk . . ."

By this time the plane was settling onto the runway. We came to a stop without incident. It was time to go. Suddenly I felt as if I had nothing in common with the Parisian woman; she would go on her orchestrated tours, I would go on to who knows what.

"Good-by," I said, rising. "Enjoy your dream . . . . But don't drink too much champagne."

"You too, *mon cher*. But be very careful."

"But not too careful," I muttered, as the crowd swept me toward the exit.

As I descended the ramp and crossed the tarmac to an open ended pavillion with a corrugated metal roof I felt the thinly veiled sun beating on my uncovered head. Within minutes, having done nothing more strenuous than walk a few hundred paces, sweat rolled down my face and soaked through my shirt. Man, this is brutal, I thought. The humidity — especially after Bogotá. It's like being in a damn greenhouse. This is gonna take some getting used to.

On reaching the pavillion I paused to consider my next move. Because Leticia straddles the frontiers of Colombia, Peru, and Brazil our flight was considered international; therefore, there was a processing line on one side of the pavillion for foreigners and a line on the other side for Colombians. Huh, now which line is for me? I wondered. I'm not Colombian but I am a legal resident . . . . I observed a handful of rifle-toting security guards stationed near the line designated for foreigners. I saw only one guard anywhere near the Colombian side. When the time comes, I thought, after I get my luggage, I'll try to get through customs on the Colombian side. Looks like less bullshit there.

By this time most of the passengers, perspiring and uncomfortable in the sultry air, had congregated in the pavillion and milled about as the baggage was brought over from the plane on a single electric cart. Once

5

the cart reached the pavillion the luggage was placed on a low metal roller and the passengers could claim their stuff. In theory it was a great system; unfortunately, a full cart carried about twenty pieces of luggage and the cargo men worked slowly — very slowly. Look at these guys, I thought. I bet they get payed by the hour. Tropical malaise. Or maybe they're pacing themselves against dehydration. Nah, it's about the same in Bogotá and it's temperate there. Oh well . . .

For ten minutes or so most of the people waited patiently and one cart load was received in an orderly manner. Then, as the second cart load seemed to delay longer than the first, I heard angry rumblings ripple through the crowd. "This is absurd," shouted a well dressed *señor* to the porters. "You cargo men should be improving with practice instead of the reverse." One of the porters gave him a sullen glance and unloaded in slow motion. The crowd edged closer to the metal roller and muttered "!*Que bárbaro*! (How ridiculous!)" and other niceties. The porters ignored them. Latin tempers began to boil.

When the cart returned from the plane for the third time several men hopped over the roller to help the porters pull luggage off the cart and place it on the roller. After a brief and feeble protest the porters accepted the aid and the cart was unloaded in the wink of an eye. Then the fun began. The following loads were taken by assault, with the crowd stampeding across the roller, snatching bags off the cart, and wandering off to customs without ever setting the baggage down. Now cries of "Wait! Let me see that bag. You have my luggage!" echoed on all sides. The situation was degenerating. Men shouted threats and made menacing gestures. Women screeched and bickered. A babble of languages. Total anarchy seemed imminent.

I looked at the nearest security guard; he was leaning on his rifle, laughing at the spectacle. The other guards were doing the same thing. Just another day at work for them, I thought.

I stayed on the periphery of the melee, chuckling along with the guards, watching the mad scramble. Just like cattle, I thought. Well, I'll sit back here and be cool. Then when my bag appears . . .

As each new load arrived and my distinctive brown leather bag failed to appear my assured complacency faded. My amusement turned to anxiety. Soon I found myself rushing the cart and searching anxiously for my bag. Where the hell is it? I thought. Have I been ripped off? Damn!

Most of the passengers had received their luggage and were straggling into queues to be checked. As I had often seen in South America, order had emerged from seeming chaos with no one the worse for the excitement. Except maybe for me, I thought, after another cart load arrived without my bag. All my clothes! All my clothes! A surge of panic rushed to my head. There were now only a handful of people waiting for baggage. I eyed the lines of passengers waiting to go through customs. No one had a bag like mine. Maybe one of the early ones nabbed my bag and is already out of the airport. Damn!

I spied one of the cargo men standing off to the side of the cart as the few remaining passengers grabbed their luggage. Since he's not working anymore maybe he can help me out, I reasoned. I approached him.

"Hi, how are you?"

He looked up and eyed me bemusedly. "Not very well. This heat and these crazy tourists."

"Yeah, well, is there much luggage left in the plane?"

"Not much. Maybe none."

"Well, I can't find my bag."

He shrugged. "One has to watch out for thieves around here."

"Thanks for telling me what I already know," I replied, and stalked off wondering if he referred to himself. "This is bullshit!"

Happily my bag appeared on the final cart load. I yanked it off the pile and carried it to a calm area away from the crowd for inspection. Some of the zippers were open and the contents of the outside pockets had been shuffled. I looked carefully. Everything was there. I heaved a sigh of relief. The Colombians are vindicated. And so am I . . . . For having the foresight to bring nothing worth stealing.

I hefted my belongings and went to the baggage inspection line. As I awaited my turn I fretted. In my one year in Colombia I had been stopped at gun point by the police and by soldiers more than two dozen times. Twice I was pulled off buses and thoroughly searched. A tribute to Colombia's problems with drugs and with revolutionary insurgents. I always passed these inspections none the worse for it but on more than a few occasions I had to do some fast talking. But why me? I wondered. Some Americans never get bothered. It must be my droopy eyelids and my slow way of talking. They think I'm stoned. Oh well, no sense getting paranoid.

I was in front of the custom's official. He looked up and gave me a cold stare. "Passport." I dropped it in his hand. The official reviewed my passport and asked me a few questions concerning my resident status.

"What business do you have in Leticia?" he asked.

"None. I've come to see the jungle."

"Watch out for the snakes."

The man gave my bag a cursory examination and passed me on with a negligent tilt of the head.

How about that, I thought. Am I slick or what? I could've gotten through with a fortune in drugs or emeralds. Of course it's easy to be cool when you know you're clean.

I walked through the gate to the road and was immediately accosted by two street urchins.

"Chu want taxi, meester?" asked the shorter of the pair as the other one made a grab for my bag.

I held tight to my luggage and eyed the boys. They were naked save for dirty bermuda shorts and looked convincingly hungry. "I don't understand that shit," I said in rapid Spanish.

They froze in their tracks and stared at me.

"Now what did you say?"

"Do you want a taxi, meester?" repeated the short one, saying only the "*meester*" in English.

"Yes." I smiled. "Like that I understand you and it is better. Of course, I need a taxi."

The boys smiled. We understood each other. The boys realized I was a gringo but not a stranger to Colombia; just as I realized they were hustling me for a living.

"Let's go," I said.

They led me a few paces down the road to a spanking new Renault taxi. I gave them a couple of pesos. The boys gawked at me as I approached the car; I had refused to let them carry my bag.

"He's all right," called the tall boy to the driver.

I got in the front seat and turned to the driver. He was a short, heavy-set black man with a perspiring face and bloodshot eyes. He regarded me listlessly. I wondered if he suffered from a hangover.

"How much to downtown Leticia?" I asked.

"What?"

I grinned and repeated the question. I suspected that he understood me but by pretending that he didn't he could make me feel foolish and intimidated. A standard ploy when dealing with foreigners and tourists.

"How much?"

"To Leticia costs $100 *pesos*, $90 *cruzeiros*, or $300 *soles*," he said. "Whatever currency you want as long as I get my money."

"$100 *pesos* is a lot," I countered, not thinking the amount exorbitant but bargaining from habit.

"Of course it's expensive. Everything in this foresaken hole is expensive." He said this without rancor, like a father explaining the sad

8

reality to his son.

"Shall we go or not?" he asked, drumming on the steering wheel with his fingers.

"All right, go ahead."

He threw the car into gear and we were off, driving in silence down a pitted, blacktop road, hemmed in on both sides by luxuriant vegetation. The man drove slowly, avoiding water filled chuck holes. The sky darkened and a few drops of rain splashed against the windshield.

"Has it been raining much?" I asked.

"Just the normal amount," he said, keeping his eyes on the road.

Whatever that is, I thought. I cast sidelong glances at the taciturn man sitting next to me. He looked straight ahead. How do I start a conversation with this guy? I wondered. He acts like I'm a spy or something.... But he's bound to know some helpful information about Leticia. I'll try again.

"You speak like *a costeño*."

Surprise flashed across the man's face. He looked at me with a glimmer of interest. "You are correct. I'm from the coast."

"From what part?"

"Santa Marta."

"Ah yeah, a beautiful place."

"In some ways."

"Well, from what you said earlier, it seems you don't like living here."

"I don't."

"If that's the case, why do you stay?"

The man stared straight ahead, at the now dusty, unpaved road, and made no reply. Maybe I shouldn't have asked such a personal question so soon, I thought. I was on the point of trying a different tack when the man said, without looking at me, "I orginally came to Leticia because of my military service. The only reason I stay is because it's simpler than going back to where I'm from."

"But surely there is something worthwhile here."

He twisted his lips. "Listen, man, almost nobody comes here because they want to — save for drug traffickers, tourists, scientists ... and fools! The rest of us are here because of the fucking circumstances of life. You understand me?"

I nodded, taken aback by his vehemence.

He eyed me. "What category do you fall under?"

"Maybe three of the four you mentioned."

9

The cabbie grunted and turned his face to the road. Well, I thought, this guy certainly doesn't work for the Leticia Chamber of Commerce. What the hell kind of a place is this? What am I getting myself into?

Our talk seemed to animate the driver. We barreled down the road now, bugs smashing against the windshield and dust sifting through the window and gritting between my teeth. A rustic collection of palm thatched wooden dwellings dotted both sides of the road. Bright colored clothes hung from lines strung between palm and platano trees. Within seconds the houses became more substantial, with white picket fences, trim lawns, and zinc roofs. Abruptly the narrow road opened onto a broad plaza lined with towering palm trees. A few dozen people sat in the shade provided by the palms — eating lunch, slapping at insects, or dozing with their backs propped against a tree trunk. The driver slowed the car and looked at me inquiringly.

"Where is the Brazilan Consulate?" I asked.

"Up ahead and to the right," he answered, waving at half of Leticia. "I tell you now, everything in Leticia is close at hand. Almost all official business is within two blocks of this plaza."

We drove half a block and he halted the cab in front of a tidy bungalow. The front lawn was hedged with an array of vivid tropical flowers.

"This is the Brazilian Consulate," he said. "But I believe it's closed until later in the afternoon. You can go and see to be sure. I'll wait."

I hopped out of the cab and tried the door. It was locked and no one responded to my knock. I returned to the car.

"You can come back after two," said the cabbie. "They should be open then."

"What time is it?"

He checked his watch, an expensive one, and said it was a little past twelve.

"It's that early!" Now what do I do? I thought. Everyone closes shop until two. I'm not hungry. Maybe I can change my money...

"Where do you want to go?" prodded the cabbie.

"Well, take me to a *casa de cambio* (money exchange)," I said. "Will they be open?"

"Probably. That's one business that usually stays open... What do you have — dollars?"

"No, *pesos*."

"What currency do you want?"

"*Cruzeiros*."

"Yes, a *casa de cambio* would be best." Without another word he

10

roared off. We turned left at the corner, sped past a military base that fronted the plaza, and stopped behind a row of parked taxis on the next block.

"Downtown Leticia," intoned the driver, pointing to the opposite side of the street at a less than imposing jumble of cafés, travel agencies, and small business establishments. "Over there you will find several *casas de cambio*."

"Many thanks," I said, handing him a crumpled $100 *peso* note plus another $10 for a tip.

"What's the $10 for?" he asked.

"For your frank commentary."

He gave a short laugh and turned to walk away. Then he wheeled and gave me a sharp look. "Be careful, man. There are many opportunists in this city."

"Thanks, man. But don't worry. I used to live in Los Angeles . . . not to mention Bogotá and San Francisco."

"All right, brother, but this is a different trip."

A wry smile played on my lips as I watched the cabbie move off and join into laughing conversation with some fellow drivers farther down the street. Opportunists, eh, I mused. But how could he know? To me that's just another word for pragmatists. And aren't I from that great land of opportunity . . . and pragmatists?

I crossed the street and entered the first *casa de cambio* I saw. I was met near the door by a balding man with a winning smile. He took me by the elbow before I could say a word and ushered me past two pretty secretaries and to a seat under the cooling breeze of an overhead fan. He faced me across his wide desk and we exchanged pleasantries; he complimented my Spanish and I complimented his choice of such pretty secretaries. One of the women heard my remark and blushed appreciatively. From the papers on her desk I deduced that she also worked as a travel agent and tour guide. She gave me an inviting smile. Maybe a hustle, I thought. Get your mind back on the business at hand. I turned to the man.

"I want to exchange my *pesos* for *cruzeiros*."

The man's eyelids drooped and his eager smile faded. "You don't have any dollars?"

"Sorry but no. I live in Colombia."

"Ah, too bad."

"But I do have $20,000 *pesos* to exchange. What is your rate of exchange?"

"I can give you $90 *cruzeiros* for each $100 *pesos*."

That sounds about right, I thought. It's even a bit better than the rate they gave me at the Brazilian Embassy in Bogotá.

"That seems fairly reasonable," I said.

"Of course it is! You can't find a better rate here . . . . When are you going to Brazil?"

"As soon as possible."

"You have chosen a good time to travel there. The *cruzeiro* was just recently devalued and prices have not been adjusted yet."

"That's good. But why was it devalued?"

"Because Brazil has a terrible inflation rate. They have to buy too much of their oil from the Arabs." He finished with a smile, apparently pleased at the Brazilian's predicament.

"Well, whatever. What I gain in the devaluation is lost for travelling at Christmas time."

"That's certain."

"Let's make the exchange, then."

I stood up to remove my belt, which contained a zippered inside lining for secreting money and documents; a useful gift from my friend Matt. I took off the belt.

"*Ay, Dios mio!*" gasped my friendly secretary.

I turned and winked at her. "Don't worry, I'm not going to lose my pants."

I extracted a thick wad of *peso* notes from the belt and laid them on the desk. Sitting in a pile it looked like a good amount of cash but there was no bill over $200 *pesos*. A glance behind me revealed that my friendly secretary was gazing saucer-eyed at the money.

"That is a fine money belt," commented the exchange man, with an appraising air. "But I don't believe the new bills will fit."

I had no idea what he meant until he handed me a $500 *cruzeiro* note. It was almost toilet paper thin but considerably larger than the Colombian bills.

"Huh, they look like checks," I said.

"Yes, it's strange money. But how will you fit them into your belt?"

"That is no problem," I said. "Watch." I folded the bills in half and stuffed what would fit into the lining of the belt; the rest I put into assorted pant's and shirt pockets. "There, you see. I never carry all my money in one place anyway."

"Good idea around here."

"I was thinking, maybe I should save $5000 in *pesos* for when I return to Colombia . . . . What do you think?"

The man chuckled. "That doesn't help my business but it's

12

probably a good idea. In most parts of Brazil you could only get one *peso* for two *cruzeiros* — if anyone would exchange at all. In Colombia it would be the reverse. Only in Leticia, and the Brazilian town of Tabatinga, can you get close to equitable value." The man shrugged. "Of course, if you had dollars or German marks, it would be a different matter and you wouldn't have a problem anywhere."

"I don't worry about what I don't have . . . . But thanks for your help." I rose.

"My pleasure, sir. And remember, if you find any dollars send them my way. Have a good trip."

"Good-bye," I said, as I approached the pretty secretary.

"Why good-bye?" she asked. "Don't you like Leticia?"

"I don't know. I just arrived."

"Why don't you stay for awhile? We have some excellent jungle tours with expert guides."

She's wearing enough gold to start a jewelry store, I thought. Two necklaces, six rings, two bracelets, earrings. She's white. Maybe from Medellin. I bet she'd be expensive.

"How much for a jungle tour?" I asked.

"$4000 *pesos*. Only one hundred dollars for a three day tour — staying overnight in a genuine Indian village.

"That's too much for me. But thanks for the information."

Well, all right. But if you change your mind, *a la orden* (at your service) for any little thing." She finished with a coquettish smile.

I left the *casa de cambio* and meandered up and down the one main street of the central tourist section. I saw a gaudy melange of sidewalk cafés, tourist information centers, travel agencies, souvenir shops, and expensive — for me — hotels. I walked among roving street vendors who were hawking supposedly authentic Indian artifacts. I dodged around glaze-eyed tourists with top-of-the-line cameras. After ten minutes of this I felt exhausted. The muggy air filled my lungs with lead and my bag seemed to have increased threefold in weight. Hell with this, I thought. Time for a few beers. . . . A moment to catch my bearings and adjust to this climate.

I took a seat at the first open-air café in my path and dumped my bag under the marble topped table. My cotton shirt was sweat soaked and clung to my skin, I smelled ripe. Oh, for a cool shower, I thought. The waiter came, dropped a menu on the table; and left before I could order a beer. Irritated, I glanced up to give him a dirty look and almost burned out my retinas. A fierce sun had perforated a hitherto protective layer of clouds. With little black dots dancing in my eyes, I looked at the table and silently cursed the waiter. When I recovered my vision I shifted my attention to the people in the café. There were only a handful of customers, most of them tourists judging from their European features. They were besieged by a steady flow of street merchants. Some of the trinkets on display were colorful knit shawls, wooden knives, plastic hammocks, and toy bows and arrows. Yeah, genuine Indian artifacts, I thought. There seems to be more vendors than tourisits . . . . Beneath Leticia's laid-back front there's frantic competition for the tourist dollar. I bet you can buy almost anything here . . . or anyone. And it would sure be a lot cheaper than in the States.

I glanced at the menu. A beer cost $18 *pesos*, or a third more than what I paid in other parts of Colombia, and the meal prices were correspondingly steep. Man, this is like being in Fisherman's Wharf, I thought. This part of town will definitely not be my hangout of preference.

I pulled out a pen and began doodling on a paper napkin. Let's see . . . . $20,000 *pesos* = $500 dollars. Minus $5000 *pesos* in reserve. $15,000 *pesos* = $13,500 *cruzeiros*. Cost of transportation to and from Manaus = X . . . . Maybe $100 dollars or so by boat. But wait, eventually I have to get back to Bogotá. There's no road so I can't hitchhike . . . . Another flight. Then there's food, lodging, and entertainment . . . . How can I make this last a month? Give up drinking? This is going to be very interesting . . .

The waiter returned, interrupting my calculations. He looked askance at the messy napkin. I ordered an ice cold beer. When he brought the beer over I made him wait for his money while I took a deep draught. It was ice cold.

"Excuse me, *señor*," I said, "why is everything so expensive here?"

"Expensive?" He arched his eyebrows. "It is not that expensive for a . . ."

Gringo with dollars, I thought.

"It is expensive compared to the rest of Colombia," I said.

"Where are you from?"

"I live near Bucaramanga."

"Ah, you live in Colombia. Well, you have to understand that Leticia is very isolated and many things have to be flown in at great expense."

"That makes sense . . . . But tell me, do you know where I can find a cheap hotel or *pensión*?"

"Of course, sir. Right down this street you can find several with very reasonable rates."

"I already checked those. For me they're not that reasonable."

The waiter gave me an almost contemptuous look. "Well, I'm referring to decent places."

"All right, man," I said, regarding him cooly. "Thanks for the information."

"Always at your order." He walked away stiff-backed.

So much for his credibility, I thought. I guess we just have different concepts about what cheap means. At any rate I got to get away from this part of town.

I drank a second beer and watched the people circulate. The rest and the beer refreshed me. The alcohol gave me a fuzzy optimism. It's time to stop thinking and follow my instincts.

I tossed my bag over my shoulder and wandered up the street in the general direction of the plaza. On the corner, across from the military base, stood a young boy selling hammocks. As I came abreast of him I nodded and smiled.

"Hey, meester."

I turned to face the boy. He struck a fawning pose, teeth shining from his mahogany colored complexion and his dark eyes glittering with anticipation.

"What do you want?" I asked.

"You want to buy a beautiful native hammock, meester?"

I shrugged. "Who knows. Let's have a look."

At first I glanced over his stock of hammocks, not really interested in buying one. Then I examined them closely; the hammocks were made of fine natural fibers. They were rainbow striped and the fabric was strong and tightly woven.

"They are good," I murmured.

The boy smiled and tapped his right foot. "Only $800 *pesos.* $20 dollars."

"They are very beautiful," I said. "And maybe worth what you are asking. But I don't have much money. What I really need is a cheap hotel or *pensión.* Can you tell me where one is?"

The boy's smile vanished and was replaced by a grimace. "Over there!" he spat, pointing toward the Hotel Amazonas — by far the most expensive place in town.

"Very funny, brother. But I can't afford that."

"Why not?" He put his hands on his hips and eyed me. "You look like a rich one to me."

I snickered. Damn this little bastard, I thought, I'm tired of these wrong stereotypes.

"Look, *manito*, (little brother) you've got a lot to learn," I said. "If I were rich would I be carrying my own bag and sweating like a pig?"

"Who knows? Maybe you are one of the many stingy gringos ."

"Maybe. Or maybe I'm not as rich as you think. There are poor people in the United States and Europe."

"I doubt that . . . . But," he continued, his taut facial muscles relaxing a bit, "if what you say is true . . . that you aren't lying to me, there is a hotel called La Villa."

"Where?"

"It's two blocks straight ahead and to the right. It's for nationals."

"How much?"

"$130 *pesos* a night. It isn't elegant, but it's clean and very safe."

"Thanks, *manito*. I'll remember you for this."

"If you want to thank me buy a hammock."

"I can't right now."

"You could."

"You know," I said, irritated by his manner, "you might have more success selling the hammocks if you weren't so rude."

"Why shouldn't I be rude?" he sneered. Then he gave me an insolent grin, as if to say, what kind of fucking idiot are you?

"All right, man, stay cool."

I turned and walked in the direction the boy had indicated, reflecting ruefully on his parting words. "Why shouldn't I be rude?" The cynical little punk almost upset me. But at least he gave me the information I wanted . . . . I hope. If he wasn't bullshitting me. Damn. He's so similar to the boys I work with in the correctional. A *Gamin*. Ancient before his time. Streetwise and cunning. He'll make a good businessman if someone doesn't kill him first . . .

A block from the main tourist drag the streets were unpaved and muddy, with great ruts eroded along the flanks. Wooden sidewalks, as if from a town of the "old west," were elevated above the muck and featured serviceable hitching posts for horses. Here hard faced men with machetes sheathed to their thighs strode to and fro, peering from beneath the rims of their straw hats. Gunslinger eyes, I thought. They look like some mean customers.

I ran into a gauntlet of small variety shops offering all manner of souvenirs. I was bombarded by attendants with cries of *a la orden*. I ignored them. Sorry. All I want is a place, almost any place will do, to strip off my stanky clothes and store this bag.

I turned the corner and the souvenir shops were replaced by rustic wooden residences with corrugated roofs. I covered the length of the street without finding the hotel. It should be here, I thought. I covered the next street. Nothing. I wondered if the boy had indeed burned me. I tried the following street. Nothing, not even an expensive hotel. Why that little punk, if I see him again . . .

I retraced my steps, walking along the opposite side of the street. This time, on the street the boy had mentioned, I encountered a nondescript building with a peaked metal roof. A small sign beside the entrance bore the inscription, Pensión La Villa. Well, I thought, he was telling the truth. Sorry, kid. I must have been in a daze. Maybe I should worry more about myself.

I scrutinized the exterior of the *pensión* and chuckled aloud. The owner must be a very enterprising and audacious person to name this sorry looking dump, La Villa. Still, I better go in and check it out. Can't forget that hotel in Cali . . . it looked a lot scuzzier than this and it was fine. Good people.

Smiling at my last thought, I bounded up a worn front stoop, pushed open the door, and entered a narrow gloomy foyer with a tile floor. It smelled vaguely of *aguardiente* (cane alcohol). I paused near the doorway, letting my eyes adjust to the change in light, and heard a chair scrape on the floor off to my right.

"At your service, young man."

I stepped forward, squinting, and finally spotted an obese, middle-aged woman. She was dressed in a colorful print gown; her bulk reclined like gelatin in a lounge chair. Startled by the apparition I remained tongue-tied.

She eyed me, curiosity apparent on her pleasant face, and asked me in slow precise Spanish, "You want a room, *mono* (literally monkey; but in Colombia a blond person)?"

I nodded assent.

"Alvaro," she bellowed, her voice like a bullhorn. "Come! Come! . . . There is a guest here." She smiled at me, flashing a gold eyetooth. "He's on the way."

Within seconds, entering the hallway from the rear door, came a trim young man with straight black hair and frank, Iberian features. He advanced leisurely and motioned for me to come forward and meet him at the desk near the end of the hallway. As I did so, he took a seat, selected a sign-in sheet from the top, desk drawer, and with pen poised he gazed at me.

"I would like a room for the night," I said in my most impeccable Spanish.

His dark eyes stared uncomprehendingly; a sardonic grin split his lips. "You . . . want . . . a . . . room . . . for . . . the . . . night?" he asked. "It . . . . costs . . . $150 . . . *pesos* . . . . You . . . pay . . . now. . . .Understand?"

The blood rushed to my face and my eyes slitted. "I understand very well what you said. And you don't have to speak to me as though I just got off the boat!"

Alvaro was initially taken aback, then a different sort of smile came to his face.

I'm tired of these people playing with my mind all the time because they can't conceive of a gringo speaking Spanish well, I thought.

"You speak *el castellano* (Spanish) pretty well," said Alvaro. "Where did you learn?"

"I have lived in Colombia for over a year. Besides this, I studied it in school and I grew up in a *latino* neighborhood in the United States."

"Americano," he muttered, shaking his head. "How strange . . . . Well, I'm sorry if I offended you."

"That's all right, man, in California they call South Americans, Mexicans."

"Who does?"

"Ignorant people."

"Oh . . . . What is your name?"

"Carrozzi. Crai . . . uh, Gregorio Carrozzi."

"Carrrrozzi," he intoned, rolling the double r as though he were a soccer broadcaster. "That is an Italian name, certain?"

"One of my grandfathers was Italian, yes."

"Ah yes, *italiano*." Alvaro nodded sagely. "That is why you speak Spanish well; you have Latin blood in your veins. For that, you are *latino*."

I stifled a chuckle. "Whatever you say, man."

Alvaro gave me a hard look. "You don't believe in that?"

"Look, man, my other grandparents were French . . . . I took two years of French in high school and didn't learn a damn thing. I learned Spanish well from necessity . . . . Nobody speaks English where I live right now."

"Yes, well . . ."

"And what you said about be being Latin . . . I remember a time in my neighborhood when a blond haired, blue eyed Mexican called me a fucking white son-of-a-bitch. You can imagine what some of the dark skinned people called me."

"That is absurd," said Alvaro. "As you said earlier, ignorant people."

18

"Well, it's more than that. Ethnically and culturally your country is more homogeneous than mine . . . . Especially where I grew up, San Francisco, we have people from almost every country in the world. Sometimes it takes a few generations for the new ways to take hold. Some groups and individuals still aren't fully integrated into the culture."

"It sounds crazy."

"A little bit," I said, smiling. "But people are still people."

"Where do you live now?"

"Well, I spend about half my time in Piedecuesta and the rest in Bucaramanga."

"Bucaramanga de Santander?"

"Yes."

"I come from Tolima," said Alvaro, smiling broadly, "But I know Santander . . . . And the people there are very similar to the people of Tolima."

"I have heard that."

"Yes, it's true. And brother, the women of Bucaramanga are so beautiful!" Alvaro released a profound sigh. "They have the finest asses in all Colombia. When I was there I fell in love with a different woman almost every week."

"Yes, there are some real beauties there."

"Are you acquainted with Tolima?"

"Yes, a little bit. I've been to Ibague and this resort town called Melgar."

"What did you think of it?"

"It's very pretty countryside and my head was turning like crazy with so many gorgeous women passing on all sides."

"I am *ibagueño*. What a coincidence, no?"

"*La verraquera, mano* (something like: far out, brother)!"

Alvaro guffawed, almost toppling from his chair.

Nothing like using a little slang and complimenting the women of a Colombian man's city to make him feel comfortable with you, I thought.

"You know *verraquera*," said Alvaro. "I don't believe it. You are a strange gringo."

"Thanks." I guess he meant that as a compliment, I thought. One thing for sure, I've made an impression on him.

We returned our attention to the sign-in sheet.

"Why are you in Leticia?" asked Alvaro. "And for how long do you plan to stay?"

"Well, actually I plan on going to Manaus if I can find a boat to take me there within the next few days.... So, I could be leaving tomorrow, or the day after tomorrow, or the day after that. I can't tell you exactly."

"Why do you want to go to Manaus?"

Now why should I tell this guy? I thought. Damn he's nosey! ... But then again, I kind of like his forthright manner. What the hell, maybe he can give me some useful information.

"Did you hear me?" asked Alvaro. "Why do you want to go to Manaus so bad?"

"I'm going because I want to take a voyage down the Amazon River; if I had more time I would go to Belém. And also, I've been studying Portuguese and I need a practical opportunity to learn and practice more."

"Portuguese." Alvaro gritted his teeth. "That is an ugly tongue.... To me it sounds like a pack of monkeys chattering away in the trees."

"I think it sounds beautiful in music."

"More or less. But I tell you something — if you really want to learn that tongue — it should not be difficult since it is nothing but Spanish very badly spoken."

"Do you speak Portuguese?"

Alvaro winced as if he had taken a shot of vinegar.

"Of course I can understand it," he said. "But I hate to speak it.... You know why?"

"I can't imagine."

"Because, except for the soldiers and the military base, one would never believe that Leticia belongs to Colombia."

"How's that?"

"How? The television is in Portuguese. Most of the radio stations are in Portuguese. And there are more people here who speak Brazilian than Spanish. It's the shits!"

"Sounds like a cultural invasion."

"Exactly. And also a physical one."

"What?"

"The Brazilians have been doing this for centuries. What they do is send in settlers to sparsely populated areas. Border areas with poorly defined limits. The settlers have large families — they reproduce like rats. But it is a gradual process. And then, before anyone realizes what has happened, there are more of them than of us. I tell you, we have lost plenty of land in Amazonas because of this illegal occupation — and so

20

have the Peruvians and the Bolivians. But," Alvaro gave an eloquent shrug, "what can one do? We are virtually abandoned by the central government."

"Well, I don't know anything about all that . . . . But what about the Peruvians? Aren't there a lot of Peruvians in Leticia?"

"Of course there are. And they steal our fish from the Amazon. But at least they speak Spanish. Although," Alvaro smiled, "the manner in which they speak resembles a singing jungle parrot."

I shook my head and chuckled. This is Latin American brotherhood, I thought. I bet Alvaro would make a great U.N. delegate . . . or OPEC minister from the Middle East. I can hear him now: Yes, we're all Moslem brothers as long as we get to fix our own profit margin. Otherwise, you're all fucking heretics and Allah will smite you! Not to mention Yahweh . . . . I can't wait to hear what the Peruvians and the Brazilians have to say about the Colombians.

Our conversation reverted to the sign-in sheet and we made excellent progress. Then Alvaro asked me my nationality.

"I am North American."

Alvaro winked at me. "I'm going to write that you're Colombian."

"Why?"

"Well, you have a funny accent but I like the way you talk . . . . So, you are Colombian and receive a discount of $20 *pesos* a day. That's a special rate for nationals."

"All right, I won't argue with that." I pulled out my wallet and started to pay him on the spot.

Alvaro waved the money away with a careless flourish. "Between friends there is no problem. You pay me whenever you want." He reached into the right top desk drawer. "You have room 9. Here is your key."

"Thanks. I'm feeling tired."

"For nothing. Go ahead and get some rest. I'll see you later."

"All right, later," I said, and hefting my bag, passed from the gloomy hallway through a narrow entranceway and into a brilliantly lit patio. I looked up and was blinded by the bright sunlight flooding through a poorly glazed skylight. I closed my eyes and inhaled deeply; the air was thick with the earthy aroma of plants, heady with oxygen. I blinked my eyes and the room came into focus. A variety of ferns and potted flowers were scattered about the area. What luxuriant plants, I thought. But why not — it's like a greenhouse in here.

Directly in front of the doorway was a motley collection of sofas and straight-backed wooden chairs, arranged theater style facing a black-and-white television that hung precariously from a roof support pillar. A dozen or so loungers were watching an apparently engrossing soap opera. At a commercial break they turned and gave me inquisitive glances.

"Good show?" I asked.

Except for a couple of giggles no one answered.

I stepped past them to the rear of the patio and found two shower stalls and a sink. The toilets were on the opposite end of the area. I inspected everything. They're serviceable, anyway, I thought. Now for my room.

Along either side of the patio ran a wood framework, the front covered by plywood and the frame divided into individual compartments by thin pressboard partitions. Like jail cells, I thought. Each room was equipped with a good quality, wood door, a small padlock, and a gold painted metal, room number. These rooms are a joke, I thought. But I don't get the nice doors and the gold numbers . . . . Either the owner got a deal on them or he wanted to add a touch of class. Maybe it raises the rent by $50 *pesos*.

I shook my head and pushed open the unlocked door to cubicle number 9. I stooped to enter. The room was nothing more than an oversized closet; yet somehow, two cots and a night table were jammed into the space. I tried to squeeze past the near cot and banged my shin against the protruding corner of the steel frame. "Shit!" I flung my bag onto the bed in the back of the room. I knelt down to examine my leg; it was skinned and had a purple welt. At least it's not bleeding, I thought. I rubbed it to take some of the stinging sensation away. While on the floor I happened to look up. The front and side partitions of the cell were about eight feet high and ended in thin air. An electric fan hung from a ceiling beam that traversed the length of the patio. My ceiling was the patio roof. This permitted air to circulate but it also made every giggle, belch, scream, fart, or whatever, audible throughout the *pensión*. Cheaper than building windows, I thought. Well, maybe the fan will drown out some of the noise. I checked the beds; the sheets were freshly laundered; the bed springs sound. This will do fine for a day or so, I thought. Now for a nap.

I stripped off my clothes, switched on the fan, and flopped on the nearest bed.

My rest was shortlived. Voracious mosquitos, who buzzed my ears and picked at my uncovered feet and ankles, drove me to distraction. A maddening itch assailed the lower part of my legs. I sat up to look. A series of angry welts adorned my ankles and the tops of my feet.

"You dirty bastards," I muttered.

I shifted my gaze to the wall. A gang of bloated insects leered back at me. "All right, suckers." I arose, grabbed my sweaty shirt, and vengefully mashed the mosquitos into bloody pulps. I shivered with disgust. That's mostly my blood on the wall, I thought . . . . Bugs are going to be a problem. Well, it's time to get going and take care of business. On to the consulate.

I selected fresh clothing — light cotton jeans, a blue tank-top, athletic socks, and my inevitable sneakers. I topped things off with a white Panama hat. Jungle clothes, I thought. Got to keep cool and think cool.

I left my cubicle and walked over to the sink by the shower stalls to throw water on my face. I looked at my reflection in the cracked mirror.

"I look like a complete idiot!" I exclaimed, startling several of the soap opera viewers. Embarrassed, I put a lid on my thoughts. Maybe I should dump this hat. It just don't look right on me. Nah, wouldn't do any good. Besides, it'll keep the sun off.

I strode from the *pensión* and headed in the direction of the Brazilian Consulate. About two blocks later I stopped to drink a beer. It's tough to get moving here, I thought. This humidity. The sweats pouring off me. Oh well . . .I called for another brew. Got to ward off dehydration, I assured myself cheerfully.

I sipped at the beer and took in the sights. A pretty girl walked past. Then another, and another, and another. . . .There seemed to be a disproportionate amount of women to men. I gawked as another sweet young girl passed. There's a fascinating mixture of races here, I thought. I think I'd go crazy here. Most of these girls are petite — the way I like. Slim and well-proportioned. Beautiful, creamy brown skin. And exotic features — almost Polynesian. But what gets me the most is the way they walk. Very sensual. Unaffected. Light-footed, graceful, and proud. They remind me of jungle cats on the prowl. Sinuous and sleek. Alert and ready for whatever. And maybe dangerous . . .

I finished the beer and walked the remaining two blocks to the consulate. I entered a plain, functional office. As I closed the screen door three men turned and eyed me. Two of them, tall and white, appeared to be European or American. The third man was spare and dark, with an impeccably groomed vandyke beard and officious countenance. The dark man greeted me in Portuguese but switched to Spanish when I responded in that tongue. He quickly divined the reason for my visit and beckoned me to come and sit by his desk on the other side of the office. I did so. Then he took a seat and with practiced

23

assurance slid two visa application forms across the desk while simultaneously explaining that I would need to give him three photographs.

"And also," he said, "I will need your passport overnight in order to run a security check. And, when you get your visa, if you get a visa, you will have to get stamped entry confirmation into Brazil from the police station in Tabatinga."

The guy speaks excellent Spanish, I thought. Clear and precise. But what's all this bureaucratic bullshit he's rattling on about? Why so much red tape for a lousy tourist visa? They didn't say anything about this in the Brazilian Embassy in Bogotá.

"Look," I said, flushing with irritation, "what's going on here? I am an American citizen with valid residence in Colombia and no criminal record. Why isn't my passport sufficient identification? I have a photo in the passport. I have no intention of staying in Brazil for a long time. They told me in the Brazilian Embassy I would only have to present my passport and everything would be arranged . . . . On the spot."

"That was the case — a few months ago. But things have changed. Before I would have checked your passport and given you a tourist card, but not anymore. Now Americans need a visa to get into Brazil."

"Why?"

"For a number of reasons . . . . But mainly because your government has been making it tough on Brazilians to travel to the United States. So . . ."

"Yeah but, look . . . . "

The consul gave a sympathetic cluck. "Sorry for the inconvenience, but it isn't my job to make regulations . . . that is for the politicians in Brasilia. Now then, if you still want to get into Brazil, would you please hand over your passport and fill out the forms."

"Huh." I slid my passport across the desk. As he took it to an adjoining room I glared at his retreating back. This is crazy, I thought. What a stupid farce. Maybe what this guy really wants is a bribe.

My ire mounted as I looked over the visa application forms; they requested the exact same information already contained in my passport. I snorted loudly and shook my head. This is too much, I thought. Fill out two duplicate forms and they don't even have a lousy sheet of carbon paper. What a pain-in-the-ass to cross an imaginary line in the middle of nowhere. I got a mind to say fuck Brazil and go to Peru instead. I don't need a visa there. Ah, don't be ridiculous.

I filled out the forms. On finishing I looked up and noticed the other two men sitting quietly on a bench beneath a finely detailed map of the Amazonas region. For the first time I examined them. Instantly my vexation subsided. A broad smile creased my face. I restrained myself from laughing aloud. The men were garbed in classic, Hollywood jungle fashion, with matching khaki designer outfits and pith helmets. The "Great White Hunters," I thought. If they were carrying elephant guns I might mistake them for props in a low budget Tarzan movie.

The shorter of the two men made eye contact and grinned back at me, perceiving my smile as a gesture of friendship. He arose and strode over to introduce himself. A barrel chested man, with wide shoulders, a firm jaw, and a shock of curly black hair.

"Are . . . you . . . American?" he asked, with an accent that was clearly stateside English.

"Yes, I am."

His face lit up and he stuck out his hand. "Me too," he said, squeezing my hand hard. "And my friend back there, also. I figured you were American because of your blue passport and those tennis shoes."

"You were right."

"What brings you to these parts?"

"Oh, I'm on vacation here . . . . But I live in Colombia."

"Yeah, you work for a company?"

"Yeah, sort of . . . . I'm in the Peace Corps."

"Peace Corps, huh. That must be a hell of a thing to do . . ."

He really sounds impressed, I thought. Maybe he's a patriot who trusts implicitly in those hoaky television commercials from the mid-sixties. If he only knew . . .

He continued to ask me a string of personal questions. His nosiness was irritating me. For some reason I felt pressured.

"Hell," he said, slapping his outsized head, "here we are talking away and we don't even know each other's names. Mine is Bobby. And this guy here is my partner and good buddy, Bill."

"My name is Craig," I said, without enthusiasm. I don't know, I thought. There's something about this guy I don't like.

Bill, a tall burly man with a sensitive face, came across the room and presented himself in a quiet way. His handshake was firm but soft, like slipping a hand into a velvet lined work glove. Then Bill faded into the background as, with little encouragement from me, Bobby dominated the conversation. This is the kind of person, I thought, who would be described as loquacious if he's a friend — and as a big mouth bore if not.

"Yep," said Bobby, "me and Bill are owners of a restaurant in Anaheim, California — a very successful restaurant. We decided to come to the Amazon for a jungle safari and some red-blooded hell raising . . ."

"Great."

"I tell you, the restaurant business is a real grind. Oh sure, we make the bucks all right, but we have to work our asses off to do it. We needed a break . . . so, we want to experience something really memorable before we go back to earning a living. Ain't that right, Bill?"

Bill smiled. "You got it, Bobby."

I also smiled. Anaheim, huh, I thought. That's where Disneyland is . . . . Maybe they have the idea their safari will be something like "Pirates of the Carribean." Let's see how serious this guy is.

"Hey, Bobby," I said. "If you're really tired of working why don't you join the Peace Corps?"

"Peace Corps? I don't know," said Bobby, shaking his head. "Don't you have to live out in the sticks without any luxuries?"

"Not necessarily. Depends on your job and where you're sent."

"What do you do?"

"I work in a reform school in a small town. The job is no piece of cake, but my standard of living is good. The best I've ever enjoyed in my life. Of course, there are volunteers who live in primitive conditions, but most of them are in the countryside. The thing is, Peace Corps Colombia is a special case."

"Why is that?" asked Bill.

"Because there's a lot of revolutionary activity. The honchos don't want to send volunteers to isolated regions because they're worried about guerrillas kidnapping someone else. So, most of the volunteers work near or in big cities. And if you're near a big city in Colombia you can get almost anything that's available in the States . . . . If you have the money."

"Wow, man, I didn't know that about Colombia. Sounds very interesting. But, I still wouldn't join. I checked into it once and they don't pay enough for my tastes. I'm used to the good things in life." Bobby smiled, as if to console me. "I'm sure it's a good thing, man. But the bread just isn't there."

I smirked. "That's not why I joined. You see . . ."

"O.K., I get you," said Bobby. "Help mankind and all that."

No, you don't get me, I thought. But that's cool.

Bobby was still babbling away. He confided to me that his Spanish was very good because he had taken it in high school.

"And," he said, "I know plenty about the culture of South American because I go to Mexico quite a bit. I've taken three vacations there in different places. Two weeks each time. Yep, you can pick up a lot hanging out in places like Cancún and Acapulco . . ."

I wondered what he picked up — language, culture, or syphilis. Probably all three.

"Yep," said Bobby, "I've been around some in Latin America. But you live here. How long have you been here?"

"A little more than a year."

"Maybe you can answer a few questions for me."

"I'll try."

"Isn't it true that all these Latin American customs officials are corrupt and easy as hell to bribe?"

I shrugged. "I've heard that. Probably so. I don't think their salaries are too good. You got a wife and six kids, well . . . but I can't tell you for sure because I've never had to pay one off . . . . I guess it depends who you deal with."

"Yep, you got a point there," said Bobby. Then he lowered his voice and moved a step closer to me. "Say, what would the chances be of smuggling a pound or so of cocaine back to the United States?"

I wrinkled my nose. I knew he'd get around to that, I thought. Somehow I just knew it.

"Man, I don't know. Depends on how slick you are . . . . And how you cope under pressure — knowing you have the stuff in your possession. I suppose if you shoved the shit up your asshole you might get away with it."

"Would you try it?"

"Me?" I chuckled. "I doubt it."

"Why not?"

"Mainly because I'm too chicken. And I don't have any rich relatives in the States. Besides, I KNOW what the Colombian prisons are like."

Bobby nodded agreement. "Yeah, it would be risky. What the hell, I make good money legit. But with a pound or two . . . think of it. I could really set something up with that. It would be bitchin'."

I coughed into my hand in reply. This is a bore, I thought. He can do what he wants. But if he is gonna do it he shouldn't talk so damn much . . . . The guy reminds me of that used car salesman who sold me that lemon. He wants something . . . . Where the hell is that damn consul man? I want to get out of here.

"Hey, guy," said Bobby. "Me and Bill have a great idea for a trip."

I rolled my eyes and kept silent.

"We're going to make a three day trip down the Amazon in a

canoe," said Bobby. "A real jungle safari . . . . We'll be travelling on the Colombian side for the most part, and we're going up some of the inlets and to a genuine Indian village. We'll stay overnight there. Bitchin', huh! . . . I've already arranged for a native guide and full provisions. It should be one hell of an adventure . . ."

I nodded. "Sounds pretty good."

"Think you might want to come with us? We can always use another good man."

"How much would my share cost?"

"Not that much," said Bobby, his face showing the first sign of uncertainty.

"How much is not that much?"

"Only $200 dollars."

I almost swallowed my tongue. He's nuts, I thought.

"Only $200 dollars," I said. "That's half my money. I can't spend that on a three day trip."

"Yeah, but . . ." Bobby's voice sputtered out. Both Bill and Bobby appeared crestfallen by my rejection of their offer — especially Bobby. His salesmanship is being put to the test, I thought.

"Look, man, I like your idea," I said in a soothing voice. "But I been planning a trip to Manaus for a long time now. I'm more interested in the Brazilian side at this point in time. And like I said, I don't have that kind of money."

Bobby's smile looked forced. "Yeah, yeah, I get you. But this is the chance of a lifetime . . . . We wanted to head for Manaus, too. But the people around here have been telling us that it's a boring trip — the Amazon is too wide to see the jungle well on the way to Manaus."

"Could be but . . ."

"And you don't get to stop at any genuine Indian villages, either! . . . Besides, me and Bobby have to get back to Anaheim soon. A boat trip to and from Manaus would take at least three weeks and we don't have the time."

I looked at my toes, ignoring Bobby's imploring face. Now what the fuck do I care if you have to get back to Anaheim or not? I thought. This guy's a trip.

I kept quiet.

Bobby took my silence as an invitation to continue his sale's pitch. It went in one ear and out the other. His spiel sounded like a telephone recording. He went on and on. I was on the verge of saying something truly sarcastic to him when we were interrupted by the arrival of the consul. I turned to him with a smile, happy for an excuse to ignore

Bobby.

"Is everything fine?" I asked. "When can I get my visa?"

The consul cocked his head and eyed me, as if unsure whether he were dealing with a sane person. I blushed. I deserve that look, I thought. For giving him a hard time.

"Sorry about earlier," I said. "I'm a little nervous."

Satisfied, the consul smiled. "You can pick up your visa in the morning provided you get the photos to us by 5:00 o'clock this afternoon."

"Good. Anything else?"

"Yes. We will have to keep your passport overnight. There are certain things that still have to be confirmed."

"What? You can't be serious . . . . You must know how dangerous it is to walk around in Colombia without proper identification."

"It's not that bad."

"Maybe not for you, but for me . . . . Man, they stop me all the time here. Without my identification they could throw me in jail — if I'm lucky. Or worse, they could put me in the army. Then I'd truly have problems if they sent me to fight the narcotics mafia."

The consul chuckled. "Don't worry. I will vouch for you if you happen to have problems. But you must have some other form of identification besides your passport."

"Yes, of course. I have a letter from D.A.S. (Colombia's equivalent of the F.B.I.) and another card from the embassy.

"Then?"

"Yes, but . . . I've still been harassed on a number of occasions — even with my passport."

"Well, I don't believe you will have any problem here."

"No?" Easy for him to say, I thought. He's never been yanked off a bus in Pamplona and accused of being a Mormon subversive . . . . Fuckin' drunk D.A.S. asshole — just wanted some cash. But he didn't get it . . .

"I don't know," I said. "I don't like the idea of leaving my passport."

"You have to . . ."

"I have to . . . . O.K., then. I suppose it's better to risk one night in Leticia then go to Brazil as an illegal."

"That's certain, *señor*. There's a lot of narcotics and other contraband in Amazonas. Sometimes mistakes are made by ignorant or overzealous individuals."

I chatted with the consul about Brazil. He turned out to be a pleasant person — certainly preferable to Bobby. He informed me that I could probably catch a boat to Manaus across the river in Benjamin Constant.

"Or," he said, "you might try your luck in Tabatinga at the Brazilian Air Force base. Too bad you don't speak Portuguese.... They sometimes give free flights to people who know how to ask correctly."

Whatever that means, I thought.

The consul led me to the map of Amazonas and pointed to some places of interest. Bobby came over and butted into the conversation; he did speak some Spanish. The consul helped things along with a few words of serviceable English. Bobby traced the course of his proposed safari on the map. The consul said that the same kind of adventure could be had on the Brazilian side. Bobby told the consul what he had told me earlier. The consul politely disagreed. I stepped away from them alongside Bill, who understood little if any Spanish, and translated for him. We soon grew bored with their discussion. Bill and I spoke of other things. I liked Bill. He struck me as a thoughtful, sincere person who chose his words carefully. His large size and dignified bearing made me think of a benign Panda. I wondered how he had become mixed-up with a blow-hard like Bobby.

"I just want you to know," said Bill, "that if your travel plans aren't concrete yet, and you would like to come on our safari . . . you are more than welcome."

"Why thanks, man. But you see, my plans are concrete. I just haven't worked out the details."

"All right, but if things don't work out . . ."

"Yeah, I'll certainly keep it in mind."

I looked at Bobby. He was still gabbing with the consul. Time to make my escape, I thought.

"Well," I said, interrupting them, "I've got many things to take care of. Take it easy. *Hasta luego*."

Just as I reached the door, Bobby, who had rushed across the room, grabbed my right arm. I shrugged him off.

"Think over what I said, huh," he told me. "We're staying at the Hotel San Jorge. Stop by tonight or tomorrow — for a beer or something. We Americans should stick together."

"All right, dude. Later."

I strode toward the central tourist area without looking back. We Americans should stick together, huh, I thought. Maybe so. But I don't trust you, Bobby. I don't like your plastic smile or your jive words. Now then, time to get those stupid photos for the visa.

The consul had mentioned a place, near the docks, where I could have my picture taken "almost instantly." I wandered around for a spell without finding it. Either his directions had been too vague or I misunderstood them. I finally ran into the familiar taxi row of the morning. The river was in front of me. I cut through a line of palm trees and high hedges. The great expanse of the Amazon River came into full view, shimmering in the dappled sunlight. For a moment I stood transfixed, wondering when and where the beckoning water would take me. Then I shook my head and looked closer to shore. Off to my right the river was clogged with boats — luxury racers with gleaming outboard motors, yachts, small launches, canoes paddled by bare chested men, barges, and a variety of mangy scows. Looming starkly behind this innocuous collection was a peeling gray destroyer of World War II vintage. Ah, I thought, the resolute protector of Colombian sovereignity. But a real eye-sore.

I frowned and shifted my gaze to the bank and on to the main dock area. It hummed with activity. Scores of stevedores were at work, loading and unloading an impressive assortment of plant, animal, and manufactured produce. Incoming and outgoing passengers, staggering under bundles like worker ants, dodged in and around the stevedores. A boat came in or pulled out seemingly every minute.

Between my vantage point and the dock was an unpaved rutted street that tumbled precipitously to the water's edge; it was lined on each side by a hodgepodge of rickety stalls — stalls fairly bristling with merchandise of any sort imaginable, even Sony televisions and bark arrow quivers. Raucous entreaties of *a la orden* filled the air. This is what I'm looking for, I thought. The main market. Leticia's *San Andrecito*. There has to be a photographer here.

I scraped through some scrub brush and started down the street. I peered into stalls and asked the proprietors where a photographer could be found. Nobody seemed to know. The more helpful ones offered to make a Polaroid shot of me for a healthy fee. I had almost reached the dock when I paused and took a good long look up and down the street. Suddenly, from behind, I felt someone bump my back with a shoulder and a hand make a clumsy stab for my wallet. I pivoted forcefully and my hip slammed into a body. A young woman sprawled past me, empty-handed. She rose in a flash and sprinted up the street. My derisive laughter followed her. "You have to be quicker than that," I yelled in Spanish.

From a distance she turned and cursed at me in Portuguese. Her

31

face looked wild and attractive, her body was slim and athletic. Invective, which I couldn't understand, poured from her mouth. Her breasts heaved and her long dark hair streamed across her flashing eyes.

My adrenalin was up. "You better find a new career," I called, and made a motion as if to chase her.

She snarled a last insult and disappeared into a crush of people.

A fucking *brasileira* (Brazilian woman), I thought. The Colombians are supposed to be the thieves. Huh. And an amateur at that. Even if she got my wallet there's almost nothing in it. A real thief usually distinguishes a good target . . . . Oh well, maybe she was hungry. If I hadn't been gawking around looking for a damn photographer she probably wouldn't have made the attempt . . . . Got to stay alert in these markets.

Resuming my quest, I reached the dock without finding a trace of a photography studio. I shook my head in puzzlement and started back up the street, thinking I might try one of the big hotels. I had almost reached the top of the incline when I glanced to the left and saw, in plain sight in the middle of the street, an elderly man fiddling with an antique, tripod mounted camera. Where was he when I passed by here before? I thought. Lunch? . . . Weird. His studio is the street. No, not weird. This is Leticia. The frontier, man. Weird is the norm.

I mosied over to arrange a session, drawing curious looks from two customers seated on wooden stools. The photographer glanced at me and left the camera. He knelt and fished around in a green plastic bucket which appeared to contain developing fluid. I stood behind him with my arms folded, waiting for him to acknowledge me. Nothing. I coughed. He bent lower over the bucket. He knows I'm here, I thought. What's his problem?

I tapped him on the shoulder and said, "Excuse me." Nothing, he concentrated on the bucket. "How are you doing? I need some photos for a visa." I moved around in front of him.

He refused to look at me, and the set expression on his face was anything but friendly. Anger welled up in me. I stood my ground. Let's see who gives in, I thought.

After a few moments he finally looked up and gave me a disgusted glance, then he stared into the bucket. "I am very busy right now," he said, keeping his eyes in the bucket. "I have many clients waiting. Why don't you come back in thirty minutes — or more."

Clients? I thought. Where? Two people . . . . Maybe I should ask him if he has a friend who's less occupied. Nah, better not antagonize the old buzzard. He might be the only one who can help me on such short notice.

"Very well," I said. "I understand. I'll be back in a short while."

He grunted. Damn fool, I thought. He ought to learn something about customer relations. Or maybe he just don't like gringos. Hell with him . . .

I stalked away from the market and meandered to the outskirts of town, finally coming to a road that seemed to lead into the bush. Then I saw a sign that said, Tabatinga 5 kilometros. Huh, nothing better to do, I thought. Maybe I should go and check out this place. Could be a photographer there . . .

A taxi pulled up and the driver asked me if I needed a lift. Without further thought I jumped in and we were off. About three kilometers down the road I saw the Tabatinga police station. I told the driver to stop. Might as well find out what kind of papers I need from these guys.

I entered the station and was greeted by a swarthy man with a thick bushy beard.

"Do you speak Spanish?" I asked, still unwilling to have my fledgling Portuguese ridiculed.

He shook his head emphatically, "No, I don't speak Spanish."

Feeling somewhat flustered, I pulled out my identification cards and, as best I could, explained that I needed confirmation for entry into Brazil.

He gazed speculatively at me, turned the I.D. cards in his hands to better examine them, and finally asked, "You are American?"

I nodded. He turned in his chair and called to an unseen person. From the rear office came a slim, blond young man with a preoccupied air about him. He came to the front desk and eyed me through horn rimmed glasses.

"Do you speak Spanish — or English?" I asked.

Again the emphatic shake of the head, accompanied by a distasteful frown. The bearded man spoke rapidly to him in Portuguese. I understood words but the meaning eluded me. The blond man examined my I.D. cards. From time to time he looked up to give me a sharp glance. I responded with twisted smiles. What's with this guy? I thought. He reminds me of a damn Gestapo agent. Must be secret police.

"You are American?" he asked. "Living in Colombia?"

"Exactly."

"That is very irregular."

"Is it?" I shrugged. "I am from the Peace Corps."

"Ah, I see."

His manner became less condescending, though not any friendlier. He explained to me, speaking slowly, that he would have to see my visa before he could verify my entry.

"It is in the Brazilian Consulate in Leticia," I said. "Can't you call there? Then you can give me something . . . so I don't have to come back tomorrow."

"No, I can't do that. Return tomorrow with the visa and everything will be arranged. Now that we know you the process will be expedited."

"All right, thanks. Bye." I got up. Man, I thought, I wouldn't want to have any trouble with that guy.

I left the station and began walking to Tabatinga. A sign posted near the station told me the town was two kilometers more. I stopped, thinking to flag down a taxi. A car pulled up; it was full of Colombians headed for Leticia. They offered me a lift. I hesitated. What should I do? I thought. A taxi costs $20 *pesos* or $15 *cruzeiros*. Twice. That's two beers . . . . I climbed into the car. Tabatinga can wait until tomorrow, I thought.

The Colombians left me on the edge of town. It was still too early to see the photographer. I decided to explore the fringes of Leticia. I moved off the main road and onto a wide footpath. My feet kicked up dust as I strolled past picturesque wooden bungalows with thatched roofs set against a backdrop of extravagant vegetation. Here the majority of the people I saw had decidedly native features — copper colored skin, slim wiry bodies, straight black hair, high cheekbones, prominent noses, and piercing eyes. Everyone was scantily clothed, shorts for the men and light shifts for the women. Now this, I thought, is more like what I expected of a town in the Amazon. These simple dwellings are probably more comfortable than my room in the *pensión*. Why I bet . . . . A green blur shot past me and fled into the bush behind one of the huts. Wow, that was a big one. I regained the thread of my broken thought. Even if there are lizards, snakes, scorpions, and tarantulas scuttling about on the ground and in the eaves.

I was thirsty again. I stopped in a local hangout for a drink. The owners insisted on speaking Portuguese to me. I learned how to say *cerveja gelada* (cold beer).

Leaving the bar and travelling in a looping arc toward the tourist zone, I ran into the Peruvian Consulate. I wanted to go in and ask them some questions but it was closed. Now what kind of office hours do they keep? I wondered. They should be open. I shook my head and moved on.

This is getting to be a drag, I thought. Everyone seems to be sleepwalking here. Routine stuff is complicated because no one has anything better to do. Or maybe they do have better things to do than routine business. But I sure haven't seen anything particularly exciting. Still, there's something in the air . . . . This place is like a smoldering volcano. Everyone looks secretive. No one looks me in the eye — almost no one. Huh, I wonder if people spend more time sleeping or daydreaming, waiting for something exciting to happen . . .

I halted in my tracks. A stockade of sorts loomed before me. Intrigued, I moved in for a closer look and discovered that it was a hotel surrounded by a fence of chopped logs. I opened the front gate and walked in, startling a uniformed security guard who had been too busy ogling some women by the swimming pool to notice my approach.

His face reddened with embarrassment; he swiveled the rifle in my direction. "What do you want here?"

I took a nervous step to the side, away from the gun. "I want to know how much it costs for a room?"

The guard lowered the rifle and smiled. "We have some very fine rooms. And the guests are of the best culture."

As he talked I looked past him to the cottages clustered about the compound. From the outside they looked ordinary. But the swimming pool was large and inviting. Man, a plunge would be nice, I thought. I scanned the women. The beautiful people. They're wearing enough gold; the latest bikinis; sipping drinks out of coconuts . . .

"Very pretty, no?" said the guard.

"Yes."

"We have rooms for as low as $1500 *pesos* a night."

"What?"

"Yes, it is that cheap. If you want to see a room go speak with the lady in the office."

I tugged at my chin. I wondered if I might pay a small fee and use the pool.

"Do you want to see a room?" he prodded.

"No, thank you. I was just curious about the price in case I want to change my hotel later."

He frowned and said, "Good. Whatever you want."

I cast a final, longing eye at the pool. Maybe I'll come back later and find out about the pool, I thought.

I walked out and checked the prices in some of the other hotels and restaurants. It was the same story. This is discouraging. Even some dive restaurants are too expensive for me. There's no getting around it — I have to get out of Leticia as soon as possible.

As I trudged toward the photography station a dank overcast settled over Leticia. Its leaden embrace depressed my spirits even more. Resignation gripped me. I'm really dragging, I thought. What could it be?. . .Jet lag? Change of climate? Too many beers? Too much bullshit? Probably everything.

The photographer greeted me with a grunt. He was busy with some peacock fop who was taking his time combing a half-bald head. I stifled a sarcastic remark and took a seat on one of the stools.

"Do you have time for me now?" I asked the photographer.

"Sure, when I finish with this *señor*. You have to wait."

"I can see that." The fop was still combing his hair. To show my displeasure I leaned back and emitted a loud yawn. As I did this splats of moisture ricocheted off my tongue and filtered down my throat. I closed my mouth and opened my eyes. Fat raindrops, like tiny mortar shells, were kicking up dust and staining the ground. Distant thunderclaps boomed like artillery. Flashes of light split the gloom.

The photographer was behaving as though he were under attack. Clutching the camera to his chest, he scrambled to cover under a nearby awning. I followed at a more leisurely pace, bringing the bucket of developing fluid with me. Wordlessly the photographer relieved me of the bucket.

"What now?" I asked.

A flash of lightning illuminated his face; for the first time I noticed a curving scar along the side of his jaw.

He shrugged. "Well," he yelled, to be heard over the thunder, "you can come back in thirty minutes or an hour . . . if it stops raining. But tomorrow would be better."

"Tomorrow?" I gave him a cold look. "I need the damn photos today."

He shrugged and pointed to the sky.

"Fuck this!" I snapped in English, and turned away.

I stomped up the incline through a pelting downpour, oblivious to the lightning that would normally send me scurrying for cover, aware only of my anger. Damn, I thought, that taxi driver was right about this place. If it isn't one thing it's another. Damn rain couldn't wait ten more minutes. Rain, hell! Damn photographer doesn't even have a proper studio — a street artist, this one. And this Leticia . . . what a worthless place! When just trying to get your picture taken can ruin your day. Ah . . .

I became uncomfortably aware that I was sopping wet. I spotted a café across the street from taxi row and made a dash for it. Might as well have a drink while waiting for the rain to stop, I thought. If it stops . . .

I flopped into a chair and called for a beer. The waiter brought it at once, but before I could stop him, he sloshed the beer into a glass. I ended up with a mug of foam. Nothing irritates me like a glass of suds. I glowered and muttered at the glass, waiting for the foam to turn liquid.

An old woman, sitting at a table across from me, watched my antics with a smile. She tried to make eye contact but I strove to ignore her. I'm not in the mood, lady, I thought. Her wrinkled face continued to smile at me. Finally she asked me if I had a problem.

"No, I don't," I muttered, sipping the foam. "I'm always like this."

The woman guffawed. "I don't believe that." She got up and came over to my table, bringing an armful of knit blankets, sweaters, and shawls. Beautiful, I thought, just what I need in the jungle.

"Good afternoon, *señor*. Would you like to help an old woman by buying one — or more — of my pretty knit fabrics?"

I eyed her dourly. She shoved her wares directly under my nose. Now that's too pushy, I thought.

"Listen, old woman, you must be crazy. What good is your merchandise in this sauna climate? If we were high in the Andes . . . I might consider buying something. But here — no!"

The woman smiled, showing a good set of dentures. "Of course you don't need a sweater or scarf." She winked suggestively. "But what about your girlfriend?" She thrust a sweater into my hand. "Look, this is the finest material that there is. And made by hand. You can't find better."

Her smile was contagious; her face impish. I was hardpressed to keep a straight face.

"I don't think so," I said.

"I give you a special price. Because I like you."

"Thanks, lady. I like you, too. But not sufficiently to buy something I don't need."

"For your girlfriend . . ."

"I don't have one."

At this supplication clouded her eyes. She heaved a sigh. "But, *señor* . . . . Ay, my God, business is so bad at this time of year. I don't have enough to eat. I feel so weak." She moved closer and proffered her left arm. "Feel my arm. Pure bone, right?"

I felt her arm. It was certainly thin, but also as tough and wiry as rawhide. This woman has plenty of vigor, I thought. She's putting on a good performance. I don't even mind her trying to con me.

"You should have been an actress. I'm sure you do well when there are more customers. But," I reached into my pocket and pulled out a ten *peso* note, "take this. I can't afford to buy anything right now."

She glanced disdainfully at the money. Then she looked directly into my eyes and said, "I don't want that. You think I'm lying about business being bad, right?"

I shrugged. "The truth is . . . I don't know. But you don't seem to me like you're starving to death, either."

She dumped her bundle squarely into my lap. "If you truly believe that I'm lying, you can take any one of these things for free."

I gazed at her, unable to speak. All right, woman, I thought. You got me. I can't take your wheedling any longer. You figured me for a soft touch, and I am. This time . . . . A smile came to my face. At least you got my mind off all the other bullshit. That merits something.

I pulled out my wallet and withdrew $200 *pesos*. "What will this buy me?" I asked, laying the bill on the table.

"Only $200 *pesitos*."

"Look," I said, an edge creeping into my voice, "don't play with my good humor. Your things are pretty but I don't need them. So, why don't you just pick something out for me — for my little nephew."

Grinning, she selected two multi-colored, wool sweaters. "Will these fit him?"

"I can't say. I haven't seen him in more than a year. But they look fine."

"Very well, then. These two for $400 *pesos*."

I shook my head. "That's enough. Here is $200. You can take it or leave it. You can give me one sweater or two. Do whatever you want. But no more negotiating."

For a moment she regarded me in silence, a strange light in her eyes.

"As I told you before," she said, "I like you. Take the two sweaters for $200 *pesos* and *listo* (finished)."

Without another word she tossed the sweaters on the table and turned to walk away.

"Old woman," I called. "Good luck. That you go well."

She grinned from ear to ear and said, "Be proud of yourself. You have robbed an old woman shamelessly."

Sure, I bet, I thought. I watched after her until she disappeared around the corner. A wry grin tugged at my lips as I thought of the woman's parting words. No matter. I felt lighthearted, almost giddy. So what if I bought something useless to me, I thought. So what if it will cost more to mail to the States than what I paid for it. So what if I spent my meal money for the day without eating yet. Who cares. That twinkle in her eyes was worth it. I turned my chair around and looked at Leticia with new eyes. The rain had ceased. The sun poked through the soupy clouds and its bright rays showcased the bejeweled vegetation. Parrots squawked gleefully in the trees. People started to come out from under cover. Maybe, I thought, just maybe I will find something good in Leticia. I ordered another beer. Poured it myself this time — and downed it with gusto.

I hit the street with a feeling of optimism. This lasted about thirty seconds, or until I almost fell on my face. The shower had turned the loose earth into a quagmire. It was impossible to walk normally. Gingerly, as if I were ice skating, I slid flat-footed down the hill. This method worked fine, for a while. Then I hit a spot that was more clay than mud and the lecherous muck sucked my shoe off my right foot. "Shit!" My shoe lay five feet behind me, mired in the gunk. I hopped back on one leg to retrieve it, splashing muddy water all over my pants and soaking my shoes and socks. My other shoe oozed slime. Great, I thought, putting on the shoes. Damn this place!

By the time I reached the spot where the photographer was reassembling his equipment I was in a foul mood.

"Well, can we do it now?" I asked him.

"Come back in fifteen minutes. I'm not ready."

Here we go again, I thought. This is . . . uh! I turned and stomped down the hill, assailed by a wild urge to hurl myself into the river and drown my frustrations. How, I thought, can having a picture taken be such a problem? There's got to be another way.

Before I reached the dock I was sidetracked at a hammock shop. I went in, attracted less by the hammocks than by a gorgeous young woman behind the counter. As I handled a few of the hammocks I looked up and saw her appraising me with cool eyes. She brought out some more from a shelf behind the counter and displayed them with a grave face. A real business woman, I thought.

"How much for this one?" I asked.

She quoted an outrageous price. The hammock was more expensive and of inferior quality to the one the boy on the corner had tried to sell me.

"Are you joking?" I asked.

"No, of course not. That's a reasonable price."

I snorted loudly. "Look, I may be a foreigner but I'm not an idiot. I've already priced some hammocks here."

"Maybe you don't know much about hammocks."

Suddenly all my pent-up frustrations boiled to the surface. I responded with sarcastic words. She answered in kind. We became embroiled in a stupid argument. I stood and haggled with her for minutes. Finally she walked away in disgust and called for her mother to take care of me. A matronly woman, once attractive, bustled to the front counter. Her hooded eyes regarded me suspiciously.

"What's the problem?"

'Nothing. Except that your prices are ridiculous. Or you're trying to take advantage of me because I'm a foreigner."

She sneered. "Then, don't buy anything. What do I care?"

"Exactly. You are right." I turned on my heel and strode from the store. Once outside and walking I cooled down. Now why did I do that? I thought. I was a jerk . . . . So the prices were too high. So she wasn't even interested in my accent. So fucking what. In the first case I expect that . . . . In the second case it isn't unusual. But it isn't like me to become frustrated so easily. I've got to mellow out . . . . That damn photo. A petty-ass thing like that.

As I walked the sound of my feet squishing in my sodden tennis shoes rasped against my ears, aggravating my bad humor. It's like an upside down Chinese water torture, I thought. I know that every step I take is chafing the soles of my feet. Fungus city if I don't dry out. And "athlete's foot" is no joke here. In the tropics almost any minor cut or scrape can become seriously infected. What a way to get sick — trying to get a damn photo taken.

Arriving at the dock, I found a quiet spot and sat down. Then I pulled off my shoes and socks. While my feet dried I watched a crew unload a cargo boat. The men, panting and sweating like dogs, carried huge bales up the incline on their backs. My ill-humor left me. Man, I thought, what was I bitching about? These guys have really got it tough. I'm just passing through.

I relaxed for a while longer. I hummed "Dock of the Bay." Well, can't waste any more time, I thought. The consulate will close. I put on my shoes and walked up the opposite side of the street, keeping a sharp eye out for another photographer; a fruitless endeavor. As I turned to see if my known photographer was set-up the sun peeked out from behind a cloud and caught me squarely in my sensitive eyes. The pain made me stagger; I stumbled over a pair of hairy white legs. I righted myself and turned around.

"Pardon me," I said in Spanish. "The sun . . ." I looked at a man squatting protectively over an enormous backpack. He had light-brown hair, a thick beard, and a set, stubborn jaw. Sitting next to him was a young woman with finely chiseled features and a pallid complexion. For a moment we stared curiously at each other. I bet they're German was my first thought. They probably speak English. Maybe they're friendly.

"Do you speak English?" I asked.

"Yes, we speak English," replied the man in a flat voice.

He sounds German, I thought. Let's see.

"Don't tell me," I said, smiling. "You two are German."

The man flushed. "We are not German! We are Dutch! You know . . . the Netherlands? Holland? You hear of it?"

"Yeah, man, I heard of it. Sorry, I didn't mean to insult you or anything."

"And you must be American," he said.

"Right."

We had a brief, desultory conversation; after my faux pas they seemed uninterested in making my acquaintance. I said good-bye and moved off. Well, so much for that, I thought. Imagine the guy getting all pissed off over a minor little error. He's from the nether lands — no doubt. Or he's got a complex. Whatever. Two more gringos passing through as far as people here are concerned. If they want to make life harder on themselves by clinging to petty vanities when someone's trying to be friendly . . . well, that's their problem. I got my own.

When the photographer noticed my approach he gave me what seemed an especially sour frown. I smiled at him.

"It will be a few minutes more," he said. "Wait here."

"Fine." I was past resentment. The afternoon is slipping away, I thought. The Brazilian Consulate will probably close early, which is to say the normal time. But I don't care. I'm tired. I leaned against a nearby wall and closed my eyes.

"Yes, man," said a harsh voice to my left, "it's a shame how ignorant foreigners are ruining Leticia. I would like to throw all of them into the river."

I opened my eyes, nervous energy surging through my body. Standing a few feet away, casting malevolent looks in my direction, was a squat black man with huge shoulders and a machete dangling at his side. Ostensibly he was speaking to the photographer, but there was no doubt for whom the message was intended. Oh boy, I thought. More fun.

I nodded to the man, pleasantly, as if I had no idea what he was saying. Then I turned and studied the wall. The crumbling masonry was scarred with cuts and nicks that resembled bullet marks. The army

41

probably shoots people here, I thought.

The man beside me continued to rant about lousy foreigners. I kept my face impassive and ignored him. But my scalp and skin tingled; I was tensed for action. Let him rave, I thought. I've bluffed my way past worse than this guy. I want my damn photo taken. I'm staying here. If it comes down to it, well . . .

"Hey, do you speak Spanish?"

Slowly I turned my head and looked at him. His bloodshot eyes bored into me.

"Who? Me?"

"Yes. You."

I looked straight into his beady orbs. "Do I speak Spanish?" I chuckled. "Of course! In fact, I'm practically a naturalized Colombian citizen."

For a moment the man looked disconcerted. He scratched his head and looked me up and down. "I don't believe it."

I shrugged. "Don't believe it, then. But how is it that I'm speaking to you?"

"All right, let's see what you know." The man began speaking in the super fast and grammatically horrendous jargon of the Colombian North Coast. He went into a rambling monologue: something about how the banana boats in Cartagena contained more than bananas. I listened with great attention, understanding maybe half of what he said. I threw in comments whenever I understood the gist of anything and laughed often. Soon the man was smiling. What truly impressed him was my knowledge of cuss words with which he liberally spiced his story. After five minutes or so, he laughed delightedly, clapped me on the back, and said: "You're not such a bad sort after all."

"Thanks. You must be a *costeño*."

"I am. From Cartagena. You know it?"

"Yes, I've been there. To me it's the most beautiful city in Colombia."

The man's face beamed with pleasure. "You are an intelligent gringo," he said. He asked me questions concerning my background. When he learned that I lived in the *departamento* of Santander he called to the photographer: "Listen, old man. You come from Santander, certain?"

"Correct," said the photographer, his face emerging from behind the camera veil. "I'm from San Gill." He looked at me, recognizing me as a human being for the first time. "Where do you live in Santander?"

"In Piedecuesta. And Bucaramanga."

The photographer nodded his head. "I know it very well. Piedecuesta is known as the *pueblo de los garroteros*, certain, (town of the stick stranglers)?"

"Exactly," I replied.

"Almost everyone carries a gun in Santander, right?" asked the *costeño* to no one in particular.

"That's the reputation it has," I said. "But they probably have more guns on the coast considering how much drug mafia operates there."

The *cartagenero* frowned. "Maybe the *mafiosos*, yes. But the ordinary people, no!" He grinned and looked at the photographer. "In Santander it is everybody. A bunch of cowboys."

"I haven't seen that many guns," I retorted. "Machetes, yes."

The photographer's stern face almost cracked a smile as he listened to our exchange. Dour by nature, I thought.

"You are almost *santandereano*," he declared.

"Not yet. But I'm content there for now."

"A wife and a few children will complete the transformation," he said. "Do you know San Gill?"

"Yes, I know it."

With this response his reserve was completely broken and the questions gushed forth. I answered like a machine: "Yes, I've been to the park with the Spanish moss; yes, the *san gileñas* are gorgeous; yes, I know the song *Si Pasa Por San Gill*; and yes this and yes that; and yes, yes, yes . . ." When are you going to take my fucking picture?

The photographer became friendly and accomodating. He beckoned for me to come over and have my picture taken, bypassing the *cartagenero* and another man.

"Do you mind?" I asked the *cartagenero*.

"Go ahead," he said. "I'm in no hurry." The other man nodded and smiled.

In his eagerness to help me the photographer managed to spoil the first batch of photos. While I waited for him to prepare another set, which took about twenty minutes, I buried my face in my hands and moped. What's the use, I thought, it's just not meant to be. I'll never get to the consulate before they close.

"Here are your photos," he told me at last. "Good luck."

"Thanks." I grabbed the pictures and ran for the consulate. On the way I looked at the photos. I was appalled by my likeness. I wore this dopey smirk, that reminded me of a punch drunk boxer, and the rain had plastered my hair into stringy knots that revealed my protruding ears and outlined my narrow head in an unflattering way. Well, hell with it, I thought. It's been a tough day . . . . But what an ugly picture. Ah, this is no time for vanity. I ran faster.

I caught the consul official, a different one, just as he was locking the front door. Slinking off a bit early, aren't we? I thought.

I pressed the photos into his hand. He seemed loath to accept them. "You are late," he said.

No, you're leaving early, I thought.

"Please," I said. "You can't imagine the trouble I had getting these."

"Well, the door is locked."

I smiled and blocked his path. "Be a good guy," I said in Portuguese. "I have to leave tomorrow."

He frowned. Then he unlocked the door and took the photos inside.

When he came out he was more agreeable. He was pleased that I knew some Portuguese.

"You can come here and pick up your visa after 10:00 o'clock tomorrow. All right?"

"Yes, fine. Thank you." I heaved a sigh of relief. "Good night."

"Ciao."

I walked to the *pensión*, reflecting on the day's events. Well, I thought, considering where I'm at I got a lot done. But what a hassle. Anyway, now that I've taken care of the routine things . . . why, I can get down to business.

CHAPTER II

SANDRA

Back in my hotel room I changed my clothes again. Imagine that, I thought, changing clothes three times in one day. That's usually my weekly average. I finished quickly. Darkness was falling and I was anxious to explore nocturnal Leticia. Besides, my stomach growled insistently, protesting our unenforced fast. Too much beer and not enough food. I patted my stomach and said, "Be patient, baby." Locking the room, I went in search of Alvaro. He ought to know of a decent place with reasonable prices, I thought.

I found Alvaro on the front stoop of the *pensión*, shooting the breeze with some neighborhood cronies. He greeted me with a big smile and introduced me to his friends. He was pleased to recommend a restaurant — Colombian, of course.

"It serves the finest *antioqueño* (a region in Colombia) food in all Amazonas," he said.

I smiled. "Does a relative of yours own it?"

"Of course not. It is simply the best."

"Yes?"

Alvaro took my skepticism as a challenge. He was galvanized to new heights of exaggeration as he described the virtues of this wondrous eatery. I was on the point of telling him that I believed him — to shut him up — when he stopped in the midst of his spiel and exclaimed, "Gregorio, look! Here comes a *paisana* (countrywoman) of yours."

Following Alvaro's eyes, I turned sideways and saw an apparition framed in the entranceway that both startled and inspired pity in me. It was a woman, of indeterminate age, who looked as though she had stumbled into the hungry maws of the jungle, been found indigestible, and then regurgitated back to the civilizaton that had spawned her. Her hair, color of faded straw, was streaked with grime and splashed carelessly over her forehead and about her ears. She wore a weathered cotton sari that draped indifferently over a rather dumpy figure. She was barefoot, her feet caked with mud. I would have thought her completely frowzy if it weren't for her smile, which brought to mind the sun breaking through a layer of clouds after a heavy rain. This, and her eyes — feline green with laugh lines at the corners. Alert eyes that seemed to take in everything at a glance.

"Hello, Sandra. Good evening, Sandra," said the Colombians. Their tone was almost affectionate. Alvaro introduced us with characteristic Latin formality. We shook hands limply and mumbled greetings. We fell silent. Sandra chatted wth Alvaro. Her Spanish, while unpolished, was serviceable, and she seemed to understand the majority of what was said to her. I wondered how much time she had spent in South America.

After completing our covert examinations Sandra and I addressed each other. Out of consideration for the Colombians we spoke in Spanish. With all eyes on us we felt on the spot; our conversation was stilted. Apart from our common nationalities we struggled to find something to talk about.

Alvaro, noting our unease, gave us a puckish look. "Why don't you speak in your own language?"

"Because then you wouldn't know what we were talking about and would probably imagine something bad about you," I said. "I've been through this situation before."

"No. What makes you think that? We just want to hear you speak English. Right?" he said, turning to his friends for approbation. They smiled and nodded their heads as if manipulated by a master puppeteer.

"All right," I said to Alvaro with a wry grin. I turned to Sandra. "English is fine with me."

"If that's what they want," she said.

Alvaro's face beamed with expectation.

"Let's see . . ." I began. "Alvaro is a half-wit turkey."

Sandra snickered. "You figured that out, huh."

"I understood everything," interjected Alvaro. "All of what you said. That English is easy."

I smirked. "Yes? What did I say, then?"

All eyes turned to Alvaro. He puffed out his chest and smiled. We waited.

"You said that you were hungry and want something to eat. Certain? . . . Don't tell me, no!"

I guffawed. Sandra cackled. Then I grabbed my stomach and made an exaggerated pantomine of someone receiving a dose of laughing gas. The Colombians, though they didn't understand the joke, were roaring with mirth. Poor Alvaro. He gazed at me, a puzzled half-smile on his face, awaiting an explanation. His sheepish look made me burst into giggles. He turned from one laughing face to another. Everyone laughed a bit harder.

"All right, all right. Tell me, what's the joke?" he demanded.

The laughter rose in pitch.

"Fine, then," he said. "If that's the way it is then I won't speak anymore." He covered his face with his hands and buried his head between his knees.

At this I took pity on him and more or less explained what we had said. Alvaro looked up and grinned.

"That English is an impossible language," he said. "But I'm certain that Spanish is even more difficult to learn for Americans. You give me two months over there and I would speak English perfectly."

"Whatever you say, Alvaro," said Sandra and I almost in unison. We looked at each other and chuckled. Alvaro's translation had been off, but he had succeeded in breaking the ice between Sandra and I.

"Man, I'm dying of hunger," I said to her. "Do you know of any good restaurants here?"

"Oh, yeah. I know of a lot of places..." She stopped short of inviting herself but the unspoken words were etched on her face. And there was something more. Something that puzzled me. Her entire demeanor bespoke a yearning for something more than a meal. What does she really want? I thought. Money? Company? Understanding? A chance to speak English?

I scrutinized her as she turned to say something to Alvaro. Bathed in the dull light emanating from a naked bulb over the entrance she looked tired and vulnerable. I was reminded of a wilted flower in need of a summer shower.... This woman's been through some stuff, I thought. I surveyed her again. But should I invite her along? I'll probably have to foot the bill and hear a tale of woe into the bargain.... Ah, what the hell. She probably can help me out with some useful information.

"Excuse me, Sandra," I said. "Would you like to have dinner with me?"

"Well... I guess so," she said, with all the demureness of a pursued woman.

A slow smile spread across my face. Amazing, I thought, how she can manage such affectation under the circumstances. Either she thinks I'm a patsy or she still has some pride.

I was anxious to leave, my stomach continued to growl. Sandra fidgeted with her hands and feet. Except for Alvaro the Colombians ignored us and talked among themselves.

"Shall we go?" I asked Sandra.

She nodded assent.

"Let's do it." We said good-bye to our acquaintances and hit the street.

"How long you been in Leticia?" I asked.

"When? This time . . . or the other times?"

"I don't know," I said, startled by the sharp tone of her voice. "Whenever. Obviously I don't know anything about you."

She gave me a sidelong glance. "Alvaro didn't tell you anything?"

"Nope. Well, he told me a lot of stuff. But nothing about you."

"Oh. Well, this time I been here for about two months. I been here a few times before, though. All together I've spent about five months in Leticia between trips to other places. This is like my base."

"I guess you know your way around, huh?"

She nodded. "And I know where not to go. That's even more important in Leticia."

"Is it that bad?"

"It can be. I mind my own business here. . . . There's a café over there that's pretty cheap," she said, waving at some bright lights a few blocks ahead of us. "And the food won't poison you, either."

"That's good to know. I didn't come here to get poisoned."

"Ya wanta go there? They got fish and stuff. It's good."

"Lead on. Since I've only been here a few hours I'll take your word for it."

"You're a trusting soul — aren't you?"

"Sometimes . . . . Anyway, I can eat most anything without getting sick."

"Well, it is a good restaurant," she said, a hint of irritation in her voice.

"Yeah, I believe you. Let's go for it."

We continued on in silence. An uncomfortable silence. I couldn't think of anything to say. Strange, I thought, normally I can bullshit with the best of them. What is it about her? Am I uninspired? Tired? Maybe bored. I stole a glance at her. She doesn't look too excited herself. Except for those eyes; they rove everywhere.

The street, consisting of souvenir stalls and small shops, was dark and silent. We traced a staggered course to avoid the numerous and treacherous potholes on the damp road. We concentrated on our feet, lost in our own thoughts. We crossed an intersection. Suddenly a yelping little boy, hotly pursued by another, raced across our path and dodged into the shadows bordering the houses. I snapped out of my reverie and surveyed the street. It throbbed with life. Groups of adults were gathered in front of their homes; all doors were wide open. The men and women drank and talked while keeping a watchful eye on their nude or semi-nude children who gamboled about like demented grasshoppers. Young lovers, holding hands, kept to the shadows as they sought the darkest nooks where they could behave with less inhibition. And from all sides, filling the sticky air and causing the gathered people to jiggle rythmically, came music. A cacophony of brassy Colombian *cumbia* and *vallenato*, of festive Brazilian *samba*, and faintly, to be sure, as if cognizant of its minority status in the tropical ambiance, the haunting flute of the Peruvian highlands.

I drank it all in and felt a bittersweet *déjà vù*. A memory of lazy summer evenings in my own San Francisco neighborhood. Of a time, the early 60's, when I was very young and life seemed simple. When I knew my neighbors and they knew me and my family. Everyone sitting on the front steps of the three story flats, drinking beer or soft drinks, gossiping, listening to music or to a ballgame, the children and teens congregating at the asphalt playground to organize games and mischief. Certainly it was no paradise; the area was relatively poor. Violence and racism were facts of life in this multi-ethnic community. That's the word, I thought. Community. There was a sense of community. The feeling that somehow or other we were all in this together. And then . . . the mid-sixties, the late sixties. Full blown race riots. Neighbors going off to Vietnam. The neighborhood overrun with heavy drugs and transients. Watching friends turn into junkies. Watching some of them die before they hit eighteen. Trying to keep your head straight when all around you the statistics have names. Digging so deep into yourself that you almost go into hibernation. Watching events with a detachment that makes you wonder if you're human. But knowing the detachment is what saves you from the craziness around you. Yes, I thought, looking at the gleeful children hopping barefooted in the mud, maybe something like that is in store for them. I hope not . . . . Huh, maybe Leticia is already worse.

We crossed another intersection and plunged into a red light district. The happy shouts of children were replaced by the rasping voices of drinking men. The folksy bungalows gave way to bamboo fronted bar-restaurants with Japanese lanterns hanging from the rafters. The pinkish illumination cast by the lanterns, while baldly suggestive, subtly softened the dreariness and squalor of the street.

Bizarre, I thought. From street to street you enter a different world.

Like crossing an invisible barrier from one dimension to another. Walk another mile and we hit jungle.

Sandra pointed to one of the restaurants with the Japanese lanterns. "This is the one I usually go to."

"Which one? They all look alike to me."

"Follow me." She lead me to the second one on the block. I paused about ten feet from the entrance and inhaled deeply. I flinched and wrinkled my nose.

"What are you doing?" asked Sandra, hands on hips.

"Well, you see, my older brother, he works in the hotel-restaurant business, always told me never to patronize a bar that smells of stale alcohol. He used to say, 'If you can smell the raunchy liquor before you get inside you can be sure the place sucks.' "

"So . . . what do you think of this place?"

"I don't know. I smell things a lot worse than stale alcohol. Might be my kind of place. Besides, I never listen to my brother anyway. Let's go in."

Sandra was shaking her head and mumbling under her breath as we passed into a brightly lit dining area. The room, rectangular and spacious, was split in half by a long, bamboo paneled bar. Piled on the shelf behind the bar was an impressive assortment of cane alcohol and other hard liquor. But what caught my eye was an insane wall mural above the bottles; it depicted a gang of pastel colored jaguars leaping with fangs bared at a herd of monkeys. The monkeys, with taunting expressions on their faces, were perched in palm trees and were armed with sticks and coconuts. Flitting among the combatants were rainbow hued parrots. Weird, I thought. But nice colors. A scene to stimulate the preying instincts. I shook my head and looked at the rest of the place. Bamboo tables with matching chairs spilled to all corners of the room. Checkerboard ceramic tile covered the floor. A variety of plants, ferns, and potted trees adorned both floor and ceiling space. A battery of fans circulated the air. The walls were wood from the floor to my waist and wire mesh from there to the roof beams.

As we stood in the doorway, unable to decide where to sit, we attracted stares from a good number of the restaurant patrons. Must be tired of looking at the mural, I thought. Man, there's some mean looking characters here.

I nudged Sandra with my left elbow. "You'd think they'd never seen a gringo before," I said.

"Not many come here. This ain't exactly a tourist bar."

"I noticed. Well, let's find a seat."

"Where?"

"Anywhere. I'm ready for a beer."

"O.K. Let's take this table here by the entrance."

"Right here? There's a lot of traffic."

"Yeah, but the entrance is also the nearest exit. This place can get really strange sometimes."

As we took our seats I scanned the room again. Ah, now I understand why they stared so much, I thought. Except for the waitresses and that woman in the corner Sandra is the only woman here. And definitely the only blonde.

Sandra noted my searching inventory and tapped me on the arm. "What do you think? Does it pass?"

"I think this place reminds me of the whorehouse-bars in Piedecuesta."

Sandra blinked and leaned across the table. "Funny you should say that . . . . In a couple of hours this place will be crawling with prostitutes. It's still early, you know. Leticia doesn't even start to wake up until 11:00 or later. But then, it goes until dawn." Sandra leaned back in her chair and eyed me with a thoughtful look on her face. "Hey! What's this Piedecuesta? And how come you know about bars like this?"

Inwardly I chuckled. Maybe she has me pegged as a good, clean-cut kid, I thought.

"Well, uh . . . I know about these bars because after 10:00 o'clock at night in Piedecuesta the only places to drink are at home or in the combination bar-whorehouses, which are right down the road from my house. They keep 'em in one area . . . . Of course, I only go there to drink with my friends."

"Yeah, sure, man. Of course." Sandra snorted, like a horse blowing out its nose. "And what about this Piedecuesta? Where's it at?"

"Oh, it's the *pueblo* (town) where I live in Colombia."

"Never heard of it. And I been all over Colombia."

"It's in the east. Pretty close to Venezuela, maybe six hours from the border by bus." Sandra gazed blankly. "Near Bucaramanga."

"Where?"

"C'mon. Bucaramanga. You must have heard of it."

"Boogeramanga," she drawled, wrinkling her snub nose. "Sounds like a place in Africa — like something east of Timbuktu."

I chuckled mirthlessly. "Everyone says it sounds like a place in Africa. Actually, it's Colombia's fifth largest city; it has about a half million people and is a nice place. It's famous throughout Colombia

51

because the people there eat these giant, winged ants."

Sandra grimaced and said, "Crawling ants?"

"Yep. They're considered a great delicacy."

"Do you eat'em?"

"I've tried them. They're not my favorite food."

"So the people eat ants . . . . That's not much to recommend a place. No wonder I never heard of it."

"There's more. The climate is excellent; the food is varied and good; and the women are pretty."

"Uh huh."

"Bolivar lived there for a while."

"So what? He lived everywhere in Colombia for a while . . . . Where'd the weird name come from?"

"It was named after an Indian tribe, Los Bucaros. They got blitzed by the Spanish with the help of a bunch of German mercenaries. So they made up for it by naming the capital of the region after them."

"Oh yeah," she intoned. "Sounds familiar . . . . What do you do there? Besides go to the lowlife bars."

"Who me?" I said, stalling while I thought of an answer that would make sense, "Well, I work in a prison for juvenile delinquents and . . . I'm helping this crazy ass nun with a construction project."

"In a prison? How'd you manage that?"

"I'm in the Peace Corps . . . so I do whatever I can."

"You're one of those, huh."

"Yep. I'm one of those. What do you mean by that?"

"You know, one of those goody-goody world savers."

I laughed. "I can see you don't know many volunteers from Peace Corps Colombia."

"I know a few. I knew a few. But anyway, tell me what it's like to work in a prison. Just what do you do?"

"Like I said . . . whatever I can. My title is Director of Recreation. But I'm a counselor, too. What else? . . . I'm the pet gringo."

"Is it bad?"

"It can be . . . . Most of the guards are brutal pricks. They carry sticks with braided ropes on the end — and they use them. But it's not as bad as I imagined. Physically it's not as cruel as the street. Mentally . . . I don't know. I'm used to it now. I guess you can get used to most anything if you have to . . . . Tell you the truth, though, I really don't want to talk about it. I'm on vacation. I want to forget all about that bullshit for a while."

"O.K. If it bugs you to talk about . . ."

"It doesn't bug me. It's just ... Hey, what's your story? What the hell are you doing here for so long?"

Sandra fastened me with a sharp look. "You get right to the point, don't you? What do you think you are? A cop?" Sandra turned away from me, a peeved look on her face, and stared out the door.

My, I thought, what a sensitive soul. I didn't mean to offend her. Hell, she asked me personal questions. Maybe she's trying to put me in my place.... I tried to look contrite as I surveyed the tired and sagging lines of Sandra's face. I dropped my eyes farther and took in her drooped shoulders and breasts. Like a tattered flag in a windless desert, I thought. She's down. Maybe I can cheer her up. Or at least get a strong response out of her so she don't look so beat.

"Sandra, I'm sorry. Diplomacy has never been one of my more noteworthy traits. I guess I got carried away because you're a captive audience." I gave her what I considered a winning smile. "And it's rare that I have one."

"Oh, is that what I am? ... I can get up and split right now," she said, her face flaming.

"Damn, woman! Relax! It was a joke. Don't you get it? ... When you work in a prison you can't have any more of a captive audience than that. Know what I mean?"

"Some joke."

Fuck it, I thought. I stared morosely at the table top. Sandra brooded. She must be thinking that I'm a tactless jerk, I thought. Maybe I am. What's the difference between forthright and tactless? Depends if they like you or not.

Our silent interlude stretched on. I clapped my hands to summon a waiter. One sauntered over.

"Do you want a beer?" I asked Sandra

"I don't know. I'm too tired to drink; it would probably put me to sleep."

"Or wake you up. It's up to you. Whatever you want."

"O.K. Just one."

I ordered two beers and asked for the menu.

"When I first came here I couldn't get used to calling waiters by clapping my hands," I said. "It seemed so rude. But now I kinda' like it. Although I still half expect a slap in the face one of these times."

"Yeah, me too," said Sandra, with a wan smile. "But that's the custom — everyone does it. So, when in Rome..."

"Right." I gazed into Sandra's eyes. "You really look tired."

"I am. I had a real tough time last night .... And I ain't had a bite to eat all day today."

"Why? What's wrong?"

"I don't know. I don't feel good. Maybe I'm comin' down with a cold — or somethin'."

Way she talks sounds like she has an incurable disease, I thought. If it's an act she's overdoing it . . .

The waiter brought our beers, interrupting my thoughts. I asked him to wait *un momentico* (one little moment).

"We'd better order now," I said to Sandra. "I got the feeling this guy will be hard to flag down later."

"O.K. I know what I want. How 'bout you?"

"Let's see . . ."

"If you like fish, they got some good river stuff here."

"Naw, I had fish on the flight."

The waiter scowled and shifted his feet. Our speaking English made him ill-at-ease; or perhaps he imagined we were commenting on his scraggly excuse for a beard.

"What do you want?" prodded the waiter.

"One moment," I said. I turned to Sandra. "When in doubt I usually go for chicken. How is it here?"

"Chicken is chicken."

"Not for a poultry fan. The Colombian variety is usally good."

"Whatever." She shrugged. "I'm gettin' the fish."

I took the chicken with rice and yucca. The waiter scribbled our orders and departed, mumbling under his breath. I understood something about "fool tourists." I smirked at his retreating back. Know how he feels, I thought. This must be a local hangout, for sure.

I took a sip of beer and turned my thoughts to Sandra. There's something very familiar about her. Not that I know her but . . . she's like a Sixties Era refugee from the Haight-Ashbury. And there's another thing. Her manner of speaking . . . it's got some country in it.

I looked at her just as she took a hearty swig of beer. She smacked her lips with gusto and wiped the foam from her mouth with the back of her hand. The image of a girl I knew in college flashed through my mind. I thought about her; her image became a type . . . . Now I get it, I thought. Sandra reminds me of some of the hard core acid-heads I used to see. Country girls from places like Yuba City or Humboldt or Mendocino who came to the City looking for some excitement. Man, I thought most of them wandered off to the sinsemilla fields in Northern California.

As I thought Sandra drained her glass. Her cheeks gained a spot of color. She looked at me.

"You speak pretty decent Spanish," I said. "Where'd you learn?"

Sandra's face brightened. "Oh, here and there. I never studied formal. Just kind of picked it up movin' around South America."

"Yeah. How long you been here? In South America?"

"Altogether about two years."

"Two years! Where abouts?"

"You name it. But I spent most of my time in Bolivia and Peru. And . . . I been all over Brazil, Argentina, Chile, Ecuador, Colombia . . .just about everywhere except Venezuela, Surinam, and the Guyanas."

"Wow, I'm impressed. Sounds like you're just the person I've been wanting to talk to. What place did you like best?"

Sandra leaned across the table, her eyes sparkling. "You been to Machu Picchu?"

I shook my head.

"No. Well, you should definitely check it out. It's absolutely spectacular. The mountains are the Inca ruins and all that . . . It's . . . Man, it's mystical."

"Someday . . ."

"And then there's Cuzco; it's such a mellow place. Lots of culture. Lots of artisans. Cool people. I was there for about five months and stayed high just about the whole time. Great dope! That, along with learning a lot of Spanish."

"That's one way to learn." I chuckled. "But what kind of visa do you have?"

"Just a tourist visa."

"You're kidding."

"No. Seriously. It's no big deal. What happens is when my tourist visa expires in one country I just cross the border to another and get myself an extension. They usually don't give a damn. Except . . ." Sandra grimaced. "Well, except for Bolivia. Those assholes won't let me back in the country."

"Why?"

"Because they say I'm an undesireable alien. They call me a *heepie*. What a sorry joke. Can you believe it?"

"Well . . ."

"I mean, the government officials are the ones who control the goddamn coke trade. Undesireable, huh. Those hypocritical . . ."

I laughed softly as she finished her tirade. Sandra had come alive.

"Maybe you're too much competition for them," I said.

"Huh!"

"You've got a good point about them controlling the drug traffic — some of them. But what the hell. Why hassle with them anyway? There's plenty of other nice spots in South America."

"Why? Because I like Bolivia! It's a gorgeous land . . . and the Indians there are really neat. Man, those poor people are so cool. They just live off the land and they never ask me for stupid things like papers or other shit like that. They just want to live and let live . . . . And isn't that what it's all about?"

"I wish it were . . ."

Sandra interrupted me. In her agitation she almost knocked over the empty beer bottle. As she talked she jabbed her head forward to emphasize her points . . . . This woman is crazy, I thought. But I like what she's done. If Peace Corps hadn't taken me I would have tried something similar. *Una locura, pues* (a crazy way to go for it). I looked at Sandra with a new respect. I felt a growing confidence between us.

"If I'm not being too personal," I said, "could you tell me how you've been getting by financially for the last few years? I mean, two years is a long time."

Sandra heaved a sigh and gazed vacantly at the wall mural for a moment. Then she turned to me, lowered her voice theatrically, and said: "I orginally came to South America by connin' my way onto a banana boat. That cost me next to nothing and got me to Lima. I had a fair amount of cash saved and was able to get by for quite a while on it." Sandra paused and ducked her head. "Then there's my mom; she sends me something now and then. And . . . occasionally I'm able to get some kind of work — tour guide or translator. Stuff like that. But, when things really get tough, — like the last week or so — well, a blonde woman never has to starve in South America."

Sandra's eyes misted ever so slightly and she lowered them and peered at a spot of grease on the table.

I tried to look sympathetic. But I was neither surprised by her admission or upset by it. She does what she has to, I thought. Her style of life makes it necessary. It's her choice.

"Where do you come from originally?" I asked her.

"I'm from Salem, Oregon. Have you heard of it?"

"Yeah, I have as a matter of fact. It's the capital, right?"

"Very good. What else do you know about it?"

"Nothing. I've seen it on the map."

"Oh. Where you from?"

"San Francisco."

"From the suburbs or from the city?"

"From the city."

Sandra smiled brightly. "That's a coincidence. I used to live there myself."

"How'd you like it?"

"To be honest with you, I really didn't like it there all that much. Frisco is a weird city."

"It's not Frisco!" I admonished, feigning anger. "What didn't you like about it?"

"Well, I lived on Eddy and Leavenworth and . . ."

"Hah! No wonder. Living in the Tenderloin . . . . Scuzzville. I wouldn't like it very much, either. Why. . ."

"Now wait a minute," said Sandra, raising her hand and giving me a wicked smile. "Don't go jumpin' to conclusions. The Tenderloin wasn't all that bad. What really got me was that damn depressing fog in the middle of the summer." She sniffled at the memory. "And those damn hills everywhere."

"Some people like those aspects of the place . . ."

"Let me finish now."

I nodded. "Go ahead."

"The worst thing about the place, for me anyway, was that I had trouble getting laid because the men spent more time lookin' at each other than they did me."

I have a jarring cackle when it comes genuinely from the pit of my stomach. This time it was a beauty and virtually the entire restaurant turned to stare at me. Embarrassed, I ducked my head, lowered my voice, and said: "I've always said that San Francisco is a paradise for heterosexual men. It's just like Colombia — three women per interested man."

Sandra allowed this comment to sink in. "Is that what you like about Colombia?"

"Sure, but for a lot of other reasons, too. I'm not sure how to explain it. I guess the best way is to say that Colombia is *folclorico* (folkloric)."

Sandra snickered. "*Folclorico*, huh. Yeah, sure. I can dig it. A little coke to wake up on and a little grass to go to sleep on."

"I'm not talking about drugs."

"No? You get high?"

"I've been known to."

"Want me to get you something? I can get you almost anything you want."

"I'm sure you could. But I'm not into that right now. When it comes to drugs I can take them or leave them — usually I leave them."

"Why? What are you — straight?"

Now it was my turn to snicker. "Depends who you talk to."

"I'm talkin' to you. No one else."

"O.K. Let me tell you a story."

"I'm listenin'."

"When I was in high school I went to class one day and this black dude said to me: 'Man, I don't know what it is you takin', but you always look like you be stoned. Why don't you pass some of that shit around? . . . ' So after that I got to thinking . . . . This guy says I always look stoned, there's other people saying I act stoned . . . . Well then, why should I waste a lot of time and money trying to get me where I'm already at?"

Sandra shook her head. "You're crazy like a fool, man."

"Funny you should say that. My best friend calls me the fool on the hill."

"The fool on the hill?"

"Yeah. Remember that old Beatle's tune?" I began humming softly. "Day after day, alone on the hill, the man with the foolish grin . . ."

"All right, I remember it. Spare me the music." Sandra brushed a few strands of hair from her eyes and asked, "What part of Frisc . . . uh, San Francisco did you live in?"

"The inner Mission District."

"The Mission!" Sandra giggled. "Shit, you are a fine one to be talkin' about lousy neighborhoods. The Mission. Man, I got hassled there more than anywhere else in the City. Now I understand why you're such a wiseass."

I flushed beet red. "O.K., now you hold on a minute. For your information, the Mission probably has the best weather in the City. And when I was coming up it was a real community oriented place. We all looked out for each other and took care of business. You had to live there — not just pass through. Besides," I said in a calmer tone, "considering the position I'm in now I couldn't have grown up in a better place."

"What do you mean?"

"I mean, I was already used to *latino* culture and there was all this graffiti scribbled around the neighborhood, which is how I learned many of my Spanish cuss words. I tell you, growing up there prepared me for Colombia. And for Latin America in general."

"Is that so?" said Sandra in a smug voice, pleased with herself for irritating me. "Well, I still got hassled there more than anywhere else. I got sick of hearin', 'Hey, baby. I got some good shit for you. What you got for me?' "

I laughed. "What do you expect? They looked at you and figured flower child. Free and easy love. Just like here probably."

"Hey man, I don't go with just any slime ball."

"Relax. I'm not saying you do; I'm talking about people's conceptions. How long were you in San Francisco?"

"Over six months."

"You must have liked something there."

"I didn't have the bread to get out." Sandra gave me a grudging smile. "It was all right; it just wasn't what I expected."

"It usually isn't. The Summer of Love ended a long time ago if it ever existed to begin with."

"Anyhow . . . what brings you to Leticia?"

"Actually, it's not Leticia that I'm so interested in. I want to take a boat down to Manaus and see a bit of the jungle. I'm not exactly sure how to go about it, but everyone has been telling me that Leticia is the jump off point. My main problem is that I'm working with limited funds."

I studied Sandra's face, gauging the effect of my last admission. She showed nothing.

"You came at a bad time," she said.

"Why?"

"Because the tourist Recreio to Manaus left yesterday. And the way things are around here . . ." Sandra shrugged her shoulders. "Who knows when the next passenger boat will come around. Bad luck."

She doesn't exactly sound broken-up about it, I thought.

"How much time d'you have?" she asked.

"I have about three weeks — give or take a few days. I'm supposed to be back at my job site by January fifth."

"Three weeks? That's not very long."

"Tell me about it."

Sandra leaned forward and looked me in the eye. "Can I make a suggestion?"

"What?"

"I think you'd be better off hangin' around here instead of goin' to Manaus. Maybe catch a boat for Iquitos, Peru, which is a much shorter trip."

"Oh yeah?"

Sandra paused for a moment to mull over her thoughts.

59

"Why would I be better off here?"

"Truth is," she said, "if you really want to see jungle and natives Brazil ain't the place to be. There's better opportunities in Colombia and Peru because they haven't developed their part of the Amazon as much as Brazil has."

"I'd have to see that for myself."

"I'm tellin' you, man! I been up and down the Amazon. From here to Belém and back again. And from here to Iquitos and back several times . . . . I been explorin' up inlets and I've slept in Indian villages. I know what I'm talkin' about."

"Congratulations. But what's that got to do with me going to Manaus? I don't have time to go everywhere."

"Then listen to me. I seen some nasty stuff. The Brazilians are rippin' the hell out of the Amazon Basin. Searchin' for oil . . . . Clearin' the land for lumber and to start giant cattle ranches. It's horrible, man. The Amazon Rainforest is the largest oxygen supplier in the world. The idiots should stop and think about what they might be doin' to the earth's atmosphere. But do they? No! All they can think about is bein' just like the United States. They want their own plastic paradise. You want to look at that shit?"

"Now hold on a minute, Sandra. You forget that Brazil has a lot of hungry mouths to feed. They got people starving in the Northeast during drought years . . ."

"Then they should develop the Northeast and leave the jungle alone."

"O.K., fine. That's easy to say. But maybe the Northeast doesn't have the resources. Your moralizing won't feed anyone . . . . But cattle can. And oil can generate income for further development which will create jobs and income for poor people."

Sandra's countenance glowed with a rosy fanaticism. "Shit! You sound like a commercial. Is that what you think happens?"

"You tell me."

"What happens is that a few assholes get rich and most of the beef gets exported. Not to mention that the Amazon could turn into another Sahara Desert." Sandra jabbed a finger toward my chest. "Listen buddy, I seen things you wouldn't believe."

"Like what?"

"For example: there's an American, in some province, I can't remember the name, that's got his own private fiefdom as big as some states."

"Yeah, so what? What's he do?"

"He strips away virgin jungle and makes cattle ranches that produce for maybe two years — then nothing! He leaves the ground bare and leached. He runs the place like a fuckin' dictator. With the blessings of the Brazilian Government, of course. So long as they get their dirty cut." Sandra took a deep breath. "And what about the natives? Well, if they don't die from diseases brought by the Brazilians . . . they just seem to disappear one way or another. Do you believe that?"

"Sure, Sandra, I believe you. It's no great secret. I've read about the same thing in major American magazines and in the Colombian newspapers. But who's going to do anything about it? What can anyone do about it? Brazil's population is expanding too fast; you can't tell some guy whose family is dying of hunger not to go somewhere where life might be better. He's got nothing to lose. If you tell him that clearing a small plot of land might contribute to the end of humanity, well, what's that mean to him? His world is ending in front of his eyes, not theoretically. He's looking out for himself and his own."

"The U.S. Government could do something about it. They could threaten to cut off the money if Brazil doesn't get its shit together."

"Sure. And the Brazillian Government just says who are you to point a finger after what happened to your Indians not so long ago. C'mon, Sandra, be realistic. Brazil wants to become a world power, too. They're going to open up their frontiers no matter what stands in their way."

The veins stood out on Sandra's neck; she seemed on the verge of an apoplectic fit.

"Dammit! Whose side are you on anyway?"

I chuckled softly. Then I quickly assumed a sober face as Sandra looked ready to throw her glass at me. That's all, I thought. I got her going enough.

"I'm sorry," I said. "I didn't mean to upset you. I have the bad habit of playing the Devil's Advocate; I argue for the fun of it . . . . Understand, I'm sympathetic to what you're saying. I agree with you. Development is a tricky business. The dangers are very real. A person involved in development can sincerely believe they're doing good without having a clue as to the long-term damages that are occurring. Not to mention the cynical bastards that are openly in it for personal gain and damn the consequences . . . . But, I don't know. It's tough. I can't see a clear right or wrong; you have to balance the good against the bad. Somebody is going to suffer."

"You make it harder than it is," said Sandra. "If we could just get rid of some of the assholes and change the system then things would work out."

"Would it? I used to think so, too. Now I'm not so sure."

"Why?"

"Because, and it took me a long time to realize it, there are always certain people who have the ability to manipulate other people; you know, the so called leaders of men. I used to think that political systems could make a difference — but not anymore. To me one is as good or as bad as another — they're all run by human beings. Human beings with all the human frailties — greed, lust for power, ambition, jealousy. And the good qualities, too. But I don't see how systems alter the basic character of man. Man makes the systems, most of them are ideally good; but a very strong person can makeover and distort a system in his own image."

"Man, you are too negative," said Sandra, shaking her head.

"Negative? I don't think so; I'm making a positive statement. I don't like wearing blinders. It's too easy to blame an abstract system for all the world's ills, not to mention my own. I don't want an ideology. I don't want to be a sheep. I dread the day when I no longer question the established order of the day in the name of duty. Yeah, duty is a convenient word — with that word you don't have to accept individual responsibility for your own actions."

Sandra was gazing at me in amazement. My brain was on fire. My thoughts seethed.

"How old are you?" asked Sandra.

"24 going on 25."

"What makes you think you know so much? I'm thirty, I don't think I have all the answers."

"Neither do I. But I came to these conclusions on my own after a lot of thought. I don't want a ready-made philosophy of life."

"What do you want?"

"I want to be able to live my life, making my own decisions about things, with as little interference as possible from the people in control."

"Now I get you, man. You're all for yourself."

"No. Because I want the same right for everyone else. I'm never going to tell anyone else what they need to be happy. You understand?"

"Not exactly."

"Look, in my case, I'm not that materialistic. I can get by on relatively little and I feel content as long as I have free time to think and do the simple things I like. To me a lot of things are an encumbrance . . . but other people don't feel that way. Fine, I don't care.

They can do what they want as long as they don't mess up my thing."

Sandra shook her head and gave me a sad smile. "You got a lot to learn, kid. They'll mess up your thing."

"Did they mess up yours?"

Sandra gave me a sharp look and guarded silence. She gazed sullenly at the residue of foam in her mug. Did it again, I thought. Mr. Tactful. Or maybe my argument disturbs her. What the hell, so the world's a mess. Probably always has been. Fuck it. Brighter minds than ours have been stumped by the mysteries and problems of existence . . . . Bring on the food and drink and we can watch Rome burn together.

The waiter arrived, rescuing us from our uneasy silence with two lukewarm plates of food. No need to exchange theories now, I thought. Just dig in and grub.

I watched Sandra go through her food with the rapidity of a famished wolf. Wow, she is hungry, I thought. But she doesn't look particularly undernourished . . . only a little shopworn and frazzled around the edges.

I ordered another round of beers; we drank them in silence. My serious mood ebbed away. Matters began to settle into a fuzzier, friendlier perspective. Sandra reclined in her chair with half closed eyes.

"Look, Sandra. Let's call a truce."

"I didn't know we were at war."

"Yeah, right. But let's not talk about politics or philosophy anymore. We're just becoming upset over nothing. Why don't you tell me how I can get to Manaus instead."

Sandra opened her eyes and regarded me. "Why d'you want to get to Manaus so badly?"

"Well, it's kind of a childhood fantasy that became a dream and a goal . . ." I had no intention of going into an involved explanation, but I found myself giving her one. I told her of my young fascination with Brazil. The strong images impressed on my mind by a third grade, out of date, geography book. Then the follow up study. The images becoming sharper, almost taking on a life of their own. In my mind I danced the *samba* with exotic ladies at *Carnaval* in Rio. I explored the Amazon and encountered savage headhunters, turgid rivers, and wild and outlandish plants, animals, and insects. I toured sprawling cities and lolled on the beaches of Copacabana and Ipanema. I moved at ease in a land of racial harmony. I saw Pelé score goals. I surveyed immense plains . . . . Brazil became a fixation.

"And besides," I told her, "I've been telling my family and friends about going to Brazil for years now. If I don't go through with it when I'm this close I'll be disgraced."

"What's the big deal? You live in South America; you can go any time. I told you right now is bad because . . ."

"I'm not going to stop on the threshold — even if I have to do something reckless . . ."

Sandra raised her hand and tried to get in a word; but I ignored her and kept talking, more for my benefit than for hers. It was almost as if I had to convince myself. The realization of a dream can be a frightening experience if it shatters the illusion of a lifetime. I needed to confide in someone. For whatever reason, this was the moment and Sandra the person. I'll be damned if I know why. Perhaps, despite our differences in lifestyle, I recognized a kindred spirit. Or was it because I realized she was a sympathetic stranger who couldn't embarrass me farther down the road? Strange how one can confide in strangers when there is only the moment to be shared and nothing to be gained but mutual reassurance.

"You know," I went on to tell her, "I mainly joined the Peace Corps because it offered me the best route to get to South America. I knew I would find a way to get to Brazil . . . . It's funny though, now I really like Colombia. It's my home. I wonder if the fantasy of Brazil can measure up to what I've found in Colombia?"

I paused to catch my breath, and Sandra, with a puckish grin, clapped a greasy palm over my mouth.

"Okay, okay! I think I got the point. Jeez, and I was thinkin' you were a quiet one at first." Sandra took a deep breath. "You got a couple of good possibilities for gettin' to Manaus. Number one: you can go to Tabatinga and see about hitchin' a ride on a Brazilian military plane. This ain't likely but it can be done if you're lucky and you catch the right person." Sandra smiled coyly. "I did it by convincin' the pilot that it would be to his advantage if he took me along."

"You're right," I said, "it doesn't sound likely. At least not for me . . . . What's the other possibility?"

"The other is that you go to Benjamin Constant and hope for some kind of cargo boat."

"How do I get there?"

"There's a launch that leaves from here to Benjamin Constant everyday . . . 'round 12:30 or so. Then you just ask around at the dock."

"What about a tourist ship?"

"Like I said, the tourist Recreio left yesterday. I wouldn't expect another for five days to a week. And you're in a hurry . . ."

"What a bitch."

"Well, you can try Benjamin. You might get a boat — but no tellin' what kind of sleazy tramp it'll be."

I nodded my head. "Whatever. I'll take my chances. What the hell, it can only enhance the adventure."

Sandra gave me a skeptical look and shrugged her shoulders. "It's foolish! I'm tellin' you, man, with your knowledge of Spanish, you could get yourself a guide here in Leticia pretty cheap. I can tell you who to go to; it won't be the usual tourist rate .... Then you canoe up some of the inlets and catch some real Indian villages — not the prefab shit you mostly see in Brazil. That would be one far out adventure."

I smiled. "I hear you, Sandra. Thanks for the suggestion. But I'm determined to go for Manaus. I want to cruise the Amazon in Brazil. And that's it! Tomorrow I'll be in Benjamin Constant ... unless those chumps in the consulate screw up my visa."

Sandra shook her head and sported the same kind of tired smile that I had seen many times before in conversations with my father and some of my former teachers — meaning, why do I waste my time with this idiot?

"You are stubborn, man. Why don't you listen?" asked Sandra.

"Because I know what I want."

"What sign are you?"

Not this, I thought. Cosmic explanations.

"I'm a Taurus."

"No wonder. Now I dig it."

"If you say so. I don't run my life according to Astrology."

Sandra's smile turned into a grimace. Oops, I thought. I did it again. Time to massage some ego — and fast.

"Sandra, since you've been all through Brazil, maybe you can tell me some things about Portuguese. I know it's similar to Spanish, but can you get by with Spanish in Brazil like everyone's been telling me?"

Sandra wrinkled her forehead. "*Português? Não! É muito diferente.*"

"I understood that. You said that Portuguese is very different. But your pronunciation sounded funny; the te at the end of *diferente* sounded like ch in English."

"Yeah, that's how it is. But that was easy to understand. The Brazilians speak super fast and they have a very nasal accent. I can only understand them when they go slow."

"I know a little," I said. "I prepared for the trip by studying a tape of tourist phrases. And I've been listening to short wave radio broadcasts from Brazil. Plus a couple of books.... But that's all textbook stuff and broadcasters who speak very clearly. What's it like talking to normal people?"

"Tough. Very tough. Lots of slang and poor pronunciation. And another thing... they have lots of words similar to Spanish but with different meanings. Then they have other words for common things that are completely different. It's easy to get embarrassed if you don't know what's goin' on."

"Give me an example."

"Let's see... well, the Spanish word for knife is *cuchillo*. Right?"

"Uh huh."

"The Brazilians say *faca*. For *tenedor* (fork) they say *garfo*. Man, it's really a bitch! Why the hell do they have a different word for every stupid little thing?"

I tried to restrain myself but I burst into laughter at Sandra's outrage. How dare they have a separate language, I thought.

"What the hell are you laughin' at?"

"Relax, I wasn't laughing at you.... I was just thinking about this joke I heard once about this group of Americans who went to France and said: 'Damn, all these frogs must be stupid. So many millions and I can't find a one who speaks English.'"

Sandra pondered for a moment. "Meanin' I'm like them?"

"Not at all. You speak Spanish and some Portuguese."

"I'll let you get by with that."

"Thanks." I ordered a final round of beers. We needed a new topic of conversation. We finally got around to talking about Sandra.

"Yeah," she said, "I figure I'll hang out here until something good comes along. I mean a decent opportunity to get something big started; not any old thing."

"Like what?"

"Oh, I don't know. Something in the tourist business maybe. There's a lot happenin' in this area."

Sure, I thought. You can be a multi-lingual tour guide, a woman about town, a drug runner.... Lots of things.

"So what are you going to do until your big chance comes along?" I asked.

"What I always do. I take things day by day. Leticia's not a bad place once you know the ropes."

"Why don't you go back to the States?"

"What for? I like South America just fine. I'm in no hurry to go back."

"Not even to visit?"

"At this time I got no desire to go back. The rampant materialism back there disgusts me. It's such a shallow value system. That's why I had to get away."

I listened impassively to all she said. I still don't get it, I thought. I have to ask her.

"But why like this? Why this self-imposed exile?"

"What?" Sandra's eyes popped open. "Well, it's like I told you . . . . I don't dig what's happenin' in the States and . . . Ah, what the hell . . . . See, I had this old man back in Oregon . . ."

"Yeah."

"We were tight. We were living together for more than seven years and we had a good thing for a long time. But then — the sonuvabitch decided to take a hike on me. And don't even ask me why. I still dug the guy. Anyway, that was about three years ago. That's when I started hoppin' around. That's why I went to Frisco and from there . . . to here . . ."

"But why South America?"

Sandra lowered her eyes to the table. "I don't know." Then she raised her head and said with an edge of spite, "I figured South America would be a good place to forget about men."

I laughed. "Is it?"

"No! They're just as bad if not worse here. But they got a different style. Still, basically the same."

Enough of this, I thought. I'm tired of arguing with her. If she's going to lump me into a category with everyone else I've nothing to say. Treat me as an individual or nothing."

"I've had some disappointments, too," I said.

Sandra yawned. "I bet." Her shoulders slumped and her chin dropped to her chest.

"Let's finish our beers and get going," I said.

"Yeah, I'm beat."

I paid the bill and we left. A block from the *pensión* Sandra was hailed by a short, mahogany colored man with curly hair and high cheekbones. He spoke heavily accented but intelligible English. He was on familiar terms with Sandra. I remained silent as they chatted. The man gave me sidelong, speculative glances. I stood with arms folded.

"Does your friend speak Spanish?" the man asked Sandra, switching to that language.

"Yes. He lives in Colombia."

"You can speak with me," I told him in Spanish. "I don't bite."

67

"O.K., meester," he said in English. "I see you speak well." He returned his attention to Sandra. "A live one," he said.

Careful with this turkey, I thought.

They exchanged a few more words and parted. The man crossed the street and moved down the block. Then he whirled and called out to Sandra: "If you don't have a bed for the night — mine is hot and available to you." He turned and strode away without waiting for an answer.

Sandra snickered. I felt an urge to shout an insult at the man's departing back. Nah, better not, I thought. What for? Sandra knows how to take care of herself.

"Who was that guy?" I asked her. "Seems like an asshole."

"Him? No, he's cool. He's a tour guide from Tabatinga. I've known him for some time; he's almost a genius. He speaks French, Italian, Spanish, English, Portuguese, and more than a little German."

"Fluently?"

"Very well."

"His English is certainly good."

"Yep. And he really hasn't had much education. But he's been workin' with the tour boats since he was seven."

"That's an education."

"Yeah, I guess . . . . The only thing about him, though . . . his main hobby in life is laying as many women as he can. And he especially goes for the gringa tourists."

"Sounds harmless enough. He can't be such a Casanova if he uses a weak approach like the one he tried on you. Poor guy sounded desperate."

"No. He can have lots of women. He was just foolin' around. We're old friends."

By this time we had almost reached the *pensión*. Alvaro and his companions were still on the front stoop. Alvaro greeted our approach with an exuberant, "*Hola!* How was the dinner?"

"All right," I said.

"Just all right? I told you to go to the *Antioqueño* one."

"Sandra's choice," I replied.

Alvaro turned to Sandra and began teasing her. He made things especially difficult for her by using numerous Colombian slang expressions. Sandra glared at him in bewilderment; her fatigued brain wasn't up to understanding even correct Spanish at that point. The other Colombians roared with laughter.

"What's he saying?" she asked me in English. "I'm more used to the

Peruvian Spanish."

"I can't understand all of it myself. He's using idioms I've never heard before. It don't matter. Just tell him, *No joda, pingo!* (Fuck off, jerk!)."

"*No joda, pingo!*" said Sandra.

The Colombians cracked-up. Alvaro laughed and continued to tease her, using even more slang. Sandra simmered with frustration, unable to respond.

I patted her on the shoulder. "I know how you feel. When I just started to learn Spanish they worked me over real well. I used to get so pissed off; but it made me want to learn faster so I could defend myself."

"Yeah, well, I ain't in the mood to learn. The Peruvians ain't so damn rude."

Alvaro hit her with another barb.

Sandra threw her arms into the air. "Fuck this bullshit! I'm goin' to take a shower and go to bed."

When I translated Sandra's words to the Colombians they became very solicitous and wished her pleasant dreams. Sandra disappeared into the dark corridor. I was left to fend for myself.

Alvaro turned to me with a grin. "You speak very well *el castellano.*" His tone was sneaky, insinuating. The others watched me with half smiles on their faces, anticipating some more diversion.

Here we go again, I thought. I'll use the standard line.

"Of course I speak well," I said. "Where I live, in Santander, most of the people are just like you . . . or worse. I had to learn well to defend myself against people *muy marmagallista* (a very obscene way of saying bullshitters) like you."

For a moment there was stunned silence. Then they exploded into a frenzy of laughter. Nothing like learning a language in depth, I thought. Beautiful slangology.

Alvaro was still shaking with mirth when he said: "Gregorio—you might seem like a gringo—but you have the *barriga colombiana.*"

I have a Colombian belly? What kind of babble is that? I thought.

"What do you mean?"

"Well, you have an accent when you speak Spanish, but you seem to know a lot about our expressions and customs. You've been among us and with us . . . . You are . . . well, *folclorico.*"

I looked at my shoes, flattered by Alvaro's comment. I guess he means I'm not a snob, I thought.

"Thank you, Alvaro. But I can't take credit for that. I owe it all to the little gangsters back in the correctional in Piedecuesta. They taught me almost everything I know."

The Colombians laughed some more. They forgot about giving me a hard time and moved on to more mundane subjects — What do you think of Leticia? What do you think of Colombia? Where have you been? . . . Then out of the blue Alvaro turned serious.

"Gregorio, we worry about Sandra. She is such good people, you know. But she seems confused by life. Why is she like that?"

"I don't know. What do you think I am — a sage?"

"No, be serious. Everyone has an idea. Myself, I don't understand. Doesn't she come from a country where you can have everything you want by working hard? Doesn't everybody have cars, and houses, and good clothes, and mountains of other things? We watch the television and see the movies. You see, to us, even the poor people over there seem rich."

At first I was taken aback and remained silent. Now I understand what he's getting at, I thought. But how do you answer? What do things have to do with happiness? It hasn't been any answer for me.

"What do you think, Gregorio?"

"I don't know what to tell you. If I knew the answers to your questions I might not be here myself . . . . Perhaps the wealth itself is a problem — or the chasing after it. A person is mostly judged by what they have and what they do rather than by who they are. Many people rebel against this and live on the margin of society. They become outcasts. Then they become disoriented and lose all purpose in their lives. Not all. But there are many people like Sandra in my city."

"I still don't understand," said Alvaro. "With all that money . . ."

"Yes, but you have to give up things to get that money. For some people it's not worth it."

They looked at me with perplexed faces. I felt as perplexed as they looked. I realized that words were inadequate; I wanted to give them the images flashing through my mind. I wanted to show them Powell and Market Streets in San Francisco, where the walking corpses of burned-out hopes stumble amidst the white-shoed glitter of credulous tourists awaiting the little cable car that climbs halfway to the stars. I wanted to give them the faces of people who started with high expectations and felt stigmatized by low realizations. Lots of competition; not everyone can have all that money. But you have to see the faces — on the buses, on the BART train, driving in their cars. Anger and frustration. They tell you in grammar school that everyone has a chance to become president: drunken generals, grade B actors, checkered liars, even Tippecanoe and Tyler too. I wanted to show them all of this and more. But . . . I glanced across the street and saw a naked child frolicking laughingly in front of a clapboard home. I looked at the circle of happy faces sitting on the stoop. The absurdity of trying to explain anything left me speechless.

"Money isn't everything," I managed to mumble. "And not everybody there has it."

The Colombians murmured among themselves. Alvaro turned to me and, lowering his voice confidentially, said: "You should go talk to Sandra. She gets lonely for her language and for someone to share ideas with."

"Really? There seems to be plenty of Americans here."

"Yes, sometimes she associates with people from the hotels.... But they don't understand her way of thinking and style of life. Go to her and accompany her, for she is so sad."

I stared at Alvaro, flabbergasted by his insight. I had sized him up as an intelligent but culturally limited person who relied too much on stereotypes. Now I saw him in a different light. My first impression was partially discredited. Suddenly I felt close to Alvaro, we had shared an intimate feeling. With a warm glow suffusing my insides I excused myself and went in search of Sandra.

I found her exiting one of the shower stalls, a towel wrapped around her torso, beads of water dripping from her body and staining the floor. I surveyed her face and was pleasantly surprised, for the faded flower had revived considerably with the infusion of water. Beneath that layer of dirt and self-abuse lay the remnants of an attractive woman. I approached her.

"Sandra."

"Huh? Oh, it's you."

"Do you want to talk for a while longer?"

A hint of surprise passed like a shadow across her face, and the hand holding the towel across her breasts tightened perceptibly. "I figured you were goin' out to look around Leticia."

"I'm thinking about it; but I haven't decided yet. I'm pretty tired myself; it's been a long day . . . . Maybe after I talk to you for a while I'll be able to make up my mind."

"Well, all right. Sure. Give me a couple of minutes to throw on some clothes and come to room 12."

I went to the sink to brush my teeth. My face was flushed and stained with perspiration. I held my right hand up to the mirror, it trembled slightly. This climate is really doing a job on me, I thought. Or maybe my nerves are shot. Probably be a better idea to just go to bed . . . . Ah, it's still prettly early.

I took off my shirt and splashed tepid water on my face and chest. The water felt clammy. I dried off and combed my hair.

I went to my room to put away my toilet articles. She's really not bad looking, I thought. I left my room and went to the dark, empty patio. I paced about for five minutes or so. That should be enough time for her, I thought. But I don't know if it's enough time for me .... Ah, get going, chicken.

I shuffled to her room and tapped on the door.

"Come in. It's unlatched," said a muffled voice.

As I reached for the door a short, very fat woman emerged from the adjoining compartment. She halted and fixed me with a conspiratorial look. "Going to visit the *paisana*, eh."

I winked in reply. She gave a long cackle and lumbered off to the bathroom.

I chuckled and eased into the room, gently closing the door behind me. I glanced about the room; it was similar to mine but contained a double bed and a wicker chair. Sandra was sprawled full length on the bed, garbed in a clean pullover dress with the hem hiked well up the thighs and not a stitch underneath.

The blood rushed to my head. I felt a mad impulse to flop onto the bed. Her closed eyes and tranquil demeanor calmed this impulse. I sank into the wicker chair.

"Sandra."

Flutteringly, as if the dim lamp light hurt her eyes, her lids opened and she regarded me dully.

"Oh, hi. I thought maybe you had decided to go out after all. I guess I kind of dozed off."

I didn't wait that long, I thought.

"Hey, no problem. I wanted to talk to you before I leave. Maybe I'll go out later. Maybe not .... But if you want to sleep I can leave now."

A flicker of a smile came to her lips. "No, I'm fine. I just needed to lay down .... But listen — if you do go out later — be careful! This town is full of drugs. And there's a lot of mean people here who get the wrong idea when strangers come around. Especially gringos who know how to speak Spanish."

"Thanks. I'll be cool. I know how to mind my own business .... Hey, why was Alvaro giving you a hard time out there?"

"Oh, that was nothin'. He's really a nice person. He just likes to come off as a hard-ass once in a while. He lets me stay here for free when there ain't too many guests .... Yeah, he's cool..." Sandra's eyes closed; her voice sounded as though she were speaking under water.

I wish she would wake up a little, I thought. If not I might as well take off.

Suddenly, from the neighboring room, came the sounds of groaning bed springs and smacking lips. Low moans and muffled cries followed. The fat woman had been joined by her obese husband. I looked at the ceiling fan, distracted by the sounds. I tried to imagine two such huge people fucking away. I wondered if it would be any more difficult with so much flesh to bypass. I smiled and looked at Sandra. Her eyes were open and her head cocked to the side in an attitude of listening. We grinned sheepishly at each other. My eyes wandered to Sandra's bare legs and thighs. They're appealing in a chubby kind of way, I thought. But I wonder where she got all those scratches and bruises. What's this woman been doing? . . . By now I felt somewhat aroused. My eyes moved frankly along her legs.

"What are you gawking at?" demanded Sandra, blushing slightly, but making no move to adjust her skirt to a more modest position.

"I was just noticing those welts on your legs." I obeyed an impulse and ran a light, probing hand along the length of her thigh. Sandra's face reddened a shade more, but she remained still, supine. I let my hand rest on her upper thigh.

"How did you get those nasty bruises?"

"Oh, the insects are terrible here."

"No, not the cuts — the bruises."

"Oh, well . . . I get loaded sometimes and have accidents. I don't always remember what went on."

Doesn't remember? She sounds almost fearful, I thought. What's she hiding? She looks so lost.

"You should be more careful," I intoned. I sat on the bed and placed my hand under the hem of her dress. "Cuts and bruises can turn real bad in the tropics if you don't take care of them." I massaged her thigh; my fingers brushed against crinkly pubic hair.

Sandra eyed me, a quizzical look on her face. "You know something, man," she said in a flat voice.

"What?"

"You're full of shit . . . . And if you're thinkin' of screwing me — it won't be much fun 'cause I'm beat."

"You're not interested?"

"I didn't say that. Why don't we wait until tomorrow and see how we feel about each other."

"Maybe you just need a nap to pep you up a little. I can wait. Don't forget, tomorrow I'm leaving Leticia."

"It'd take more than a nap. If I just had some coke . . ."

I fell silent, no longer interested. How many times have I heard this shit? I thought. If I just had some coke. The magic crystal. Not this time. After all, she's right. She's too tired. I might as well be jacking-off.

"Yeah," continued Sandra drowsily, "we can have breakfast together and talk some more. I want you to meet . . ."

A rap on the door interrupted Sandra. Before either of us could say a word, Alvaro burst into the room. He took in the scene with a quick, searching look, his face impassive.

"Gregorio, Sandra, pardon me."

"What's happened?" I asked.

"A Peruvian woman has just arrived from Iquitos and we don't have a place for her."

"So?" I replied

"Well, why don't you take this room with the double bed, which is more comfortable, and Sandra can share your room with the other woman since there are two cots."

I shrugged and looked over to Sandra. She elevated herself on an elbow, blinked like an owl, and said to me in English: "Yeah, I gotta go. Like I told you earlier, I don't have to pay here."

"Whatever."

Sandra got off the bed and kissed me lightly on the lips. "We'll have breakfast in the morning," she said, patting me on the shoulder.

Oh yeah? I thought.

She padded out of the room before I could answer. Alvaro remained in the doorway, a rueful grin on his face. "Sorry, brother. I didn't mean to interrupt anything."

"Don't worry." I said. "You didn't interrupt anything."

"Well, sleep well."

"Thanks. Same to you."

Alvaro left the room. Now what the hell was that all about? I thought. I don't get it. Maybe Sandra and Alvaro are in business together . . . or something. He sure wasn't protecting her virginity . . . . He must be telling the truth. Well, he did me a favor by ending the charade. Now I can rest up for tomorrow — and in a much better bed at that.

I thought of Sandra's parting words. Breakfast, huh. We'll see about that. I don't mind buying her a meal or two . . . . People have done it for me when I was in need . . . . But I can't be worrying about meeting her at certain times and all that. I don't know what's gonna happen tomorrow. She didn't even wait for an answer . . . she just assumed. I don't like that. She of all people should know better than to make assumptions. Well, guess I can't blame her for trying.

I thought about taking a jaunt around Leticia. I lay on the bed; the wide mattress was firm and comfortable. Nah, why go out. This is nice. I saw plenty of bars in Cali.

I got up, stripped to my shorts, and flopped on the bed. Wait a second, I thought. I left my bag in the other room .... That's all right. There's nothing worth taking. I'll get it in the morning...

CHAPTER III

BENJAMIN CONSTANT

I passed the night in fitfull bursts of slumber; between the heat, the mosquitos, and my turbulent thoughts I had a rough time of it. I rose at dawn, feeling leaden and dim-witted. I went to take a shower. The *pensión* lay dormant. The cold water cleared the cobwebs from my mind. I dressed quickly and locked up my room. For a long moment I stood in the patio. Should I wake up Sandra? Company for breakfast would be nice . . . . Nah, I don't have time to wait around for her to get up and get ready.

I slipped from the *pensión*. To my surprise there was a slight chill in the air. The sky was laden with pregnant clouds, ready to unleash a deluge. A drop of water hit the tip of my nose. I started walking fast, in the opposite direction of the evening before. As I moved along the deserted street fat raindrops splattered into the dust with ever increasing frequency. Within seconds it was pouring, and I ran for the first shelter I saw, the covered porch of what appeared to be a small café. The building sat on stilts. Wooden tables and chairs were arranged in neat rows on the porch. Seeing no one, I selected a table near the center of the area and made myself comfortable.

I watched the rain slant down and form small gullies in the street. The effect was soothing; I began to doze.

A short time later the sound of an opening door shook me from my stupor. I turned to see a man emerge from the bowels of the café, a dish towel draped over his right arm. He spotted me and moved closer, a startled look on his face. Guess he didn't expect a customer so early in the morning.

For a silent moment we eyed each other. He was a young man, slight of build, with those tantalizing, almost Polynesian features indicative of Inca ancestry.

"Are you open for breakfast?" I asked.

He nodded hesitantly, as if sorry to begin work. "Yes, we're open. What can I bring you?"

"Are there *huevos en pericos* (scrambled eggs with tomatoes and onions)? And *cafe con leche?*"

"Yes, of course, sir. It will take but a moment to prepare. I'll be right back."

He left to place the order. His accent is different, I thought. His Spanish has a lilting, singsong style. It's softer than the usual Colombian tone. Wonder where he's from? . . .

When the man returned, his moon face brimming with curiousity, he engaged me in conversation. Reluctantly I turned my attention from the soothing rain.

"And what is your nationality?" he asked.

"North American. And you?"

"I am Peruvian. From Lima. But I've been in Amazonas for years . . . . Have you been to Peru?"

"No, not yet. I expect to someday . . . . Have you been to the United States?"

"No. And I don't want to. I would prefer to go to the Soviet Union."

"Yes? Why?"

"Because I know something about your country. I am university educated . . ."

"And, so?"

He was off and running at the mouth. In a calm and reasonable manner he delivered a textbook Marxist analysis of South America's ills, placing the blame for these troubles fully on the shoulders of the capitalist United States. I weathered the harangue in silence—having had practice with this attitude in Bogotá — waiting for him to finish.

"So what do you say concerning these revelations?" he finally asked me.

I scratched my head before answering. "Is it true that the Peruvians are stealing the Colombian's fish from the Amazon River?"

He stared at me, nonplused. I smiled to encourage him.

"No, that no!" He spluttered a few words. "That's a lie! We do not steal their fish!"

"That's not what they tell me."

"And you believe them?"

I shrugged my shoulders.

"Listen to this! I'll tell you about the Colombians. It's that they are very lazy . . . and don't have any boats of their own. While we Peruvians . . . we are great fishermen. So of course we take the fruits of the river which are there for those who can harvest them . . . . And then, the Colombians, who are great thiefs, come with guns to confiscate our hard earned catch. That's how it is here."

I gave the man a sad look. "You are all crazy. Certain?"

For a moment he flushed with anger, then he realized the irony of my remark. A sheepish look came to this face. "I can't excuse the excesses of certain Americans and their companies," he said. "And the C.I.A. . . . ."

"Neither can I . . ."

"But I have to admit that the jealousy between the South American countries is absurd. We are our own worst enemies. But," he shrugged, "it is deeply rooted over centuries of conflicting national interests . . . . And because of the blind pride that is the curse of the Spanish blood. But, what is one to do?"

"You tell me. I have enough problems in my own life. And one of those is that I'm very hungry."

The man chuckled and went to the kitchen, returning seconds later with my breakfast. During the meal, which was delicious, he left me in peace. How stupid, I thought. If he wasn't such a chauvinistic nationalist and ideologue we could be friends. He seems like a reasonable person.

When I finished breakfast he came for his money and gave me some advice. "Be sure to visit Peru," he said. "As everyone knows — it is the most beautiful and interesting country in all South America . . . . Maybe in all the world."

"I would like to, but I'm going to Brazil."

"Brazil?" His eyes narrowed. "It is a great country. Huge and varied. But is has nothing as magnificent as Machu Picchu . . . . And . . ."

"Yes, but I have little time and money for this trip."

"Well, at least go to Iquitos. It has much to offer." The man kissed his fingertips. "The *loretanas* are incredible."

"What's a *loretana?*"

"The women of Loreto. Iquitos is the capital . . . . Why, man, the girls are so hot there that they throw the man out of bed if he can't make love five times in the same night."

"Be serious. I would die."

"But what a way to go," said the man, laughing.

I got up to leave. "Remember," he said. "only a fool would lose the opportunity to visit Peru."

I walked off, chuckling to myself. I must be a fool, I thought. I'm not going to Peru — at least not this trip. And what he said about the *loretanas* . . . . Whistling, I retraced the block to the *pensión*.

I entered the corridor and stopped dead in my tracks. My skin tingled and I stared shamelessly. For sitting in the lounge chair, smiling at me, was a petite young woman with nut brown skin and smoldering dark eyes. She wore a clinging dress which caressed the curving lines of her body, enhancing the femininity of her every little twitch. Sensuality seemed to ooze from her pores. I was struck. I felt the urge to take her by the hand and lead her to my room without saying a word; it would have seemed natural. But my cursed internal voice was saying, "Don't forget Manaus! Don't forget Manaus! Use your head instead of what's dangling between your legs. Be strong."

She caught my eye. Her smile and gestures were enticing.

I lurched forward. "Good morning," I said, as I tried to ease past her.

"Good morning," she said, reaching out and touching my arm with her finger tips. "Do you speak Spanish?"

Her touch was like a feather; my knees went weak. "Yes. I speak."

"Good . . . . Why are you in such a hurry? Why don't you sit down and chat with me for a while."

Instantly my resolved vanished; all thoughts of Manaus were banished. Her touch had ignited me. I flopped into the chair beside her. I slid over and leaned lightly against her shoulder. She smelled fresh, as though she had just stepped from the shower. Wisps of her dark, straight hair tickled my cheek. She spoke softly, in what I came to know as the singsong Peruvian jungle accent. Her voice was melodious and sexy. My mind floated; I understood only a small part of what she said. Wake up, I thought. I gave my head a violent shake.

"Are you the Peruvian woman who came last night and took my room?" I asked her. "The room with the gringa?"

"Yes. I shared the room with a blonde woman. She was very nice . . . . It was your room?"

I nodded.

"I want to thank you for your generosity in letting me have it."

"For nothing. It was my pleasure. Besides, I received a very comfortable bed in the bargain."

"Yes?"

"Uh huh. A double bed with a good mattress. Really too good for only one person."

"Ah, yes?" She licked her full lower lip. Then she spoke of other things. I was oblivious to her words; I had conjured a vision of steaming forest, a lazy stream, chirping birds, and me and her like Adam and Eve.

Then I felt her hand give mine a gentle squeeze and her words filtered into my consciousness.

"It was so difficult for me to come to Leticia with nothing but Peruvian *soles*," she said. "How is a person to survive in a place like this? It is so expensive."

"Is it that much more expensive here?"

"Why, compared to my Iquitos, everything is at least double here." She gave me a wistful smile. "But perhaps for you Leticia is cheap."

"I wouldn't say that."

"No?" She exhaled slowly. "If I could only find a man — a sympathetic man. I like foreigners. Someone who will show me a good time and buy a few things for my poor little son in Iquitos. If not . . ." Her eyelids drooped and she hung her head. "I will have to return to Iquitos faster than planned and lose the price of the passage down the river."

"Ah, I see." I looked into her dark eyes. She smiled and ran a caressing finger down the length of my arm. I quivered with excitement. I could wait for the Recreio, I thought. Maybe go later and fly out of Manaus . . .

Suddenly the front door banged. Sandra bustled into the corridor and took in the situation with a disgusted glance.

"I see you met my roommate," said Sandra in English. "Ya have breakfast yet — or what?"

"A pleasant day to you, too," I said. "Yes, I've already eaten."

"Why didn't you wait for me?"

"Mainly because I have a lot to do today. Some of us have to get up early."

"Oh, you're real cute. And just what exactly do you have to do?"

"Like I told you at least ten times last night, I'm going to Benjamin Constant. Today! . . . Right now I have to go to the consulate and pick up my visa. Oh yeah, but first I have to get my bag from your room."

"Don't worry, man," she snapped. "We ain't touched it."

"Thanks, I appreciate that . . . . I'm glad you showed up, Sandra. Your friend here was beginning to distract me."

Sandra's face turned to stone.

"Good-bye," I said to the Peruvian woman. "I have to go now." She gazed in befuddlement from me to Sandra. I stepped past her and glanced at Sandra; her eyes glared daggers. I shook my head and strode into the patio without looking back. What the fuck does she think? I thought. That one meal together constitutes some kind of contract. She's really grasping at straws. She's got nothing to hold me here.

I entered the darkness of room 9 and my temper cooled. Maybe I shouldn't of been so sarcastic to her, I thought. But I can't stand people trying to control me. I made my intentions perfectly clear last night. I don't want to play games with her. And she can damn well fend for herself . . . . Maybe better than me.

I checked through my bag; the contents were undisturbed. I slung it over my shoulder and went to look for Alvaro. I found him in a small office near the entrance of the *pensión*. Never saw this before, I thought.

"Good morning," he said, looking up from a pile of papers. The room was a mess.

"Your office, huh?" I asked.

"It's going to be. I have plenty of work to do to fix it up . . . . What are you up to?"

"I have to go to the consulate and see about my visa. Can you take care of my bag?"

"Of course. But why don't you leave it in your room?"

"I might have to leave in a hurry."

"Then you are leaving today? For sure?"

"I expect so. You want the money for the room now?"

"No, pay me when you return. Leave the bag on the floor there." He looked down at his papers. Suddenly he seemed distant.

"Thanks, man," I said. "Later."

He looked up and smiled. "We'll talk before you go."

I left the *pensión* and headed for the consulate. On the way I spotted one of the Americans from Anaheim, Bill, approaching me from the opposite side of the street. He had a preoccupied, aimless air about him, and a baby spider monkey was twined around his neck. I stopped and stared. They make quite a picture, I thought. Both outside their natural habitats and clinging to each other for mutual support. They look kinda cute . . . . Could be father and son.

I crossed the street and called out a greeting. Bill looked up, a perturbed expression on his face. When he recognized me he smiled.

"Hey, how's it going?" he asked. "What's up?"

"Pretty good," I said. "I'm on my way to the consulate to pick up my visa. Want to come with me? Or are you busy?"

"No, I'm not busy; I was just thinking . . . . Yeah, sure, I'll walk over with you."

"Good." We started walking. "Where'd your friend come from?" I asked, touching the monkey's shaggy fur.

"He's a native," said Bill, in his gentle voice. "I bought him from a little kid a few days ago for $300 *pesos*. Imagine, the kid's walking around the streets with a monkey and he sells him to me . . . . That would never happen in the States."

"$300 *pesos*. That's dirt cheap."

"Yeah, I thought it was a great bargain . . . . Until I found out how complicated it is to get him back home. There are all kinds of regulations . . ."

"Why don't you claim him as a political refugee?"

"Very funny . . . . But seriously, he'd have to go through quarantine in Miami for several weeks. And even then I'm not sure I could pull it off legally . . . . It would really be a big hassle. I can't afford the time and money involved."

"Why don't you sell him, then?"

"That's what I'm thinking about doing. But not to just anyone. I want to find a good home for him." Bill reached up and scratched the top of the monkey's head. "He's a real sweet guy. I just wish to God I could keep him myself."

Bill patted the monkey's back as though he were burping a baby. The monkey responded by wrapping his prehensible tail and spindly arms even tighter around Bill's neck. Then for good measure he tongued Bill's cheek.

This is true love, I thought.

"I just don't know what to do," said Bill.

"Why don't you take him to the edge of town and let him go? He might be old enough to take care of himself." And find a more appropriate mate, I thought.

"No . . . I don't think so," said Bill. "And besides, if I do that I lose my original investment. After all, seven bucks is seven bucks."

Give me a break, I thought.

As we were passing a bar, catty corner to the military base, a man called to us in Spanish.

"What did he say?" Bill asked me.

"He wants to talk to you about buying the monkey."

"If I talk to him will you interpret for me?"

"Sure."

The man came out of the bar to meet us, a bottle of beer in his hand.

"Tell him I want at least $500 *pesos* for him," said Bill. I relayed this information to the man.

The man laughed and shook his had. "Tell him that is too much. There are plenty of monkeys around Leticia. I would go into business myself if I could get that."

I told Bill. "Ask him how much he'll offer," said Bill.

"No more than $300 *pesos*," answered the man. "That's a fair price."

"I understood that," said Bill. He considered the offer with furrowed brow. "I'd like to make some profit out of this . . . . Let's see if we can negotiate with him. Ask him why he wants the monkey."

I did as Bill asked. The man grinned wryly and took a long pull from his bottle. Then he explained to me with great seriousness why he wanted the monkey. I exploded into a paroxysm of laughter.

"What? What is it? What did he say?" demanded Bill.

I controlled myself with effort. "The guy says . . ."

"Well, come on."

"The guy says he'll keep the monkey for a while and try to fatten him up . . . . So he can sell him later at a better price. But, if worse comes to worse, and he can't get a decent price for him . . . well, he says he'll make soup out of him."

For a moment Bill was frozen. Then his eyes bulged and he stared blankly. Then he shook his head, eyed the would-be buyer reproachfully, and moved off with long fast strides.

The man looked at me in bewilderment. "What happened with that crazy gringo?"

"He decided not to sell the monkey," I said. "Later."

I trotted to catch up to Bill. "Hey! Wait up!" I yelled. He continued at a rapid pace, his head straight. I caught him and tugged at his sleeve. He stopped and looked at me, his face contorted with anger.

"Bill, listen. You have to understand one thing . . . . Monkey meat is considered a delicacy in Amazonas."

"A delicacy?" he muttered, scowling. "The savages! The savages! . . . Well, they won't get this monkey!" He cuddled the monkey to his chest and with his free hand fondled the dark, sloping forehead. "The nerve of him. Savages!"

We had almost reached the consulate before Bill calmed down.

"So what'd you do last night?" I asked him.

Bill ducked his head. "I was going to tell you . . . . I ran into a prostitute last night and . . ."

"Oh, wait a minute, please. This sounds juicy. Why don't you let me take care of business inside first, then you can take your time and tell me all about it."

"All right. I'll wait for you outside."

I entered the consulate and was greeted by yet another new man. He had a weasly face; one of those born bureaucrats. He seemed irritated when I spoke to him in Spanish.

"I don't speak any Spanish," he said.

Then why do you work in Colombia? I thought.

I continued to speak to him in Spanish and he understood me well enough to fetch my visa, though he did so with a noticeable lack of grace. I received my visa from his reluctant hand and examined it carefully. I was pleased to note that I had been given the maximum of ninety tourist days, starting on December 11, 1979. The other consul came through for me, I thought.

"Thank you very much," I said in Portuguese.

"For nothing," he said, now all smiles. "Good luck. Have a wonderful trip to Brazil."

What a freak, I thought, as I walked out the door.

"How did everything go?" asked Bill.

"Fine. I got exactly what I came for."

"Great . . . . Oh, by the way, what do you say to having breakfast over at my hotel? Bobby's over there waiting for me."

"Breakfast?" I mulled it over. Bobby, huh. I don't know if I want to see that guy. Well, the launch isn't supposed to leave until 12:30 . . . and it's only about 10:00 now. Ah, why not.

"I've already had breakfast," I said, "but a cup of coffee sounds good."

Bill smiled. "O.K. Let's go, then." We turned and started for Bill's hotel. A light drizzle fell.

"This weather is bad," said Bill. "You never know from one minute to the next if you need an umbrella . . ."

Suddenly I stopped in my tracks. "Wait a minute," I said. "What about that story you were about to tell me before I went into the consulate?"

"About the girl last night? Well . . ." Bill ducked his head with boyish shyness — boyish charm. I bet this guy gets all the women he wants in the States, I thought.

Bill leaned toward me, striking a pose of confidentiality, and said: "Last night me and Bobby were drinking in a bar near the hotel and we picked up a couple of whores . . . . Or it might be more accurate to say that they picked up on us. Anyway, we had a few drinks with them — a few laughs. I didn't understand much of what was going on; I had a number of drinks and they didn't speak English. Bobby did the talking. So, after a while he tells me everything's set. Bobby decided to take his girl back to the hotel room . . . . But I didn't want to do that because there's four of us there and, you know . . . it's kind of embarrassing with other people watching."

"Yeah." I nodded. "I understand."

"Anyway, Bobby took off with his and I stayed in the bar with the other one. I tell you, my head was spinning. I was tipsy and I couldn't understand a word this broad was saying to me. But she was grabbing me all over the place and getting me super horny . . . . Anyway, she finally got frustrated trying to make me understand and she just grabbed me by the hand and yanked me off the bar stool. She led me outside and to the dirt road that hooks up with the road to Tabatinga . . ."

"Oh, oh . . ."

"Yep. I went with her; I couldn't help myself. I'll tell you something — that woman felt hot. And she was wild looking. Exotic. As we walked she was kissing me and feeling me up all over the place and, wasted as I was, I was doing the same to her . . . . So anyway, I don't remember when or how, we just kind of fell off the path and into the vegetation along the side of the road. Then she had my zipper down and playing with my prick. I almost went out of my head. I was doing my damndest to strip her clothes off." Bill paused and tossed his head in a sheepish manner. "I guess I was too loaded. I was fumbling around — it was so damn dark — not getting anywhere when . . . she suddenly starts screaming at the top of her lungs. Almost scared the shit out of me. But it got me even more excited, too. Anyway, I finally got her panties down and I was trying to get it in her when she started struggling like a mad woman. She kept up with these piercing yells . . . . We were wrestling around in a shallow ditch of some kind. And the yells, and her odor, and her struggling . . . it had me wild. Then, I thought I heard someone coming through the vegetation and I loosened my grip on her . . . . Well, she was quick to take advantage of this. She belted me in the face and rolled away from me. Then she jumped up, kicked me in the side, and . . . scat! She was gone down the road and me too drunk to get up and do anything about it."

"So what happened then?" I asked.

"Nothing. I just lay there for a while, looking up at the sky, trying to get myself back together. When I felt a little better I got up and went back to the hotel. I went to bed thinking that the entire mess was pretty strange but really no big deal. Then this morning, I checked my pockets and found $700 *pesos* missing. She must have got it while we were rolling around." Bill assumed a look of righteous indignation. "But the worst of it is . . . is that she took off without putting out."

"That was cold."

Bill ran a hand through his black wavy hair. Consternation was mirrored in his eyes. "Why do you think she did that to me? I'm not a bad guy."

My stomach churned with supressed mirth but I maintained a straight-face. "Well, it was probably nothing personal. Just business, you know. You were drunk and she saw a good opportunity to get by without straining herself. . . . . You have to understand, you're a walking target here. To her you're a gringo — and gringo means money. You're a tourist to be exploited, and since you don't know the set-up and the language you're especially vulnerable. So, you have to be extra cautious . . . . You might even consider yourself lucky that that noise you heard wasn't some friend of her's coming to stick a knife in your ribs or to club you over the head. You might be lucky she got away from you."

"Yeah, well, I can see that. But it was still dirty pool because I would have paid the slut." A whimsical smile came to Bill's lips. "But what the hell, I only lost about $20 bucks or so. Less. It could have been a lot worse."

"Sure. And think of the great story you can tell your grandchildren someday. Just change the plot a little bit."

Bill laughed and gave the monkey an affectionate squeeze. "Well, it's hard to know who to trust anywhere," he said. "And here in South America . . . I'm just a babe in the woods. I've a lot to learn and not enough time to learn it in."

"You and me both. I've been here a year and I'm just scratching the surface of things. Each country is so different. Hell, each region of Colombia is different."

"So how do you know who to trust?"

"I don't; I rely on my instincts."

"That's what I should have done last night. In the bar I had a bad feeling about that girl." Bill heaved a sigh. "You know, even though she ripped me off, she sure seemed hot. I really wanted her. I don't know . . . I look around and it seems like a lot of women are hot and passionate in Leticia."

"I get the same feeling."

"But why?"

I shrugged. "Maybe it's the climate."

"I don't know . . . . But they sure seem different from the women in the States. Or at least different from the women in Southern California."

"How so?"

"They seem less blasé. They seem to get excited easier. I've been with a couple on this trip... What do you think? Are the Colombian women where you live hot like the ones here?"

I rubbed my chin and considered his question. Have to keep in mind, I thought, where Bill's from. Anaheim—White Bread City. These Latin women must seem very exotic to him. Hell, the ones here seem exotic to me. They have a mystique, even among the South Americans.... Huh.

"Where I live it's more conservative," I said. "I can't compare Amazonas to anywhere else I've been in Colombia."

"Well, give me a general impression."

"In general.... Sexually.... Yeah, it's been all right. Man, I'm no Casanova, but I've had some good times with the Colombian women."

"What do you like about them?"

"Fewer head trips. Well, different head trips. It's hard to explain-.... It's a different culture; women are brought up to treat men with... well, there's less competition between the sexes."

Bill regarded me silently.

"I don't know, man. The people seem closer to the earth. Maybe that's just my perception. Maybe the women here need to read more books. Maybe someone has to come down here from the North so that they too may enjoy the benefits of enlightened neurosis."

Bill gave me an odd glance. "What are you talking about?"

"Well, there seems less emphasis on mechanics—and less over-analyzation..."

Before I could finish we were interrupted. A short wiry man stepped from the shadow of a doorway and addressed Bill in a garbled Spanglish that I couldn't understand. Bill looked at me, a puzzled expression on his face.

"I speak Spanish pretty well," I told the man. "You can speak to me normally if you want."

The man eyed me suspiciously. "Who are you?"

"I'm his friend," I said, nodding toward Bill. "What do you want to tell him?"

The man peered from side to side. Then he grinned and said out of the corner of his mouth, "A pleasure to meet you. Are you American, also?"

"Yes."

"Well, I'm the guide for the jungle tour. I want to tell this man here that we can probably leave within three days."

I translated. Bill smiled happily and said he would tell Bobby.

"Good, meester," said the man. "Tell your friend talk me soon." Then he turned to me. "If you want to go on the trip, also—we could do it for $200 dollars."

"$200 dollars? Forget it. I can't pay that much."

"Well, for special customers we can do it for $100." He winked. "I don't have to say anything to these others. What do you say?"

This guy is a weasel, I thought. I bet he'd let me come along for $50. But I don't trust him.

"No, thank you," I said. "I already have other plans."

"What are you guys talking about?" asked Bill.

"Nothing. He just wanted to know if I wanted to go on the trip."

"Oh. Well, let's go. Bobby's waiting." Bill turned to the guide. "We go now. I give your message to my friend."

"Yes, meester. O.K."

We left the guide and headed for the hotel. I wondered if I should tell Bill what I thought of their guide. Nah, what's the use, I thought. Bobby is the one I would have to convince.

We reached the hotel without further incident and found Bobby in the coffee shop saving a table for us.

"Hey, guy," said Bobby, rising to pump my hand. "What a time I had last night!"

"Yeah, I heard."

Bill went outside to hitch the monkey to a wooden post and I took a seat across from Bobby. He was still wearing the safari outfit but had exchanged the pith helmet for a black cowboy hat. Before I could order a coffee he launched into a lurid account of his encounter with the prostitute.

"It was fucking bitchin'," he chortled. "I humped her on the floor right in front of my other two roommates. I think they got off on it as much as or even more than I did." He clapped me on the shoulder. "It was so bitchin'!"

"I'm surprised you could get it up with an audience on hand," I commented, wondering if he notched his belt after each conquest.

"Hey, you know, I couldn't—at first. But later I got the old whanger in gear and really laid it to her. She was yelping and moaning like nothing I've ever heard."

"Yeah."

"Yep! I'm beginning to like this place pretty well. It's not Anaheim-... but it does have certain attractions. Now I'm ready to see some of them Injuns in their mud huts."

I almost laughed in his face, thinking of his "native guide." He'll see some Injuns all right, I thought. And they love to see fools like this. He'll find out . . .

Bill came to the table and took a seat next to me. "We saw the guide," he said to Bobby. "He says everything should be ready in a few days. You have to go see him and make the final arrangements."

"That's great!" said Bobby. "I can't wait."

"Why don't you change your mind and come with us?" Bill asked me.

I looked at his earnest face. I like this guy, I thought. But Bobby . . .

"You guys already know why I don't want to go," I said. "But to tell you the truth I have another reservation."

"What's that?" asked Bobby.

"I don't think too well of your native guide."

"Why?" asked Bobby. "He comes highly recommended by the owner of this hotel. I think he's a nice guy . . . . And besides, he says he can show us some real neat spots . . . . Where we can camp overnight with natives. And they'll sell us artifacts and all that."

"That's all probably true," I answered. "I just have a gut feeling that the guy isn't gonna give you what you're paying for . . . . He reminds me of a barker in front of a strip joint—promise you the world but give you watered down drinks . . . . But, hey, it's just a feeling. I've been wrong more than my share of times."

"You probably are this time, too," said Bobby quickly.

I smiled. "Well, you're the ones that are going to find out."

"Yeah, that's true," said Bobby, his voice less sure. "But why don't you come along with us and find out?"

I don't get it, I thought. Why do they want me to come along so badly? They don't even know me . . . . I guess Bobby isn't as sure of himself as he tries to sound.

For the next half hour the two of them took turns trying to wear down my resolve. I drank one cup of coffee, then another. Bobby droned on and on. I yawned from boredom. Though it was still early I itched to get away. Enough of this, I thought.

"Listen," I blurted, cutting Bobby off. "If I can't find any transportation to Manaus within two days I'll come back and consider this jungle tour seriously."

"Yes, think about it," said Bill. "It would be nice to have you along."

"I will."

"What did you do last night?" asked Bobby.

"Oh, not much. I had dinner and went to bed early. I was kind of tired from the plane ride and from running around Leticia."

"Not much happening, eh?" snickered Bobby.

"Nothing that would interest you," I said evenly.

"By the way," said Bobby, "what did you say the name of your hotel was?"

"I don't remember telling you.... But it's called Pensión La Villa."

"La Villa, La Villa," he muttered. "Yeah, that's the place." His face grew pensive. Bobby leaned closer to me and almost in a whisper said, "You know, the owner of this hotel told me that the place where you stay at is run by thieves. You better move out of there; a lot of low lifes hang out there."

I laughed long and hard. That's a good one, I thought. Coming from Bobby.

"What are you laughing at?" Bobby demanded, red faced.

"Maybe I'm where I belong."

"What?"

"Look, man, what's the nationality of the hotel owner here?"

"I think he's Brazilian," said Bill.

"That figures," I said.

"Why?" asked Bobby.

"Because the Brazilians and the Colombians have a rivalry going here. They all talk bad about each other.... When they're not talking bad about Americans."

"The owner here has been great to us," said Bobby.

"I bet," I said. "Anyway, how much are you guys paying for your room?"

"$250 *pesos* per man," said Bill.

"And there's four persons in the room?" I grimaced.

"Right," said Bobby. "But it is a very nice room."

I glanced around at the interior of the coffee shop. "Maybe you guys are getting a better deal. My hotel doesn't have any of this fancy imitation wall paneling. Or a nice coffee shop like this..." With higher prices and worse coffee than that dump I ate at this morning, I thought

"Is the decor of your room like this place here?" I asked.

"Sure! It's paneled and everything," said Bobby.

"Well, I pay $130 *pesos* for my own room. But it is pretty funky.... I guess one has to pay for class."

"Damn right!" said Bobby. "We learned all about that in the restaurant business in Anaheim."

I looked up at the wall clock. Time to start marching, I thought. I stood up.

"All right, you guys," I said. "I got to get moving. If things don't work out for me today in Benjamin Constant I might be seeing you again . . . . Good luck."

"All right, guy," said Bobby. "But don't wait too long or we'll be gone. It's gonna be a bitchin' trip!"

I hope you're gone, I thought.

Bill accompanied me outside and firmly clasped my hand. "Good luck," he said. "If I don't see you again it was nice knowing you."

"Thanks, man. The same to you. I won't say be careful who you deal with here—you already know that . . . . Bye."

While walking away from the hotel, I turned for a last look and saw Bill with the monkey in his arms. The monkey gibbered loudly and bit at the leash that was still fastened to the post. Bill, in an effort to calm him, stroked his head and crooned words of comfort. Even after they faded into the thick mist rising from the ground this image remained vivid in my mind and followed me to the *pensión*.

I almost collided with Sandra as she came rushing from the *pensión* with her eyes on the ground. We stopped dead in our tracks and looked at each other. Sandra scrutinized my face; her own was expressionless. Silently we made peace. She smiled and I grinned to reassure her.

"No hard feelings?" I asked her.

"No, man, what for? . . . You're bound and determined to go, huh?"

I nodded.

"I'm sorry that you're going," she said. "I mean that! But, I know that's what you want to do. Sooo . . . I got to go now and hustle up some food. But I just want you to know that if for some reason the trip doesn't come off . . . come back and see me. I should still be around."

"Can I lend you a few *pesos?*"

"No. I can take care of myself."

"I know that."

Sandra stepped forward and kissed me lightly on the lips. I took both her hands in mine and squeezed hard.

"I hope you find whatever it is you're looking for," I said. "Maybe . . ."

"Don't go gettin' heavy on me, I don't need a social worker."

"Sorry. You're right . . . . I guess sometimes the best way to say good-bye is by not saying anything."

"Could be."

I gazed into her expressive green eyes. "You know, I kind of enjoyed arguing with you. You're a bright person. I respect your opinions. Maybe we can do it again sometime."

Sandra rolled her eyes. Then a wistful smile came to her lips. She knows what I'm trying to say, I thought.

I released her hands. "Bye," she said. "Take care of yourself."

"You too."

She trudged away without a backward glance. For a moment, I watched her receding sandaled feet and felt a vague sadness. The mist enveloped her. I turned and went to Alvaro's office.

"Hi," he said, greeting me with a cheery smile. "Have you changed your mind about staying for a while longer?"

"No. I would like to pay the bill now."

"All right. Let's settle it."

I paid him the exact amount. He accepted the money wordlessly. He put his head down and shuffled the papers on his desk. I picked up my bag and eased toward the door.

"Good-bye, Alvaro. Thanks for everything."

"What?" Alvaro was up and next to me in a moment. "Why are you gringos always in such a hurry?" he asked, taking me by the elbow and leading me to a chair. "Relax a bit. The launch won't be leaving for a while yet."

I plopped onto the chair. "Maybe I'm afraid that if I wait around I might decide not to leave."

"Why don't you stay, then? You have friends here."

"Because I can't."

Alvaro nodded, an understanding look on his face. "I know, I know .... You have something gnawing at your insides. But anyway, can you do me a favor?"

'What?"

"I would like you to deliver a letter for me to a friend in Manaus."

"A Colombian friend?" I asked, feeling flattered by his confidence.

"Yes, a Colombian. Will you do me the favor?"

"Sure!" I smiled. "Do you trust me so much or is the postal service so bad?"

Alvaro chuckled. "A little bit of both .... But there is one minor problem ... "

"What?"

"I haven't written the letter yet," Alvaro cackled.

"All right, that's normal. Certain?"

Alvaro winked, sat down at his desk, and with an intent look on his face began to write. "Don't worry," he said, without looking up, "I'll be done quick."

Despite his assurance I fidgeted in my seat. Though I had plenty of time before the launchs' scheduled departure I was anxious to get away from the *pensión*. I knew that the longer I stayed the harder it would be for me to leave. I was torn between my fantasy of Brazil and the reality of the moment—the reality of having met some good people who genuinely wanted me to stay, and whose company I found agreeable. Leticia, I thought, could be one hell of an adventure! But I have to go . . .

I watched Alvaro write for a few minutes before retiring to the cool dark corridor, the better to brood.

I was alone only moments. The tantalizer from Iquitos spotted me and came over to chat.

"Did you get all your business taken care of?" she asked, tapping on my hand with her fingers.

"Yes, I'm all set. Ready to go."

"When are you going?"

"Today."

"So soon? . . . That doesn't please me."

"Me either. But I only have so much time to do so many things. I have to choose what's most important to me."

"Yes, this is true. But . . . you know, on one of my other trips to Leticia I met a man . . . . American, like you. A real gentleman. Well, we had a wonderful week together. I must have pleased him well because he was very good to me. He was so generous. We ate in the finest restaurants; he bought me beautiful clothes and other presents; he gave me money for my little son . . . . Yes, it was a beautiful week." A faraway look came into her eyes and she sighed. "He was a true gentleman, that one. A man who knew how to make a woman feel appreciated. A fine person . . . . I think maybe you could be like him. No?"

"I doubt it."

Iquitos laughed good-naturedly. "I like you. You are very frank."

"Some people say rude."

"No, I don't believe that . . . " She rambled into a long monologue about her life in Peru. Her musical voice tickled my ears; it soothed me and made me feel drowsy. I detected nothing false in her manner. I felt comfortable with her. She reminds me of a curious child, I thought. But not a naive one . . . . It's like life is one continuous adventure to her, with limited expectations, but exuberant gusto for the stolen moments of pleasure . . .

Her laughter tinkled in my ears. "I like you," she said. "Do you like me?"

"Yes, I like you."

She lay her hand on my arm. "We could make an arrangement . . . "

Again I heard the tinkling laugh. I looked up at a gleaming smile. I gazed into her dancing, dark eyes and saw a hint of pain. A yearning to drift off with her and learn to share her joy for some of the simple things in living came over me. She's another good reason to stay in Leticia, I thought. It would be so nice—to bask in sweet inertia. Why not? . . . Then that other desire, the more potent one, surged up and flooded my mind and washed away the driftwood of my scattered and impulsive longings. I must go now, I thought.

"You tempt me almost too much," I said to her. "But it's impossible. I have to go."

"Why? Don't I please you?"

"Yes, but . . . Ah, forget it. It's impossible right now."

Iquitos changed the subject; I fell silent. By and by Alvaro emerged from his office and handed me a sealed envelope. I rose to receive it and we shook hands. Then, impulsively, he gave me a big *abrazo* and said, "Take much care on your voyage." He looked me squarely in the eyes. "I wish you were staying here a while longer. . . . But remember, if you ever pass through here again . . . you have a home here. Do not forget — *la barriga colombiana*." Alvaro laughed. "One more thing . . . . Be sure to keep my letter in a dry place. I don't want the piranhas to get it."

"Good-bye," I said, bending down and kissing Iquitos.

"You are going now?" she asked, a startled look on her face.

"Yes." Funny, I thought, I told her a few minutes ago I was going.

I reached into my bag and pulled out the two small sweaters I had bought from the old woman at the café the day before. I thrust them into Alvaro's arms. "Listen, *mano*, keep these for me until I pass by here again. But if I'm not back within a month I probably won't be back at all . . . . And they are yours."

"Thank you," he said. "But you will return one day."

"Who knows? . . . I don't. I hope you are right."

We shook hands again. "That you go well," he said. Iquitos gave me a wistful smile. I turned and trudged to my rendezvous with the launch.

I reached the dock without mishap. Then, from the top of the incline, I spied the launch puttering backwards. Panic surged through my body. This is absurd, I thought. I've never seen anything leave early here. I raced down the incline to the water's edge. Frantically I waved and shouted for the boat to return. It moved stolidly away from the shore; the farther it moved the more my shoulders slumped. I shouted a few choice words at the boat. A passing stevedore watched my manic exhibition with a disapproving expression.

"The boat isn't leaving," he said. "It's just going to take on more cargo. It will return to the berth shortly."

"Oh." My face flamed with mortification. I started to thank the stevedore but he turned away from me, a disdainful smirk on his face, and headed up the incline.

What a bastard! I thought. Hasn't he ever made an honest mistake before? For a moment I glared at his receding back, then, for the first time, I became aware of a large group of waiting passengers. Most of them had shied away from close proximity with me and were regarding me with that half-pitying, half-amused expression usually reserved for nuts. Some of them were even pointing me out to friends who hadn't seen my performance. I turned my face to stone. The phrase *gringo loco* came clearly to my ears. Feeling quite subdued, I set my bag on the ground, sat on it, and slouched down as low as possible, wishing the earth would swallow me.

After what seemed an interminable wait in the hot sun the launch taxied back to the boarding area. A steel ramp was shoved into place and the passengers jockeyed for position in line. I stepped back from the crowd and examined the ship. It was a barge-like, ungainly vessel, double decked and loaded with cargo. What a tub, I thought. But it looks serviceable enough.

I slipped into line and was one of the first passengers to board. I sat on a wooden bench in the open air, on the bow of the lower level. I watched the passengers stream aboard, pushing and shoving as they vied for good spots on the crowded deck. The majority of them appeared to be country folk; they wore straw hats and light durable clothing that could stand up to hard physical labor. I imagined they came to Leticia to buy commodities that were unavailable in the outback. Men, women, and children walked bent under heavy loads. They carried large woven baskets filled to the brim with produce, both fresh and dried; they lugged sacks, bales, boxes, suitcases, wire cages, hammocks; they dragged wooden carts with metal rollers and protesting farm animals with ropes. Chickens, pigs, monkeys, parrots, linen, machines, seeds, and every imaginable tool and trinket in existence seemed to parade past me. By the time the ship embarked its decks resembled a floating marketplace.

The smells and sounds emanating from this collection were equally varied. I listened intently. Most of the people were speaking Portuguese. I concentrated on the unaccustomed sounds, trying to understand. I felt a sinking feeling in the pit of my stomach. I can't understand a damn thing, I thought. Whatever it is they're speaking is nothing like the well-enunciated language I know from the Brazilian radio broadcasts. This is how the country folk speak. . . . So what the hell, I'm here in part to gain a practical knowledge of the Brazilian language. Might as well get to it.

I pulled out my pocket edition of Portuguese self-taught and reviewed such key phrases as: Where is the bathroom? What is there to eat? Where can I stay? I love you.

A dark, rather prosperous looking man sitting next to me on the bench became intrigued by my mumbled words. He smiled encouragingly and kept trying to catch my eye. At first I thought he might be trying to hit on me and I ignored him. Then I realized he was merely curious. I set the book down. Might as well get some real practice, I thought.

"How are you, sir?" I asked him, smiling.

"What?"

"How are you?"

"Ah, fine, fine. Quite fine. And you?"

"All right."

"What are you doing?" he asked, pointing at my book.

"I am learning Portuguese."

"You want to learn Portuguese? That is fantastic!" The man became enraptured and went into a long spiel of which I understood maybe forty percent. His recurring themes were, "We Brazilians are warm, friendly, and free people. Portuguese is one of the world's most beautiful tongues. *Brasil é uma maravilha* (Brazil is marvelous)." I was happy to agree with him. I expected everything to be marvelous.

"Why are you here?" he finally asked me.

"I am going to Manaus. I want to see the Amazon."

"That's good. I am from Manaus."

"Oh. Why are you here?"

"I came to see my woman and children."

"You live here?"

"No!" He chuckled. "I live in Manaus with my wife and children. I came to see my other woman and children. I used to live in Tabatinga."

"Oh." I glanced around the deck and listened to the strange murmurings. "I don't understand," I told him. "I can understand you a little bit . . . almost fine. But I don't understand nothing these other people say."

"Well, I'm a dentist . . . . A dentist. Understand?"

I nodded.

"These people are peasants," he said. "They don't speak proper Portuguese. They speak *portulhon.* That is the dialect of Amazonas."

"I understand . . . . Where are you going now?"

"To Manaus."

"Do you know a cheap way for me to get there?"

"Of course! No problem. You can fly on the same plane I am going to take. It would only cost $5000 *cruzeiros.*"

I flinched. "That is too much money for me."

The dentist gave me a skeptical look. "Really?"

This guy's no practical help, I thought. He said peasant like he was saying nigger. Oh well . . .

After his initial interest wore off the dentist showed signs of impatience with my lack of functional Portuguese. When he spoke at a normal rate of speed or tried to express a complex idea I was unable to understand him. We lapsed into silence.

I looked for some other diversion. We had left Leticia far behind. The launch churned a muddy brown swath through the waters of the Amazon. I groped around in my travel bag and took out my Instamatic camera. I trained it on the river. No good. My view was partially blocked by the forest of passengers ranged along the railings. I zipped up my bag and rose from my seat. The dentist looked at me in surprise.

"I am going to sit there," I said, pointing to the near side. "To take pictures."

"All right," he said. "Go." His look was reproachful.

What a reaction, I thought. Maybe he's some kind of honcho or something.

I found a seat with a clear view of the river. A pretty young girl sat nearby. For the moment I scanned the expanse of the river with eager eyes. So, I thought, this is the Amazon. The river teemed with small fishing craft; some of them, manned by burly straw hatted men, were no more than fragile canoes. The fishermen stood proudly against the wind, cutting heroic figures. The sun bounced muffled rays off the scattered dark clouds, burnishing the water in silver. As the gentle swells bore us along I saw some giant fish burst from the water and into the air. They seemed to eye us coldly before dipping below the surface. Looking across the river, far off, almost mingling with the horizon, I saw a smattering of thatched huts that delineated the shore from an otherwise solid backdrop of vegetation. I focused my camera, thinking to snap a photo, but the spray flecking my face discouraged me. It's too far for a good shot anyway, I thought. This cheap camera don't make it for long range stuff. I put the camera in my bag.

From the corner of my eye I noticed the woman beside me stealing curious glances. She'd be more fun to practice Portuguese with than the dentist, I thought. I caught her glancing my way and gave her a smile. Quickly she averted her face and fixed her eyes on a magazine she held on her lap. A tinge of red spread across her cheeks. She opened the magazine to a marked page and resumed work on a crossword puzzle. I tried to look at the puzzle but her ripe breasts, which peeked through the low cut of her blouse, distracted me. My eyes moved up the graceful curve of her neck to her face. How fresh and innocent she seems, I thought. She reminds me of an angelic young nun reciting psalms .... Words quavered on my lips but I remained silent. Suddenly I felt shy. I caught her glancing my way again. Again she averted her face. I wondered what she was thinking.

I twisted around and swept the river with my eyes. Nothing new. I turned and surveyed the passengers. One man, sitting on the other side of the deck directly across from me, stood out from the rest. He was a tall man, over six foot, lean and wiry. His black straight hair cascaded down to the middle of his back. His high cheekbones and coppery skin showed Indian heritage, but his green eyes and certain other features indicated Caucasian blood. He wore patched and faded jeans and an embroidered cotton shirt of a style popular among Colombian street artists and hippies. I had noticed him earlier, expensive camera gear slung over his shoulder, pacing from one end of the deck to the other and up and down the stairway between decks. At the time I idly wondered why he didn't sit down and relax. Now as I observed him, he fidgeted in his seat and cast long glances toward Leticia. For an instant our eyes met and a look of mutual recognition passed between us — the recognition that we were strangers among strange people heading for an unfamiliar place. I almost got up to walk over and speak to him, to dispell the mystery of his unusual appearance and to reassure our shared doubts, but I remained rooted to my seat. The timidity that had first assailed me when I wanted to talk to the Brazilian girl was still with me.

I watched the girl work on the puzzle; by doing this I learned to spell a few words of Portuguese. From time to time I looked out over the river. The calm water and the jungle shore passed monotonously. The passage dragged on. If not for the rocking of the ship and my hard seat I might have dozed. Finally, about two hours after departure from Leticia, an old woman carrying a burlap bag came around to collect the fares.

Minutes later a town slid into view. Low slung, boxy brick houses thickly covered the inclined earth that rose above the busy dock area. I saw several large cargo ships and dozens of small craft at anchor. There should be one boat for me there, I thought.

As we drew closer to shore my nervousness mounted. Well, this is it, I thought. I'm about to land in Brazil. Now what? . . . After that little chat with the dentist I know my Portuguese isn't good enough to communicate well with these people. And they don't even want to hear Spanish. I don't have any contacts here. I'm a rookie again. Just like I was when I first got to Colombia . . . . But what am I so nervous about? Things will work out.

The engine slowed almost to a halt and the launch was shuttled into place alongside a group of cargo vessels. Husky stevedores pushed a steel gangplank into position. The drone of the engine ceased. Everyone gathered their things and prepared to disembark. I wiped perspiration from my forehead and fingered the leather carrying strap on my bag. I caught the dentist's eye and sidled over to him, wanting to ask him if he knew of a good and reasonably priced lodging in town. Before I could say a word the gate opened and the passengers surged forward. The dentist gave me a cold nod and moved into the crush of people boiling toward the gangplank. I should have expected that, I thought.

I spied the hippie looking guy with the expensive camera equipment. Inspired by something bordering on desperation I jostled my way through the mob to him.

"This is a bitch, no?" I said to him in Spanish.

"Yes," he said, after a glance at me. "Like walking with a herd of cattle."

"Are you Colombian?"

"Yes. And you?"

"North American. But I live in Colombia."

"I see. Why are you here?"

"To look around. Maybe get a boat down the river. And you?"

"I have some business here. I'm going to meet a contact who will show me around. A Colombian who lives here."

"What is your name?"

"Jairo."

As we continued talking the press of the crowd funnelled us ashore. We were soon joined by another Colombian off the ship who was an acquaintance of Jairo. Having nothing better to do, I decided to tag along with them. We broke clear of the crowd and stood near the prow of the launch, waiting for Jairo's contact to show. Jairo and his friend huddled together and talked. I was ignored but no one suggested I leave. I could feel the heat of the scorching sand through my shoes. I turned to watch the bustle of the stevedores about the dock. They scuttled from the ships to the beach like two legged brown crabs. How do they do it in this sapping heat? I thought. Must be good genes.

"Where is that son-of-a-bitch?" asked Jairo. He seemed nervous.

I shrugged and turned back to the activities on the beach. I watched two stevedores, short of stature but with powerful muscles undulating under a sheen of perspiration, bowed under the weight of huge bales, move to one of the ships and swing their cargo up and over the side as though it were air. That's impressive, I thought.

My reverie was broken by the arrival of a lanky, copper skinned teenager. His straight black hair looked as though it had been cut by placing a bowl over his head and lopping around the edges. He was clothed in jeans, T-shirt, and sneakers.

"Where were you?" asked Jairo.

"What do you mean where was I?" he said. "The boat just arrived."

"A while ago," said Jairo. "It's damn hot here."

"All right, man. Calm down. I'm here." He looked at me. "My name is Hector," he said with an affable smile. "Welcome to Benjamin Constant. Welcome to Brazil."

"Thanks," I said.

"Is he coming with us?" Hector asked Jairo.

Jairo looked at me.

"If it's all right with you," I said.

"Let's go," said Jairo.

Hector took us in tow. We ascended the incline that led away from the landing and strolled through uniformly dusty streets. Jairo, to my great curiosity, snapped photos of the functional, cement brick buildings characteristic of this river port. He also questioned our guide about the population, commerce, and diversions of Benjamin Constant. I kept quiet and looked around. My spirits sagged as we continued the tour and encountered more and more of the same things —drab brick buildings, acrid dust, sultry air, and the low hum of insects. The streets were virtually deserted. Most of the townspeople were home taking siestas to avoid the afternoon sun.

So this is the paradise of my dreams, I thought, blinking to wash the salty perspiration from my eyes. What a dump! . . . Why Leticia, for all its squalor, has a rustic simplicity that blends with its tropical environment. It has some character . . . . This place is like a festering sore eating away at the jungle. There has to be something better than this.

"Excuse me," I said to the guide. "What is your name?"

"Hector."

"Do you come from here?"

"No. I come from Leticia."

"You like it here?"

"Yes, pretty well."

"How long have you lived here?"

"Over two years. But I go to Leticia often to see family."

"You like it here better than Leticia?"

"I like them both about the same but I get more guide work here."

"This place seems like a bore to me," broke in Jairo. "This town is ugly."

I chuckled.

"It's not that bad," said Hector. "It's calmer than Leticia — less drugs and violence. The people are nice once they know you . . . . And the soccer is much better here."

"So what?" snorted Jairo. "I like a little excitement in my life. From what I've seen so far I prefer Leticia."

"Was it difficult for you to learn Portuguese?" I asked Hector.

"At first, but I picked it up fast."

"As native Spanish speakers it's easy for us to speak Portuguese," said Jairo. "The languages are very similar."

"That's true," I said. "But I understood almost nothing of what those people on the boat were saying. And if I tried to talk to them in Spanish they gave me funny looks."

"That's because you are not a native speaker," said Jairo. "I haven't had problems. If I speak Spanish the Brazilians will understand me."

"I don't know . . . "

"I know. Believe me."

"Why are you taking so many pictures of the buildings?" I asked Jairo.

"For my job. I am a photographer and reporter for a newspaper in Cartagena. I'm doing a story on Amazonas."

"Seems like a good job. Do you get to travel around all the time?"

"Yes. Quite often."

"How long are you going to be around here?"

"A few weeks. I want to make a vacation of this assignment."

"Were you born in Cartagena?"

"No. I was born and raised in Rio Hacha. That's the capital of La Guajira."

"I know. I've heard of your city. A policeman in the town where I live used to work there . . . . He told me that he made a lot of money there but he was happy to leave."

Jairo laughed. "I can imagine. Police don't receive much respect in La Guajira."

"Yes, that's what he told me," I said. "You know, once he was making a drug investigation — big shipments of marijuana. Anyway, he chased two North Americans to this field in the country where an airplane awaited them and, well, he caught up to them just as they were about to board and trained his rifle on them and told them to put their arms in the air. So they turned and raised their arms but they were laughing. Then, he said he felt something cold and hard pressing against the back of his head and a voice said, 'What do you want, sonuvabitch? $20,000 *pesos* or a bullet in the head? It's the same to me . . .' Of course he took the money."

"Yes," said Jairo, a serious look on his face. "That is a typical story from La Guajira. We are overrun with *mafiosos*. It's a shame that we are best known for drug trafficking because there are many beautiful things in La Guajira. Unfortunately, our rugged coast line, inaccessible deserts, and close proximity to the United States make La Guajira the ideal place to traffic. And the central government can do nothing to control it . . . . I tell you, Rio Hacha is incredible! You can see Guajiro Indians — they were in the Stone Age not so long ago—driving around Rio Hacha in Mercedes Benz. They walk the streets openly with machine guns and other weapons. Incredible! These indians have gone from being fishermen and hunter-gatherers to full-fledged *mafiosos* in about a decade. Modern times. Things change too fast.

Rio Hacha is booming. The amount of money coming into the city is scary. But as I mentioned, this wave of prosperity isn't without its disadvantages. I left my city because it has become so dangerous due to warring Mafia factions that only a fool goes out after dark."

"I believe you," I said. "Peace Corps has prohibited us from traveling to La Guajira."

"From what you guys are saying," said Hector, "I like Benjamin Constant even better."

"Don't tell me there are no drugs here," said Jairo.

"Of course there are," said Hector. "But it's not a big problem. Not like Leticia or Rio Hacha."

Jairo laughed mirthlessly. "Wait a few more years. Abuse is spreading like a plague."

I gave Jairo a skeptical look. "You don't use any drugs?" I asked.

"Of course. I like high quality grass and cocaine. But I know when to stop. I use drugs to enhance pleasure, not to escape from reality."

We continued to swap stories as we circled the town. After an hour or so we paused in the shade of a store awning to rest. I was drenched with sweat and my eyes burned from the dust. The buzz of insects from the nearby bush sounded harsh in the stillness of the street. A lone boy sat on a pile of stones under the shade of a banana tree, licking a popsickle.

Jairo and the other Colombian went into the store and bought a soda. I waited outside and chatted with Hector. When Jairo emerged from the store he took a swig of soda and pointed to the boy under the tree. "See that boy," he said to me. "I'll prove to you that anyone who speaks Spanish can understand Portuguese and vice versa."

"Go ahead," I said.

"*Hola! Hola*, boy," called Jairo.

The boy looked at him.

"Lend me five *pesos*," said Jairo in rapid Spanish.

The boy stared at him, his forehead wrinkled.

"I don't think he understands you," I said.

"Of course he does," said Jairo. "Lend me five *pesos*, you stupid kid!"

The boy gazed at us, a blank look on his face.

Hector spoke to him in Portuguese, translating Jairo's words. The boy grimaced and eyed Jairo for a moment. Then he rose and scurried away.

I looked at Jairo and smirked.

"He understood," said Jairo, his voice wavering. "He just didn't want to give me five *pesos* . . . "

Hector and I exchanged a knowing glance but we guarded silence.

We resumed walking and in a short time came to the top of the rise overlooking the wharf. We saw passengers filing onto the launch for the return trip to Leticia.

"What time does the launch leave?" Jairo asked Hector.

"Very soon . . . . But why? I thought you and your friend were going to stay for the night."

"Maybe. You see, I've been invited to a big party in Leticia . . . "

I don't think they want to stay, I thought. That episode with the boy seems to have shaken him a bit. Now he knows Brazil is different from Colombia . . . . I don't know if I should stay myself. Everything is so up in the air. And this town looks like a real nothing . . . . But there might be a boat going to Manaus. I have to check.

"Well," said Jairo, gazing at the launch, "I have all the photos and information that I need for my story on this town . . . "

"But you haven't interviewed any of the residents," interrupted Hector. "Don't worry about the language, brother. I can interpret for you."

"No, I have enough. What's there to know? This place is shit!"

"All right," said Hector, "whatever you want. You better hurry or the boat will be gone."

"What about you?" asked Jairo, turning to me. "Are you staying?"

"Yes. I'll see if this place is shit or not."

"As you wish. You could come to the party . . . "

"Thanks, but no."

"All right. *Adios*."

Jairo and his friend turned and started trotting down the incline to catch the launch.

"Good-bye, jerk," muttered Hector.

"What's wrong?" I asked. "Didn't he pay you?"

"Yes, I was paid . . . . I didn't like him."

"Oh . . . . Listen, can you take me to a cheap *pensión*?"

"Sure," he replied in an eager voice. "I know just the place."

"Let's go, then."

As Hector led me to the *pensión*, which was a block away, he told me about himself. His manner was airy and confident. He spoke with the self-assurance of one who has been around and seen something of the world. A cocky kid, I thought. How much of it is an act?

When we reached the *pensión*, or *pensão* as it's known in Brazil, he told me to wait at the entrance.

"It's better if I go ahead alone and arrange things," he said. "They know me and will give you a good price."

"How much is a good price?"

"More or less $100 *cruzeiros*."

"All right. Find out."

Hector went in and spoke briefly with a middle aged white woman. I saw him point me out to her. She looked at me and nodded her head. I felt useless. I should have gone with him, I thought. Hector came back whistling a tune.

"I fixed it fine for you," he said. "$80 *cruzeiros*." Then he struck an expectant pose, as though waiting for a tip.

"Thanks, man, the price is fine . . . . Ah, one more thing. Do you know if there is a ship leaving for Manaus within the next few days?"

"A ship to Manaus? I doubt it. I haven't heard a thing and I have friends who work on the docks."

"Can you find out for me?"

"Yes, I can check it out."

"I'd appreciate it . . . . And I don't care what kind of boat it is. A cargo ship would be fine."

"I'll look into it . . . . By the way, I'm a very experienced guide. I've shown many, pardon the word, gringos around this area before. So, if you decide to stay here for awhile, I just want you to know that it would be a pleasure for me to assist you with anything you desire."

"Can you take me for a hike in the jungle?"

"Of course! Just last week I took a group of Europeans on a river expedition."

I studied his face. He seems earnest enough, I thought. I like his enthusiasm. But I don't know . . . . Ah, why not? At the moment I have no better option.

"All right, Hector. Can we go for a hike in the bush on the outskirts of town?"

"Yes, of course. Or something much better than that. I have friends who . . . "

"No, wait a moment. For now a short hike is the only thing that interests me . . . . Right now I want to take a shower and clean up and take a nap. Why don't you come back in a couple of hours. When the sun is cooler. Then we can go for a walk. How's that?"

"Perfect. Right now while you rest I'll go check on a boat. No problem." Hector's eyes glowed with elation.

"Fine. See you."

Hector skipped away, whistling lustily as he headed for the wharf. I looked after him with an amused smile on my lips. He must think he's got a real sucker this time, I thought. Well, we'll see . . .

I stepped into the *pensão* and felt a cooling rush of air from a battery of overhead fans. The proprietress, a matronly woman with Germanic features, came to attend me. I tried out a few of the Portuguese phrases I had learned from the tourist tape. The woman grinned delightedly.

"You speak Portuguese," she said.

"Not really."

"Yes, you speak." She asked me a few personal questions. I answered as best I could, using Spanish words when I couldn't think of the Portuguese ones. She seemed to understand me fairly well. I had considerable trouble understanding her. Still, her gracious manner put me at ease and I spoke with confidence. After satisfying her curiosity, she escorted me to the room closest to the front door and told me to call her if

I needed anything.

The room was small but varnished wooden shutters opened onto the street. The bedsheets were clean and smelled fresh. The room was newly remodeled. The ceiling and walls were covered by porous panels of a synthetic material. The tile floor was immaculate. The overhead fan featured a varying speed control dial on the wall by the light switch. Everything clean and modern, I thought. Not bad for two bucks. Now where's the shower?

I found a clean towel draped over the straight-back chair beside the single bed. I picked it up and sallied forth to find the bathhouse. I wandered from the lobby to the kitchen, asking passing maids for directions. They giggled and directed me to the rear of the building. I ended up in the backyard where I found a maid washing clothes. She looked up from her work, a startled expression on her face.

"Do you know where the shower is?" I asked her.

"What? The what?"

"The shower. The shower. You know, to wash." I held up my towel.

"Oh, the shower," she said. "Can't you see? It's right there." She pointed across the yard at two splintery wooden stalls without roofs.

"That?"

"Yes. That's it." She gave me a funny look.

This isn't what I expected after seeing the room, I thought. Guess they're remodeling little by little . . . . Good idea, though. The bather can enjoy the sun while taking a shower. And if it's raining — no need to waste water.

I stepped into the far stall and removed my clothes. I draped them over the door. I turned on the water; a miserable trickle came from the pipe. "Damn!" I followed the drops of water to the floor. The cement was covered by rusty stains that made my feet itch on sight. Better hurry, I thought.

I got under the tepid sprinkle. The water cooled my burning skin. The soap was fragrant. One of the maids sang as she hung clothes. Her voice was soothing and melodious. Before long, as the trickle of water slowed to a drip, I was dozing on my feet. A yell from the adjoining yard snapped me awake. Man, I thought, I'm even more tired than I realized.

I wrapped the towel around my waist, draped my clothes over my arm, and padded back to my room. On the way one of the maids said something to me. I was too weary to respond.

Once in the room I set the fan at medium velocity and tumbled onto the bed. I stared up at the whirling blade. My mind spun with it. I reviewed the events of the past two days. Got to slow down, I thought.

Everything's moving so fast. People, places, time . . . a kaleidoscope. Sandra's green, cat eyes. I'll never forget those eyes. . .

CHAPTER IV

LOST IN THE BUSH

Vaguely, as though from a great distance, I heard a steady rapping sound. It's like a woodpecker, I thought, stirring groggily. Or a beaver tamping down the mud on its dam. I wish it would shut-up . . . . I sat up on the bed, remembering where I was. A voice called me from the other side of the door. It's Hector, I thought. He hasn't forgotten our appointment after all.

"Wait a moment," I called.

"Yes, but hurry," he answered.

What's the hurry? I thought as I got out of bed. My brain was still fogged with sleep. I pulled on my clothes. I opened the door and faced Hector. He looked at me with surprise.

"Do I look that bad?" I asked him.

"You look hungover. Did you sleep?"

"Yes, for a while. I feel better now. I just have to wake up."

Hector's face was sympathetic.

"What's happening?" I asked him. "What did you find out?"

"Well, I have some bad news . . . . I checked around the wharf and with some of my friends who know about such things and — to their knowledge—there are no boats leaving for Manaus until the end of the week. Maybe Saturday."

"Are you sure?"

"Yes! Positive! . . . But one never knows."

"What do you mean by that?"

"Somebody wants to go home early. Schedules change."

"But it's unlikely."

"Exactly."

Damn! I thought. Looks like I'll have to scrap my plan and go back to Leticia. So much for Manaus . . . . What a bitch! But what the hell, I'll wait around Benjamin Constant for a couple of days and do some checking on my own. I'm still not so sure about this Hector. He might be a little con artist . . . . Let's see what develops. Maybe a favorable whim will blow my way and everything will work out. If not . . .well, I know I can have a good time in Leticia.

"What do you want to do this afternoon?" asked Hector, interrupting my thoughts. "I can show you more of Benjamin Constant . . ."

"No, let's go for a turn in the jungle like we planned. Just wait a moment while I put on these boots."

"All right, if you like. But there's one problem."

"What?"

"It's pretty late to go into the bush. We have only a few hours of daylight left and . . . the jungle is very dangerous in the dark. There are snakes and spiders and scorpions . . . . I think it would be better if we go early in the morning."

"No. We can just go to the outskirts of town for a short hike. That's all. Nothing special."

"Yes, we can do that."

"Let's do it, then."

We left the *pensão* and headed for the outskirts of town. After a few blocks of dusty walking, I wanted something to drink.

"How's the beer in Brazil?" I asked Hector.

"It's good."

"Let's stop and get one."

We stopped at a neighborhood store. I ordered a beer. Hector asked for a soda. The man gave me a large tall bottle. The beer was called *Antarctica*. I like the name, I thought. A taste of the frozen south while sweltering on the Equator. I took a swig. The beer was cold and good. Tastes better than Colombian beer, I thought.

Hector drank a *Guaraná*, a carbonated fruit drink.

"Do you drink beer?" I asked him.

"Sometimes. But not when I'm working . . . . Anyway, I prefer *Guaraná*. Beer tastes bitter to me."

We left the cool gloom of the store and walked. The beer had buoyed my spirits and refreshed my tongue and throat. We passed the center of town with its public buildings and swung left toward the river. Hector was a conscientious tour guide. He made several detours to show me such points of interest as the hospital, the high school, and the homes of town personages. I grew bored. This whole town seems to be cheap brick and corrugated metal, I thought. Everything is bland and uniform.

As we ascended a gentle slope that paralleled the Amazon the road, shaded by huge trees, grew muddy. The houses along the sides of the road thinned out and the vegetation thickened. Several abandoned houses were overgrown with vines and brush. The mud sucked at our shoes.

"Pretty soon, right?" I asked Hector.

"Yes, pretty soon."

Hector walked slower and slower. He kept finding excuses to stop. He cast longing gazes back to the town.

"Let's go," I urged him. "It's getting late."

"Yes, you're right, we should come back in the morning."

"Why? Just a short walk, man. What's the problem?"

"No problem." He shuffled forward.

All the bragging he did earlier, I thought, about what an experienced guide he is. He doesn't seem to have a clue.

Opposite the last of a string of modest residences we reached a narrow footpath that led into the bush. A boy about Hector's age sat with half-closed eyes on a log beside the trail.

"This is a friend of mine," Hector said to me. "He lives here and goes into the jungle every day. I'll ask him how it is today."

Hector greeted his friend and introduced me. Then they spoke for several minutes. Concentrate as I might I was able to understand only an occasional word. I watched Hector's face. He maintained a grave countenance as he talked and gestured toward the bush. His friend chuckled several times. I folded my arms and waited. At last Hector finished talking and turned to me.

"Well?" I asked.

Hector's shoulders slumped and his eyes were downcast. "Bad news," he said. "My friend says the ground is very treacherous because of unusually heavy rains . . . . He thinks it would be advisable to stay on solid ground and away from the forest."

"Really?" I stepped onto the footpath and tested the ground. "It doesn't look that bad. It's no worse than the road we came here on."

Hector avoided my eyes. "The mud is much worse the farther you go. That's what my friend says."

"The plants don't hold the ground? . . . I don't understand, Hector? What is the problem? You told me you had plenty of experience as a guide."

"I do! The problem is with the mud."

"Look, man, I have boots for the mud. And you should be used to it. It must rain here all the time . . . . But I don't care. If you think it's too dangerous—no problem. We can do something else."

"You think I'm afraid?"

"I don't think anything. What do you think?"

Hector stared at the shrubbery for a moment. "Let's go." He turned and followed the footpath; I was right behind him. We entered a maze of weeds and brush.

"This isn't really jungle," said Hector. "It's reclaimed farmland that they are letting lie fallow for a year or so."

"It's still thick," I said, pushing a vine away from my face.

"This is nothing. Wait until later."

After five minutes of walking, the footpath disappeared and we plunged into dense foliage. Though I was covered with insect repellent, swarms of bugs dove at my face. I swatted at them and forged ahead. Hector moved fast, threading a meandering course. Within minutes I was breathing heavily and my lungs burned. The heavy, sweet air was suffocating. The plants tore and scratched at us with thorny fingers. Myriad snags and pitfalls lay hidden in the bush. Trailing vines and sucking mud worried our feet, trying to trip us up and send us to the ground where stinging ants with horny mandibles awaited. The ants were monsters.

"You should have brought a machete," I called to Hector.

"I don't have one."

He continued on, forcing the pace. I puffed along behind him, too proud and stupid to ask for a rest. He's getting back at me, I thought.

Hector halted next to a huge, lichen covered tree and waited for me to catch up.

"This is where you really have to watch yourself," he said. "This kind of zone is more dangerous than the area we passed through . . . . Here you have venemous snakes, spiders, scorpions, even frogs. Look before you step and watch the trees."

"All right."

"Do you want to go back to town?"

"No! This is what I came to see . . . . Are there jaguars here?

Hector laughed. "No, not this close to town. Thank God . . . . Are you tired?"

"A little bit. But I'm fine."

"I'll go slower now."

Hector started forward; I stepped gingerly after him. His warning words and the gloom of the forest played on my mind. My scalp tingled and my senses were heightened. Every rustling limb caught my eye. I heard jabbering monkeys and the whir of insect's wings. I imagined a jaguar leaping from the camouflage of a tree and onto my unprotected back. I could feel the claws digging into my flesh and the teeth at my throat. Don't be ridiculous, I thought. There are no jaguars here. And even if there were there's better things to eat than me.

As we continued on and nothing untoward occurred, my anxiety lessened. I became entranced by the richness and variety of the flora and fauna. I marvelled at nature's imagination and flair for adaptation. We reached an open space under a tree and I paused for a closer look. In the immediate area I saw ferns with leaves like flapping elephant ears—trees with thick gnarled limbs, spiraling their branches into the sky and forming a canopy that blocked out the sun—bright red berries—poisonous fruit—beckoning enticingly from a bed of emerald. Multi-colored dragon flies, with a metallic glint, hovering, then buzzing away, like helicopters. A praying mantis, the size of my thumb, in meditative pose, green as the leaf it sat on, waiting for something to fall into its clutches. I saw all this and much more. I craned my neck from side to side, letting my senses drink until they were satiated.

"Let's go," said Hector, a worried look on his face. "It's getting late. This is no place to get stuck after dark, believe me."

We resumed the hike. Hector took a circular route and we left the forest and returned to overgrown brush. We must be close to town, I thought.

Then we blundered from one blind rut to another. Everything looked familiar but nothing was absolutely the same. Hector muttered to himself and walked faster. We're travelling in a circle, I thought.

"Hector, what's going on?"

"Nothing. Everything is under control."

Oh yeah, I thought. This guy seems about as well versed in jungle craft as me. I hope I didn't make a big mistake with him. I don't feel like sleeping in a tree.

I caught up to Hector and walked beside him. He kept his eyes glued to the ground.

"Don't worry," he said. "There's a trail that cuts through here and leads back to town. I should find it at any moment."

"All right, Hector, I believe you. Take your time."

We wandered on. Hector made several detours and backtracked three or four times. He continued to assure me that everything was fine but the concerned look on his face belied his words. I remained silent, not wanting to upset his concentration. Then he backtracked again and I could no longer contain myself.

"Where are we going, Hector?"

"The main path is just ahead of us," he replied, forcing a smile. "I am sure of it. I just spotted a landmark I recognize."

"I hope so . . . "

A moment later we encountered a narrow path and followed it to a broad clearing.

"Now I know where we are," said Hector. "There's no problem." The relief was evident in his voice.

I breathed easier.

"What's going on here?" I asked Hector, surveying the field.

"They are preparing this zone for cultivation. They came through here a few days ago with machetes and axes. Soon they will burn."

"It looks weird."

Fallen timber, like wasted corpses on the field of battle, lay dormant and forboding on the exposed black loam. Five foot high mounds of earth and twigs rose eerily over the vegetation rotting in the hot sun.

"What are those mounds?" I asked Hector, walking over to examine one.

"These are ant hills," he said.

"Ant hills?"

I took out my camera and snapped a few pictures. I took one of Hector posing next to one of the ant hills. Then he took one of me. Hector's self-assurance returned. He chattered about his dual life in Benjamin Constant and Leticia. "I hope to open my own tour agency someday," he said. "The problem is, I'm not sure where I want to live. Leticia has more business, but also much more competition—established competition. It would be difficult. Here in Benjamin Constant I have many friends to help me get started."

"Think it out well," I commented. "But it sounds like you have the right idea."

"I think so."

We rested and chatted for a while longer. I liked Hector for his enthusiasm and cheerfulness. He was starting to grow on me. I just hope he gets us out of this bush without further problems, I thought.

While we talked, dark ominous clouds congregated overhead. The sky turned blue-gray and a damp wind rustled the high grass and bushes.

"We'd better get going," said Hector, eyeing the sky. "Here dusk hits like lightning. There is almost no twilight; it's light one minute and dark the next. And these clouds will make it happen even faster."

"I'm ready . . . . Now, are you sure you know which path to take from here?"

"No problem. This clearing is the landmark I was searching for." Hector pointed his long skinny arm to the bush. "We follow that footpath left by the cutters and . . . no problem. We're back in town having a drink."

We followed the path into the bush. Within a few hundred yards it disappeared under fresh growth.

"Now where?" I asked.

"Relax, man. From here I don't need a path."

You don't convince me, I thought.

We moved into heavy undergrowth. Hector again seemed to be leading us in circles. Less and less light seeped through the foliage. I slapped at insects and cursed under my breath. Then I stumbled head-long over a vine. As I went down I grabbed at a branch and had my hand raked by thorns.

"Shit!"

Hector hurried back to me. "Are you all right?"

I picked myself up. "Yes, I'm all right. But I'm not sure you know where you're going. This doesn't look anything like what we passed on the way in."

"Because it's not the way we came in. This is a different route. I know where we are."

We stumbled forward, clawing the plants out of our faces, until we hit a screen of impenetrable vegetation. Hector decided to double back. Now I was truly worried. We thrashed through the bush for another fifteen minutes or so. Finally Hector stopped and turned to me, a look of dejection on his face.

"We're lost," he said. "Which way do you think we should go?"

"Which way do I think we should go? . . . "

My impulse was to take him by his scrawny neck and ring it. What a fucking worthless guide, I thought. He's got us stranded in the middle of nowhere . . . . Got to keep cool. Yelling at him might get him flustered and make things worse. I counted to ten to control myself before I spoke.

"Look, Hector, you are the guide. You come from here. I don't know where we're at . . . . Now, before we take another step, look around and think about where we are before we get any farther from town. Take your time."

Hector gave me a reproving look, as though I were the one who had screwed up. "You don't have any idea?"

"How the hell would I know where to go?"

"All right. It's only a matter of time before I relocate the correct path. I got sidetracked somewhere."

"Fine. But what's a matter of time? . . . Do you mean hours, days, or months? I can just imagine us trying to sleep in the crotch of a tree.

Yeah, just like Tarzan."

Hector giggled. "Don't worry, I'll find it soon."

I hope this is his idea of a joke, I thought. But it ain't funny.

We moved ahead with greater urgency. Every minute brought night closer. Hector croaked reassurances, but as we blundered from one dead end to another, his voice betrayed less and less conviction. I remained silent. If I hound him he might panic, I thought. Just stay cool. We can't be far from town.

Again Hector doubled back. He looked confused. I caught him glancing back at me from time to time with a reproachful look in his eyes. He must be cursing the day fate sent this idiot gringo to plague his existence. As for me I'd like to thrash him for his lies. Experienced guide, huh.... But it's my fault, too. I could see he didn't want to go into the jungle and I pushed him into it.

As we tripped along Hector slowed his place. Both of us were winded and arm-weary from pushing the vegetation aside. What we need is a seeing-eye dog, I thought. Or a trained monkey.

Panting and sweating, we broke through the trees and brush and onto a field of head high grass. Without a word we halted. Hector stood on his toes and spun like a top, trying to get his bearings. The grass rustled in his face, blocking his vision. It seemed to mock us.

"We must be close to town," I said. "This land has been worked."

"I don't recognize it," said Hector. "But we must be close.

A sudden gust of wind rippled the grass. Thunderheads rumbled in the distance. The moist air seemed to crackle with energy. The sky was gloomier. Hector and I exchanged serious looks.

"Well, what do we do?" I asked him.

"I know we are close. We still have time and light enough for another attempt."

"But if we can't find the way back? . . . We have to do something. We need some kind of shelter for the night."

"Let's not think about that yet. We can still find our way back."

"We have to think about it. We need to do something before nightfall. We need light."

"I don't know what to do," said Hector. "I've never stayed in the forest overnight."

"Me either. At least not this one.... We'll need a fire. I have matches."

"Let's look for a trail. We still have about an hour of light."

"All right."

I felt calmer. I was already anticipating the worst. Looks like we're really in for an adventure, I thought. This is a lot more than I bargained for. We need to . . .

Suddenly, from somewhere in the grass, came the sound of cracking twigs.

"What now?" I exclaimed. "Some kind of strange animal?"

"Sshish!" whispered Hector.

We listened intently. Hector's face cocked forward as though he were a bloodhound on a hot scent. I stood frozen. Adrenalin pumped through my body. The sounds moved closer. We swiveled our heads, trying to localize the thing.

Hector blurted something in Portuguese.

After a moment of silence he was answered.

Hector called out again. Though I understood nothing his voice carried a hint of relief.

Again we received an answering call.

Hector looked at me and smiled. "Everything's all right now."

We peered in the direction from which the call had come. A moment later, emerging from the cover of the waving stalks, out trudged a rustic backwoodsman. On one shoulder he bore two saplings and on the other an antique rifle. An olive drab army cap sat upon his head, framing a grizzled, sun-spotted face. He grinned shyly at us, showing greenish teeth. Man, I thought, ugly as you are I'd like to give you a kiss. Moses come to lead us out of the wilderness. And just in time.

The woodsman never broke stride. He gestured to us to follow him and walked straight into the bush. Hector, grinning and confident once again, fired sentences at the man. I understood nothing. The man made only token responses. He was in a hurry.

"Do you know him?" I asked Hector.

"Of course. I know almost everybody in Benjamin. His name is Simon. He's good people."

Simon strode unerringly through the baffling tangle of vegetation. His step was light and sure. Nothing like experience, I thought. I should have had him for a guide.

Hector despaired of conversing with Simon and turned to me.

"You know," he said, "I was never really lost. I know this route we're on now. I was only momentarily confused."

"Whatever you say, Hector."

"You don't believe me?"

I laughed, an insult dying on my lips. I don't know how to say unmitigated gall in Spanish and I don't want to tell him he's full of shit, I thought. I'm just glad we're getting out of this.

116

Within twenty minutes we were on the dirt road leading back to town. We had been within shouting distance.

"Ask Simon if he wants to go for a drink," I told Hector. "I'm inviting."

Hector asked him. The man laughed and gave Hector some kind of explanation.

"Thank you," said Simon, speaking to me. "I can't. Thank you."

"Thank you," I said.

"His wife is waiting for him with dinner," said Hector.

"It's all right," I said to Simon. "Thank you."

Simon smiled and walked off. His grizzled face was imprinted on my memory. Well, I thought, thanks to him we escaped cheaply from that stupidity. I stared at Hector for a moment. I should get on his case. Ah, what the hell. Nothing happened.

"You want to go for a drink?" I asked him.

Hector looked surprised. "Of course. Let's go."

We retired to a neighborhood store that also served as a bar. I ordered a beer for myself and a *Guaraná* for Hector. While we drank I teased him.

"Man," I said, "if you're going to run a tour agency you have to do better than today. That could have been dangerous. If you can't guide someone in the forest you have to get someone that can."

"That's what I wanted to do," said Hector. "But you were in a hurry; I didn't want to disappoint you. For real jungle tours I have partners who help me."

"You should have told me that. I would have waited."

"It was late. And I didn't think I needed help for a little hike . . . . Anyway, nothing happened."

"Luckily. Next time you might not be so lucky."

"No, I've learned something today. Give me another chance. I'll bring a friend who is an expert in the jungle."

"I thought you were an expert in the jungle."

"Well, I'm more of a translator and businessman. Let me take you out tomorrow and I'll really show you something."

"That's what I'm afraid of." I chuckled to take the edge off my words. "If you show me much more than you did today it might prove fatal."

"Just give me another chance. You'll see."

"All right. Maybe."

We finished our drinks and headed for the *pensão*. On the way we passed a vacant lot where a gang of young men were playing soccer on a dirt field. One of them called Hector. We stopped. The young man came over and talked to Hector.

"They want me to play," Hector told me. "This is my team.

"Do you want to play?" the man asked me.

I looked at the rock strewn field. "No, I want a cold beer."

The young man laughed. "Later."

"Can you find the *pensión* by yourself?" Hector asked me. "I want to stay here and play."

"Sure. No problem. Go ahead and play."

"Should I come by the *pensión* tomorrow morning to see what you want to do?"

"Well...Yes, come by if you want."

Hector smiled. "Good. Until tomorrow." He turned and raced onto the field.

Maybe I'll be gone by the time he gets there, I thought. I don't know about this kid.

I walked off and found the *pensão* two blocks from the vacant lot. No problem, man

CHAPTER V

STOWAWAY—SORT OF

I opened the wooden shutters and looked out on the street. Night had fallen and the townspeople were coming out of their homes. I looked at the sky. Glimmering Venus was visible. She seemed to wink at me. Maybe it's an omen, I thought. Something is going to happen tonight. Hopefully something good . . . . How bright the stars are here. Clear skies and clean air.

I felt restless and hungry. I closed the shutters and left the room. The front of the *pensão*, a sitting area with lounge chairs and old magazines, was moribund. I went to the dining room and found the staff eating supper.

"Good evening," I said, looking at the food spread on the table.

"Good evening," said the *dona* (mistress). "Are you hungry?"

"Yes."

"Would you like to eat with us?"

"What is there to eat?"

"What we have here. There is plenty."

I saw a tureen of clear broth, white rice, bread, and one boiled egg for each diner. Plenty? I thought. Maybe for you but I want something more substantial. I haven't had anything solid since early this morning in Leticia. But if it's cheap enough I could have a snack and talk to these pretty maids for a while.

"How much?" I asked the *dona*.

"Only $80 *cruzeiros*."

"No, thank you. It's still too early for me to eat."

"All right." The *dona* looked offended.

I left the dining room and walked to the front door. Now I understand why the rooms are so cheap, I thought. Charging $80 *cruzeiros* for that pap seems out of line. I'll go out in a little while and find something. Maybe make an evening of it.

I stood in the doorway and watched the people pass. I tapped my right foot to the music issuing from many of the open front doors of the

119

houses on the block. The corner store was jammed with drinking men. This place is waking up, I thought. Maybe there is some action here — it is a port. But where can I go?

I was bursting with suppressed nervous energy. I felt unsettled and scatter-brained, as though I had drunk too much strong coffee. I paced from the sitting room to the dining room and back several times. Finally I sat on one of the lounge chairs and thumbed through a magazine. I was joined by one of the other guests. After a short interval he struck up a conversation with me.

"So you are from the United States," he said. "I have been there. I was a sailor on a merchant ship."

"Did you like it?" I asked.

"Yes, to visit. I like here better. It's calmer."

"Probably so. I don't know."

"Do you like Brazil?"

"This is my first day."

"Your first day!" The man smiled and produced a bottle of clear liquid. "Have a drink to celebrate your first day in *Brasil*."

"What is it?"

"*Cachaça* (cane alcohol)." He took a draught and passed me the bottle. "To celebrate your first day."

I took a sip. The fiery liquid burned my throat and shot to my head. "It is strong," I said.

The man laughed. "Have another shot. It will help you learn to speak *brasileiro*."

I took another shot. The liquor was harsh but the effect on my head was good. This would be better mixed, I thought.

The man knew a few words of English and tried them on me. Unfortunately my Portuguese was much better than his English. Our conversation petered out after about five minutes. The man gave me a last shot of *cachaça* and left. A nice guy, I thought. I feel more settled now — ready to go out . . . . But first I better change these muddy pants. They smell of jungle rot.

I retired to my room. While changing clothes I was overtaken by a bizarre sensation. The combination of nervous energy and alcohol had done something to me. I felt detached from my body. I looked at the mirror hanging on the wall over the bed and saw this strange but familiar person languorously move about and change pants under the dim, artificial glow of the electric lamp. Except for my sight my senses seemed to be deserting me. It was as if I had become a disembodied spirit, or an actor in a film watching himself on a slow motion replay.

"This is crazy," I said aloud. "The booze wasn't that strong."

Weird, I thought. My voice sounds like it's coming from underwater. What's happening to me? . . . I better go out and get some air. Get some food.

I left the room and hit the street. The sensation of self-detachment persisted as I walked. My thoughts became fuzzy. My mind went numb. I gave no conscious thought to where I was headed, nor did I care. I was adrift, floating, like a wind tossed paper wrapper. A stray light caught my eye and pulled me up the street. A shouted oath, a burst of laughter, led me down an alley. Bright Christmas decorations and loud music brought me to the town *praça* (square). Faces were caricatures. I saw everything as absurd. I laughed. People gave me funny looks. I laughed harder. I walked faster and the bright lights dimmed. Tree branches swayed and leaves rustled in the gentle breeze. I felt sweat drying on my forehead as I stopped walking and looked about.

I was on the edge of town. Behind the last row of houses the darkness was thick and the brooding trees were silhouettes. A delicious aroma of roasting beef tickled my nostrils. I noticed the building directly in front of me. Through mesh-screened windows I saw a spacious, well-lit interior with rows of tables and chairs. It's a restaurant, I thought. Just what I need.

Without further delay I entered. Save for a lone man drinking a beer, I was the only customer. This made me hesitate before I sat down. I surveyed the room. The decor was simple and agreeable; a backdrop of soothing pastels with a lush variety of plants hanging from the ceiling and potted ferns scattered between the bamboo furnishings. The red, stone tile floor was clean. The overhead fans provided good air circulation and a comfortable temperature. The place made me feel at ease.

I stepped forward and was met by two waitresses. They led me to a table in the back in full view of the kitchen.

"What would you like?" asked one of the waitresses, a teenage girl.

"I don't know. I want to see the menu."

"The what?"

"The menu. The list."

"We don't have one."

"What do you have to eat?"

The girl rattled off a list of things. I looked at her and shrugged my shoulders.

"I don't understand you," I said.

The two waitresses looked at each other and giggled. I smiled and said every Portuguese word for different foods that I knew. I don't mind making a fool of myself if it's the only way to get my point across, I thought. The girls giggled some more. I must be butchering their language. But they don't seem to mind. It's like a game.

Finally the cook, a young black woman, scolded the girls from behind the counter.

"Come with me," said one of the waitresses. "The cook will show you what there is to eat."

She led me to a glass plated cooler and left me with the cook.

"This is the fresh meat and fish that we have today," said the cook, tapping the glass with her hand. She pointed to each cut on display and pronounced its name in Portuguese. I repeated after her. In the end, through a combination of words and pantomime, I managed to order a meal of grilled beef, salad, and rice.

"And to drink?" she asked. "Water? *Guaraná*?"

"A beer."

She laughed. "You already know that word well."

I took my beer and sat at the table closest to the grill. I took a long pull. Now this is the way to learn a language, I thought.

While the steak fried I continued my conversation with the cook. She asked me about my background and plans and filled me in on information of local interest. She was easy to talk to and understand. Her speech was slow and precise without being choppy. She was patient. When I had trouble formulating a sentence she would smile encouragement and fill in the gaps. She was a natural teacher. Within five minutes she taught me several new and useful words. For a foreigner like myself it was a pleasure to hear her. If I stay in Benjamin Constant, I thought, this will be a good place to come to. They make me feel like a king.

The food was ready; I was served a heaping mound of rice and a generous portion of meat for $60 *cruzeiros*. I ate slowly, savoring every juicy morsel.

I was about halfway through my dinner and working on my second beer when I spotted Hector and a friend at the front door. He saw me at about the same moment and rushed over to my table, chattering something as he came. His bony face was alight and his eyes sparkled. He was blowing and sweating like a racehorse. He babbled something in mixed Spanish-Portuguese. I eyed him bemusedly.

"I can't understand what you're saying, Hector," I said.

Hector was unable to catch his breath. He choked on his words.

"All right," I said. "Why don't you sit down, calm yourself, and order something to drink for you and your friend. My treat . . . . Then you can tell me what's going on."

Though they sat down, Hector squirmed with agitation as he fought to recover his wind.

"Bring us a *Guaraná*," called his friend to the waitress. She brought a bottle and two glasses. I filled one of the glasses and passed it to Hector. He gulped down a swallow.

"Drink," I urged his friend, who was watching me saucer-eyed. He filled his glass and drank.

I resumed eating. Then I noticed Hector's friend staring at me as if I were an alien from another planet. This irritated me. I leered at him until he averted his gaze. Then I turned to Hector.

"Are you ready to talk?" I asked him.

He shook his head and took another drink.

Maybe this is serious, I thought. What can he have to tell me that would bring him here in this state?

I watched him take another swallow of his drink. He seemed to have recovered his breath but he remained silent. Now he's playing games, I thought. I looked at him and shrugged my shoulders. Then I cut off a piece of steak and started chewing.

"Where have you been?" he burst out. "I've been looking all over town for you."

Slowly I raised my head, annoyed by his preemptory tone of voice. "You must not have looked very hard," I said. "Except for a short walk, I've been here and at the hotel all evening."

"I went to the hotel. Nobody knew where you went."

"When I left ... I didn't know where I was going. I just knew I wanted something to eat .... And now, if you please, I want to know why you were looking for me."

"Because I have some important information ... " He paused for effect, really hamming it up.

"Go ahead," I said. "What is it?"

"There's a cargo ship leaving for Manaus this very night."

"What? Are you sure?" How can I take this guy seriously? I thought.

"It's certain!"

"If it's so certain why didn't you know about this earlier when you checked at the dock?

"Nobody knew." Hector leaned forward. His face was earnest. "What happened is that the captain decided on short notice to cut his stay and take off tonight. He's got a cargo of lumber and they finished loading it ahead of schedule. He probably wants to get home early for

Christmas holidays. Who knows?...Anyway, you have to hurry! They're going to leave soon."

What time is soon?"

"I don't know, man ... . But very soon."

"Can I finish my meal?"

"Of course! If you want to risk missing the boat."

"I'll risk it. I'm hungry."

This is crazy, I thought. Why should I spoil my dinner with a head-long dash to a ship that might not be leaving for days? How did he miss this information earlier? There aren't that many big ships in port. Maybe he didn't check. . . . Still, he certainly looks like he's telling the truth. Hell, what reason would he have to lie?... A prank? Nah. He's telling the truth . . . . But this food is so good. And I haven't felt this mellow in days. Damn the boat! If it leaves it leaves.

I forked rice into my mouth and washed it down with a long swallow of beer. Hector squirmed in his seat as he watched me.

"Who told you the boat is leaving tonight?" I asked him between gulps of food.

"One of the sailors on the boat is a friend of mine. He told me. Don't you believe me?"

Yes, I believe you. I just don't think the boat will leave in the next hour."

"Maybe, maybe not. But there are arrangements to be made."

"Hector, relax. Order another soda."

"I don't want anymore soda."

"All right. Give me ten minutes of peace and we'll go. I just want to finish this plate."

Hector folded his arms and stared at the table. The mound of food on my plate shrank. Hector's friend, a dark sturdy youth with kinky hair and the look of a soccer player, asked me breathless questions about the wonders of the United States. I answered him between mouthfuls of food. I distracted Hector by having him translate for me when I couldn't express or understand something. This way I was able to finish the bulk of my dinner with relative calm. Still, Hector's worming contortions in his chair and nagging tongue finally got the better of me. The food lost its taste. I left a portion of rice and salad on the plate and swilled the remainder of the beer.

"All right," I said. "I'm ready. I'll go pay the bill and we can go."

"Hurry. I'll wait for you outside."

I went up to the cook and gave her the money. "Thank you for everything," I said. "The food was good. You give me a good image of

Brasil."

"Are you coming back?"

"I don't know."

"Good luck."

I left the restaurant and found Hector and his friend in animated conversation. "Let's go," I said.

"I can't," said Hector's friend. "I have to go home. Have a good voyage. Luck."

"Same to you."

"I'll see you tomorrow," said Hector. His friend turned and walked off.

"Now we have to get moving," said Hector. "Let's go."

"I'm right with you. On to the *pensão* to get my stuff."

Hector turned and almost at a trot started down the hill. I mosied after him. I felt bloated and lazy. Before long Hector was a good half block ahead of me. Then, realizing he was alone, he turned and glared at me until I caught up.

"You must hurry!" he said. "Don't you realize that? The boat may leave at any moment."

"I can't hurry, man. I'm full." I smiled. "It's very bad for your health to rush around after a heavy meal."

Hector gave me a dirty look.

"O.K. I'll try to move faster."

Now we walked side by side and I quickened my pace. Still, I didn't exactly rush. I'm not ready for this, I thought. It can't be real. I no sooner resign myself to not going then he comes along with this. If he said tomorrow—fine. I'd be ready. But this? . . . Well, what's that saying? . . . Expect nothing and be prepared for everything. Especially when dealing with someone like Hector.

As we drew closer to the *pensão* Hector walked faster. I finally caught some of his urgency and actually passed him. I went into the *pensão* and speedily packed my bag. Forewarned by Hector, the *dona* was waiting for me at the front door when I came out with my bag in hand.

"You are leaving so soon?" she said.

"Yes. Hector says there is a boat for me that leaves tonight."

"Congratulations. I hope you have a good trip."

"Thank you. I hope there really is a boat. If not, maybe I'll see you later."

"Just give me $40 *cruzeiros*," said the *dona*. "Since you are not going to spend the night I'll only charge you half the price."

I was shocked. "Why, thank you. Thank you. That's very kind of you." I shook her hand.

"Good luck to you," she said. "Have a good life."

"The same to you."

"Let's go," urged Hector, tugging at my arm. We walked out of the front door and turned to go down the hill.

"Eh! Where are you going, mister American?" It was the Brazilian sailor who had given me the *cachaça*. He looked crocked. "Let's go to the bar and have a drink."

"I can't," I said. "I'm going to catch a boat for Manaus right now."

"Right now? That's too bad."

"Not for me."

He laughed. "Good luck. Enjoy *Brasil*."

Hector had started walking down the hill before I finished speaking to the sailor. I hurried to catch him.

"Who was that?" he asked me.

"Some guest at the hotel. We shared a drink."

We pointed our noses towards the winking lanterns of the wharf and walked in silence. I watched the action on the street and was surprised. The night, as was the case with Leticia, seemed to imbue Benjamin Constant with a more vibrant, almost magical, personality. Hundreds of flaring light bulbs were strung on wires along either side of the street and fireflies arced through the humidity, vying with the stars in brilliance and ionizing the air. The buildings no longer struck me as pastel, brick piles, but rather as quivering juke boxes — shaking its inhabitants, like so many dice, out on the street to dance, sing, play, laugh, quarrel, gossip, weep, love, shout—to live.

"Is it always like this here?" I asked Hector.

"Like what?"

"This live. It's like a *carnaval* on this street."

"This is normal. There are many bars for the sailors on this street .... And many prostitutes to service them."

"It's still live."

"Away from this area most of the town is quiet. This zone can be dangerous."

"Or fun?"

"I suppose."

We passed the red-light district and hit a darkened warehouse street. As we drew closer to the murky river the din and glow of the town was muted and, the vivid memory of which, made the shadows flitting among the tethered ships even more forboding. Here was a gloom to skulk behind, and a stillness to provoke murmurs.

"When we hit the beach keep your eyes open," said Hector. "Here there are often assaults on drunken sailors."

"Don't worry. I already had that feeling."

I felt my senses, already jarred awake by the tumult of the street, shaking off the lethargy that had gripped them earlier and acquiring an acuteness that transcended their norm.

We halted on the lip of the embankment that separated the road from the beach. "Listen," whispered Hector. "We have to find a certain ship over there and speak to the captain about your passage. The smell of fresh lumber should lead me to it."

"Fine. Let's do it. I'll follow you . . . . But just one question . . . "

"What?"

"Why are you whispering?"

"I told you—the thiefs! Let's go."

We leaped from the embankment and sank into the gravely sand. As we shuffled toward the boats Hector took an angled course. The sand grew firmer and moister. We walked along the shore. Soon a great mass loomed out of the darkness.

"This way," said Hector, taking my arm. He pulled me onto a wooden pier that jutted well out over the river. We walked along the pier. Now the inky water seemed to surround us; it smelled of petroleum and emitted an uncomfortable coolness. Hector halted suddenly; I bumped into him.

"Careful," he hissed.

"Sorry," I said. "Where are we going?

"See that light over there?" Hector pointed to a beacon that seemed far away.

"Yes."

"That's your ship."

"How do we get there? We can't walk on water."

"We have to climb over the cargo flat."

"What cargo flat?"

"I don't see it. Huh, we must have passed it. Let's go back."

We retraced our steps along the pier.

"Ah, here it is," said Hector. "Careful. We have to climb down."

We jumped from the pier to a metal flatbed. The sweet aroma of fresh hewn lumber perfumed the night. We took a few steps forward and I banged my nose into a wall of wood.

"Careful," said Hector. "Follow me. There's space to walk around the corner here. Along the side."

"All right, man," I said, rubbing my nose. "I hear you already."

I groped around the stack of lumber and followed Hector. We tightroped along a narrow corridor formed by the lumber on one side and the river on the other. My bag was giving me problems. It threw me off balance. I kept my left hand on the wood for support and carried the bag out over the water in my right hand. My arm began to ache. This is no picnic, I thought. This damn bag is heavy. I can't see a damn thing.

"Watch it," said Hector. "There's a pole here."

I eased around a thick metal stake used to keep the cargo in place.

"Thanks for the warning," I said. "Is it much farther?"

"Not too far. You want to rest?"

"Yes." I rested my bag on top of the steel pole; it was flat-topped. I looked at the ship's lamp ahead of us; it seemed farther away than before. Hector came over to me.

"We're about halfway there," he said. "Are you ready?"

"Sure. Let's go." I hefted my bag and followed him. "There's no problem except for this damn bag."

As we eased forward I kept my eyes on the lantern. The light seemed to recede as we advanced. This can't be, I thought. It's an illusion. My imagination is running away from me. I focused my eyes on Hector's white shirt. I lost track of time. Then Hector's shirt disappeared.

"We're here," he said, from behind the corner of lumber. I rounded the bend and dumped my bag on the deck. The flat was bound to a white tugboat by steel ties.

Hector's face was purplish in the indirect glow of the ship lamp. "Wait for me a moment," he said. "I'll go in and make the arrangements with the captain."

"Why alone? I think we should both go so the captain knows who's coming."

"No! It would be better if I go alone. Believe me."

"I don't like people making arrangements for me when I can do it myself."

"Trust me," said Hector, eyeing me unswervingly. "It's better like this. I'll talk to my friend."

"All right, as you wish," I said, shrugging my shoulders. "No sense arguing about it and wasting time. Go ahead. I'll wait here."

Hector leaped across the narrow gap separating the flat from the tug and clambered over the guard rail. In seconds he vanished from sight.

I waited impatiently, wringing my hands against an imaginary chill. I stared up at the spot where Hector disappeared and listened for sounds coming from the tug. What's taking so long? I thought. Are they giving him problems?

I turned and faced the town; its bright lights and muffled sounds were oddly comforting. Ah, there's no problem, I thought. I can always go back there if things don't work out . . .

"Eh, man! Wake up!"

I turned in time to see Hector leap from the rail and onto the flat.

"What's the word?" I asked. "Good or bad?"

"Well, I don't know yet. The captain is still in town. But my friend says you can probably have a place . . . . You just have to wait around and talk to the captain when he gets back. That is, if you still want to go."

"Of course I want to go. I wouldn't have come with you if I didn't want to go."

"Well, I have some things to do in town. I can't wait around with you. You'll have to speak to the captain yourself."

"That's no problem, man." I snorted. "Believe it or not, I can take care of myself."

Hector chuckled. "Very well, then . . . . There's not much more I can do here. So, I guess I'll get back to town."

"You don't want to stay and wait with me for a little while?" I asked in a teasing tone of voice. "I thought you said the boat was leaving at any moment."

"Probably not until midnight. My friend says the captain is in a bar with some friends . . . . I would like to wait with you but I'm in a hurry. You can deal with the captain."

"Probably. I was just kidding you, Hector." Impulsively I stuck out my hand. "All right, man, thank you for all your help. You really did show me something."

"For nothing. It was my pleasure. I want you to leave with a good impression of this place."

"Let me give you something for helping me find this boat." I started to reach for my wallet.

"Forget it," he said, raising a hand to stop me. "You were my guest. Have a good voyage."

Hector turned on his heel and, whistling a popular tune, faded into the night. I was alone.

I picked up my bag and looked at the tugboat. Time to get on board, I thought. I remained frozen in my tracks. My body tilted forward but my feet refused to budge. . . . What is it? I'm nervous. I got too dependent on that kid. I paced along the flat for a minute or so. . . .This is ridiculous. What am I worried about? Ah, fuck it! Either they take me or they don't . . . .But I'm sure not going to find out here.

I slung the bag over my back and climbed across the steel tie. Then I dropped the bag onto the boat's deck and sidesaddled over the guard railing. I picked up the bag and strode forward, following the railing. I passed a small cabin and came to the heart of the boat, the cargo hold, an open area that encompassed about a third of the vessel's length and the broadest part of its width. The first things I noticed in the dim light were five brightly colored hammocks, of various makes and sizes, hanging from hooks on the ceiling beams. Backpacks and assorted travel gear lay piled on the floor beneath the hammocks.

I stopped walking and leaned against the railing. How strange to leave this stuff unattended, I thought. Where are the owners?

I took a deep breath. The heavy odors of machine oil and gasoline were in the air but a more pungent aroma dominated and made my nostrils twitch. That smell is very familiar, I thought. But I just can't place it. Huh . . .

I was about to continue my exploration when a young man sauntered in from the shadows of the stern. On seeing me he stopped, a surprised look on his face. For a long silent moment we eyed each other. He was short and wiry. His dark hair reached to the nape in the back and almost to the eyes in the front, framing a round face with high cheekbones. He advanced a couple of steps closer and the overhead naked bulb shone full in his face, revealing a set of piercing brown eyes. Our eyes locked momentarily. Then he appeared to relax and a genial smile came forth. I returned his smile at once.

"Are you a passenger?" he asked me in Spanish, with the same lilting cadence, though less pronounced, that I had heard from the Marxist Peruvian in Leticia.

"I hope so. I guess that will depend on what the captain decides."

"Don't worry. There should be no problem with him." His grin was a mile wide. "You speak Spanish. That makes me happy. I wasn't sure I would have anyone to talk to. But where are you from?"

"I'm from the United States. I speak Spanish because I work in Colombia."

"Ah, that's good. My name is Fernando. I come from Lima, Peru." We shook hands.

"Welcome to the *Magalhães*, he said.

"The *Magalhães?* What's that?"

"The name of the ship. Strange, no?"

"Very strange, at least the sound. I wonder what it means?"

"Who knows?"

"Well, I hope I get to take a trip on it."

"Don't worry. I'm sure he will let you come. If you have the money for passage."

"How much?"

"$1000 *cruzeiros* to Manaus."

"That's reasonable."

"For me it's expensive. But the price includes meals."

"What kind of meals?"

"I don't know. We'll find out tomorrow."

I glanced around the hold. "Where does everyone sleep?"

"All the passengers sleep in hammocks."

"All of the passengers?"

"Well, most of them, that I know of. My hammock is right there alongside those others." He pointed to a meshed string hammock a few feet from us.

"Are there any *camarotes* (cabins) for passengers?"

"I don't think so. This is a small ship; even most of the sailors sleep in hammocks."

"Shit!"

"What's wrong? Don't you have a hammock?"

"No. And the worse thing about it is that everyone in Leticia was trying to sell me one. I was too stupid to buy one."

"That's too bad. But I'm sure you can find some place to sleep."

"Where? I don't see any place."

"There's no problem. You can sleep on the floor under my hammock if necessary."

"Well, we'll see. First I need to talk to the captain. I want to make sure he's going to take me before I do anything."

"I'm sure there's no problem. He likes money."

"Is he anywhere around here by chance?"

Fernando tilted his head and a quizzical look came to his face. "Well, it's possible that he's above deck in his cabin . . . . But I last saw him a couple of hours ago in a bar saying good-bye to some friends from the town."

"Was he drinking much?"

"I don't know. But he seemed to be laughing and having a good time."

"Are we supposed to leave today or tomorrow?"

"Tonight. It's certain."

"And the captain of the ship is out drinking and expects to navigate at night?...That's crazy, man!"

Fernando chuckled. "He's probably only drinking a little bit. Anyway, there's no problem. I'm sure if he gets too drunk one of the mates can handle the ship."

"That's true." As long as he doesn't get stupid, I thought. I don't like this set-up. I need to get away and think.

"Well," I said, "I'm going to see if the captain is in his cabin."

"Go ahead." Fernando walked over to a ladder at the front of the hold. "Climb this to the second deck. You will find his cabin up front on the left hand side."

As I slowly ascended the ladder the unlit gloom of the top deck enveloped me and affected my thoughts. Maybe it would be better to abandon ship without talking to this dude. I mean, if he's tanked...that's tempting fate. And I don't have a hammock.... I don't know about this.

I stepped around the ladder and groped my way along the railing to the lighted pilot's cabin. It was empty. No one here, I thought. I must have passed his sleeping quarters.

I backtracked a few steps and found a varnished door. This must be it, I thought. I raised my hand to knock. Then I hesitated, hand poised aloft. I needed to think.

I turned from the door and leaned on the railing. I peered out over the black water. A cool breeze dried the cold sweat on my forehead. I thought and thought. What should I do? No hammock to sleep on. Maybe a drunk captain. From my readings I know the Amazon's reputation as one of the most treacherous rivers in the world. How was the description in that article I read?... The mighty Amazon, possessed of tricky currents and channels, booby trapped with shifting sand bars, and subject to violent tropical storms, has run aground or swamped innumerable vessels that have dared to test its power. In some cases boats have gone down and nothing was salvaged but cleanly picked bones.... Lovely description. Too much hyperbole. But I remember reading about a boat going down and losing over three hundred people a few months ago. Of course, it was overloaded. I don't know. I should just talk to the captain. This boat seems sturdy enough.

I turned and rapped on the door. No answer. I rapped again. No answer. Too bad, I thought. I wanted to get this over with now.

I walked around behind the cabin and found an open sided wooden lean-to. A large ice chest and two hammocks lay under its shelter. I looked at the hammocks and shook my head. Must get cold and breezy up here at night, I thought. Wonder if anyone sleeps here or they're just for relaxing during the day? Well, there's nothing up here, might as well go below.

As I descended the ladder I saw Fernando, still leaning against the railing, in animated conversation with a bearded white man. That guy looks familiar, I thought. I got off the ladder and moved into the light. . . . Well, what do you know. It's none other than the Dutchman I met in Leticia. The one who got all pissed off when I asked him if he was German.

"Eh! I remember you," said the Dutchman.

"And I remember you," I said.

Fernando looked from me to him. "You already know each other?"

"We've met," I said.

"Glad to haf you aboard," said the Dutchman, vigorously shaking my hand. "Now I haf someone I can speak to in English."

"Thanks. I hope they let me stay aboard."

"Sure they will. The captain is a goot guy."

"Does he speak English well?" Fernando asked me.

"Yes. He just has a little accent."

"I also speak Spanish," said the Dutchman in that language. "In Europe you haf to know at least three languages," he added in English.

"What other languages do you speak?" I asked him.

"German, of course. And a goot bit of French."

"Do you know many Frenchmen who agree with you when you say you have to know at least three languages in Europe?"

For a moment the Dutchman gave me a blank stare. Then he understood and guffawed.

"What's so funny?" asked Fernando.

"He say good joke about French people," said the Dutchman. He tried to translate the joke. I understood him only because I already knew what he was trying to say. Fernando looked at me with a puzzled expression on his face. After the Dutchman finished speaking, I retranslated the joke for Fernando. The Dutchman turned red and gave me a dirty look.

"Ah, now I understand," said Fernando. "That's funny."

"I say the same thing," said the Dutchman. "Why you not understand me?"

Fernando and I exchanged looks. This boy has a fragile ego, I thought. He may know enough Spanish for basic things but he definitely doesn't speak it.

"I speak French pretty well," said Fernando, ignoring the Dutchman's question. "I used to work in the French Embassy in Lima."

"How is this man's Spanish?" the Dutchman asked Fernando.

"He speaks well. But he has an accent. Maybe because he lives in Colombia."

"Ah, you live in Colombia," said the Dutchman, turning to me. "I didn't know that."

"By the way, my name is Craig," I said.

"Mine is Jaap (pronounced yap)." Jaap half turned and stretched his arm toward the woman who was gently rocking in her hammock. I had noticed her earlier when she poked her head over the lip of the hammock to watch our byplay. "This is Betti."

She sat upright, almost tumbling from the hammock, and extended her long white hand to me.

"A pleasure to meet you again," I said, taking her hand. Her grip was limp, but her sharp, gray eyes bored into me. I was startled by her appearance. She was wan and very thin. She looks ill, I thought. Or maybe she's frail. How is she going to hold up on a trip like this?

Throughout the introductions Fernando maintained a smiling face. He seemed to be enjoying himself immensely.

"Does Betti speak English, also?" he asked Jaap.

"She speaks very well."

Fernando's smile widened. "I too speak a leetle English. Not much. A leetle." He reverted to Spanish and said, "This is tremendous! You three can teach me some English during the voyage."

"And you can teach me some more Spanish," I said with a wry smile. "I still have a lot to learn."

Jaap and Betti were conversing in Dutch.

"Look at them," I said to Fernando. "Imagine what it's going to be like around here when the Brazilians arrive. We have at least four languages."

"Yes. It is truly going to be a Tower of Babel."

"It already is. Especially when you take into account what we've been talking about."

"What?"

"Nothing. I was thinking out loud."

What do you know, I thought. I wanted to concentrate on Portuguese and apparently none of the passengers speak it. Worse, this guy Fernando wants me to teach him English. . . . But I like him. He seems open and friendly. I think we're going to be friends. As for Jaap and Betti . . . I don't know. They seem to take themselves very seriously. Ah, who knows what to expect from chance traveling companions? . . .

A young woman entered the hold, interrupting my thoughts.

"Hi! How are you?" said Fernando with enthusiasm. *"Como vai você?"*

"Fine," she said, ducking her head and sitting on the long bench at the front of our area.

"She's a little shy," Fernando said to me.

"Who is she?"

"She's a passenger. Brazilian."

She dipped into a colorful knit purse and pulled out a ball of twine and two long needles. Without looking up she began knitting.

"What are you making?" Fernando asked her in Spanish.

"What?" she answered, a confused look on her face.

"What are you making?"

"I don't understand you."

Fernando smiled. "That's all right. It looks nice."

The girl shook her head and resumed darning.

"She is pretty. No?" whispered Fernando, nudging me with his elbow.

"Let me look at her."

I studied her profile. Tightly curled, boyishly-cut black hair outlined a high forehead that made her eyes, lips, nose, and mouth seem disproportionately small. Her face struck me as plain, almost homely. Yet, she possessed lustrous brown skin and a well-rounded plumpness that was attractive—suggestive of robust health and vitality.

"Well, what do you think of her?" prompted Fernando.

"I think you must be horny."

Fernando chuckled. " I am. But what do you think of her? Pretty?"

"Man, if you think she is . . . than she is. Depends on your taste."

"You don't think she's pretty?"

"What's the difference what I think? . . . It's what you think. Personally she doesn't attract me that much."

"You wouldn't take her if you had the chance?"

"I don't know. It would depend on the situation."

Fernando changed the subject. Jaap left Betti and came over to chat with us.

"How long will it take to reach Manaus?" I asked Fernando.

"The captain told me four or five days."

"How did you find out about this boat?"

"A Peruvian friend is a loader on the docks . . . . He told me this morning. It was a surprise. The boat wasn't supposed to leave for a few more days."

"How did you find out about the boat?" I asked Jaap.

"We asked at the docks this afternoon. A sailor sent us to the captain of this ship."

So, I thought, Hector was telling part of the truth. Doesn't matter. He came through in the end.

To communicate well among the three of us we had to switch back and forth from Spanish to English. The burden of translating fell on me. It was tiresome work. My head began to throb.

Betti took scant interest in our conversation and soon fell asleep in her hammock. The Brazilian girl stayed quiet. I would look over and catch her glancing at us, wide-eyed and blank faced, listening to the strange accents and languages. If I made eye contact with her she would duck her head and play with the ball of yarn. Fernando tried to talk to her but she put him off by saying she couldn't understand him. When he persisted she said, "Leave me alone. I don't speak Spanish." Fernando chuckled and left her alone. "She's playing hard-to-get," he told me.

I grew impatient waiting for the captain.

"Fernando," I said. "Could you find that bar where you saw the captain?"

"Sure. It's on the main street of the town."

"Do you want to come with me and show me where it is so I can talk to him and get everything settled?"

"I can tell you how to get there. But I don't want to go."

"Why?"

"I don't think it's a good idea to leave the ship right now. We could miss him on the way over. It's better if you wait for him here. Don't worry. He should arrive soon."

"Come on, man. I'll buy you a drink."

"Well . . . No. I'll tell you how to get there."

"That's all right. I'll wait. Maybe you're right."

"I'm tired," said Jaap, yawning. "I am going to sleep."

"Me too," said Fernando.

They took off their shoes and climbed into their hammocks. I leaned against the railing and waited. Within minutes the Brazilian girl put away her yarn and needles and prepared for bed. She pushed the bench flush against the wall and covered it with a blanket. Then she stretched her plump body full-length on the narrow bench and threw a blanket over herself. I watched her in amazement. Precariously balanced as she was, she closed her eyes and went right to sleep. Look at her, I thought. That's one tough girl. But how is she going to stay on that bench if the ship starts rolling? This I got to see. Anyway, I guess I can find a place to sleep as good as that.

I eyed the floor space under the passenger's hammocks; it was clogged with travel gear. And, I thought, what if one of the hammock ties snaps and I end up with somebody on my head or back....If I have to I can sleep there but I might as well look at the rest of this tub first.

I walked past a wooden partition that cleaved the hold in two and headed aft. Directly behind the partition was a wooden deck about two feet high, six feet wide, and eight feet long. Oily rags, cans of gasoline, crates of oranges, boxes of bananas, and miscellaneous tools and sundries were stacked on it. Suspended over this mess was a small hammock. The hammock puzzled me. Looks like it was made for a midget, I thought.

A large hammock hung at the foot of the deck. Two more hung in the aisle across the way. Coiled ropes and steel implements lay on the floor near the railing. Also jammed against the railing were these large black blobs. They emitted the acrid odor that I had noticed when I first boarded the ship. Really have to watch your step around here, I thought. This place is positively claustrophobic . . . . What the hell are these blobs? I whacked the closest one with my fist. My knuckles bounced off and came away streaked with a black sticky substance. I sniffed at the back of my hand. I know this smell. I just can't place it.

While I pondered the blobs Fernando joined me.

"Let's go," he said. "I'm on my way to the bathroom. You can see the rear of the ship and get some air."

We walked past the deck and the floor narrowed and bowed.

"This is the bathroom," said Fernando, indicating a door to our left with the word *banho* inscribed on it. "And that's the kitchen." He pointed to a door opposite the bathroom on our right with the word *cozinha* inscribed on it. "This ship has everything."

"Yes, only the best," I said. "Too bad everything is like a closet."

Fernando went into the bathroom. I walked out to the stern and inhaled the fresh air, trying to dispel the odor of machine lubricants from my nose. An aromatic breeze came in off the river. The temperature was comfortable.

I looked about the stern—to my right was a stainless steel sink; to my left a huge metal drum. There doesn't seem to be an open space anywhere on this ship, I thought.

I reentered the hold and met Fernando coming out of the bathroom. We walked toward the middle of the ship. I stopped and pointed at the raised wooden deck with all the junk piled on it.

"What's this roof?" I asked him.

"It's the casing over the engine room. You know, you could sleep here if you want. Just move some of these things to the side."

"Yes, I could. But won't it be noisy?"

"Maybe. It shouldn't be too bad. It's better than nothing."

"I don't know . . ."

"You should have brought a hammock."

"Thanks."

"That you sleep well," said Fernando without irony.

"You too. Good night."

Fernando returned to his hammock. I studied the clutter of objects on the roof. I haven't seen any better place, I thought. This will have to do.

I selected a spot on the extreme edge of the roof, under the midget hammock, close to the deck partition. I wedged out a space large enough for my body by shifting two crates of oranges to the middle of the roof and by stacking some cans and dirty rags atop the crates. This, in addition to the other things already stacked there, formed a tidy mound. We better have calm sailing, I thought.

I ran my hand over the surface of the wood; it was well-varnished and, save for the grooves between the planking and some nicks and scratches, quite smooth. That's a break, I thought. At least I won't have to worry about picking splinters out of my ass.

I fetched my travel bag from under Fernando's hammock and pulled out a mosquito netting I had purchased in Bogotá. I doubled it twice and spread it over the roof to serve as a mattress. For a headboard I grabbed a carton of bananas and placed it against the partition. The bananas smelled overripe. I made a pillow by balling up some old shirts. There, I thought, all set. Let's see how it feels. I pulled off my shoes and set them next to the crates of oranges. I sat down and carefully settled my back and legs onto the hard wood. Not too bad. If nothing else I ought to come out of this trip with a straight spine.

I cupped my hands against the back of my head and stared up at scarred ceiling beams. The ship was silent as a tomb. I could clearly hear the shouts of drunken revelers drifting in from the town. My right calf started to cramp. I kicked it loose. My body was tensed like a coiled spring. Relax, I thought. Try to get some rest. I closed my eyes and thought about what I would say to the captain when he showed up. If he shows up. Maybe he'll get too wasted and sleep it off in town. And if he does come will he give me a berth? This ship seems awful crowded. Fernando doesn't seem to think there'll be any problem . . . . I hope he's right. Ah, why worry about it. I'll find out when the time comes . . . . My thoughts spun slower and I drifted into a stupor—a limbo state between sleep and consciousness.

A gutteral shout roared in my ears. My eyes shot open and the short hairs on the back of my neck stood on end. Standing over me, fixing me with a look of absolute fury, was a short stocky man with powerful knotty muscles. I stared into his bloodshot eyes; the pupils were shrunken and intense with rage. His face was twisted into an ugly mask. His tightly curled short hair seemed to throw off sparks. Garbed only in Bermuda shorts, young and strong, he looked like a boxer moving in for the kill.

I lay motionless. He chattered at me in a highly nasalized Portuguese. It was an insane garble. I understood only a few words; but it was enough to know he was insulting me and wanted me off the ship. I raised up on an elbow and regarded him with what must have been a look of consternation. Why, I thought, is this asshole yelling at me? We haven't even been introduced.

I watched him closely. My scalp tingled and my muscles bunched. I was ready if he attacked me, but I sat still and tried to understand what he was saying. He was talking so fast his lips were flecked with spit. Finally he quieted down and took a step back. He glared at me for what seemed an eternity. To break the impasse I shrugged my shoulders and shook my head.

"I'm afraid I can't understand what you're saying, fool," I said to him in English in an even voice. "So your insults are a fucking waste of time."

For a moment he glared at me with increased fury. I thought for sure he was going to spring at me. Then, after giving me a final baleful look, he turned on his heel and strode into the galley. For the next minute or so I heard him muttering and banging pots together.

As the initial shock of this meeting wore off I grew angry. Not a very friendly welcome, I thought. I don't know what the hell his problem is . . . but if he thinks I'm going to be intimidated by a little shouting he's crazy. I'll leave when and if the captain tells me to.

I tried to piece together the words and phrases I had understood. I suspected he was upset because he felt there were already too many passengers on board the ship. It's a good thing I didn't understand most of what he said . . . I might have gone off on him. This time my ignorance was an advantage.

My nerves still jangling, I lay down and gazed at the ceiling. Then . . .

"What the fuck?" I yelped.

Something, with the agility of a monkey, had vaulted over my prone body and into the midget hammock, giving me a sharp blow on my prominent nose with a trailing heel. Maddened with pain and surprise, I lashed out and swiped the hammock with the heel of my left hand. I felt a solid thump and heard a short muffled cry.

For a breathless moment there was silence; the hammock swayed to and fro. I sat up and waited. A small head peeped over the border of the cloth hammock and surveyed me. It was a little boy.

"What happened?" I asked him in Portuguese.

"Pardon, *senhor*. Pardon," he said.

"It's all right. You startled me."

He smiled and said something in very fast Portuguese. He was a cute child—big white teeth and bright eyes glinting from a smooth brown face. He had an intelligent, alert look about him.

"I am Jorge. But they call me Jorzinho. Or *menino* (little boy)."

"A pleasure. I'm Craig."

"What?"

"It's difficult in Portuguese. Call me Gregorio."

He laughed and said something I couldn't understand.

"Who is that man in the kitchen?" I asked.

"He is my father."

"Your father? . . . What does he do here?"

"He is the cook."

So that's what it is, I thought. More passengers, more work for him. That's why he was mad.

I wanted to ask Jorge some more questions but I failed to make him understand that he would have to speak slow and clear if I were to comprehend him. He chattered like his father. Also, it was difficult for him to understand me. I'm too tired for this, I thought. I gave it up as a lost cause and said good night. I settled back onto the mosquito netting. All right, I thought, what next?"

The cook emerged from the galley and, after giving me a hard look, climbed into his hammock. Quiet descended over the ship. Again I heard drunken shouts from the town. The time dragged. The cook began to snore. I tossed and turned on my improvised bed. It's no use, I thought. I can't sleep. Where is that damn captain? This wait is killing me . . . . Ah, what's the use of wondering? Resignation seeped into my consciousness. I was drained, both physically and mentally. Every time I had begun to relax some new situation that needed to be dealt with had arisen and my taxed system had responded with fresh jolts of adrenalin. Now, I thought, there's nothing left. If the captain comes right this minute and tells me to get off the boat . . . well, it really doesn't matter.

That's the way it goes. I just want to know one way or another.

With this decided I fell into a light slumber.

I woke to the sound of scurring feet. I rolled onto my side and watched the bustle through hooded eyes. Muscular young men in bermuda shorts appeared on all sides. Two of them went through the hatch near my feet and descended to the engine room. Others scooped up equipment and headed for the top deck or to the steel flat. This is it, I thought. It's time to cast off. Now where's the captain?

Seconds later a man with an imperious countenance appeared. He stopped a few feet from my head, gazing aft, a steady torrent of commands issuing from his mouth. Without moving I looked him over. He was dressed in white bell bottom pants, a burgundy pullover shirt, and white deck shoes. He stood tall and straight. A generous paunch further marked him as a man of stature.

This must be the captain, I thought. I started to get up but on an impulse I remained still. Hell with it. He's busy right now. Maybe he won't notice me until we shove off . . . or — better yet — until tomorrow. Then he'll have to either throw me off, which is unlikely, or allow me to continue with them to Manaus. Yeah, let him notice me.

He strolled past me, seemingly without noticing, and proceeded to the hatch. He leaned over and barked orders to the two sailors in the engine room. Then he straightened up and motioned another sailor to the second deck. Meanwhile I assumed the fetal position, trying to look as inconspicuous as possible. This is ridiculous, I thought. I should just get up and talk to him.

Suddenly the captain was back near my head. Though my left arm was crooked in front of my face, my hand over my eyes, I could see between my fingers. The captain leaned down and scrutinized me. I lay like a stone and studied his face. He didn't look drunk, only pleasantly buzzed and very alert. His eyes bored into me. It was an excruciating war of nerves. My muscles tensed and my calf started to cramp again. That's it, I thought. I have to talk.

Then, as if he had spotted what he was looking for, a smile flitted to the captain's face. He nodded his head and turned away. After issuing a final command to a sailor out of my sight he moved off to commandeer the pilot's cabin.

I released an audible sigh. My body was coated with perspiration. I sat up and massaged my calf. He must have noticed me the first time, I thought. And known I was awake, too. I don't think he misses much. He just wanted me to sweat a while. That's cool, though, I could be a psycho for all he knew . . . . Now I can relax. That little smile and nod of the head told me I'm in.

The cramp in my calf subsided. I settled more comfortably against the wood and closed my eyes, feeling much better about things in general.

At that precise moment the boat's engine ignited with a coughing roar, the sudden explosion from below almost dislodging me from my narrow berth. As the engine warmed the noise increased. It's like a buzz saw, I thought. I sat up and covered my ears with my hands. Within seconds the water pump chimed in—lending a rasping staccato note to the din. . . . This is insane. I'll never be able to sleep with this racket.

I took my shirt off and wrapped it around my head. I lay down. The wood vibrated from the action of the machinery. My head shook and my teeth chattered. I grabbed two more shirts and added them to my pillow. This extra insulation helped some, but not much. I sat up and wrapped the shirt tighter around my head and ears. Then I lay down, cupping the back of my head against my fingers and covering my ears with the heels of my palms. This helped, for the moment.

The interior lights of the ship were extinguished. The boat was sliding into motion. The noise of the engines retreated to the background of my consciousness as I concentrated on the movement of the boat sliding through the water. It felt as though the particles of motion were passing from the wood to the bare skin of my back. Such an eerie sensation—as if I had become a living part of the boat.

The ship came about. We began to gain speed. I rolled onto my side and gazed through the railing at the dark water sluicing past. We were headed on a slanted course toward the center of the river. A cool breeze flooded the hold. The fresh air rushed over and through my body. I felt lightheaded and intoxicated. I was a child on a wild roller coaster ride. The lights of Benjamin Constant winked in the distance. We were on our way.

Soon the thrill wore off. The cool air chilled my sweaty skin. The racket from the engines became intolerable. A sledgehammer began pounding inside my skull, the pain diffusing through my body as a throbbing pulse. I got up and put on a shirt.

I have to do something, I thought. This is like a torture device. I'll lose my mind if this goes on much longer. I paced along the side of my bed, thinking. What do I do? What do I do? . . . I need some cotton — or some kind of earmuffs. The shirt isn't enough. How about a different place to sleep? . . . There is no other place to sleep. Damn! I don't want to stay awake all night. Wait, I got an idea.

I dug around in my bag and fished out an old T-shirt. I tore some thin strips off it and rolled them into balls. I inserted the balls into my ears. I nodded with satisfaction; the engine noise was substantially reduced. I wrapped a thick bathing towel around my head for insulation against the vibrations. I lay on my pallet. Much better, I thought. As if on cue the water pump shut off. Minutes later the captain cut the power to cruising speed. We reached our shipping channel and straightened out. The engine noise subsided to a dull hum.

I still felt a vague thumping near the core of my skull but the pain was tolerable. Nothing to do now, I thought, but wait until I get used to this constant noise and attain a higher pain threshold. Hell, if I could take downtown San Francisco and Los Angeles at the peak commute time I should be able to handle this. I have no choice. . . . I'll just pretend I'm a masochist.

I settled down to sleep. Then I encountered new problems with the location of my bed. Sailors, on their way to the toilet and to the engine room, walked past me at a steady rate. They came and they went. Several brushed against my shoulder. The water pump ignited at sporadic intervals, according to the amount of water accumulated in the bilge, and belched for minutes at a time. The damn thing sounds like a lawn mower, I thought. This, along with my restless thoughts, kept me from much needed sleep. I lay awake and stared at the ceiling. I'm gonna be dead in the morning. Nothing like first class travel . . .

I heard titters from the other side of the partition. I rolled over and looked. I saw two women, one with an attractive figure, whispering and suppressing giggles as they inspected the passengers in the hammocks. My, I thought, they look like a fun loving duo. I wonder what they're doing here. Where do they sleep?

The women finished their inspection and came toward me. I rolled onto my back and feigned sleep. They walked past without stopping and went to the toilet. They were gone for what seemed a long while. On the way back they paused to give me a look. Through half closed eyes I watched them whisper and point. They were both dressed in shorts and light blouses. The one with the attractive figure stepped close and positioned one of her shapely thighs within three inches of my nose. I repressed a strong urge to reach out and grab it.

"He's not asleep," I heard one of them murmuer.

"No?"

I smiled. They giggled and moved off, leaving a wake of cheap perfume.

Too bad they left, I thought. I was about to say hello. Guess I'll meet them tomorrow. . . . I can't wait for tomorrow. . .

CHAPTER VI

BOAT LIFE

As the first gray slivers of dawn filtered into the hold the cook slipped from his hammock and entered the galley. I was right on his heels to use the bathroom. After taking a long satisfying piss, I went to the stern. I sat on the edge and dangled my bare feet into the wash kicked up by the propeller. Despite having slept poorly I felt wonderfully alive and enjoyed the cool sensation of the water rushing between my toes.

The cook emerged from the galley and went to the sink to fill a coffee pot with water. I watched him warily. He greeted me with a grimace that could have been a smile. I grinned and nodded to him. He filled the pot, the excess water draining over the side through a rubber hose, and returned to the galley without a word. At least he's not hostile like he was last night, I thought. I guess he's resigned to my presence.

I put the cook from my mind and squinted out over the expanse of water at my feet. The surface was gently ruffled and gray, with silver dapples. My eyes rose to the sea of vegetation that stretched to the horizon. So green and mysterious, I thought. What secrets are contained in its depths? ... Then the sun caught my eye—a red-orange ball lifting free of the jungle's verdant bosom and scattering fleecy clouds on the way to its post in the heavens. Meanwhile, the sky, like a white-spotted chameleon, changed from a dank gray to a very light blue that was almost indistinguishable from the color of the river.

I gazed in sublime wonder, at peace with myself and ready for the new day. That was gorgeous, I thought. I hope I can preserve this image in my mind forever. I've always loved a pretty sunrise and the early morning softness. A time of regeneration and fresh hopes — a moment to savor before the uncertainty of another day ...

"How beautiful! No?"

I wheeled, startled from my reverie by a soft voice behind me. It was Fernando. We looked at each other and smiled.

"Yes," I said. "It was very beautiful."

Fernando excused himself to use the bathroom and I turned to face the river. The wind picked up and whipped the chill from the water into the air. I shivered and took my feet out of the water. I was still cold. I went inside to get a shirt.

When I returned to the stern I found Fernando, the cook, and three Brazilian sailors sipping hot coffee.

"Good morning," I said in Portuguese.

The Brazilians nodded their heads and mumbled, *"Bom día."*

"Do you want *café da manhã* (breakfast)?" the cook asked me.

I nodded. He handed me an enameled tin cup with smoke curling from the rim and motioned for me to help myself from a can of crackers sitting on the red oil drum. For the moment I ignored the crackers and slurped the black coffee. "Ah!" I scalded my tongue. But I relished the heavily sweetened liquid as it went down and warmed my insides.

"Aren't you going to eat?" asked Fernando, smiling, cracker crumbs dribbling from his lips.

"Yes. After I drink my coffee."

Fernando chatted with me in Spanish. The sailors looked on un-comfortably, almost suspiciously. I watched them out of the corner of my eye. They spoke quietly among themselves—simple, work-tough-ened men, with lean, well-proportioned bodies and guileless faces. Two of them were short and stocky like the cook; the other, who wore bright green bermuda shorts, was about my height, six foot. They don't look unfriendly, I thought. Just a bit self-conscious.

Fernando smeared a cracker with margarine and passed it to me. I bit into it. The cracker was dry and tasteless; the margarine made it go down easier and gave it some flavor. The cook came around with a large thermos and gave us a second cup of coffee. In minutes we devoured every cracker in the can.

"Is that all for breakfast?" Fernando asked one of the sailors.

He nodded.

"I hope we have more and better for lunch," Fernando commented to me.

"Me too."

While we drank our coffee I remained relatively quiet. After my exhilaration from the sunrise passed the lingering effects of the turbu-lent night caught up to me and left me flat. The sailors were equally taci-turn. Fernando talked to everyone but received terse responses. After the second cup of potent coffee, however, the caffeine took hold and our eyelids lifted a notch higher. Soon, thanks to the efforts of Fernando, through the simple device of exchanging the names of common objects and obscene words in three languages, our reticence started to break down. The cook joined in and told a few jokes. Though his extremely nasalized Portuguese was unintelligible to Fernando and I, we laughed along with the sailors as the cook capered on the bow and made weird facial expressions. We were getting along quite well. Then I noticed Jaap and Betti stirring in their hammocks.

"Better get over here," I called to Jaap in English, jokingly. "The food's almost gone."

Jaap hustled over to the stern at once, scowling suspiciously. "Where my breakfast?" he demanded in Spanish. "Where my breakfast for me and my woman? I pay."

The cook eyed him sternly. "What did you say? I don't understand. What?"

"Breakfast . . . . Food. Food for us," Jaap said in a milder tone.

The cook grunted and entered the galley.

Jaap stood nonplussed.

He's lucky the cook didn't understand him at first, I thought. Or he might have got tossed overboard.

"Vat's going on?" Jaap asked me in English. "You already haf eaten?"

"Yes."

"We haf a right to our share of the food. We paid the fare."

"Relax, man. He probably went into the kitchen to get you guys something. What do you expect? . . . Breakfast in bed?"

Jaap muttered something in Dutch and calmed down. A few minutes later the cook handed Jaap a cup of coffee and brought out a new tin of crackers.

"Thank you," said Jaap, smiling.

The cook grunted.

"Betti," called Jaap. "Betti. Come here . . . "

Betti shambled over, causing a stir among the sailors. She wore a thin, almost transparent, pullover nightie, which revealed her small titties, and powder blue panties that showed her pipestem legs all the way to the crotch. Curly black pubic hairs wriggled out from under the fabric and into the open air.

The cook greeted Betti with a gentle smile and special deference. He offered her coffee. She refused.

"Water," she said. "Hot water. Water?"

The cook went to get her water and Betti pulled a packet of tea from her knit bag.

"What kind of tea is that?" I asked her.

"It is mint tea . . . . Coffee is bad for one. This keeps me healthy."

The cook gave Betti her cup of hot water. Jaap settled down by the sink and dangled his feet into the water. Betti sat next to him, Indian fashion, giving the standing sailors an excellent view of her crotch. The sailors fell silent. The sailors would look toward her, amazement etched on their faces, and then look nervously away, as one might when seeing an accident victim on the street. Betti seemed oblivious to these half-curious, half-scandalized glances. She daintily sipped her tea and gazed at the river. I glanced from the sailors to Betti to my feet, chuckling under my breath. What a show for these guys, I thought. I wonder if they're aroused by her sexually or horrified by her undernourished appearance . . . . I'm more struck by her bony body . . . . And her lack of sensitivity. Or maybe ignorance is a better word. I mean, it might be all right to parade around almost naked in front of strangers in Holland— but it sure isn't here. Especially in front of sailors on a cramped ship . . . . This is the tropics. The people are volatile. I hope she gets a clue somewhere along the line. Maybe I should give her a friendly warning. . . . Nah, I get the feeling they'd resent any advice. Let's see what develops.

We loitered on the stern, sipping coffee and shooting the breeze. The sailors seemed particularly sluggish. These three must have been on the night watch, I thought. I know how they feel.

After a while Betti shivered in the cool breeze. She got up and went to her hammock. She returned wearing jeans and a woolen shirt. The show was over. The sailors, as if on cue, left the stern and went to get their toothbrushes. The passengers did the same. Soon we were all assembled on the stern, scooping water from the river with our hands to rinse out our mouths and spouting streams of white into the muddy brown water over the side. It was like a ritual of sorts. I was careful to keep the water from spilling down my throat. No telling what kind of funky microbes this water has, I thought.

After brushing, everyone dispersed to different parts of the boat. I hustled over to my sleeping niche and grabbed a towel from my travel bag; I wanted to get into the bathroom and take a shower before someone beat me to it. I rushed over to the bathroom, ducked inside, and fastened the latch. Made it, I thought . . . . Yuk! Damn it's rank in here! Whoever used the bathroom last must have been eating a lot of beans lately.

I looked around. The bathroom was the size of a small closet. The toilet bowl took about half of the space and a small sink took most of the rest. The shower nozzle hung over the toilet and came to the level of my chest. A sewer drain in the middle of the floor completed the all-purpose water closet.

What a joke, I thought. How am I going to get comfortable to take a decent scrubbing? Let's see . . .

I held my nose with one hand, turned on the shower with the other, bent from the waist, and ducked my head under the shower flow. The sink jammed against my ass; my contorted posture caused pain to shoot through my lower back. Only a few stray drops of water reached my lower body. This isn't working, I thought. About the only thing I'm doing is screwing up my back.

I straightened up and stared at the shower nozzle. What do I do? What do I do? Wait . . . . Now I know.

I sat on the toilet and let the water cascade over my head and upper torso. The water was cool and pleasant. I leaned back against the wall and propped my feet on the sink. I stretched my legs out. Now I luxuriated. I grabbed the soap and sudsed up, taking my time. I shampooed my dirty stringy oily hair. Someone rapped at the door.

"One moment," I called.

I rinsed off and turned off the shower. I rose and ran my hand over my damp hair and scalp. "What the . . . " My hair was no longer oily —it was sandy. This damn river water, I thought. I should have known better. It's too silty. My hair feels like I've been wrestling with someone on the beach. If I keep taking showers I'll be able to plant a flower on top of my head. Guess I won't be shampooing my hair for a while.

I stalked out of the bathhouse with a towel wrapped around my waist. No one was waiting at the door. Great, I thought, I hurried for nothing. My sandy scalp itched, irritating me further. Then the water pump switched on, that infernal mechanical stutter combining with the engine noise; the sound bored into my head. I clapped my hands over my ears. I can't take this! It's either going to make me deaf or drive me to the edge of insanity—whichever comes first. I have to find some relief from this . . . . Fast!

Fernando approached me, smiling and pointing toward the forward end of the ship. His lips were moving.

"I can't hear you," I shouted.

He cupped his hands around his mouth and yelled into my ear. "Let's go climb over the wood to the front end of the flat. It's much quieter there—and there is an unobstructed view of everything."

"What a good idea!" I exclaimed, patting him on the back. "You go ahead. I'll join you soon. After I change my clothes."

Fernando turned and left. I went over to my travel bag and rummaged through it, looking for a clean shirt. Nothing. I began tossing my stuff out of the bag and onto the floor. I dug down to the bottom of the bag before finding a reasonably fresh shirt. Time to find a laundry, I thought. I slipped on the shirt and basketball shorts. I stuffed everything back into the bag and dumped it under Fernando's hammock. I was on my way out when the chubby Brazilian girl descended the ladder and stepped in front of me. She jabbered something at me.

I stared at her, a silly grin on my face. She repeated her message. "Speak slower," I said. "I don't understand."

She flailed her arms and repeated once again. I strained my ears in concentration but I still couldn't understand her. Two missing teeth near the front of her mouth made her words come out in a whistling lisp.

"Don't you understand me?" she asked. "What is your problem?"

My face burned. I felt stupid. "One more time."

She shook her head and windmilled her arms. "The captain . . . the captain wants . . . "

Finally I understood, more from her emphatic gestures than anything else, that the captain wanted to speak to me and was waiting above deck in his cabin.

"The captain wants to talk to me?" I asked her.

"Exactly."

"Thanks."

This has to be about money, I thought. I returned to my travel bag and picked out my passport. I extracted $1000 *cruzeiros* from my money belt and folded it in my right hand. In case he tries to con me and charges me more than he did the other passengers I'll be ready, I thought. I'll lay this money on him before he even tells me the price.

As I climbed the ladder to the upper deck, the engine drone diminished and bright sunlight bathed my eyes. After the darkness of the hold I was momentarily blinded; I blinked my eyes several times. Things swam into focus. I saw the captain leaning against the railing outside his cabin. He was staring at the river and seemed lost in thought.

In the light of day he doesn't seem so impressive, I thought. He was short and his body looked soft. He wore the same tight burgundy turtleneck as the night before, which accentuated his pot belly, white slacks, and leather sandals.

I scuffed the deck with my foot to catch his attention and stepped forward. The captain turned and called out a greeting. His eyes, brown and alert, ran over me at a glance. His face was dark and clean shaven, with sagging jowls and an easy going dissolute look about it. His close cropped black hair receded from his high forehead. Man, I thought, this guy looks like he does some heavy partying.

"How are you?" he asked cordially, giving my hand a firm shake. He motioned toward his cabin. "We can talk in here."

We went inside. The cabin was dark and very small, with barely enough space for the two of us to stand between a combination desk-easel and a compact bunk. The captain reached across the desk and pulled open the red curtains, revealing a sliding glass window that opened to the pilot's cabin. One of the mates was at the wheel. He turned and nodded to us. Light splashed onto the desk; it was littered with maps, papers, and shiny nautical instruments.

The captain engaged me with small talk as he shuffled through some papers on the desk. I scanned the interior of the cabin. It was done primarily in crimson and black and remained gloomy despite the light coming through the window. Portraits of naked mulatto women, in erotic poses, leered at me from the walls. The bunk was covered with a crimson spread and the night lamp had a red bulb. The air reeked of masculine cologne. This place would do credit to any whorehouse boudoir, I thought. And what about those two ladies I saw last night? . . . I wonder where they sleep . . .

"Do you have your passport?" asked the captain.

Wordlessly I placed it on the desk. He ignored it for the moment and continued sorting through the pile of papers in front of him. At last he sighed with satisfaction and held up a travel form of some kind. He opened my passport and examined it. Then he asked me a few questions, writing my replies on the travel form.

I understood the captain pretty well. His Portuguese was precise and well-enunciated. He was evidently well-educated, experienced in dealing with foreigners, and intelligent. He must be sharp to be able to understand the Portuguese I'm throwing at him, I thought.

"You speak a little Brazilian, eh," said the captain with an approving smile.

"Very little."

"No. You are speaking almost like a Brazilian. Where did you learn?"

What a bullshitter, I thought. But nice of you to say that.

"I used to listen to short wave radio broadcasts of *Radio Nacional de Brasília* in Colombia," I explained. "And I have a book."

"I congratulate you."

"Thanks."

He asked a few more routine questions and looked at my passport again. Then he frowned as though he were about to perform an unpleasant task.

"Now—about your passage. The fare is $1000 *cruzeiros*."

I nodded and pointed to the desk; I had placed the money down before he finished telling me the price. The captain gave me a speculative glance. Then he counted the money and smiled. Still, I knew my gesture hadn't been lost on him.

"I already spoke with the other passengers about the passage," I said. "That's how I knew the price beforehand."

"*Tudo bem,*" said the captain, pocketing the money. "I don't have to explain everything to you."

Tudo bem, I thought. There's that phrase again. I've been hearing it constantly . . . . This time I get the sense of it — it means everything is cool. Now I can use it myself.

The captain made out a receipt and passed it to me. "All right," he said. "Thank you." I absently filed the receipt in my passport. I bid the captain good-bye and left the cabin. Just as I was about to climb down the ladder, I spotted the two women I had seen the night before in the hammocks behind the captain's cabin. I stopped in my tracks and smiled at them. They lay still, their hammocks gently swaying, unsmiling, regarding me speculatively.

"*Tudo bem?*" I ventured.

One of them, with a nice creamy complexion and a cute but hard face, eyed me coldly. The other, somewhat older and plainer, smiled guardedly. Neither of them spoke.

Not very friendly, I thought. Why are they so suspicious? And how much do their tickets cost? Huh?

I gave the cute one my best guileless smile. It seemed to irritate her; her face hardened even more. Whatever, I thought. I nodded amiably and went down the ladder without another word. I guess I'll find out what they're all about later.

Back in the hold I dropped off my passport and, in case of nothing better to do to pass the time, picked up my Portuguese handbook. I went to the prow of the tug and leaned on the railing, gazing at the gap between the boat and the cargo flat. The water beneath me churned as though it were in a giant washing machine. Have to be careful, I thought. I straddled the railing and eased onto the other side. I used the steel framework of the tie as a bridge and climbed across to the steel flat. Now I was confronted by a fifteen foot high wall of lumber. Rather than climb over the lumber I decided to skirt around the corner. The space between the cargo and the rushing water was narrow, about three feet. The flat pitched and rolled. I held onto the lumber with my left hand and took a few tentative steps. Farther ahead I saw water splashing onto the walkway and spattering the wood. That was too much. I halted, assailed by vertigo. Take it easy, I thought. One false step and I end up in the river. There's no rush. Maybe I should go back and climb over the lumber . . . . Ah, c'mon, I have at least three feet of space to walk on. That's plenty. I've walked along much narrower things than this — and at dangerous heights. No problem. So what if there's no guard rail . . . . I just need to get my sea legs.

I took a deep breath, felt the queasiness subside, and moved on. Spaced at regular intervals along the length of the flat were solid steel hydrants with flat tops designed to keep the cargo from sliding off the flat in rough weather. I was soon walking confidently from one hydrant to the next. In a couple of minutes I reached the front of the cargo bed. Here there was a good six feet of space between the lumber and the edge of the flat. Before I could enjoy the additional area a small wave washed over the prow and almost dislodged my barefoot grip on the metal. I backed against the lumber and grabbed on.

"*Hola!*" called a voice from above and behind me. "Why don't you come up here? The view is much better and you won't get as wet."

I turned and saw Fernando. He was perched near the top of the lumber pile, smiling, like a king surveying his domain.

"You're probably right," I said. "But let me look around here first."

Another swell licked around my ankles and splashed water into my eyes.

"I've seen enough," I said, scrambling onto the lumber. I found a comfortable seat next to Fernando. We exchanged pleasantries. Then for a while we spoke sparingly, our attention absorbed by the scenery.

I was mesmerized by the river. The surface was smooth, as though the current were negligible, but it was strewn with jungle debris that must have been forcibly torn from the banks by flooding and erosion. Entire trees, huge logs, and large bushes were swept along as if they were mere chips. Our ship, by virtue of its motor, traveled faster than the refuse. From time to time a log or a chunk of driftwood would collide with the flat and send a hollow thumping sound into the air. The ship's engine noise, muffled by distance and the rush of the wind, had become a whisper. The sluicing sound of the water against the flat was a gentle murmur in my ears. The river was hypnotic. For a time I forgot where I was and what I was doing there. I had to tear my eyes from the water to keep my mind from drifting with it.

I looked toward the near shore. I was startled by the height and smoothness of the bank; it loomed well above the water line, like a great wall with vegetation running along the top, and was scoured by the erosive action of the river. Here and there the gnarled roots of unfortunate trees lay exposed, seeming to claw at the air to regain the foothold that would prevent their majestic leafy bodies from tumbling into the river during some future storm. Past the front line of trees and bush I could see nothing; the vegetation was too dense. Our course was too far from shore. The land seemed a solid mass of trees with spiraling branches and shrubbery. I felt momentarily depressed. I guess I'll have to wait until we stop before I see anything in detail, I thought. Oh well . . .

Then the sun, playing hide-and-seek behind scattered clouds all morning, came into the open and bathed us in bright warmth. My disappointment vanished. I took off my shirt and basked in the rays. The wind began gusting, sharp and fresh, cool against my skin and pleasant in my nostrils. I filled my lungs with air and savored its scent and taste. A sense of well-being pervaded me. I stretched my arms and upper torso and sighed with pure animal delight.

"The air tastes sweet here," I said to Fernando. "It's intoxicating me."

"Yes, I feel the same. The Amazon is the world's grandest arboretum; the oxygen is pure."

"Whatever the reason I feel great. I've never enjoyed the simple act of breathing so much. The Amazon . . . "

For the first time the full significance of where I was and what I was doing came home to me. I've done it! I thought. I'm on the Amazon. The promise I made to myself so long ago is now a reality . . . . I've done it! . . . No matter what else I do the rest of my life I can reflect on this moment and draw strength from it—knowing I can finish what I start out to do, knowing I did it despite all the people who said I couldn't or shouldn't do it. Well, the hell with them — I'm here. Now for the rest of Brazil.

I swiveled my head and looked to all sides. I opened my ears and listened.

"You know," I said to Fernando, "except for this boat there's absolutely no evidence of man here. It's strange for me to see such virgin land."

"Yes, strange and beautiful. Every year there's less and less land like this; they're doing away with it at an incredible rate of speed . . . . We're fortunate to make this trip before the Amazon is totally raped and exploited . . . . Imagine, someday this may fade into the oblivion of historical legend. The great Amazon jungle will be a myth."

"I don't want to imagine that. Maybe something will prevent it."

We fell silent. I gazed at the curtain of foliage on the shores and the turgid water of the river. It seemed limitless. This has to endure in one form or another, I thought. At least some of it.

"Well," I said, "one good thing about being here is that you can forget about the problems of the world. I haven't read a damn newspaper in three days. I like that."

"Why? It's good to stay informed about what's happening in the world .... Anyway, there are world problems here, too."

"That's true. What I meant to say was that I don't have to read about how the United States and the Soviet Union are threatening to destroy each other — to prove once and for all who has the most humanistic regime. What a joke."

"Do you really think about it that much?"

"I try not to — but in my country you don't have much choice. You hear about it all the time."

"In Peru, also. If the superpowers have a war it will affect everybody. That's the way it is."

"Yeah, well, I always wondered what it would be like to grow up in a place or time when none of that mattered. . . . Sometimes I think I was born in the wrong era. I would have been better off in a simpler world."

Fernando chuckled. "No offense, but I think you're romanticizing things. Every period of history has had its great problems — plague, wars, drought, famine. Modern civilization has done much to eliminate those problems . . . "

"For now. But they still exist and . . . "

"Yes, but there is progress. I believe we are reaching for something better."

"I'm not talking about that."

"What are you talking about?"

"I'm talking about living in an era or place where you worked for the essentials of life. Where success was predicated on a harmonious balance with nature. Where you didn't have to worry about paying rent, paying taxes, balancing your budget, securing meaningful employment, fighting for ill-defined ideals, wearing appropriate clothing . . . . None of that shit! A place and time where you have the space and spirit to recognize the beauty and mystery of nature and the universe. Do you know what I'm trying to say?"

"I think so. Something like what some of the Indian tribes had?"

"Yes, something like that. I want to keep my life simple. I don't want my mind cluttered up with a lot of shit."

Fernando laughed. "That's not very practical thinking in the modern world."

Now I laughed. "Being simple isn't practical?"

"No," Fernando said seriously. "Not if you want to survive in a big city like Lima. Do you think you could survive in the jungle?"

"No. I'm from a big city, too. I'm not equipped for the jungle. At least not a natural one."

"Then?"

"It would be fun to try to survive here for a while—if I had the right teacher."

"It would be a dangerous challenge."

"That too . . . . Ah, what's the difference? It's a fantasy. But just coming here and being on this boat is a fantasy for me. Right now I feel like I'm enjoying a spasm of liberation. My mind feels free. Anything seems possible."

A thrill of emotion surged through me and struggled for expression. It started in the pit of my stomach and rose up through my throat and to my mouth until I could no longer suppress it. I stood up and shouted out over the water, "Fuck it all! Freedom! Life!"

I sat down, feeling joyful, purged. Man, I thought, I've been wanting to do something like that for a long time.

Fernando looked at me and smiled. "I don't know what you said — but you look like you feel well."

"Then you know exactly what I said—because I feel very well. The words weren't important." I patted him on the back. "I think we're beginning to know each other."

For a time we sat in comfortable silence. We basked in the sun and relaxed. Then Fernando brought out a glossy sheet of folded paper. I watched him curiously.

"Look at this," he said, unfurling the paper and spreading it on the plank between us. It was a map of the Amazon Region. He pointed to a dot on the river a few centimeters from Leticia and said, "We should be about here. Our first stop will probably be in São Paulo do Olivença . . . . Here. Sometime early in the afternoon."

"I hope you're right. I'm anxious to see how people live along the river. Maybe even see a few natives."

"By natives, do you mean Indians?"

"Yes."

"It's doubtful that we'll see any real Indians. What natives are left stay far inland—away from the river and contact with civilization. They can't survive otherwise."

"It's that bad?"

"Yes."

"That's screwed!"

"Yes, of course," said Fernando, shaking his head sadly. "But their time has passed. Progress must have its way. If they don't adapt to the new ways they will become extinct. It's not quite as bad in my country — yet. But Brazil is determined to move ahead fast."

"So I hear."

"It's true. Unfortunately some people have to suffer."

"Maybe in the end everybody suffers."

"Maybe."

"That's a good map you have," I said. "Where did you get it?"

"From the Brazilian Consulate in Iquitos . . . . Free."

"What nice people."

Fernando grinned. "It was the only thing I got for free from them . . . . I had a very difficult time securing a work permit. It took considerable persuasion and a little bit of palm greasing—but I did it."

"Then you have a work permit, not a regular tourist visa?"

"Yes, it's not so unusual. Many Peruvians work in the Amazon Region of Brazil. We are good and relatively cheap labor." Fernando snickered. "Especially those without legal documents."

"I know what you mean . . . . It sounds like California. Especially like the city and neighborhood where I grew up in."

"Yes? What kind of illegals do you have there?"

"You name it . . . . We have everything. Chinese, Mexicans, Central Americans, South Americans, Filipinos, Italians, Germans, whatever . . . "

"Well, anyway, I have some Peruvian friends working in Manaus with whom I am going to make contact. I expect them to help me find a place to stay and work for a while. As I would help them if they needed it . . . . Who knows, maybe they can help you."

"Maybe they could . . . "I smiled. "But I already have work in Colombia that I'm satisfied with."

"Yes, but one never knows what opportunity might present itself." Fernando winked. "They say the Brazilian girls are very beautiful and very persuasive."

I laughed. "What they say and how it is are not always the same . . . . I know that from Colombia. But I'll try to maintain an open mind."

"It would be well that you do."

Fernando returned his attention to the map and traced his finger along the main blue line of the Amazon River. The map of Brazil looked like a large human heart, and Fernando a surgeon plotting to remove a clot from a vital artery. He recited the names of all the towns on the map between Benjamin Constant and Manaus and estimated our arrival time at each one. I listened to him in silence. Everything has been so jumbled on this trip, I thought. I can't imagine things smoothing out and following any sort of schedule. This is a waste of time.

As Fernando rambled on with his estimates I yawned and turned away from the map. I watched the swells splashing onto the front of the lumber stack. My mind drifted. Eventually Fernando folded up the map and put it away.

"So," said Fernando, "what has brought you to South America?"

"It's a long story."

"We have plenty of time."

"Well . . ."

"Hey, you guys! Vat are you doing?"

We turned and saw Jaap, dressed only in bathing trunks and sandals, regarding us from the top of the lumber pile.

"We're just talking and enjoying the scenery," I answered.

"Betti and I are on top of this wood taking the sun," Jaap intoned. "But I am quite bored . . ."

"Already?" I replied.

"I haf a game called 'Mastermind,'" continued Jaap. "Come up and join us and we can play."

Jaap folded his arms across his chest and tapped his right foot as I translated his message for Fernando.

"Let's go," said Fernando enthusiastically. "It should be fun."

We climbed to the top of the lumber pile and found seats. Jaap and Betti explained the aim and rules of the game. It was very basic — it consisted of one player designing a pattern with colored pegs on a small, rectangular board with holes in it. The other player must then try to figure out the hidden pattern by matching the design on another board within a specified number of moves. Then the antagonists switch roles. The player who figures out his opponent's pattern with the least moves is the winner and is declared "Mastermind."

"Do you want to play me first?" Jaap asked me. "I haf already beaten Betti."

"No," I said. "Play Fernando. I don't like table games that much. I'll watch."

"Vhy don't you play? It's a goot way to make the time pass."

"So is talk. So is sex . . . . No, man, I don't feel like playing right now. Fernando will play . . . . You want to play 'Mastermind', right?" I asked, turning to Fernando.

"Of course, I'm ready. But what does this 'Mastermind' mean?"

"Huh, it's something like *Hombre Genio* (genius man). Yeah, that's it! You can play Jaap to see who is the Genius Man of the passengers."

"All right," said Fernando. "We will see."

We squatted down around the plastic boards and pegs.

"I'll begin," said Jaap. Within minutes Fernando and Jaap were engrossed in the competition. I tried to talk and joke with them but their attention remained riveted to the game. I felt like an intruder. These guys are too damn serious over this stupid game, I thought. I was afraid of this. You'd think they were playing for money . . . . I turned to Betti.

"So how do you like the trip so far?" I asked her.

"It is interesting," she said, her eyes glued to the game boards.

"What do you mean, interesting?"

"Oh, you know, different from Holland. Quite different."

"No, I don't know. I've never been to Holland."

"No? That is unfortunate." She gave an impatient toss of her head and spoke to Jaap in Dutch.

All right, lady, I thought. Whatever you like. Man, this is a bore.

I stood up. "I'll talk to you people later," I said. "I'm going to read for a while. Let me know who wins."

No one answered. I returned to my spot near the front of the lumber stack and opened my Portuguese book, reviewing several chapters before setting the book aside with a sigh. This is a waste of time, I thought. I already know this book by heart. The written words alone aren't enough. I need someone from here to practice with—to learn the intonations and sounds no book can convey. To learn the slang and regionalisms of Amazonas so I can bullshit with the local people easier. Fuck! Why aren't any of the passengers Brazilian?

Pensively I stared at the near shore. A wall of unbroken green stretched to the horizon. Yelps of glee and protest drifted to my ears from the Mastermind contestants. The contest was heating up. How can they take that game so seriously? I thought. Still, it might be fun to watch their reactions to the twists of the game . . . . After another minute or so I got up and joined them.

"You missed it," said Jaap, his face flushed and smiling. "I beat him two games to one. I am the Mastermind."

"Of what?"

"Of the ship."

I grinned crookedly. This guy's serious, I thought. Bizarre.

"He was lucky," said Fernando in Spanish. "And besides, he has more experience with this game than I. It wasn't fair. But I'll beat him later."

Now it's your turn," said Jaap to me.

"My turn for what?"

"To face the Mastermind."

"Nah, you be Mastermind. I'm too lazy. I submit to your domination."

"Vat? . . . I think you are . . . how do you say . . . Chicken."

I laughed. "Your English is good, man. Why don't you play with yourself and quit bugging me."

"Come on. I haf beaten the others . . . "

Suddenly one of the sailors waved from the pilot's cabin and yelled to us to come in for lunch. Instantly all thoughts of a game were forgotten. We scrambled over empty soda and beer cases along the top of the stacked lumber, lowered ourselves to the flat, and climbed across the tie and into the tug.

The cook stood waiting for us beside a fold down table. With arcing sweeps of his soup ladle he motioned for us to take seats on the bench the Brazilian girl had slept on the night before.

We exchanged pleased glances as we sat down. The rude wooden table was set with a white cloth, a vase of flowers, ceramic plates, and assorted bowls of food. Steam seeped from the covered bowls and filled the air with succulent aromas. My mouth watered.

"Eat," said the cook.

The food was hearty and plentiful. We ate *feijoada*, a Brazilian staple made of black beans, chunks of spicy meat, seasoning, and whatever else the imagination of the particular cook thinks appropriate, white rice, *farinha*, and a jellied guava dessert. We washed the spicy *feijoada* down with boiled river water that had been chilled in the freezer. After we started eating, the cook brought us a can labeled *"Leite em po."* I was puzzled. *Leite em po* meant powdered milk, but the can was filled with strange knotty balls. I picked one of the balls out of the can and rolled it between my thumb and forefinger. It was like paste. I popped the ball into my mouth and bit down on it. I flinched with pain. The core was hard as a rock.

"What is this shit?" I asked Fernando.

"It's strange, no?" Fernando tasted one of the balls. "I think it's powdered milk. The humidity has condensed it."

"I almost broke my tooth on it. It's too hard."

"Mix it into the food. The moisture should soften it. I'm going to try to eat it because it contains many vitamins and minerals that the other food lacks."

159

I sampled a chunk that Fernando had soaked in his watery rice. This one was softer but it disgusted me.

"It must be old," I said. "It has no taste at all."

"Well, no, it has no taste. But it is good for the health."

"Maybe you're right, Fernando." I ate another insipid pellet. "If I keep telling myself that it's good for me, I might even be able to convince myself that it tastes good."

Fernando grimaced as he bit into one of the hard ones. "That I doubt."

Jaap and Betti were smart. They let us experiment with the *leite em po* and then refused to try it. Naturally I called Jaap a chicken. All in good fun.

About halfway through lunch we were joined at the table by a young Brazilian man. I had noticed him earlier and assumed he was part of the crew. He glanced shyly at us and silently filled his plate.

"Are you a passenger?" I asked him.

"I am," he said. Then he dropped his eyes and filled his mouth with food.

Great, I thought. If he has as much time on his hands as we do maybe he can teach me something of his language.

During this first meeting, however, he barely said a word. He responded to our friendly overtures with self-conscious smiles and a perplexed lifting of his thin black eyebrows. From time to time he would look up from his food and stare at us wide-eyed as we bandied words in three languages. He reminds me of a child at the zoo or the circus for the first time, I thought. Well, he'll get used to us.

After lunch we went to a small forward cargo hold and grabbed a bunch of bananas. We each ate a couple and rubbed our full stomachs.

"That was a goot meal," declared Jaap. "I hope this class of service continues."

"Pretty damn good," I agreed. "The *feijoada* had a nice flavor. But the rice was watery."

"Well, that stew had too much meat for me," said Betti. "I normally don't eat red meat. But under these conditions . . . "

"You can always gif the meat to me," said Jaap.

"Shall we go back to the wood?" I asked.

Betti and Jaap yawned. "I'm going to take a siesta," said Fernando. The three of them retired to their hammocks.

I shrugged and returned to my spot at the head of the lumber stack. It's much quieter and less uncomfortable here than on my bed, I thought. Might as well enjoy the peace and quiet when I can get it.

I reclined against a short stack of lumber and stretched my legs. Sun rays filtered through a light mist, a breeze cooled my brow. With drooping eyelids I watched the river slip past. Soon an enormous island appeared dead in our path. I became alert. The ship veered and we skirted close to one of the island's flanks. Narrow strips of beach gave way to lush forest. The cries of birds and other creatures rang clear. I could distinguish individual ferns and trees with grotesque spiraling shapes. A band of monkeys frolicked among the branches on the fringe of the trees. They emitted strange and piercing calls as the boat chugged by them. Perhaps the ship annoys them, I thought. It must be as mysterious to them as their jungle is to me. I gazed at the curtain of vegetation. The island passed interminably, like a green unbroken freight train. Before I saw its end Fernando came around the corner of the lumber stack.

"What happened to your nap?" I called to him.

He frowned and shook his head. He climbed up to join me before answering. *"Carajo!"* he exclaimed. "That engine noise made it impossible for me to sleep . . . . It's like some screaming banshee."

I chuckled.

"What's so funny?"

"The way you described the engine noise. I like that."

"It's terrible. I don't understand how the sailors can take it all the time."

"They probably go slowly deaf. That's how they get used to it."

"Well, I don't want to get used to it."

"No. Me either . . . . So tell me, how is it that you're on this boat in the middle of nowhere?"

Fernando burst into laughter. "What? . . . Do you want a life story or a simple confession of woe?"

"A simple story would be fine."

"All right, then." Fernando paused, a grin tugged at the corner of his mouth. "Let's see . . . as you already know I was born and raised in Lima. I suppose you could say that I'm more or less a product of a middle class environment. My father is a retired army officer and my mother is a housewife . . . . Anyway, I was attending the university — I'm 21 years old by the way — when I realized how routine and boring life seemed. Every day, every month, every year began to merge and blur in my mind. Go to school, work, study, the usual round of parties, friends, the family, and then more of the same. You know, an endless cycle. The same program . . . "

"Uh huh. And?"

"Well, I felt discontented and restless. Everything bored me. I

161

needed to break out of the mold . . . . I thought and thought. What is it that I want to do? What is it that I need to do? Finally it came to me . . . . I decided to set everything aside, let myself go, and embark on an ambitious journey."

"As you have. You're a long way from home."

"Yes, but there's more. I propose to continue my journey until I reach Paris, France."

"Paris?"

"Yes. And I plan to do it insofar as possible by water. Flying would be too easy. And too expensive."

"That's fine, by boat. Do you have enough money?"

Fernando chuckled. "I don't know how much enough money would be . . . . Right now I have a little over $500 *cruzeiros*."

"What? That's nothing, man!"

"I know that this is very little money—but I don't expect money to be a problem."

"How's that?"

"Well, it's like this, I've always been a very lucky person . . . . And besides, before leaving Peru, I managed to secure a work permit for Brazil. I'm sure I'll be able to gain some kind of employment when the necessity arises. And as long as I'm on this boat I certainly don't need any more money."

"That's true, but a little more money would help. Trying to make it to France on the equivalent of $15 dollars will be a good story." I shook my head. "You're a fool or a magician. I don't know which . . . . But I like your attitude. I hope you succeed."

Fernando laughed. "It's not as difficult as it would seem."

"Yeah? So, what's your plan? Do you have a plan?"

"Of course. Look, I used to work in the French Embassy in Lima. I speak French well. Believe me, I had plenty of practice because none of those Frenchies ever wanted to speak Spanish..."

"I can imagine," I said, thinking of my mother's parents. "But that was good for you to learn French better."

"Yes . . . . Now, when we arrive in Manaus, I have some Peruvian friends who are already working there. They can help me find a place to stay and some work. I'll earn some money and look around. Then I'll get a berth on a boat that will take me to Belém. From there I go to French Guiana, where, with my knowledge of French, and a letter of recommendation from the embassy, I should be able to gain employment. And, eventually, a ship that will take me to Europe . . . . Simple, no? *Voilà!*'

I laughed. "Seems easy, the way you describe it . . . . But would it bother you if I put some doubt in your nice easy plan?

"Go ahead."

"All right, you know there are many dangers and a lot of insecurity involved. Why should everything go smoothly and happen just right for you? . . ."

Fernando started to protest.

"One moment," I said. "What if you can't locate your friends in Manaus? What if they have problems of their own and can't help you? . . . What will you do then? Why should things necessarily go well?"

Fernando chuckled. "Why shouldn't things go well? As I told you, I'm a very lucky person."

"Yes, but luck can change in a moment. You could end up on the street begging handouts."

"That's true. But if that's the worse thing that happens to me, it isn't so bad . . . . And anyway, who are you to lecture me on the insecurity of my trip? What about you?"

"Well, uh, if necessary, if I get into bad trouble, I can ask for help from the organization I work for. Of course I wouldn't like to do that but . . . it seems to me you don't have any backing at all, man. You better think about that."

Fernando looked thoughtfully out over the river and murmured, "I have thought about it." After a long moment he turned to me and said: "You know, youth is something that passes very quickly. I want to catch it now and savor it . . . . When I made the decision to embark on this journey I felt the time was right to do something I had thought about for a long time — if not, the time might never be right. The opportunity would pass me by . . . . That, and it's time for me to leave my comfortable nest. I want to go out and face the world without the help of my family and friends . . . . Call it a test of manhood, call it whatever you want. I feel the need to do this thing. I like the adventure and the challenge. And as for the insecurity. . . well, there is insecurity every moment of one's life; in one way or another." Fernando shrugged his shoulders and smiled. "And besides, I've come quite a distance already. I think returning to Lima right now would be almost as difficult as continuing on to France. You understand me?"

I nodded. Yes, I thought, I understand you too well.

"Listen to what's already happened to me on this trip and you will better understand my confidence," said Fernando. "When I left Lima and headed for Amazonas via the *Rio Marañon*, I had a fair amount of money. Then, due to some unfortunate circumstances and my own care-lessness, my savings were quickly dissipated . . . "

"Carelessness?"

"Well, I met some congenial people in this great town and I was having a good time . . . . Before I could tear myself away I spent most of my money."

"Sounds good. Tell me the details."

Fernando hung his head. "I'm embarrassed by what happened. I lost my head."

"All right, I think I get you. That almost happened to me in Leti-cia . . . . So what then?"

"So, luck was with me, one of my chance companions, who helped me spend my money, paid me back by finding me a job. Within a week I earned enough coins for the passage to Benjamin Constant. On arriving there, virtually broke, good fortune was with me again. I was befriended by two Peruvians and a Colombian. They gave me a place to hang my hammock and helped me to locate work."

"What kind of work did you do?"

"I had two jobs; I worked on the docks as a cargo loader and as a doorman at a discotheque."

"How was the work?"

"Ah, so so. Loading the boats wasn't too bad — except for the low pay . . . . But I didn't much like the job at the discotheque."

"Why?"

"You know, the usual kind of problems. Drunks trying to screw around with you. Assholes trying to sneak in. I almost had to fight sev-eral times and I wasn't getting enough money to risk my neck . . . . And there was another thing that bothered me. I couldn't believe the number of women who were prostitutes. And such young women."

"Really?"

"Yes, most of them were barely more than children."

"Frontier zone."

"I suppose . . . . Anyway, between my two jobs, I made enough mo-ney to pay the passage on this boat. I tried to talk the captain into letting me work my way to Manaus but he would have none of that . . . . So, here I am, my passage paid but with small savings in my pocket."

"Well, you've certainly come a long way already," I said. "You've al-most convinced me that you're going to make it."

"I will make it. I just don't know how many months before I reach Paris."

I laughed. "Go for it . . . . What do you plan on doing when you reach Paris?"

"Paris will be my base; I have friends there. Primarily I want to travel around Europe and become acquainted with the way of life."

"Uh huh."

"And later, after I satisfy my wanderlust, if possible, I hope to enter the university in Paris and study law. I believe that living and studying there would give me a better insight into the culture than merely travelling from place to place. Don't you think so?"

"Of course. If you maintain an open mind . . . . You have some ambitious plans, man."

"Yes. I want to move forward. I don't want to waste my life."

"I see."

Fernando peered at me. "And you?" he asked. "What made you leave a paradise like the United States to live in Colombia?"

"Paradise?" I gave a rueful laugh.

Fernando ignored it. "Did you do it for your career?"

"No, not really. I've been interested in South America for a long time. If I hadn't joined Peace Corps I would have figured out some other way to get here . . . . I wanted to travel, experience other cultures, learn other languages, and maybe help a few people along the way."

"That's all?" Fernando eyed me skeptically.

"That's enough for now." I laughed. "Maybe later I'll find better reasons to be here."

"What is the main purpose of this organization you work for? This Peace Corps?"

"Officially? . . . Or what I think?"

"Both."

"Well, according to Peace Corps, we're in Colombia to assist in the development of an emerging industrial nation — or something like that. And, more importantly, to raise the consciousness of the people."

"What do you mean by raise the consciousness?"

"Well, the way I have it figured . . . "

"Yes."

"I suppose we're there to show Colombians that North Americans don't eat babies for breakfast. Then later, I go back to the United States and tell gringos that Colombians aren't savage Indians living in the jungle and chewing coca leaves all day. Understand?"

"Not really." Fernando giggled. "That is absurd."

"Sure, it's absurd to you because you know better. Obviously it's an exaggeration. But you'd be amazed by some of the conceptions that people have . . . . Or I should say the misconceptions. It's incredible."

"Fine, but what are you supposed to do about that?"

"All right, for example, you go to the university in Lima."

"Yes."

"Among people you know, what percentage of them think that Peace Corps is a front for the C.I.A., or that almost all North Americans come to South America only to exploit its people and resources?"

"There are many who think that way."

"Exactly. Many people in Colombia feel the same way. I'm supposed to show them something else. I'm supposed to show them that North Americans are good people — not *cucos* (boogie men) . . . . Now, in the United States, the majority of people, when and if they think of Colombia at all, they think of drugs, violence, political instability, Third World country . . . . The best things they associate with Colombia are coffee and emeralds. They know little of the cultural diversity and natural beauties or any of the other fine things I've experienced there. It's my job to inform as many people as possible—after I inform myself. So, more than anything, my job is public relations. Something like a goodwill ambassador. A dispeller of stereotypes."

"That's fine," said Fernando. "But does this program have any real value for development?"

"I can't speak for the program in general. What is valuable? What is useless? Development is a tricky business."

"Then, are you doing anything worthwhile?"

"For me, the experience itself is worthwhile. It's beautiful. But for others it can be a nightmare."

"But are you doing anything concrete to improve the standard of living there?"

I looked at Fernando's earnest expression and was unable to repress a chuckle.

"Why are you laughing?"

"Because you talk like many people in the United States."

"Why?"

"It's like, go on down there and show those poor people how to live better . . . . Making the assumption that we know how to live better. I don't think anyone can make that assumption."

"But I'm talking about change for the better. Technical advancement and modernization."

"All right, I can't answer your question. I don't know if I'm doing any good. I don't even know if I want to change anything. The only thing I can tell you for certain is that I'm learning much from the Colombians and I hope that they learn something from me."

"That's fine," said Fernando, impatience creeping into his voice. "But what exactly are you doing?"

"That's what I'm trying to tell you, man—I don't exactly know! There are no specific guides to measure my work."

"But . . . but . . . "

"Look, man, this is how I look at my job: I'm supposed to help reform a bunch of unwanted street kids, who have been dumped in a shit prison in a small town, by giving them an organized recreation program. That's fine, nothing wrong with recreation. But here's the thing that kills me. . . I'm supposed to counsel the guys to be good little boys and follow the norms of society; then the majority of them get out of prison and have to return to the street because they have nowhere else to go . . . . Well, it's tough to be a good little boy and survive on the streets. It's tough to be a good little boy and survive in the prison. Shit, it's tough to be a bad little boy and survive in those places. So, I think, is there a real choice for them? Is it a matter of right or wrong, or a matter of survival? Is what I'm supposed to be telling them worth a damn thing? Is anything I do with them worth a damn thing? The contradictions were driving me crazy."

"You can't worry about those things," said Fernando. "You do your job."

"If you know what your job is?"

"So what did you do?"

"I became more pragmatic. I accepted my limitations and did what I could. For the most part I simply try to entertain the kids and make their stay in the prison less unpleasant with movies, and games, and sports, and conversation, and whatever else I can think of. As for reforming them . . . well, I tell them to know the consequences of their actions and be ready to accept them. That's all. So you see, it's not the kind of job where you see the results of your work very often. Doubt and frustration are normal."

"I don't understand you," said Fernando, frowning. "If it's like that —why don't you go back to your own country?"

"For what? I'm enjoying my time in Colombia. I can't see that I'd be living any better in the United States than I am in Colombia right now . . . . I've worked with juvenile delinquents in the United States and it's equally frustrating. Maybe more so. It's the nature of this particular kind of work; I don't think the country has much to do with it."

Fernando, still puzzled, wrinkled his forehead. "Yes, but . . . isn't it true that even the poorest people in your country have cars and good clothes and many other things that are beyond the reach of most people in my country? Don't tell me you can't make more money there in your profession." '

"Ah, now I understand what you're talking about . . . . Look, man, it's not as easy there as you seem to think. You have to work very hard for your toys; sometimes you think you're working for the machines instead of the machines working for you. There is much pressure to produce. . . . Anyway, it's another misconception that all North Americans are well off. In San Francisco, which is one of the richer cities, there are people living in the streets begging for money and food. The streets aren't paved with gold."

"That may all be true; but don't tell me the poverty is nearly as bad as in most of the countries of South America. The United States is one of the most, if not the most, advanced industrial societies of the world . . . . Anyway, I see nothing wrong with working hard for the good things of life. That's the way it should be."

"That's it! What I'm trying to explain to you. You just said it."

"What?"

"Things, man! Things! Working hard for things. This is the mentality I was trying to escape by leaving the United States."

Fernando shook his head. "I don't understand. What's wrong with nice things? They enhance the quality of life."

"Yes, certainly they do . . . but you pay a price. Too high a price for me."

"Like I said, I don't see anything wrong with working hard."

"I'm not only talking about that—although the work in general is very demanding."

"Then what?"

"To be successful, as the word is defined in the United States, you have to sacrifice much of your individuality. You have to sublimate yourself to the system and not ask too many questions — even when you think something is stupid — if you want to get ahead."

"So what? That's like anywhere. You can't have everyone doing whatever they want."

"All right, fine," I said. "Like anywhere. But in some places more than others. At least in Colombia I'm not bombarded with propaganda to the extent I am in my country. I suppose because Colombia's not as organized and efficient—yet."

"Propaganda?"

"Yes, advertising, that sort of thing. Commercials depicting the good life. Measure your personal value by what you own, not by what you are. To me it's a joke. But that's where the emphasis is. Everything and everyone is a commodity. Learn to sell yourself—that's the motto."

"Well, if you don't like that system, you don't have to follow it. At least your country is free and gives you the opportunity to make a choice. In many places one doesn't have that luxury."

"Listen, Fernando, in my country if you don't follow the system you're not likely to survive. There is tremendous pressure to conform .... Ah, it's no use. I can't explain it to you; you would have to go and live there and see for yourself. Maybe it would be a paradise for you .... I'm not trying to tell you the United States is a bad place; it has many good things. I'm just trying to give you an idea of the reality as compared to the image."

"You're speaking strangely for an American. My image of the United States is that it's the country of hopes and dreams for many people all over the world."

"Sure, of course, the image is that. The Statue of Liberty and such .... The rags to riches immigrants. But what about the other side of the story? What about the failures? My neighborhood was full of them. The country has major problems — crime, drug addiction, racism, violence, industrial pollution. That's also part of the story. You don't just live there and make money and buy things and live happily ever after."

Fernando appeared lost in thought.

"What do you think, Fernando?"

"Well, wherever you have people there will always be problems. Adam and Eve screwed up paradise. Problems are relative. I think the United States has less than most other countries."

I chuckled. "Yes, and some that other countries can't even imagine. Hell, why say more. You'll get a taste of an advanced industrial society when you get to Europe. See what you think. It should be different, but not too different from my country."

"So it's modern civilization that bothers you."

"Certain aspects of it bother me. I already told you a few of them."

"What do you propose to take its place?"

"For everyone?"

"Yes, for everyone."

"I propose nothing. I'm no genius to try to run other people's lives. I merely propose that people think for themselves and respect the ideas and way of life of others — within reason .... Anyway, the world will take care of itself. If modern civilization continues to evolve as it is maybe the world will drown in its own garbage. Then we can start over."

"Man, you talk like there is no hope for the world. How can you live with such a negative attitude?"

"Is it negative to think about problems and accept them and try to deal with them? Or is it negative to ignore them and pretend everything is fine, or it's better here than there? You tell me."

"So what are you saying? Who has the answer? Do you think the Soviet Union and communism is better? Do they have the answer?"

I laughed mirthlessly. "What I'm saying is that I don't think any one person or any one system has the answer for everyone. To me that's the biggest problem. Too many people think they have the answer and they want to impose it on everyone else, instead of taking care of their own life. For example, look at Hitler — he thought he had all the answers. And the shame of it is that many people believed him."

"What about the Soviet Union and communism?"

"I don't know. I've never been there or lived under that regimen. But if they truly preach blind obedience to the state, I wouldn't want anything to do with it. When the system becomes more important than the people it's supposed to serve it becomes dangerous. Any system. Or any one person . . . . I hate all fanatic nationalists or fanatic religious people regardless of whatever label they use to serve themselves. They use slogans and statistics to manipulate people for their own ends in order to attain a historical niche for themselves. Fuck that! It doesn't suit my temperament to just go along because some power crazy fool says it's right for everyone. If that's the case I might as well be a robot . . . . Well, what do you think?"

"There are things that are good for everyone. I believe in order and progress. Most people are untrustworthy and must be controlled at the expense of certain freedoms."

"But who makes the order? Who defines progress? . . . To an Amazonian Indian your civilized paradise could be hell . . . and vice versa."

Fernando shook his head. "If things were the way you wanted all order would dissolve and anarchy would be the result. We would regress. History will take its course."

"That's for sure. History will take its course." The strong and charismatic will survive and dominate, I thought. And perhaps destroy everything to satisfy their lust and greed. Ah, the hell with it. We'll only go round and round if I say it.

Fernando was regarding me with a curious look. "How do you see yourself in all this? If you don't like organized society how do you keep from feeling alienated?"

"Well, I do feel alienated sometimes. I don't like crowds but I do like people . . . . I don't know. I'm a loner by nature. I've come to terms with myself."

"A lone wolf?"

"Yes, something like that. I've always admired wolves."

"Why?"

"Because they only take what they need and no more. And they run in packs or can stand alone . . . . They represent true freedom to me."

Fernando fell silent. Embarrassed by my outburst, I did the same —for a while. Time and the river slipped past. We spoke of personal impersonal subjects such as family background, friends, education, and travel anecdotes. Meanwhile, our course veered and we were chugging toward the south bank. Isolated huts began appearing at irregular intervals. The boat drew closer to the shore and straightened out. Soon a town came into view. Our speed slackened. Fernando whipped out his map.

"This must be São Paulo do Olivença!" he exclaimed. "I believe we're going to stop here. Now we can go and see something besides trees and water."

"What I want to see is a cold beer," I said. "Let's hope we can get one here."

The ship came about and we backed toward a small clearing with a tiny pier. The town sat a few hundred feet above and beyond the shore. The captain cut the engine and we coasted to the landing. Fernando and I got up and hurried to the prow of the tug. Various sailors left the shade of the boat and boiled to activity around us. We got out of their way as they grabbed stout ropes and wooden planks. A thrill ran through me as I felt the bottom of the cargo flat scrape along the muddy river bottom. Before we came to a complete stop two agile sailors leaped to shore and lashed the ship to a number of thick wooden stakes. Another sailor lay boards across the gap between the flat and the bank to make a gangplank. The tall sailor with the green bermuda shorts climbed atop the lumber stack and picked up a case of soda. Within seconds the sailors formed a human chain and began passing cases of beer and soda to dry land.

"Damn," I said to Fernando, "these guys work well and fast."

"Yes. This is an experienced crew."

"The way they're working it doesn't look like we're going to be here long. Do you think we have time to get off and look around?"

"I don't know. Let's find out."

We lowered ourselves to the cargo flat and approached the nearest sailor.

"Help? Help you?" asked Fernando.

171

"What?" replied the sailor, continuing his work.

"Help with the work?" said Fernando, pointing to one of the cases.

The sailor looked at us, grudgingly pausing from his task. "No, no. Thank you. This is our work."

"How long are we going to be here?" asked Fernando in Spanish.

The sailor's eyes rolled, his face went blank.

"How much time here? How much time here?" I asked him in Portuguese, motioning to the town.

"Eh?"

"How much . . . "

"I don't know. One moment." He turned and yelled something at the tall sailor. The tall sailor yelled back. A rapid exchange followed. Fernando and I looked at each other; we understood nothing. The sailor turned back to us. "*Uma hora.* One hour. You can go."

"Thanks."

We fairly leaped across the planks to shore. We found a narrow path at the edge of the clearing and scrambled up the damp incline. When we hit level ground we paused to catch our breath. I was dripping perspiration and spots danced in front of my eyes. Insects hummed in my ears.

"A little farther," said Fernando. "The town is just past this bush."

"Let's go slower," I said. "It doesn't pay to rush in this climate."

"True. But the beer will taste better."

"It'll taste good anyway."

We walked ahead and broke through the trees. The town lay before us; we surveyed it with eager eyes. Scattered clumps of board houses with corrugated metal roofs and some barrack-like storage sheds lay on terraces cut into the sloping hillside. A network of intersecting dirt paths connected the groups of buildings.

"What is this?" I exclaimed. "It looks like a military base."

"It reminds me of a mountain camp for prisoners," said Fernando. "Without the barbed wire."

"Some town. I expected more than this."

We edged toward the first group of buildings. Nothing stirred.

"Where are the people?" asked Fernando. "It may be siesta time but there should be someone out and around."

"Maybe they got wiped out by bubonic plague."

Fernando snickered. "Or died of boredom." He wiped his brow. "*Puta!* It's hot."

"Uh huh. Well, let's go. If we can find a store in this ghost town I'll invite you to a beer."

As we reached the first group of buildings a lone man emerged from one of the storage sheds. Without noticing us he turned and headed down another path. We called to him but he kept on. Fernando hustled after him and headed him off at a fork in the path. I followed close behind. The man stared at us with a surprised look on his face. We asked him where we could find a cold drink. After a few moments of confusion he understood us. He pointed up the slope to a long square building that looked like most of the others. We thanked him and hiked up the slope.

We entered the building and were greeted by a pleasant draft of air from the overhead fans. The room was cool and spacious. It was a combination general store and recreation room. A large pool table dominated the center of the room, flanked by matching sets of bamboo tables and chairs. A high counter ran along the length of the back wall. Behind the counter were rows of scantily stocked shelves and a huge white refrigerator. We headed for the refrigerator. No one seemed to be minding the store.

When we reached the counter we saw the attendant seated at the far end reading a book. The attendant was a startlingly pretty young girl.

"Service," I called.

Unhurriedly she rose and came over to wait on us. She was gorgeous; a dark haired, dark eyed, petite young woman in full flower. We gaped at her.

"What would you like?" she asked us.

A dangerous question if I were to tell you the truth, I thought.

"Two cold beers," I said with a smile.

She stared at us with frank curiosity. "What? I don't understand."

"Two cold beers, please," I repeated. "Do you have it?"

"Yes, of course. Now I understand." She laughed. "You talk funny."

"Thanks."

She laughed as she went to get the beers; her laughter was happy and open.

"What a beauty," said Fernando.

"Uh huh."

She returned with two bottles of *Antarctica* and placed them before us. I took a long pull.

"Cold as the name," I said to Fernando. "Just what we needed."

"Among other things," he answered.

As we drank our beer the girl stayed near us and studied from a primary level reading book. We did our best to distract her and she encouraged our attentions by setting the book aside. We asked her questions, trying to make her understand us. She would listen to one of our broken sentences, squinting as if in great concentration, then surrender to happy laughter. It was somehow entertaining. This little game carried us through our first beer. By the time we started on our second beer I was ready for something else.

I took her reading book and asked her to instruct us in Brazilian pronunciation. She agreed readily and took on the job with enthusiasm, reveling in her role as teacher. She would read a sentence or phrase; I would repeat it. Whenever I managed an intelligible pronunciation she would nudge me encouragingly and her face would beam with pleasure. Now this is the way to learn, I thought. I wish I could take her with me.

Fernando participated in the lesson by using Spanish pronunciation for the Portuguese words. After a while I gave him an irritable glance. Why is he doing that? I thought. Is it that stupid rivalry? . . . Or are his ears for language bad? How well does he really speak French? Huh . . .

As we were finishing our second beer Jaap burst into the room and hurried up to the counter.

"Where haf you fellows been? The boat will be leaving in a short while."

"We've been right here having a few cold ones," I said. "Want one?"

"No. There is no time. We must go."

"Has an hour gone by that fast?"

Jaap didn't answer me. He was looking at the canned goods on the shelves behind the counter. He smiled. "Oh, look at all the things they haf here . . . . Good things! Sardines! I think the boat will wait a few minutes."

By way of grunts and hand signals Jaap showed the girl what he wanted. He bought a can of crackers, tins of sardines, guava marmalade, and, for a mere twenty *cruzeiros*, a serviceable straw hat. He placed the hat atop his head and gave it a jaunty tilt.

"This is goot; it will keep my nose from burning . . . . So, do I look like a Brazilian?"

"You look more like Huckleberry Finn," I said. "But it's a sharp hat."

As Jaap paid for his goods I turned and saw a man standing near the entrance. He eyed us suspiciously and appeared to be upset about something or other. I turned and said something to the girl. Then I turned to watch the man's reaction. He knocked a chair over and came to the counter with a dark scowl on his face. He spoke to the girl and stepped behind the counter. Her face turned serious and she pointed to the counter top in front of us. The man surveyed the items we had purchased and almost smiled. He grabbed a beer from the refrigerator and moved away from us to the far end of the counter.

"Who is he?" I asked the girl in a low voice.

"My uncle."

"Ah, that's why."

"Why what?"

"Nothing."

I glanced at the man. He was watching us without being obvious about it. Guarding the family treasure, I thought. He must have thought we were being too friendly . . . . Doesn't matter, man. We have to go now.

Fernando and I said good-bye to our lovely and exuberant teacher. Jaap scooped up his booty. We returned to the *Magalhães* at a trot.

Two of the sailors gave us sour looks as they hauled the planks onto the flat after us.

"We must have delayed them a little," I said to Fernando. "But that sure didn't seem like an hour."

"It wasn't an hour. Don't worry about it."

My mind was buzzing from the beer and the heat.

"I'm going to sit in the shade in the boat for a while," I said to Fernando. "And you?"

"All right, let's go."

We rounded the corner of the lumber and stopped in surprise.

"It looks like we have some new passengers," said Fernando.

There in front of us, snorting and oinking as they devoured a mound of green bananas, were four pigs. The animals were tied to a single rope that restricted their movement to the twenty square feet or so between the front of the cargo and the end of the flatbed connected to the prow of the tug. Further, they were fastened in such a way that if one pig wanted to move then all of them would have to move — or be dragged.

"The captain must be bringing them along to sell later," I said.

"Or to eat," said Fernando.

"You think so?"

"Maybe. Fresh meat."

"They sure are runty."

"No. Young and tender."

We stepped gingerly past the area occupied by the pigs, avoiding the slick mash of squashed bananas, urine, and shit they had concocted.

"What a mess," said Fernando. "Now we have to be very careful when we cross back and forth."

We climbed onto the tug and went into the hold. I spied little Jorge. He was sitting on one of the mysterious black blobs, watching the receding shore as we pulled out onto the river. Inspired by my lesson with the girl, and no doubt by the beer I had drunk, I went over to talk to him.

"What is that you are sitting on?" I asked him.

He looked at me and grinned roguishly. "What?"

"What is that you are sitting on?"

He mimicked my voice in an ugly way.

"I don't speak like that," I said.

He mimicked me again, and added some nasty sounding words of his own. Then he laughed—a hyena laugh.

"All right, you little chump," I said in English, "two can play this stupid game. You're a sorry little punk with no manners."

Jorge's mouth fell open and his face took on a forlorn expression. He spoke to me in a conciliatory tone.

"That's better," I said in Portuguese. "What are you sitting on?"

Jorge grinned and mimicked my voice.

I should belt him one, I thought. No, I can't do that. I'm a juvenile counselor . . . . Jorge gave me his hyena laugh. I burned. One little slap, I thought. No! The adult thing to do is to tell him he's a naughty boy and walk away with dignity . . . . Jorge mimicked my voice. That's it!

I raised my hand as if to strike him. He cringed back. I brushed my upraised hand through my hair and turned away with a laugh.

"Wait," said Jorge, tapping me on the back. "What do you want?"

"What is that? What do you call it?"

Jorge showed his even white teeth and pounded the blob with his fist. "*É borracha* (bo-hash-ah). *Borracha.*"

What the hell is that? I've never heard that word before, I thought.

Jorge noted my perplexion. He pounded the blob again and again. *"É borracha! Borracha! Borracha!"*

I shook my head. "Sorry, I don't understand."

Jorge yelped his frustration and ran off. Well, he's lousy teacher material, I thought. Huh . . . . I'd still like to know what this garbage is . . . . I sought out Fernando and found him by the galley.

"What is this?" I asked him, kicking one of the blobs with the point of my toe.

"This?" Fernando looked surprised. *"Es caucho natural* (natural rubber)."

"Oh, natural rubber. That's why it seemed familiar."

"I would have expected you to know that."

"No, not like this. We don't have too many rubber tree plantations in California."

"No, I suppose not." Fernando laughed. "I thought they had everything in Califoirnia."

"That's what you thought."

"Well, this rubber is taken directly from the trees — as sap — and crudely processed by . . ."

"Excuse me. Do you want to go out to the wood and continue our conversation? This damn engine noise is getting to me."

"All right."

We left the tug and took our places near the front of the woodpile. Jaap and Betti followed close behind us. Soon Jaap brought out the "Mastermind" game. Fernando was eager for a rematch. The contest resumed in earnest. Betti and I were ignored. This time she grew bored by the game and engaged me in conversation.

As the sun dropped, shadows crept across the flat and it grew chilly in the shade. Betti and I moved away from the players to a spot on the lumber still bathed in sunshine. We settled down and stretched out.

"How do you like South America so far?" I asked her.

"Oh, some things I like and some things I don't like. . . . It's interesting and curious. Beautiful and ugly . . . "

"Uh huh." She speaks excellent English, I thought. Fluent and precise—with just a hint of a British accent that sounds cute.

"You speak excellent English," I told her in a matter-of-fact tone of voice.

Betti smiled and smoothed her hair. "I should speak well . . . . I have studied for twelve years. And, of course, all my teachers were from Great Britain."

"I see."

"Where did you learn to speak Spanish? In school?"

"Mostly in Colombia. I took an intensive language course in Bogotá and I picked up the rest living there."

"Colombia?" Betti grimaced. "We found Colombia to be a rather dangerous country. Quite inhospitable at times."

I chuckled. "It can be. But . . . " As I gave her my impressions of Colombia, I noticed that she didn't understand all I said. I made a conscious effort to speak slower (though my normal speech is deliberate) and to eliminate slang words and expressions. I finished talking and looked at her expectantly, awaiting her comment on my impressions. To

177

my surprise her gray eyes glinted irritation.

"Why were you speaking to me like that?"

"Like what?"

"As though I were some sort of child."

"What? . . . No, no, you got me wrong. I just thought that . . . "

"Your tone of voice was patronizing."

"Now wait. I just thought that you might be having trouble with some of my expressions and manner of speaking. Just like I have trouble with Spanish sometimes."

"Nothing of the sort." Betti drew herself up haughtily. "The reason I cawn't understand all you say . . . is because you do not speak English . . . but rawther American. Which, needless to say, lacks the style and correctness of the true British language."

I smiled. "You're absolutely right, Betti. American is different from the English spoken in England. Different enough . . . . But then again, I've never met an English person who couldn't understand me. So that leaves your problem with me unsolved."

Betti thought this over for a few seconds. Then her face blanched. "Well, to tell you the truth . . . the United States does not interest me in the least! Nor the manner of speaking there!"

"That's fine." I'm sure no one in the U.S. is losing any sleep over what you think, dear, I thought. But why hassle over stupidity like this?

"Look," I said, "let's start over. I'm sorry if I sounded patronizing."

"Very well."

"Well, how long do you two plan on traveling? What's your ultimate destination?"

Betti's face brightened. "Eventually we are going to Surinam."

"Surinam. I wonder what that country is like?"

"We have heard it is quite exotic—a wonderful quaint country with many strange customs. But where the people speak Dutch."

"Yes."

"But of course, before we go to Surinam, we plan to see much more of Brazil. At the very least we will go to Rio and São Paulo and another large city called . . . Belo . . . "

"Belo Horizonte."

"Yes, that's it. Jaap is thinking of purchasing some emeralds there."

"Emeralds? I didn't know they have emeralds there. . . . Are you sure? I think Colombia is a better place for emeralds."

"Well, perhaps so. But he is interested in some sort of precious stones they have there."

"How long do you plan on staying in South America?"

"It will depend on our money; but possibly as long as six months."

"Wow, you'll be travelling for a good spell . . . . Most of the time in Brazil?"

"Yes. But we want to have a good look at Surinam. At any rate we have to return to Holland from there. And six months is the absolute limit because Jaap must return to his job and work."

"Yeah, work. Can't ever forget about that . . . . Still, along with the travelling you've already done, it sounds like the trip of a lifetime. An exciting one you can tell your grandchildren about."

"It has definitely been exciting . . . . I am not sure the tropics agree with me. The heat and filth. The poverty."

"It takes some getting used to — some people never do become acclimated."

Betti sniffed. "Who would want to?"

"Do you plan on learning any Portuguese?"

"Portuguese?" Betti curled her lower lip. "I don't believe so."

"Why? I mean, since you'll be travelling in Brazil so long you might as well."

"Frankly, I find it a horrid language. To me it sounds more like Japanese than it does Spanish."

I chuckled. "Maybe it's only like this in Amazonas."

"I don't care. I really do not need to learn any as Jaap speaks Spanish."

I grinned at her, my stomach convulsing with mirth. She's a winner, I thought. I can't believe she said that. But she did. If she only knew how bad Jaap's Spanish is—let alone Portuguese. Man . . .

"What sort of education do you have?" Betti asked me. "Are you university educated?"

"Yes. I studied sociology and recreation and creative writing and anthropology and whatever else caught my fancy."

"What kind of work can you gain with that?"

"I don't know. I never specialized. But it got me in the Peace Corps. Right now I work with juvenile delinquents."

"Oh. That sounds commendable."

"How about you?"

"Why, I attended one of the best universities in northern Europe. My specialty was English. But I studied other languages, and art, and history, and economics, and music, and . . ."

She sounds like she's interviewing for a job, I thought. Finally she finished.

"That's quite an extensive liberal arts background you have," I said.

"Nothing out of the ordinary—for northern Europe."

"Is that right?"

"Of course! . . . Permit me to be frank, and don't take this as a personal reflection on you, but I think the United States must be providing a wholly inadequate education to the majority of its people."

"Really? What makes you think that?"

"Because most of the Americans I have met are almost completely ignorant of the Netherlands."

"How many Americans do you know?"

"More than enough to make this judgment."

"All right, if you say so."

"I am certain. What do you know about Holland?"

"Hmm . . . Let's see . . . it's one of the low countries. The Netherlands. Windmills, dikes, wooden shoes, tulips, uh, Heineken beer, ships, sailors . . . . In general known to be stubborn and shrewd business people. South Africa. The Dutch East Indies. The Boer War. Wasn't it a Dutchman who bought Manhattan from the Indians for $24 dollars? . . . "

Betti giggled. "You know a little more than most."

"Gee, thanks. So I passed your test?"

"Not yet . . . . What type of government does the Netherlands have?"

"Uh, some kind of social-democratic, paternalistic, common market, NATO, whatever. I suppose it's pretty liberal—a friend of mine who visited there told me that the government supports artists. Another one, a German, told me many Germans go to Amsterdam to buy pornographic material."

"Yes, we are quite liberal . . . . One more question: who is the head of state of the Netherlands?"

"I have no idea."

"There! You see! But I know that Carter is the president of the United States."

"But I know that Holland's national soccer team is known as 'The Clockwork Orange', and I know the names of several of their players, which only shows you that I'm more interested in sports than I am in politics. Nothing more."

Betti looked confused momentarily. "Well, another reason I say Americans are receiving an inadequate education is because very few of them speak another language aside from English . . . "

"You mean American."

"... Why, in Holland, and in most of northern Europe, one is required to study two or three different languages. This is one of the principal reasons we are culturally superior to the average American."

For an instant my lips narrowed to a tight line and a sarcastic retort leaped to mind. Betti smirked at me. I turned away from her and looked at the river. Why bother, I thought. We might as well be playing "Mastermind." She babbles about the cultural importance of learning other languages but she can't be bothered with Portuguese .... I repressed a chuckle.

"Well?" asked Betti. "Have you nothing to say?"

"What can I say? I can't agree or disagree with what you say."

"Why not?" Betti's patrician face smirked at me.

"Because," I said softly, "you're talking about formal education and cultural standards that ... well, whose standards?"

"Oh! Why world standards, of course."

"Which world are you talking about? ... Right now we're in the middle of the Amazon. I think that here this cultural superiority you speak of is less important than the ability to recognize what is good to eat and what isn't."

"Oh! Stop being impossible! You know very well what I mean—or you know even less than I first thought."

"Fine, yes, I know what you mean. But it doesn't mean anything to me. It's mental masturbation ... "

"What?"

Before I could continue, a cool breeze whipped off the river and fanned us. Betti pulled her knees up against her ankles and shivered. Goose pimples bubbled on her arms and legs. "Oh! It is cold," she said.

Suddenly she looked naked and vulnerable. Behind the arrogant tilt of her jaw and the flashing challenge of her eyes crouched fear and doubt. The fear of an unknown land and a strange culture. The doubt of one's ability to deal with situations when the accustomed norms don't apply. I've seen that look, I thought. I saw it in the eyes of quite a few people in my Peace Corps group when we arrived in Bogotá. I felt it myself .... Let her cling to these familiar things if they give her some comfort. In the long run they won't do her much good here ... but she has to find that out for herself.

"What were you saying?" asked Betti.

"What was I saying? ... Oh, yeah, you're probably right in saying that foreign languages aren't pushed in the U.S. like they could and maybe should be .... But I think the situations are pretty different. The U.S. is a huge country and, historically, it's been almost self-sufficient and it's been isolated. Europe is a relatively small area with many countries and many languages. I would think the necessity to learn additional languages is much greater considering proximity and economic considerations . . . . Is that reasonable?"

"Yes, but it's no excuse."

"Well, I suppose most Americans are content in their own little world and don't want to be bothered to learn another language. Hell, I can't speak for them. For myself I would try to learn the language of whoever I come in contact with if I'm going to spend much time with them. At least something . . . to give me a better rapport with them and enable me to get along with less problems."

"Of course, of course," said Betti, running her hand through her hair. "But one cannot learn everything. One has to be selective."

"Selective . . . . Yes, of course."

I studied Betti from head to toe and marveled anew at her skinny body.

"Have you been having trouble with the food in South America?" I asked her.

"Oh, yes. It has been horrid. I have been so sick at times. I have lost much weight . . . . It has gotten to the point that I am almost afraid to eat."

I clucked sympathetically. "It's difficult at first. And it can be a vicious cycle — you can get sick from eating, or weakened and sick from being afraid to eat. It takes the body a while to adjust."

"How long did it take you to adjust?"

"Well, I've been pretty lucky. I haven't gotten sick from the food or water—yet. But I have gotten sick from other things."

"How do you suppose you've managed not to get sick from the food?"

"I'm not exactly sure . . . . Either I have a resistant system or I've kept the amoebas at bay by eating plenty of raw onions and fresh pineapple."

"Raw onions? . . . Fresh pineapple? . . . How curious. And what are those supposed to do for you?"

"In general they're good foods, that I know. As for keeping the stomach healthy, well, some of the Colombians in the village I live in swear that they are the best things for controlling amoebas. They claim that the acid and the roughage of the pineapple cleans them out of the intestines. The onion more or less the same." I laughed. "Plus the obnoxious smell."

"How curious. That sounds like one of those . . . how do you say?

". . . One of those . . . "

"Old wives' tales?"

"Yes." Betti snickered. "How curious."

"Maybe it is curious, but I'll take their advice until I find out it doesn't work. It certainly hasn't hurt, and I like fresh pineapple . . . . I told a few of the Peace Corps nurses about this and they laughed. Most of them kept getting sick, too. But they have their pills . . . . Anyway, the nurses are a bad example."

"Why?"

"Because they're so paranoid about what they eat. I think the stress from their paranoia is doing them in more than the unhygienic food and conditions."

"But one should be aware of possible problems to prevent illness. I worry very much about the unsanitary conditions here."

"Sure, you don't want to eat a piece of meat that has flies crawling all over it . . . . But awareness is one thing and paranoia is another. You can't worry so much about the food that you don't eat enough to keep your natural resistance up . . . . And hell, you can get bad food anywhere."

"Very unlikely in Holland."

"O.K." I sighed. "I'll take your word for that. But we're not in Holland."

We fell silent. Jaap and Fernando finished their contest and came over to join us. Soon twilight descended, then the swift curtain of darkness. The lamps at the front of the tug switched on. They glowed like twin lighthouses, drawing us from our now windy perches to the boat. The cook was spreading the tablecloth as we entered the hold.

"Sit down," he said. "Sit. It is time to eat."

We settled down and got comfortable. Within minutes the food was served. Dinner was identical to lunch, though the portions were larger. Save for Betti, we ate ravenously and, at the beginning, quietly. Then as the meal progressed a feeling of easy camaraderie and intimacy grew among us. The naked bulb on the wall just above our heads seemed to provide a bulwark against the inky mysterious world outside our circle. Good cheer and optimism enveloped us like a cocoon. Jaap was jovial and expansive. Betti's face was vibrant as she spoke in Dutch. Fernando kept up a patter of cheerful talk. The Brazilian man watched us with wide eyes and an easy smile. I relaxed and was relatively quiet, well-pleased with the company and the meal.

We lingered at the table long after the plates had been removed, sipping water, relishing the sense of well-being. We discussed the events of the day and looked forward to the morning with keen anticipation.

"The trip is going very smoothly," said Jaap. "My compliments to the captain. I think we will make Manaus on schedule."

Jaap brought out a tin of crackers and guava marmalade. "Haf some dessert. To top off a goot dinner."

"Thanks, man," I said, "that's generous of you."

"Think nothing of it."

We ate crackers smeared with marmalade and drank more water. Conversation continued lively for another hour or so. When our talk started to peter out my mind drifted to the other passengers. A memory of cheap perfume lingered in my nostrils from the night before.

"Have you seen those other two women that are on the boat today?" I asked Fernando.

"Yes. I saw them earlier. But they seem to stay upstairs almost all the time."

"It's strange that they haven't come down to eat . . . . Neither has the captain."

"The captain probably eats in his cabin. As for the women," Fernando shrugged, "maybe they ate earlier. Or maybe they're not hungry."

A short time later our questions were answered when the cook carried a tray with three servings of food up the ladder.

"Now I understand," commented Fernando. "We are entertaining royalty. They don't want to associate with the common people."

"You're crazy," I laughed. "The captain probably just wants to have an intimate meal with them."

"Well, that's possible . . . . I can't blame the captain for that. But how unsociable of them not to descend and converse with the passengers for a while."

"Is conversation the only thing that you're interested in?"

"What do you take me for?" Fernando drew himself up with feigned outrage. "I am a gentleman. Do you think I would betray the confidence of my host?"

"Of course, if you have the opportunity."

Fernando gave me a broad wink and retreated to the bathroom. I pulled a magazine out of my bag and started reading. One by one the hammocks were untangled and the passengers drifted off to bed. Though I was tired I continued to read, dreading the thought of trying to sleep in my noisy space.

Fernando rolled over in his hammock and looked at me. "Would you turn off the light when you're finished reading?" he asked.

"Am I bothering you?" I asked.

"No, but the light bothers me."

"All right."

I put the magazine away and turned out the light. Then, unable to repress a sigh, I went to my sleeping area and settled in among the oil cans and the soiled rags, with the humming engine and the raucous water pump to play me a lullaby.

Chapter VII

RIVER LIFE

I stirred groggily to my second day on the river. It had been another exhausting night of fitfull slumber due to that damned rasping water pump. I stood up and stretched. A numb exhaustion pervaded my body. Feeling like a zombie, I went aft to receive the *cafe da manhã*.

I sipped my scalding coffee and gazed at the river; it was shrouded by a light mist that dulled its reflective surface, making me think of a steamy bathroom mirror. My brain must be full of that mist, I thought. I can't clear away the cobwebs. But that figures . . . . When's the last time I had a good night's sleep? . . . Four days ago? Yeah, four days ago in Bogotá.

I munched my crackers and washed them down with the coffee. One by one the other passengers came over and joined me. After greeting them I kept silent. Their light conversation irritated my raw nerves. Morosely I watched the red sun burn off the translucent veil over the water. As soon as I finished my second cup of coffee I slipped away without a word and headed for the cargo flat.

I sat at the front of the lumber stack and covered my eyes with my hands. A dull throbbing pounded at the base of my skull. This feels like the day after that tequila party a few years ago, I thought, remembering that day with horror. What can I do to relieve this?

I lay down on a wide board and tried to doze, but the contact of the wood against the back of my head intensified the throbbing that had spread to my neck and shoulders. I sat up and closed my eyes. I kneaded my neck and shoulder muscles with the tips of my fingers. I listened to the soothing sound of the water breaking against the metal flat. Slowly the dull throbbing subsided and my muscles and nerves relaxed. I was just starting to enjoy my solitude when Fernando arrived and sat down beside me. He wore his usual wide smile and was in a mood to talk. I discouraged him with short impatient replies. I hung my head and stared at my feet.

"What's the matter?" he asked me.

I glanced at him. He regarded me with a sober expression on his face. He must think I'm being a real asshole, I thought.

"Nothing, man. I'm just tired."

"Man, what's the matter?" he repeated, his voice sympathetic. "Is it something I did?"

"No, it has nothing to do with you. I had a bad night from sleeping over that fucking water pump and I would prefer to remain quiet for a while. That's all."

"That's fine, then. There's no problem. Just relax and take it easy."

We fell silent. I was grateful to Fernando for respecting my mood. Quickly I slipped into a comatose state. Hunched over, my mind blank, I watched the small waves wash over the front of the flat. Now and then a small trunk or other bit of debris thumped against the heavy metal. The sun climbed higher and warmed my bones. A short time later the heat became uncomfortable. I took off my shirt and stretched my arms.

"Starting to come back to life?" asked Fernando.

"Yes, a little," I said, yawning. "How long was I sitting here like a zombie?"

Fernando shrugged. "Who knows? An hour—a little more. Time is losing its meaning for me on this trip."

I know what you mean. I . . . " My eye was caught by a movement below us at the right corner of the lumber stack. Fernando turned and followed my eyes. It was the Brazilian passenger, standing in place, peeking at us from behind the lumber. We watched him for a few seconds, amused by his shyness. Suddenly the Brazilian man's face looked flustered; he realized we had spotted him. He came around the corner and took a few hesitant steps along the flat. Then he stopped and looked at us, a beseeching expression in his eyes. I smiled at him. He turned and looked at the river; then he glanced back at us.

"Good morning," said Fernando in Portuguese.

"Good morning," he replied gravely.

"Come here. Come here," said Fernando, patting a spot on the plank beside him. "Sit with us and talk."

The Brazilian teetered from one foot to the other.

"Yes," I added, "come up and join us . . . . *Tudo bem.*"

The Brazilian mumbled under his breath and lurched forward, stepping from plank to plank as though he were treading on hot coals. He reached us and took a seat next to Fernando. He lowered his eyes and gazed at his brown, calloused hands. A log banged against the flat.

Poor guy, I thought. I'll put him at ease by speaking Portuguese.

"How are you?" I said. "It's a great pleasure to make your acquaintance. I would like nothing better than to learn some Portuguese from you."

He listened politely, a wistful look on his upturned face.

Better go back to basics, I thought. He doesn't seem to understand a thing I said.

"What is your name?" I asked him.

He smiled. "My name is Eloi. And you two?"

"He is Fernando," I said, tapping Fernando's shoulder.

"Fernando," he said. "And you?"

"My name is Craig."

"Kwoig?"

"All right, Gregorio."

"Gregorio, yes. A Brazilian name."

The three of us took it from there, the conversation wheezing along. Communicating with Eloi was like trying to crack a top secret code. He could say anything, even a simple phrase, and would have to repeat himself several times before we understood even the gist of it. Fortunately he seemed to understand us somewhat better than we understood him. We plodded on. Eloi's initial reticence passed and he spoke steadily. We encouraged him, using liberal doses of Spanish. Slowly, torturously, we pieced the bits of phrases, the phrases, and the sentences together. We began to learn a few things about him:

Eloi was on his way to Manaus . . . . To reunite with his wife and two infant children . . . . He had been away from them for six months . . . . He had left them to look for work . . . . He had found work . . . . As a cargo loader . . . . In various ports along the *Solimõ*es (Amazon) . . . . He had saved some money and sent the rest of it home . . . . In Manaus he usually worked as a taxi driver . . . . He was anxious to get back home to his family . . . . He didn't like travelling much . . . . He was 21 years old . . .

Straining to understand him, my headache returned. Damn! This is a bitch! I thought. Why can't I understand him better? He sounds nothing at all like the captain . . . . None of the other Brazilians have been this difficult to understand . . . . Even the chubby girl with the missing teeth was easier than this. Or maybe I'm too tired.

Eloi noticed my mounting frustration. "What's the matter?" he asked me.

"I can't understand you well . . . . It's frustrating."

"Don't worry if you can't understand me well . . . . I speak a strange Portuguese."

"Strange?"

"Yes, strange."

"How so?"

"It is not good Portuguese. It isn't correct . . . . In Amazonas we called it *Portulhon.*"

"*Portulhon*? Is it a dialect?"

"A dialect?" Eloi wrinkled his forehead. "I don't know . . . . Yes, a dialect . . . . The way we speak along the river. It is very different. Even some Brazilians — especially from the south — don't understand us well."

As we continued talking, I asked him to pronounce certain words I already knew. His pronunciation sounded slurred and garbled compared to the radio announcers I was used to hearing. Well, I thought, it's like learning English at Oxford and then going to Louisiana and talking to the Cajuns. It's going to take some getting used to . . . . Maybe if I get my handbook I can get him to say the words and repeat after him . . . to get a better picture and feel for this Amazonas lingo. Right now I'm lost.

"I'm going to the boat to get something," I told them. "I'll be right back."

I walked along the side of the flat toward the tug. Before reaching the end I pulled up in surprise. Two of the sailors were hunched over the railing, watching something below them and to the left, on the side of the flat where the pigs were tethered. My sight was blocked by a projecting stack of lumber. The sailors pointed and licked their lips; they spoke in low tones.

Strange, I thought. What the hell's going on? They're so intent on whatever it is they're looking at they don't even know I'm here.

Without further thought I crossed the steel tie and vaulted over the railing. I set my feet on the deck and turned to look at the front of the flat. There below us, on a bed of fermenting bananas and excrement, the lone runty boar had mounted the sow closest to his end of the rope and was humping her. The boar's eyes were glazed in ecstasy, oblivious to his gawking human audience. The sow looked stoic. The other two pigs were flopped in the shade, unconcerned. The sailors looked on raptly, lips parted.

The sailors looked funny in their seriousness. A guffaw escaped me. With a start they became aware of me. The sailors turned their heads and eyed me, a mixture of embarrassment and hostility coloring their faces, as though I had caught them masturbating in a public toilet. I smiled at them and said, "*Tudo bem?*"

They grunted a response and turned back to the pigs, quickly forgetting me. The lovemaking was reaching a climax. The boar humped faster. The sailors leaned forward even more, their faces avid and, almost envious. I could feel their raw desire, and how, for the moment at least, they wished they could be that boar, or in a similar position with some woman. Suddenly I felt uneasy, sheepish, as though I had intruded on forbidden territory; a part of the sailor's lives that was none of my business. I turned and went into the hold. Man, I thought, this is going to be a long trip for some people. I chuckled. Maybe for all of us . . .

I stayed inside for a while, rearranging the clothes in my travel bag, thumbing through the worn pages of my handbook, anything to kill some time. When I finally left the tug the voyeuristic sailors were gone and the boar and sow were sprawled side by side, dozing on a patch of squashed bananas, the morning sunshine bathing their mottled pink hides. I paused to admire them for a moment. Well, I thought, they certainly look like a content couple. I'm glad some things around here are content.

I returned to my companions on the lumber. I opened up the Portuguese book and showed it to Eloi. He glanced at it without interest. I picked a page at random.

"Look," I said to Eloi, pointing to a word on page 32. "How do you say this in Amazonas?"

Eloi gazed at the word indicated by my finger, a glum expression on his face. "You don't want to learn Portuguese the way I speak," he said.

"Why not?"

"Because I speak in a manner that isn't very pretty. It isn't correct. It is bad Portuguese."

"That's not important to me . . . . I don't care if it's pretty. I don't care if it's correct . . . . What interests me is to learn to communicate here and now. In this part of Brazil . . . . I can learn to speak correctly later. Now I need basic communication. Understand?"

"Yes, but . . . all right. I'll try to help." Eloi shook his head.

"Thanks. Now, how do you say this?"

Eloi looked vacantly at the printed words. Finally he mumbled under his breath.

"What?" I said. "How do you say it?"

This went on for several minutes. Eloi would attempt to read certain phrases, but he mumbled badly and sounded even more distorted to me. My frustration grew, as did Eloi's unease. Eventually he stopped talking altogether and looked down at his sandaled feet.

"What's the matter?" I asked him.

"It's that I . . . it's that I . . . I don't have much education. You understand? . . . I'm not educated . . . . I attended school a very short time."

"Ah," I said. Of course, I thought. What an idiot I've been. The man can't read and here I am badgering him to explain nuances of his language from a book. Real smart of me . . . . Well, enough of this.

I tossed the book aside. "We don't need this."

"That's right," said Fernando. "There are many words we need to learn that one doesn't find in a book . . . . By the way, Eloi, how do you say *joder* (to fuck) in Portuguese.

We laughed.

"It's almost the same as Spanish," he said. "In *brasileiro* we say *foder*."

From this point on our class went smoother. Eloi taught us Amazonas cuss words and slang and Fernando and I taught him the English and Spanish equivalents. It was enjoyable. I gained a working knowledge of common and useful words. Then, as the session continued, my concentration wavered. Despite a fragrant breeze to cool us, the equatorial sun was beating into my head and scorching my skin. I fell silent. Then my head dropped onto my lap and stayed there.

"Listen, man," said Fernando, nudging my shoulder.

"Huh? What?"

"Are you tired?"

"Yes . . . . I'm sleepy."

"Well, your back and shoulders are starting to burn. . . . If you want, go inside and take a nap. You can use my hammock."

"Are you sure you're not going to want it soon?"

"Yes, I'm sure. Go ahead."

"Fine, then. Thanks. See you guys later."

I returned to the tug, rubbing my eyes and yawning as I went. I entered the hold and found Jaap and Betti reclined in their hammocks reading books.

"What are you reading?" I asked, addressing both of them. Absorbed by their books, apparently, neither one answered.

"What are you reading?" I asked in a louder voice.

Jaap looked up irritably and showed me the cover of his paperback book.

"Zen and the Art of Motorcycle Maintenance," I intoned.

"Very goot," he said. "Haf you heard of it?"

"Yeah, I have. But I never got around to reading it . . . . Is it good?"

"Yah, yah, I like it . . . . It is interesting."

"Can I check it out when you're finished?"

"Yah, sure. If we don't get to Manaus before I finish." And with that he buried his nose in the book; Betti never bothered to look up from her's.

Well, I thought, since neither of them is inclined to talk . . . it should be easy to sleep. I stuffed my ears with wadded scraps of cloth and climbed into Fernando's hammock. The hammock, made of thick woven string, like a net, was comfortable. My stiff back melded into the pliant cording and I stretched my arms over my head and twisted my torso to loosen up my spine. "Ah, that's better," I murmured. The water pump was quiet. The engine noise was a comforting hum, like the drone of a bumblebee on a lazy spring day. I swayed to and fro, relaxed, watching the river slip past. Much better, I thought, closing my eyes. This is more like what a tropical vacation should be. Now if I only had a cool drink . . . on a wide sandy beach . . . with coconut palms . . . some fresh seafood . . . a native girl . . . and . . .

****

I shot awake. My senses alert, my blood racing. I heard a muffled jumble of high pitched squeals, shouted words, and laughter. I looked around. Jaap and Betti were gone; I was alone in the hold. "What the hell's going on here?"

I pulled the scraps of cloth from my ears and slipped from the hammock. I stood poised for a moment. The sounds, increasing in volume and frequency, were coming from the flat. I rushed toward the sounds . . . . When I reached the prow of the tug I almost ran into Jaap. He had taken a few backward steps, his eye glued to the camera lens, to get a better angle on something happening below us on the flat. I put out my hands and caught him about the waist.

"What's going on?" I demanded breathlessly.

He turned to face me, a wild look in his eyes, and shouted, "Look! Look there! It is incredible!"

I scrambled past him to the railing and peered down at the flat. There, the huskiest of the sailors had one of the sows by the ears and was dragging her to the side of the flat away from the other pigs. The sow— the very one that had been screwing a short time before—squealed and thrashed about in a desperate effort to escape. The sailor, hardpressed to hold her, sweated and heaved, his muscles bulging from the strain. He had a curious, almost sheepish look on his face.

Near the struggling pair stood the cook, his face a grotesque mask, a stream of chatter issuing from his mouth. He swung a hand mallet in slow purposeful arcs with his right hand, with his left hand he directed the sailor. Several times he interrupted his chatter to emit a cackle — a piercing maniacal cackle that sent shivers down my spine and raised the short hairs on the back of my neck.

I'm glad I'm not that pig, I thought.

The tableau took on a dream-like quality. From the corner of my eye I saw the other pigs, frantic with terror, straining against their bonds. If they could have broken free they would have leaped into the river where an equally certain death awaited them. But at least the wait would be over, I thought. The little boar stopped tugging at the rope and tried a different tactic; he reared back on his haunches and slammed his snout into the wall of lumber, again and again, in an attempt to burrow through the wood. Finally he gave it up and stood huddled against the wall, his nose bleeding and his face lacerated.

Fernando, Eloi, and two sailors were atop the lumber directly over the action. They braced their hands on the edge of the top plank and leaned over for a better look. Their faces were frozen into anxious grimaces.

By now the sailor had hauled the sow to the far end of the flat. The cook, smiling, his eyes bright, closed on the pair with deliberate steps. He advanced to within a few paces of the struggling sow and stopped. "Hold her well," he said to the sailor, grinning. Then the cook took a step back and thrust out his deep chest. He inhaled and flexed his arms. He exhaled a long cackle, raised the mallet over his head, and held it there. He swiveled his head and pivoted on the balls of his feet, looking at us for approval. One of the sailors yelled encouragement. Jaap trained his camera directly on the cook. I turned my head and spat into the river. Get it over with, I thought.

The cook lowered the mallet and took a few sidearm practice swings. The squealing of the pigs died down a bit. The rush of the water between the tug and the flat seemed to roar in my ears. The cook's face turned grim and businesslike. He motioned to the sailor to turn the sow so that her forehead was exposed. "Hold her well," he said. The cook stepped forward and measured his target with a half-swing. The sow whimpered and twisted her body. Her head was gripped in a vise by the sailor's hands. Abruptly the cook pulled the mallet back and let fly. There was the sound of a dropped melon. The cook had delivered a precise, crushing blow to the forehead. The sow lay on her side, unconscious, twitching convulsively, blood oozing from her mouth and ears.

A tremendous clamor went up from the other pigs; the scent of blood driving them to a heightened frenzy. Jaap pounded me on the back and exclaimed, "Vait until my friends in Holland see these pictures. They von't believe it! . . . It is really something, no?"

I gazed at Jaap's face — it was bright red and his eyes glittered. Startled by the intensity of his reaction, I could only stare dumbly at his parted, quivering lips. Wow, I thought. Talk about getting off on something. . . . Then, though my stomach churned, I returned my attention to the flat.

The cook unleashed a machete and fingered the handle. He flourished it in the air, the sun glinting off the polished steel. He licked his thick lips and set himself beside the wheezing animal. With the point of the machete he lined up a spot on the sow's throat. He thrust the blade home with dispatch. The sow's body gave a great shiver, as if shot through with an electric current, and a death squeal was stilled in mid-throat and came out as a pathetic moan. A geyser of blood sprayed the cook's feet and ankles. With barely a pause the cook knelt down and disemboweled the dead animal with expert strokes of the machete. As he worked he spoke calmly to the sailor. His demeanor was tranquil. He had changed from killer to cook in a heartbeat.

Well, at least he was quick once he got to it, I thought. The man definitely knows his business. She didn't seem to suffer too much — except for the terror. I wonder . . .

Jaap was nudging me with his elbow, a demented look on his face. "It is . . . it is . . . it is incredible!" he said, snapping a photo of the carcass. "They von't believe this in Holland ven I tell them about this. . . . But I haf the proof. Here!" He patted the camera. "I haf the proof. But they von't believe it."

As I watched and listened to Jaap, a strange mixture of irritation, disgust, and amusement welled within me.

"Why shouldn't they believe it?" I asked him. "Don't they butcher hogs in Holland? Don't they know where bacon and ham comes from?"

Jaap was too busy clicking his camera and yelping in Dutch to answer me—if he heard me at all. Suddenly Betti appeared at Jaap's elbow.

"You missed the show," I said to her.

"What? What has happened?"

Before I could answer she put her hand on Jaap's shoulder and drew his attention. She gazed tenderly into his face and murmured to him in Dutch. Jaap responded in an excited tone and gestured toward the flat. Betti squeezed past us to the railing and looked down.

At that moment the sailor dragged the body of the sow to the lip of the flat. He seized a side of the sliced belly in each hand and pulled them apart as the cook scooped out the entrails and dumped them into the river. Blood dribbled from the carcass and ran over the side. The water boiled from the splash of discarded innards and the tussle of scavenging fish. The rank death odors of blood and excrement filled the air. The live pigs squealed madly.

Betti watched as if in a trance, her lips curling with repugnance. Soon her pallid face turned a light shade of green. Jaap put his arm around her shoulders and talked in a cheerful voice. He pointed directly at the split belly. Betti swallowed thickly and slid out from under Jaap's arm. She fled to the hold. Seconds later came the sound and odor of her retching over the side.

The cook finished cleaning the inside of the carcass. He then took a bucket and poured water over the outside of the body to rinse off the blood and the dirt. He wrapped the body in a clean white towel and with the help of his assistant carried it to the galley. Jaap snapped a photo as they walked past us. The cook smiled for him.

Another sailor came with mop and bucket and began swabbing the gore drenched deck. Soon there won't be any trace of the killing, I thought. The deck will shine and the pig will be eaten. Just like that.

For some reason, I suppose to record each phase of the operation, Jaap was still taking pictures. I stood beside him, trying to decide whether to go back to the hammock or to head for the lumber. I was about to head for the lumber when the sailor, who was swabbing the deck, slipped on a piece of intestine and skidded toward the river. For a moment the sailor teetered on the edge of the deck. Jaap let out a yelp and I sucked in my breath. . . . The sailor would have a fine time trying to ward off the blood crazed fish following the pig remains. I saw the look of panic on his face. With a desperate twist of his hips he managed to throw his weight forward and sprawl onto the deck, landing with a hollow thud on his knees and belly, his right calf dangling over the foaming water. The sharp click of Jaap's camera rang in the sudden hush.

"Damn! You almost had a prizewinner there," I said.

"Yah. He was lucky not to fall in. Incredible."

For a long moment the sailor lay still, pressing the tips of his fingers against the hardened steel. He inhaled deeply.

"Are you all right?" I called to him.

Gingerly he rose to one knee. He looked up and gave us a relieved glance. He craned his neck and eyed the water, his right calf still projected off the deck. "Damn!" he said. "Almost." The sailor made the sign of the cross. He dragged himself away from the edge of the flat before rising to his feet. He picked up the mop and bucket and resumed his work, staying well away from edge of the flat. What a way to die that would have been, I thought.

I tore myself from the railing, climbed over the tie, and stood on the deck. The three remaining pigs squealed at my approach and cowered in a tight group against the wall of lumber. I stopped and looked at them for a moment. They never showed fear of me before now, I thought. Well, I'm not going to kill them. Not me. But I suppose I might have to eat them, which is more or less the same thing.

The pigs' squealing faded to whimpers. I edged around them and walked along the aisle toward the front of the flat. I saw water splashing onto the deck ahead of me and my stomach churned. I halted and closed my eyes. The sight of the sow's terrified eyes came back to me. I saw the sailor teetering over the foamy water. My mind raced out of control. . . . I wonder what time lunch will be served? . . . My stomach is shot. . . . But why has this affected me so much? . . . I've seen animals slaughtered before . . . people too . . . . But this was too much of a show for the paying customers—a Roman spectacle. A cat playing with a cute little mouse. A snot-nosed kid pulling the wings off a butterfly. A man with the power of life and death. The shitted on flunky with the whip. . . . And this was the same sow that had been screwing so contentedly only a few hours before. How patiently blissful her eyes were then . . . then terrified . . . then amazed . . . then glazed . . . then nothing. Like a burned out light bulb. Maybe the light will come back if the cook stuffs a bright red apple in her mouth. . . . Maybe she conceived right before dying. First one life then two lives then no life. Maybe the fertilized egg is resting in the belly of some fish who is going to use the energy of the food to make some more eggs . . . some of which will be eaten by fish and others which will become fish who will eat other fish and who will be eaten by bigger fish and on and on. . . . Who knows where that spark of bliss, terror, amazement, nothing will end up? Maybe it will give life to a billion lives. . . . And what about the live pigs? Are they still cringing with fear, awaiting their own executions while the spark of their sister is fanned throughout a billion bodies? That boar, gleefully humping one moment, his lover butchered before his eyes the next moment, each moment intensifying the next moment and the boar seeking the ultimate climax by fighting to burst the bonds of his fear by hurling himself into the river and take his chances with the unknown. . . . But what are you thinking? Haven't you always been told that animals have no reason. The spark in their eyes is only the glint of mucus. Wasn't it instinct and fear that told that boar he'd have a better chance in the river than he would against the human scythe that's laying waste to the Amazon? . . . And if the sailor had fallen into the river he would have fed a lot of fish. Maybe his bones would have made it all the way to the Atlantic to feed some lobsters; just like being flushed down the toilet and into a giant sewer. Hell, in the end, everything makes it to the ocean.

I felt the sun, hot and penetrating against my skin; I looked at the sky and saw it emerging from behind a billowing cloud. I shook my head and blinked my eyes to clear my thoughts. "Get moving," I said in a soft voice. "You're thinking too much . . . or is this tropical sun frying my brain? Whatever. Get moving."

I walked to the end of the flat and found Fernando waiting for me in our already accustomed spot. He was alone.

"How was your siesta?" he asked me.

"Fine, until it was interrupted. . . . What did you think of the show?"

Fernando grinned and rubbed his hands together. "Well, now we're going to have fresh pork to eat. I've been craving a bit of fresh meat."

I laughed.

"What's so funny?"

"You really know how to put things in perspective."

"Aren't you pleased to have some fresh pork?"

"Pork . . . . I never have liked pork that much — except for ham. And sausage once in a while."

"I like pork very much."

"That's fine."

"What don't you like about it? What's wrong with it?"

"I don't like the taste that much; that's my main reason."

"Well, I enjoy the taste of pork very much."

"I know, you already told me that."

"Maybe you've never had it prepared properly. There is nothing like the baked pig we prepare in Peru."

"I've had it prepared many ways. Look, man, I eat it if I can't get something else."

"Is there some other reason you don't like pork?"

"Yes. Several nutrition books I've read say that pork is bad for you." I chuckled. "And also a few million Moslems and Jews."

Fernando gave me a shrewd look. "Were you ever a vegetarian?"

"Oh, not really. I played around with being one for about six months . . . just before leaving the United States for Colombia."

"So you were a vegetarian."

"Not a very good one."

"But why? Are you one of these people who are against killing animals?"

"Well, I'm not into killing animals for sport, but, no, nothing like that. If I had to eat, I would kill an animal. . . . Anyway, if you think about it, plants are living things, also. Everything is interrelated and dependent."

"Then why?"

"Because I wanted to see if becoming a vegetarian would make me healthier so that I could live longer . . . "

"And what did you find out?"

"Well, I can't say for certain if I was any healthier when I was trying to be a vegetarian. I felt good. . . . But I've felt pretty well during periods when I've eaten meat. For me the results were inconclusive."

"What made you give up the experiment?"

"Lack of willpower. I really like the taste of certain meats — especially chicken. Plus, when I got to Colombia, I realized that I needed the protein and the vitamin B 12 to balance my diet. The substitutes weren't readily available like they were in San Francisco. . . . And I got bored. Man, a typical dish where I live in Colombia is loaded with starches — potatoes, rice, platano, and yucca. Sometimes all in the same plate. I needed the meat that goes along with it."

"But you might not live as long," suggested Fernando, with more than a hint of irony in his tone.

"Live as long?" I chuckled. "I don't worry about my old age as much as I used to."

"Why not? One has to prepare for the future."

"Because I came to the conclusion that there are too many other factors that could make this question academic. . . . Besides, too much worrying is the very worst thing for your health. I don't want to make myself sick."

"That's a good point," said Fernando. "Now I've thought about vegetarianism — but I like meat too much to give it up. However, I think it could be beneficial . . . "

We discussed vegetarianism until they called us to eat. Apropriately lunch was meatless; pork would be served at dinner. For lunch we dined on small bowls of tired bean soup, *leite em po*, and a whopping portion of watery rice. The meal was insipid and we ate with little enthusiasm. Throughout the meal Jaap muttered in Dutch. After the cook cleared away the dishes we remained at the table, listless and disgruntled.

"Are we going to stop in any town today?" Jaap asked Fernando.

"I'm not sure. Let's see." Fernando pulled out his map and spread it on the table. He traced his finger along the river; it came to rest on a dot called *Fonte Boa* (Good Source). "Fonte Boa," he drawled. "That's the next town on the map. But I calculate that we won't reach it until tomorrow—or tomorrow night."

Jaap grunted and his face turned sour.

"What's the matter?" I asked him.

"I want to buy some food. I can't lif on this garbage . . . . I thought there was to be pig for lunch."

Damn, I thought. They already ate all that stuff he bought yesterday?

"Dinner should be better," I said to Jaap.

"Hah!" He turned and spoke to Betti in Dutch. Without another word the couple rose and retired to their hammocks.

Fernando and I left the table and took up our posts as scouts on the front of the lumber stack. Eloi stayed on the tug to take a nap. For an hour or so we talked, Fernando correcting some of the flaws in my Spanish. Later we got up and did a few exercises to keep the juices flowing. Then, as the afternoon deepened, we lapsed for the most part into silence, watching the flat cut a swath through the muddy brown watercourse. Several times, from ennui and the hypnotic effect of the rushing water, my head dropped into my lap and I dozed. After the last of these catnaps, Fernando nudged me with his elbow and pointed to the shore on our right.

"We changed course while you were sleeping," he said. "It seems that we are going to shore for a stop."

"Oh yeah." I rubbed the sleep from my eyes and roused myself. We were moving at reduced speed toward the near shore but I saw only an impenetrable wall of foliage. Fernando and I exchanged puzzled looks.

"I don't see any sign of people," I said. "Do you?"

"No, nothing."

The tug edged us closer to shore and a tiny clearing, a machete hacked wedge in the vegetation, became visible. Beyond it was a thickly jungled slope. We ground to a halt, the flat almost parallel to the shore. I spotted a precipitous footpath at the base of the slope leading into the forest.

"What could this be?" I asked Fernando.

"Let's go and see."

We hurried to the tug. The crew was in another flurry of activity. Jaap was already ashore, unslinging his camera. We were about to follow Jaap when Eloi, unperturbed by the bustle, sauntered out to meet us.

"What's happening?" Fernando blurted.

Eloi, speaking slowly and repeating various phrases, informed us that there was a settlement on the hill above us, and the captain wanted to see if he could purchase fresh fruit.

"Are we going to be here for a while?" I asked Eloi.

He grunted. "I believe so; and I don't like it. Travelling like this, we'll never get to Manaus in five days."

"We're going ashore," said Fernando. "Will you accompany us?"

Eloi shrugged.

Without another word or a backward glance at Eloi we rushed ashore. Jaap had already disappeared into the bush and we went after him. Sliding and scrambling on the steep path, the trees and bush closing around us, our feet making sucking noises in the soggiest places, we managed to overtake Jaap just as we topped the rise. Together we pushed through a thin layer of underbrush and came upon a large clearing. We halted, panting and sweaty, to catch our bearings. Spread before us was a carpet of scraggly, green and yellow growth, gashed by irregular footpaths of gray dirt and pockmarked by the blackened remains of campfires. A few feet beyond the front clearing, against a backdrop of tall trees and bush, were an assortment of thatched, wooden huts; each one raised upon stout flood stilts and connected by rude bridges. The huts could be entered only by climbing makeshift wooden ladders.

"I don't believe we'll find a Hilton Hotel here," I said to Fernando.

"No, I suppose not."

Suddenly I felt an eerie sensation. I swept the clearing with my eyes. I became aware of many other eyes, peering at us from behind vegetation and through the unglassed windows of the huts. I focused in on the eyes and was gradually able to make out the bodies. To the left of us, to the right of us, maybe even behind us, staring at us, boldly, curiously, fearfully, were children. Everywhere! A tribe of Munchkins. Almost all barefoot and bareheaded—boys and girls of varied size, age, and color —the infants naked, most of the boys garbed in shorts and T-shirts, and most of the girls in light dresses. "Shall we go forward?" I asked. "I think we've been spotted."

We walked slowly into the clearing. "Where would the adults be?" asked Fernando.

"Working?" I replied.

Slowly the children were coming out into the open.

"This is incredible," said Jaap, sighting his camera. He advanced a couple of paces ahead of us and raised the camera to his eye, ready to fire. The childrens' eyes widened. We must seem like creatures from an-

200

other world to them, I thought. Really, I guess we are . . .

A bare-chested little scamp called out to the other children and approached us boldly. We stopped walking and smiled at him. Jaap refocused his camera.

"Good day," Fernando said to the boy. A look of confusion crossed the boy's face and he scampered away.

"He must have thought we wanted to eat him," I said to Fernando.

"Yes, or take him as a slave. What a reaction."

We moved forward and drew abreast of Jaap. "Get any good pictures?" I asked him.

Jaap lowered his camera and turned to me, his face elated. With his free left hand he clapped me on the back and exclaimed, "Look! Look! Look at the Eendians! . . . I vould haf never believed it."

For a moment I regarded Jaap with furrowed brows. He's serious, I thought. Indians? Where? Maybe he's been taking stuff we don't know about . . .

Jaap turned and set his camera on the "Eendians." I looked at Fernando; his face was red and puffy from suppressed laughter. Looking at him made me snicker. That did it. We burst simultaneously into peals of laughter. Jaap wheeled and gave us a murderous stare. His cheeks and neck swelled with blood and his eyes popped.

"Vat is it?" he bellowed. "Vhy do you laugh? . . . They are Eendians!"

We were shaken by fresh spasms of laughter. He looks like a bullfrog in heat, I thought. This is too much.

Fernando and I almost collapsed at this point. Jaap gave us a last furious look. Then he turned and scurried forward. He gestured frantically to the "leetle Eendians" to pose for a photo or two. The children sidled away from him. Jaap spoke in mangled Spanish and shook his camera at them. The nearest children moved farther away from him. At a safe distance they stopped and faced Jaap, regarding him as though he were an escaped loony. My stomach cramped from mirth; tears rolled down Fernando's cheeks.

"Poor Jaap," said Fernando, managing to control his voice with great effort. "I don't want to shatter his illusion . . . but I'm afraid he's mistaken some *mestizo* colonists for indigenous Amazonian cannibals."

"Yeah, something like that. . . . But it's crazy, man! A couple of the sailors look more like genuine Indians than these people. . . . But I bet you that by the time Jaap gets back to Holland, he'll be convinced he was the first white man to ever see them."

"The first? What about you?"

"Well, me, him, and Columbus."

"Since Columbus."

While we joked a man had emerged from one of the huts. He started in our direction, scrutinizing us, then stopped. As Jaap continued his antics with the children, the man scowled. I saw him finger the hilt of a gleaming machete and lurch forward toward Jaap. The laughter died in my throat. Uh, oh, I thought.

"Hey, Jaap!" I called. "Settle down, man. You're making people nervous."

"Vat? Vat do you say?" He gave me an angry look.

Silently I pointed in the direction of the man. Jaap turned and saw him; he also saw the machete. He lowered his camera and became more subdued. The man took his hand from the machete and relaxed noticeably, although he still eyed us with suspicion.

At this moment I heard footsteps behind us. We turned and saw Eloi.

"What's happening, friends?" he said. "Why did you leave in such a hurry?"

"Good question," I answered. "We're glad to see you. These people seem to be afraid of us. Maybe you can do better."

"Afraid?" Eloi smiled. "Let's go."

With Eloi as our emissary we headed toward the huts. Eloi addressed the first wide-eyed boy we came to and quickly won his confidence. Fernando and I listened to the exchange.

"Do you understand any of what they're saying?" Fernando asked me.

"Barely a word or two. It's discouraging."

Eloi finished his chat with the boy and asked us to accompany him on a tour of the village.

"Sure," said Fernando. "Let's go. Maybe we can pick some fruit."

I hesitated. I'd like to try talking to this boy myself, now that he knows I'm harmless, I thought. I'm not gonna learn much if Eloi does all the talking for me.

"You guys go ahead," I finally said. "I'll be along."

Eloi looked surprised; he started to say something. Then he gave me a long look and shrugged his shoulders. "*Tudo bem*," he said, and walked off.

"Aren't you going to come with us?" Fernando asked.

"In a while. . . . I want to talk to this boy first. Go ahead. I'll catch up."

Fernando turned and followed Eloi to a grove of trees on the edge of the clearing. I was left with the boy. He stood with his arms folded, regarding me gravely. We exchanged a few simple words. Once he realized I could understand some Portuguese he relaxed. Now I can get down to business, I thought.

"Do you have fruits here?" I asked him.

"Yes, of course."

"For sale?"

The boy flashed a toothy grin and nodded his head.

"What kind? Where?"

He fired the words at me with machine gun rapidity. I shook my head, baffled. He smiled and started walking. "Come with me," he called over his shoulder. He led me along one of the dirt paths into the trees fringing the embankment and on to a park-like clearing with scattered shade trees. Ahead of us, bathed in sunshine and clustered about a rough picnic table, were a group of children and a stout matronly woman.

"Is that your family?" I asked the boy.

"What?"

"Your family. Your family."

"Yes, my family. My mother and brothers and sisters."

The group spotted us and fell silent at our approach. As soon as we reached the table the boy introduced me. Two of the older children tittered, the others gaped at me.

"A great pleasure to meet you," I said, nodding my head and smiling.

This time almost all of the children giggled. "What did he say? What did he say?" they asked each other.

I flushed. The mother hushed the children. Then she turned to me with an encouraging smile.

"A great pleasure to meet you, *senhora*," I said.

The woman's smile remained, but puzzled wrinkles etched her forehead. Forget the pleasantries, I thought. I'll get right to the point.

"Do you have any fruits for sale?" I asked her.

"Eh? . . . What is it?" There was no sarcasm in her manner. Her face, agreeable and attractive, was cocked to one side in deep concentration. One more try, I thought.

"Fruits? Do you have fruits? . . . Uh . . . oranges, lemons, pineapples, uh . . . you know, fruits."

The woman looked at me with raised eyebrows, a silly blank grin crossing her lips. How, I thought, can't she understand me? Dammit!

It's the same fucking word in Spanish! The same pronunciation!

"Fruits! Fruits! Fruits!" I barked in English.

"Ah, *frutas*," said the woman.

"Yes, *frutas*. That's it. . . . Do you have any?"

"Of course we have them." Her cherubic face smiled at me. "Yes, we have them. Many . . . "

The silence lengthened. I guess I'm supposed to offer her something, I thought. But what?. . . Money? Out here in no-man's land? I could but . . . I looked at the circle of bright-eyed inquisitive children. I was smitten by an inspiration.

"Wait for me one moment," I said to the woman, waving my arms. "One moment. I'll be right back." I turned and trotted away, leaving them with flabbergasted looks on their faces.

I'll trade the "*Geo Mundo*" (a Latin American version of National Geographic) for fruit, I thought, as I huffed and puffed to the tug. It has an article about that colonial boom town, "*Ouro Preto*."

I went to the hold and turned my bag inside out looking for the magazine. Damn, I thought, it's gone. Who ripped me off?. . . Wait, I lent it to Fernando. That's right. . . . Hurriedly I searched under the hammocks. I found the magazine under Fernando's dirty clothes. Got it! They'll probably like this better than money — it has beautiful pictures.

I raced back to the clearing. Then, as I approached the picnic table, keeping the magazine hidden behind my back, I slowed to an amble. The woman and children, obviously puzzled by my behavior, stared askance.

"*Tudo bem*," I said, bringing the magazine from behind my back and holding it up. The children cooed with pleasure and jostled each other and came toward me to get a better look. With a flourish I handed it to the woman. The children crowded around her, their eyes and lips budding like spring roses. The woman leafed through the magazine until she hit an article about Guyana — an article featuring the style of dress and African roots of the culture.

Laughing and talking, the children pointed to the pictures, excited by the brilliantly colored clothing and the ornate headgear of the depicted Guyanese women.

"What beautiful dresses!" exclaimed the woman.

"Yes, but look at this," I said, wedging past the children to the woman and turning the pages of the magazine to the story on Ouro Preto. "This is a Brazilian city. Look at the beautiful buildings."

The woman glanced at the photos of baroque colonial architecture.

"Pretty. Very pretty," she said in a flat voice, and turned the pages back to the Guyanese women. "What gorgeous colors," she sighed. "What do you want for this magazine?"

"Oh, I don't know." I scratched my head. "I'm sorry that the words in the book are in Spanish."

"That's no problem," she said. "We can read Spanish if we have to.... And the photos, so beautiful!"

I glanced at the children. They gazed at me appealingly. Those expressions when they first saw the magazine were priceless, I thought. Certainly worth this magazine. Hell, I'm finished with it; they can have it.

"Take it," I said to the woman.

"Thank you.... And for you? Maybe you want some *mamãos*."

"*Mamãos?* What? What did you say?

"Yes, *mamãos*. We have many."

I stared at her. *Mamãos*, I thought. What is she trying to say? That sounds just like the word the kids in Colombia use for cocksucker ...

The woman went into an involved explanation. She drew figures in the air with her hands and made sucking noises with her mouth. I don't get it, I thought. Is she offering to suck me off? Nah, no way. It's something else. But what?

Finally the woman sent one of her sons into a nearby thicket. We forgot about the *mamãos* and chatted about simpler things. Within minutes the boy returned, staggering under a load of enormous papayas. He dumped them out of a burlap sack and onto the picnic table in front of his mother.

The woman picked up one of the yellow fruits and rolled it in her leathery palm. "This is a *mamão*," she said. "Have you never seen one before?"

"Yes, of course." I snickered. "I eat them all the time in Colombia.... There they call them papayas."

"Why do you laugh?"

"Because ... because ... ah, it's not important. It's just that *mamão* has a much different meaning in Colombia."

"What does it mean?"

"Don't worry, it's not important."

"*Tudo bem*." The children giggled at my evident embarrassment.

"What's so funny?" I asked them.

"You," one of the older ones responded.

At this moment, Fernando, munching on a guava and spitting the seeds onto the ground, strolled out of the bush and joined me.

"Look what we found," he said, handing me a guava. "We found plenty; you should have come with us to pick fruit."

"I've been picking fruit here," I answered, pointing to the huge papayas on the table.

"Well done, man. Where did you find them?"

"They found them," I said, nodding my head at the giggling children.

"I see, the easy way. We had to work for ours."

"It wasn't so easy."

Fernando grinned. "Well, come with me. I'll show you around the village and maybe we can add some mangos to our collection."

"All right, one moment." I addressed the woman. "Can you watch the *mamãos*? I'll be right back."

"Go. *Tudo bem.*"

I followed Fernando and he led me on a quick tour of the perimeter of the main clearing. Actually, calling this place a village was pretentious; it was more like an outpost on the edge of the rainforest. Aside from the central cluster of huts, a dozen or so in all, there were an abundance of guava, mango, papaya, banana, and lemon trees, a small field of corn, vegetable gardens, hammocks strung between shade trees, and roaming about freely, a handful of runty pigs and mongrel dogs. As we strolled about I was struck by the fecundity of the rainforest. The fruits were huge and juicy, the wild vegetation vivid and lush. A sickly sweet aroma permeated the humid air—an aroma of death, decay, regeneration, nascent life, and growth, taking place on a simultaneous plane and with a ferocious rhythm. Man, I thought, or at least this kind of man, is truly an intruder here. The insects attack in hordes. The stilted homes are evidence of the river's periodic wrath. The forest snakes vines into any open area that isn't constantly cultivated or tramped on, trying to reclaim lost ground. The diseases must be terrible. . . . But these people are sturdy and tough—fecund as the jungle, resilient as the vines. Bright-eyed children everywhere . . .

"Listen, Fernando," I said, thinking aloud.

"What?"

"Why do you suppose these people come to live in this hot little space between the river and the jungle?"

"I don't know. There's nothing here." He shrugged. "Maybe it's better to take your chances here than in one of the slums of the big coastal cities. At least here you have the opportunity to grow and gather your own food."

"Yeah, that's something . . . a chance to own land and have some space. But there must be more to it than that . . . "

"Sure, desperation."

"Yeah, well, that and something more."

"Like what?"

"I'm not sure. . . . But it seems to me that you'd have to be a pretty independent and self-reliant person to come and live in isolation like this."

"Yes, or crazy."

"They don't seem crazy to me. . . . It must be an intense life."

"It's a simple life; things are less complicated here. But it must get boring at times."

"Who knows? . . . I'm not so sure that being free to make all your own decisions would be so boring. You make the wrong choices out here and the consequences could be immediate and fatal. You don't have much to fall back on."

"Well, I wouldn't want this kind of life. Would you?"

"I don't know, but I'm not going to stay here now."

"Ay, look!" yelped Fernando, tugging at my arm. "There goes the captain and his men."

We walked faster and intercepted them as they were crossing the main clearing. Each sailor carried a crate of mangos or oranges. The captain was empty handed.

"Are we going now?" Fernando asked the captain. Without breaking stride the group marched on. The captain ignored us.

"Are we going now?" I asked the trailing sailor.

"In a few minutes. You better be there."

"Let's go," I said to Fernando. We hurried back to the small clearing to pick up the papayas. The family was still in place, waiting for us.

"We have to go now," I said to the woman.

"Yes." She motioned to her son. He thrust one papaya after another into our waiting arms.

"No more already!" I said. "This is too much."

"We have plenty," said the woman.

"*Tudo bem*." I turned to Fernando. "No sense taking any more, they're already ripe. They'll just spoil."

"They are generous people," he said.

"Yes. I bet they'd give me a piece of land if I asked for it. . . . Well, we better get going."

We bid the family good-bye. Three of the small children escorted us to the boat. With great solemnity we shook hands with each one.

"Come back for a visit anytime," said one of them.

"All right, but no promises," I said. Fernando chuckled. We went straight to the front of the flat. The engines roared to life. As we pulled away from the shore the children stood and waved. For a long while they remained immobile on the bank, gazing at our departing wake. Watching the children until they disappeared from view brought back memories from my own childhood. The many times I had stood on San Francisco piers and with wondering eyes followed the vessels heading for the Golden Gate, imagining the lands and people to be seen, dreaming of voyages I would make some day.

Fernando and I settled down to eat some papaya. We were soon joined by Jaap and Betti. Eloi had disappeared again.

We whiled away what little remained of the afternoon by discussing international politics. For me it was the usual stuff. Despite varied and clever arguments, all of them second hand to be sure, we were unable to come to a general accord on The Utopian Policy that would satisfy our different wants, temperaments, and national interests. Still, it was all in good fun and made the time pass, and, the one thing we positively agreed on, was that we were hungry.

"I certainly expect dinner to be much better than lunch," said Fernando.

"Yeah, it won't take much to improve on that," I said.

"That's right," said Jaap. "It better be an improvement or there vill be hell to pay. There vas nothing for me to buy in that village. Just fruit."

"The fruit is fine with me," said Betti.

As the afternoon waned the air grew increasingly sultry. Scudding storm clouds, like the gathering hosts of an army, assembled to our rear and along our flanks. The sky darkened. A stiff wind made our shirts flap. The river grew choppy, the waves pounded against the flat and inundated the forward lumber. Finally, one large swell soaked us to our knees. Hastily we retreated to the top of the lumber pile.

Now on our feet we surveyed the pursuing storm. The view was magnificent. A few kilometers to our rear the rain was coming down in sheets. The jungle writhed and rippled in the wind. Lightning flashed from the gray clouds and seemed to explode in the treetops. The thunder rumbled across our wake.

"Do you think it will reach us?" I asked Jaap.

"I don't know. I hope not."

"Yeah, it looks kind of nasty."

"Yah, for this kind of craft it vould be . . . "

Another bolt of lightning, closer this time, rocketed past. The thunder vibrated our ears. Random drops of rain began to touch us. To our left an advance phalanx of clouds were moving in on our boat. A chill gust of wind swept over us, knocking me off balance.

"It's getting bad," said Fernando.

"Yes," I said. "But it looks spectacular."

Betti gathered her wrap tight against her body and spoke to Jaap in Dutch. He listened, nodded, turned to us and said, "We don't have enough clothes to stay out here. We are going in to shelter."

"That's a sensible idea," I said. "See you later."

"Are you not coming in?"

"Not yet. . . . I want to watch this a while longer."

Jaap grunted and started to say something. He looked at me as though I were crazy.

"I have never in my life had such a view of a building storm," I told him.

"I vould stay out longer if not for Betti," he said in a low voice.

"Yeah."

Jaap shook his head and went to Betti. They retired to the tug. Fernando remained. For several minutes we stood together and watched lightning shoot across the sky.

"Did you see that one?" yelled Fernando.

"Yes, what a thing! It's like a fireworks show."

Suddenly a great bolt seemed to explode in our faces. The light hurt my eyes. The thunderclap was like a sonic boom. I felt Fernando tugging at my arm.

"Why don't we go inside the boat now," he said, talking into my ear. It's cold. . . . The rain is coming harder and harder. We're getting soaked."

"Go ahead," I said, my eyes glued to the panorama before me, his voice a distraction. "I'll be in shortly. I want to watch the show a bit longer."

"But it's crazy, man!"

I turned and glanced at him. His face looked strained and earnest.

"Don't worry," I said, turning away from him.

"But this lightning could be dangerous and . . . "

Man, I thought, can't you understand? I want to be alone with this storm.

"It's fine, Fernando. I'll be fine."

"Fine, as you like." He started to walk away. "Just don't be foolish. Until later." He was gone.

At last, I thought, alone with my thoughts. Now I can concentrate on this storm. I've never seen anything like this. Such startling clarity.

I raised my face to the sky and scanned the horizon. Flashes of light crackled from the bosom of the gray black clouds and shot bursts of illumination over the expanse of jungle and water. The thunder boomed and reverberated. The wind and rain pummeled the forest and whipped the river to a froth. Exhilaration coursed through me. The ionized air seemed to dance in waves against my tingling skin. I spun myself like a top and shook my arms. I was one with the elements. My mind was ablaze.

It's like travelling in the eye of a hurricane, I thought. The storm is all around but it's barely touching us. Just a little rain and wind and electricity . . . but more than enough to feel the larger storm. Will it reach us before we can outrun it? . . . I tried to gauge the distance between us and the mass of trailing clouds. I whirled about and looked downriver. A shaft of sunlight was knifing through the overcast and silvering the river, a beacon of salvation, urging us on. We need to beat the storm to the light. I can see the rainbow. . . . It should be a good race. A roller coaster ride with no limit. I love it! . . . Maybe this is why some people choose to live along the river.

I set my face into the teeth of the wind and breathed deep. I wagged my head to and fro to watch the advance of the storm toward the sunlight. It struck me, perhaps an illusion of boundless space, that the violent forces on our path were being funneled to an apex where the turgid waters of the Amazon met the sun splashed bowl of the horizon. Nature was glorious in all its raw power. The boat was a chip in the torrent. I felt terrified and uplifted, cursed and privileged. Alone with the wind.

A lone black cloud swept overhead from our right flank and the rain pelted down. Within seconds my clothes were plastered to my skin and a soggy clump of hair lay against my left eye. I brushed the hair away from my eye. My exhilaration was sopping away. A gust of wind chilled me to the bone. That's it, I thought, shivering. I've seen enough. It's time to find a warm corner.

I returned to the dry hold of the tug, feeling numb and subdued. The other passengers, including the chubby Brazilian girl, who had kept her distance from us, were huddled about the table, quiet, listening to the storm with anxious faces. The muffled thunder seemed closer, but the tug, despite creaking like an old rocking chair, rode smooth. I saw two of the sailors lounging near the galley. Their faces looked unconcerned. I went to my bag under Fernando's hammock and got a dry shirt. Then I sat down amid the luggage and buried my face in my hands, reflecting on what I had seen and felt.

I was soon pulled from my reverie by the sound of footsteps on the ladder. I looked up to see the two women passengers, who had made infrequent and aloof appearances, coming down to join us. Well, I thought, looks like the storm's shaken a couple of peaches out of their tree. The lightning and wind would be pretty bad up there.

The young mulatto woman with the creamy smooth skin was the first to hit the deck. I nodded my head and gave her a thin smile, wary from the indifference she had shown me at our previous meetings. To my surprise, she smiled back and asked how I was doing.

"*Tudo bem*," I said.

"What is your name?"

I told her. "And you?"

"I am *Nazaré*."

"How is it?"

"Na-za-ré."

"Oh, Nazaré."

"Correct. . . . My friend is Milene."

I nodded to the older woman now standing next to Nazaré. "A pleasure," I said. She nodded back.

"And your friends?" asked Nazaré. "What are their names? . . . And nationalities?"

I stood up and led the two women to the table. I introduced each of the passengers to the two women and gave their particulars. Nazaré seemed impressed.

"Do any of them speak *brasileiro*?" she asked me. "Like you?"

"He doesn't know how to speak Portuguese, either," interjected Eloi. "Only Spanish."

"And English!" I said, giving Eloi an irritated glance before turning back to Nazaré. "He is right. I don't really speak Portuguese. . . . But I am trying to learn."

"No, you speak. Why does he say that? You can speak."

"Only a little bit."

Nazaré smiled and spoke to me at a normal conversational level. I was lost. The blank look on my face must have told her as much. With an impatient toss of her head she turned from me and began talking to the chubby Brazilian girl. Eloi smirked at me. Way to screw me up, buddy, I thought. I went over to Eloi.

"Why you do that?" I asked him in a low voice.

"I did it for you," he said, his face serious.

"For me? Thanks a lot. Now why. . . "

"She is an evil woman."

"What? Why do you say that?"

"Because I know. She is bad. It's better that you don't get too involved with her. . . . Believe me, she is trouble." Eloi turned and walked away.

For a moment I stood looking after him. Weird, I thought. Now why would he tell me some shit like that? . . . She doesn't seem so evil to me. Yet . . .

Shaking my head I joined the others by the table. The ice had been broken; Nazaré and Milene were mingling with the foreign passengers. They became especially intrigued by Betti. After a while they managed to corner Betti against the railing and — employing words, sign language, pantomime, and Jaap — tried to find out from her why she was so skinny. Poor Betti. Jaap was the first to abandon her. Nazaré and Milene peppered her with questions. Did she have an illness? Was she recovering from an illness? Did she have intestinal worms? Did she work too hard? . . . Betti squirmed against the railing and worked her hands. She had no idea what the women wanted from her. The Brazilian women grew frustrated. They exchanged irritated looks. Betti arched her back and tap danced in place. She wore a tight grin and nodded her head at anything the Brazilian women said. Finally Nazaré and Milene looked at her with pity in their eyes.

"I don't think she's very intelligent," Milene said to Nazaré.

"Or maybe she's very sick and can't think well," said Nazaré

Betti nodded her head. I watched and laughed to myself. Serves her right, I thought. Doesn't need to learn any Portuguese because Jaap speaks Spanish, huh. . . . Maybe she won't be so arrogant after this . . .

At that instant Betti looked over and caught my eye. I saw mute appeal mirrored in them. My amusement and indifference wavered. Ah, that's enough, I thought. I got up and went over to her.

"Can I join the party?" I said to her in English.

"Yes, please. Do you understand what they are saying to me?"

"More or less."

"Tell me."

"Well, they want to know why you're so thin."

"Oh, is that it! Why, I say. . . tell them that it's because of the horrid food here, of course! So unhealthy."

Nazaré and Milene eyed me expectantly.

"She says that she is having problems with the food in South America," I told them. "Especially the food in Colombia."

Nazaré and Milene exchanged wondering glances. Using their own well-fleshed bodies as reference, I could understand why.

"What's wrong with the food here?" Nazaré asked in a sharp tone.

212

"What did she say?" Betti asked.

"That it's too bad the food doesn't agree with you." Then I turned to Nazaré. "Nothing is wrong with the food here. I like it. . . . But for her it is very different. And I believe she is sick from much travel."

These explanations seemed to satisfy everyone. The women separated. I breathed a sigh of relief.

Darkness had settled over us. The cook turned on the light and prepared the table for dinner. We sailed on calm waters. The brunt of the storm failed to catch us. Only an occasional distant roll of thunder trailed in our wake. I sat down to dinner with the others, hungry as a bear.

Then the cook brought in the food — boiled pork. Steam rose from the platter and moisture beaded the pale flesh. The meat stared up at me like a congealed glob of grease. . . . An image of the thrashing sow leaped to my mind. It looks gross, I thought. Even under normal circumstances I don't like this stuff. And now . . .

Jaap and Fernando were smacking their lips and moaning with pleasure. "Fresh pork," said Fernando. "What a treat." Jaap was already filling his mouth. Fernando served me a portion of pork. "Enjoy it," he said.

I filled my plate with rice and beans and started in on that. A round bone in the center of my cut of meat seemed to watch me like a sightless eye. My stomach churned and bile rose in my throat. I closed my eyes and thought, Eat it! You have to eat it! It has protein and nutrients that the other foods lack.

I opened my eyes and cut a piece of meat. I forked it into my mouth and chewed. Yuk, I thought. It's almost flavorless. Banana fed pork. . . . Boiled pork! Where did that fucking idiot learn to cook? . . . I forced down about half my allotment of meat.

Fernando had finished his portion and was casting sidelong looks at mine. "That was delicious," he said, wiping his mouth with the back of his hand. "I wish there were more. . . . Say, why aren't you eating?"

"I am eating," I said. "But this pork has no flavor. . . . No sauce, no pepper, no nothing!"

"To me the natural flavor is delicious."

I glanced at Fernando's plate; he had eaten only a small portion of his beans and rice. I patted him on the shoulder. "Fernando, brother . . . how would it be if I give you this pork for your rice and beans?"

Fernando's eyes glistened. "You don't want the meat?"

"I'll trade you for it."

"Well, I don't know. . . . All the beans and half the rice."

"Done."

"All right, what a deal! Thank you, man. Thank you."

"For nothing."

I watched Fernando devour the pork with great relish. The rice and beans filled me up. Both of us were satisfied. Jaap took Betti's portion of pork; he was satisfied. Betti and Eloi remained hungry.

"That wasn't enough food for all of us," said Eloi.

"There is almost nothing I can eat here," said Betti.

For dessert I brought out two papayas. With Jaap's Swiss Army knife we peeled the skins and ate our fill. The papayas were sweet and juicy and very ripe. "Eat all you want," I said. "They'll spoil in a day or two anyway."

Shortly after dinner we fell silent. Everyone seemed tired and preoccupied. The feeling of camaraderie and good fellowship enjoyed among the passengers the evening before had waned. The novelty of the trip and the company was wearing off. Soon all the passengers went to bed.

Man, I thought, it's been a long day. . .

CHAPTER VIII

SHIP ETIQUETTE

I finally managed a fair night's sleep, I thought, as I lay on my back, savoring the aroma of strong, fresh brewed coffee. Almost as used to the discomfort of this miserable bed as a pregnant woman must get to having a big belly. I sat up and stretched, noting with satisfaction that, after the snap and crackle of taut ligaments subsided, my muscles were losing the soreness the hard cramped bed had first induced in them.

I got up and joined the other passengers on the stern. As we partook of our usual breakfast of crackers and coffee, I watched the red sun struggle to break through a thick mist that made the river look like steaming mushroom soup. I wish it were mushroom soup, I thought. I could use some. I surveyed the other passengers strung out along the stern. They all appeared bleary-eyed and lethargic — even Fernando. I don't get it, I thought. I feel fine. Maybe the mist is working a subtle influence, casting a pall over them . . .

Suddenly, from somewhere on the river, a faint cry came to our ears. We looked at each other. "Did you hear that?" Six pairs of eyes strained to see through the fog. The cook let out a great shout. It was answered, after a tantalizing pause, from somewhere off to our left. We faced in that direction. The cries came faster and closer. Then, we discerned a dark shapeless mass. As it drew nearer, shedding the mist as though it were an outworn veil, the form swam into focus. It was a boy in a dugout canoe, paddling resolutely and giving lusty shouts whenever he could catch his breath. The only word from him that I could understand was *peixe* (fish).

The cook bellowed at the boy, urging him on. He cackled gleefully and hopped up and down. *"Peixe! Peixe!"* he yelped, turning to us. "He has *peixe*."

The cook summoned one of the sailors and dispatched him to tell the captain to slow the boat and come to the hold. Within seconds our speed slowed to a crawl. The boy caught up with us and drew the canoe alongside. He tossed a coil of rope to the tall sailor. The sailor wound it

215

around the nearest cleat, securing the canoe to the tug. The boy, he couldn't have been more than ten, scrambled aboard. He chattered greetings and pointed excitedly toward his canoe. We crowded forward and peered over the side, six silvery fish glistened at us from the bottom of the bobbing canoe.

"Wow!" I exclaimed. "Look at those fish! They must be between three to four feet long and at least 25 pounds. . . . A couple might even be 35 pounds."

"Fantastic!" said Fernando, licking his chops. "Now we're going to have fresh fish stew. And I've eaten this fish before—it's very tasty."

"They're monsters, eh," I said to Betti. "I've never seen such large fresh water fish."

"I hope they are good to eat," she said. "Fish is one thing I like very much."

Jaap had gone to fetch his camera. Eloi was chatting with the boy. Fernando gazed reverently at the fish. "We are going to eat very well with this added to the menu," he said to me.

While we waited for the captain, who was taking his time, the cook gave the boy a cup of coffee. He was working on his second cup by the time we heard footsteps on the ladder. Everyone turned. The captain strode aft, a broad grin on his face, looking quite dapper considering the early hour. He went straight to the cook and spoke to him in a low voice. Then he turned to the boy, his every look and gesture patronizing, and asked to see the fish. The boy, eager as a puppy, led the captain to the canoe. For a long moment the captain regarded the fish with an impassive face. The boy watched him intently, bouncing from one foot to the other. Finally the captain frowned and looked down at the boy. He made a few remarks, sneered once or twice, and generally gave the impression that he considered the fish worthless. The boy sagged, crestfallen.

"I can only give you $25 cruzeiros for each fish," said the captain.

The boy looked down at his feet.

$25 cruzeiros per fish, I thought. Did I hear right? . . . He has to refuse that. I can buy a beer for $18.

The boy looked up. "Give me $30 cruzeiros for each fish."

The captain shook his head.

"My grandfather told me to get at least $30 cruzeiros."

The captain laughed. "Then tell your grandfather to come himself next time. $25 cruzeiros, no more."

"I have to think . . . "

The captain turned to the cook with a sarcastic grin and spoke to him in a rapid undertone. The cook snickered. The boy looked from one man to another, a woeful expression on his face. The captain reached into his pocket and pulled out a thick wad of bills. Wordlessly he counted out $150 *cruzeiros* and thrust it at the boy. The boy accepted the money. He slunk away from the captain and climbed down to his canoe. The captain winked at the cook, a triumphant smile on his face, before turning on his heel and going above deck.

"Did you see that?" I asked Fernando. "The captain burned that poor kid . . . and enjoyed it at that. What a shit!"

"Well, to tell you the truth, I wasn't paying much attention. How much did the captain give him?"

$150 *cruzeiros* for the six."

"That's all? . . . Well, I suppose they don't need much money out here."

"I don't know about that. . . . But what bothered me was that the captain went out of his way to humiliate the poor kid. He didn't have to . . ."

Fernando shrugged. "Forget about it, man. It's unfortunate but it has nothing to do with us."

"Maybe. . . . But it could have something to do with us if we ever have to deal with the captain again."

"Then, let's hope we don't have to."

The boy, with the assistance of the tall sailor, was hoisting the fish aboard the *Magalhães*. All the bounce had gone out of him. He was silent and workmanlike."

"That's it," said the sailor, swinging the last fish onto the stern. "*Tudo bem.* That you go well." He untied the canoe and tossed the line to the boy. Wordlessly the boy cast off. He faded like a ghost into the swirling mist. Then we heard one last cry, "*Filho da puta, capitão* (son-of-a-bitch, captain)!"

The cook examined the fish and selected two of them. He brought the fish to the sink and began cleaning them. I stood and watched him for a few minutes. He wielded a long carving knife with dexterity, slicing neat fillets. The knife went up and down, in an out, flashing dully against the gray morning sky.

I soon joined Eloi and Fernando out on the woodpile. Eloi, normally taciturn, was in a mood to talk. To our surprise he went into a monologue, hardly pausing to see if we understood or not. We let him go on with only occasional interruptions. I filtered his words as best I could and tried to capture the essence. . . . He reminded us that he was 21 years of age and was already saddled with the responsibility of a wife and two children. He had thought, six months earlier when he left Manaus, that he would be able to earn enough money as a cargo loader to buy his own taxi when he returned home. But things hadn't gone as he hoped. The pay had been lower and the work more difficult than he had been led to believe by the agent in Manaus. It wasn't a total loss. He had saved some money, but not enough to warrant a longer stay in backwater river ports toting lumber. He was tired of working for other people . . .

"And I miss my wife terribly," he said. "And my children. I barely know the youngest. She is . . . "

As Eloi rambled on I noticed that his bare calves and feet were peppered with innumerable black dots.

"What happened to your feet and legs?" I asked him.

"What?"

"Those black marks," I said, pointing to his left calf.

"Ah, that's nothing."

"Nothing?"

"Just bites from flies and mosquitos."

"All those?"

"Yes, of course. The insects along this river are ferocious. Very ferocious. . . . I received most of these while working the docks in Benjamin Constant."

"From mosquitos?"

"From flies mostly. The flies are worse—the black flies."

"Don't they give you pain?"

"No, not anymore." Eloi shrugged, his face stoic. "After a while you become accustomed to them and they have no importance."

"No importance . . . "

"Yes," interjected Fernando. "I understand him. One develops a kind of natural immunity to the irritation. . . . Isn't that right, Eloi?"

Natural immunity, eh, I thought. Oh yeah? The few bites I've received since I got here are itching and bugging me like hell. But maybe I just need to expose myself to a few hundred more and I'll become immune also. . . . If I don't die from loss of blood first.

Eloi and Fernando were discussing home remedies to relieve insect bites. I fell silent and studied Eloi's face. It intrigued me. It showed traces of black, white, Indian, and Oriental blood. A real melting pot man, I thought. I burned with curiosity.

"Eloi," I said, "excuse me. Why . . . why do you look a little bit Oriental?"

"You think so?" he responded, genuinely surprised.

"Yes. Especially around your eyes."

"You are right. My grandfather . . . you understand? Grandfather?"

I nodded.

"One of my grandfathers was Japanese."

"Uh huh."

Eloi went on to explain that his grandfather came to Brazil at the turn of the century in the vanguard of a wave of immigrants from Japan.

"Tell us more," urged Fernando.

Eloi described his grandfather as something of an adventure seeker and character in his youth. He had plied the Amazon and its labyrnthine tributaries as a fisherman, treasure hunter, and gatherer of natural rubber in the boom days of the region. Later, in his forties, with little money to show from his years of prospecting, he married a Brazilian woman of mixed race, infuriating his Japanese relatives, and settled in Manaus to raise a family . . . . Eloi was rolling again, telling us the story of his mother and father. His parents were simple, hardworking, religious people with many mouths to feed. Condemned to poverty by the almost yearly arrival of a new child, they made up for their lack of money by showering their children with love and affection. Eloi loved and respected his parents. Still, he held a sneaking admiration for his not so respectable Japanese grandather . . .

Eloi would have continued his narrative but he was interrupted by the arrival of Jaap and Betti. They stood for a moment at the corner of the lumber stack, equipped with soap and towels, and conferred. Then Jaap strode along the front of the flat until he came directly in front of us. He halted, looked up at us, smiled engagingly, and announced in English, "We are going to take a bath here . . . . Because it is better than the shower." He then presented a reasonable facsimile of this message in Spanish

On finishing he regarded us expectantly, as if waiting for our approval. Betti was taking off her wrap, revealing a black bikini. The three of us looked at each other, then at Jaap and Betti, puzzled as to why taking a bath required a formal statement.

"Sure, man," I said, "Why not?"

"Of course, go ahead," said Fernando. "That's a good idea. That shower is garbage. Later I might take one here."

Jaap smiled. "Yah." He passed the word to Betti. She ginned like a Cheshire cat and casually stripped off her bikini. Jaap dropped his trunks. They stood naked in the breeze.

I shook my head and smiled. I glanced at my companions. Fernando sat frozen, his mouth gaping open. Eloi stared at some invisible object on the river, his hands trembling ever so slightly. Jaap and Betti knelt at the edge of the flat and tested the water with their fingers. It's in character for them to do this, I thought. Bathing in the nude right in front of us when they could do the exact same thing along either side of the cargo in complete privacy . . . . I bet this was Betti's idea. Another chance to show the poor savages how civilized northern Europeans are . . . . Well, they can take their clothes off in front of us — but when is either one of them gonna make a real effort to open up and communicate with us? We can play Mastermind forever and never get anywhere.

Jaap and Betti had plopped their bare asses on the peeling deck and were sitting with their legs dangling over the side and into the water. An occational swell would rush up to their waists. Betti gripped the edge of the flat with both hands, her knuckles white. Jaap hummed a tune. He sat sidesaddle and kicked water at Betti. Seems like a dangerous way of taking a bath, I thought. They could easily slip overboard — or have a chuck of driftwood nail them.

"Hey, Jaap!" I called. "Jaap!"

"Vat?"

"Don't you think you're asking for trouble sitting there like that?"

"Vat?" he replied, irritated, finally turning to look at me. "Vat do you mean?"

"You know, from the driftwood. We're moving pretty fast."

"No, I do not think so. I can see the wood coming . . . . And this is best for getting wet."

"O.K., man, if you say so."

A few minutes later a small log slammed into the flat, about a foot from Jaap's left ankle. It arrived partially submerged — no one saw it coming. The metal was still reverberating as Jaap drew his legs from the river and pulled Betti away from the edge. Then he stood still and stared at the river as though it had betrayed him.

"What happened, man?" I called.

"Huh, nothing . . . . Nothing at all."

"You all wet now?"

"Wet? Yah, I am wet. I am wet now."

"That's for sure."

Jaap turned from me and went to Betti and took the bar of soap from her. Betti was already well-lathered. She gathered a glob of suds in her hand and rubbed it onto her twat. With great deliberation she worked the suds in and around, bending over and widening her stance to give us a better view. Whether she was aware of it or not, her movements were quite sensual. She looked up and caught me watching. I winked. She answered with a a demure smile. She's too much, I thought.

I looked sidelong at my South American companions. Eloi, mute now, was facing the river, but every few seconds his eyes moved furtively to Betti's skinny ass. Fernando looked peeved, an uncertain scowl clouding his normally pleasant expression. I looked at Betti and chuckled, struck by a thought.

"Just think," I said, nudging Fernando with an elbow, "I know places where you would have to pay $6 dollars a drink to see this sort of thing."

"Yes," he said, "there are appropriate places for this. But . . . they must have mistaken this deck for the Costa Azul of Spain, or the south of France, or . . . "

Several beaches I know of near San Francisco," I said, trying to calm his irritation. "It's nothing, man. Just custom. They have to bathe nude somewhere, their own beaches are too damn cold."

"*Hein*," nodded Eloi in agreement. "It's nothing. We have nude beaches in Manaus. And then you have Rio—as you must know, that city is scandalous."

"Well, we also have some near Lima," said Fernando in a more cheerful tone. "But those beaches aren't for everybody." He shook his head. "These Dutch people must be pretty liberated."

I burst into laughter.

"Why are you laughing?" asked Fernando.

"I was just thinking about something."

"What?"

"Oh, about three months ago, I met a group of Danes who were travelling around Colombia. We let them stay at our place for a few days, and one night, we were sitting around partying with them and they started talking about some other European countries . . . . Anyway, they told me that they found Holland conservative and uptight compared to Denmark."

"Then the Danes must be super liberated," said Fernando, laughing. "I'll have to go there."

"Well, I don't know," I said. "Everything is relative. In the three days I was with those Danes they didn't seem especially liberated to me. They seemed about normal — whatever that is . . . "

"Have you been to nude beaches?" Fernando asked me.

"Oh yeah, a couple of times to see what they were all about."

"Did you like it?"

"It wasn't bad. People didn't act much different than they do at beaches where you wear clothes." I chuckled.

"What now?" asked Fernando.

"I just remembered that time I was jogging along a beach outside San Francisco and I ended up on a nude beach for homosexuals."

"What?"

"Oh, sure, they are so liberated where I come from that they have nude beaches for heterosexuals and homosexuals."

"You're joking."

"No, seriously. These are official beaches . . . . See how advanced and organized we are. Of course, if you go to the wrong beach, you could be molested."

"That's crazy, man!" laughed Fernando.

Eloi failed to understand everything; I rephrased it for him in quasi-Portuguese.

"What?" he exclaimed. "That is degenerate! Degenerage!"

"Well, degenerate is a strong word," I said. "Maybe . . . "

"That is the most liberated thing I have heard of," said Fernando.

"You really think so?" I asked.

"Yes, I do."

"Well, my idea of truly liberated is that you can go to any beach any way you want and no one cares."

Fernando shook his head. "I don't think the world is ready for that kind of liberation."

"That's all right. I'm not sure I am, either . . . . Eh, what about you, Fernando, have you gone to nude beaches?"

"Well, uh, only once . . . . You see, I believe that nude bathing is wonderful for health purposes . . . and for a feeling of unencumbered physical freedom but . . . "He glanced at Betti. "I think it detracts from the development of an erotic imagination."

"Yeah, why?"

"Because I believe that most people look better with clothes on than completely naked. One should leave something to the imagination."

"Then, you're saying that imagination and anticipation is worth more than actual physical beauty?"

"Something like that."

"In some cases I can agree with you—clothes can definitely cover defects and enhance good points but . . . on the other hand, I've known

222

people who couldn't care less about clothes and they still looked good. I don't know, they just seemed more natural and sensuous without clothes."

"Naturally, man, no one can deny natural beauty .... But a little illusion never hurts."

"I prefer the substance."

"Of course, of course, but ... " As Fernando pursued his argument, my eyes wandered over to Betti. There she stood, naked, casually rinsing the soap off her pale skin. I was unmoved. She's a case in point for Fernando's way of thinking, I thought. She has very attractive features—with the right clothes she could be a model. But right now her skinnyness looks unhealthy. I wouldn't want to get jabbed by one of those bones.

I tried to imagine us together making love. I can't even imagine a tepid hard-on, I thought. Maybe with the lights out. Now that Brazilian woman, Nazaré, is another story ...

A joyful shriek snapped me from my daydream. Jaap had filled an old coffee can with water and was dousing Betti's hair. She backed away from him, spluttering with gleeful protest, and vowed to get even. Jaap laughed heartily and tossed her the coffee can. "Come," he said. She filled the can and poured water over his body. She massaged the soapy residue off his skin with her hand. Jaap purred under her touch like a great cat.

A faint smile came to my lips. There it is, I thought. It doesn't matter what I think about Betti—Jaap loves her.

Jaap and Betti finished rinsing off and redonned their bathing suits. They picked up their towels and went to the top of the lumber stack to sunbathe, wise enough not to test the sensibilities of the sailors by doing it in the nude.

Time and the river meandered along. The mist burned off and the sun shone hot. Eloi returned to the tug to take a nap. Fernando and I talked. Around mid-morning Fernando grew restless and began taking periodic strolls along the length of the lumber.

"Why don't you sit down and relax," I suggested, after one of his walks. "You remind me of a tiger in a cage."

Fernando sat down with a sigh. "I can't relax today. I have too much energy and nothing to do with it."

"Save it for our next stop."

"Whenever that is .... We must have bypassed Fonte Boa."

"So what?"

"So, the next significant town would be *Tefe*, and I don't think

223

we'll get there until tomorrow."

"Maybe we'll stop in some other village."

"Maybe." Fernando stared into space. "I wish *La Gordita* (the chubby Brazilian girl) would be friendlier with me."

"Oh, so that's it . . . .The Dutch people's show got you horny, eh?"

"No, it got me hornier . . . . I told you before that I like La Gordita."

"Yeah," I chuckled, "you like her so much you don't even know her name."

"No, she told me her name."

"What is it?"

"It's a . . . a . . . it's one of those weird Brazilian names. I can't remember. Anyway, La Gordita suits her better. My loveable La Gordita."

"Well, she's a pretty shy girl."

"That's fine. I like that. I know how to handle shy girls."

"Then what's the problem? . . . She just won't give you a tumble?"

"I don't know. But whenever I try to talk to her, she acts like she can't understand a thing I'm saying."

"Hah, maybe she understands too well . . . . And maybe she already likes someone else. I see her talking to the sailors sometimes."

Fernando sighed again. "I just wish she would give me a chance to know her."

An hour or so later Fernando went for another walk. He came back in a hurry. "Man," he said, his face flushed and his eyes dancing, "you won't believe it . . . "

"What?"

"La Gordita and that curly haired one are sitting by the soda cases taking the sun."

"The curly haired one? You mean, Nazaré?"

"Yes, that's right."

"Interesting . . . .Well, man, now's your chance to get to know La Gordita. Go over there and tell her how you feel."

"What? You're crazy! . . . Just like that?"

"Sure, why not? What have you got to lose?"

"Only my pride."

"Yeah, big deal."

"Big deal? . . . Why don't you go over there and talk to them?"

"All right." I stood up. "I'm going."

Fernando sat down.

"Are you coming?" I asked him.

"No, I'll wait for you here. The situation is too obvious."

I shrugged. "Whatever . . . . Pass me my camera, please." Fernando handed me the Instamatic. "I'll see you in awhile."

I climbed to the top of the lumber and walked toward the soda cases. About halfway there I halted and called out, "Good morning." The two women looked in my direction.

"Good morning," said Nazaré.

I pretended to take her picture.

She giggled. "What are you doing?"

I moved closer. "You are so pretty . . . . I just want a photo of you. That's all." I put the camera to my eye and pushed the lever. Nazaré turned away just as the shutter clicked. "Why?"

"No pictures," she said, smiling. "I only let special friends take pictures of me."

"Maybe we can be special friends," I answered, walking right up to them. "I would like to see . . . "

"Maybe."

I gazed at her. She wore a sleeveless, low-cut top and white bikini shorts. Her figure was full and shapely, her skin flawless. I practiced Fernando's theory—Nazaré looked more desirable by the second.

"You are American, certain?" Nazaré asked me.

"Yes. You remembered."

"The majority of Americans have much money . . . . Isn't that so?"

"I laughed. "This one doesn't have much money. I can't speak for the rest of them."

"You have money. If not, how could you travel?"

"How can you travel? This boat isn't exactly luxury."

Nazaré paused to think this over.

"Let's not talk about money," I suggested. "Let's talk about us."

La Gordita giggled.

"You don't speak Brazilian well enough for that," said Nazaré.

"Teach me. That's why I'm here."

She gave me a sharp look. "I think you already know too much of the wrong things." She turned from me and spoke to La Gordita. They gossiped and giggled. I was dismissed. All right, I thought, it's a start.

I shambled back to the front of the lumber stack.

"What did you find out?" Fernando asked me before I could sit down.

"Not much . . . . La Gordita never said a word to me, and the other one — she mainly wanted to know how much money I have. She thinks all Americans are rich."

"What did you tell her?"

"I told her that this American isn't rich."

"It's like I thought," said Fernando, nodding his head. "I believe they are prostitutes."

"You think La Gordita is a prostitute?"

"No, no, not her. The curly haired one and her other friend. Those two. Not La Gordita."

"Well, maybe. But what makes you think that?"

"Didn't you just tell me that she only wanted to know how much money you have?"

"Yes, but prostitutes aren't the only women who have asked me about that. That doesn't prove anything.... But, it's a funny thing, Eloi told me yesterday that this Nazaré is an evil woman."

"An evil woman?"

"Yes, just like that—real strange. He didn't say anything else. It was like a warning."

"Fine, that clinches it for me.... If Eloi said that, he must know about her from Benjamin Constant. She's a prostitute. I'm almost certain."

"Whatever, I don't care."

"Do you like her?"

"No, I can't say that I like her. I don't know her.... But I am attracted to her."

"What do you plan to do about it?"

"Plan?... I don't plan anything. I'll just wait and see what develops, and if an opportunity presents itself... I'll be ready."

The sun reached its zenith and began its descent. Fernando and I joined Jaap and Betti on top of the lumber and took the sun. The Brazilian women returned to the tug. The sun dropped in the sky. Our growling stomachs told us that it was past the normal lunch hour. We fretted and complained. Finally Jaap went to the tug to check on the delay. He returned shortly.

"I don't know vat the problem is," he reported, "but they haf not even started the lunch yet."

"Huh, wonder what it could be?" I said. "They've been fairly punctual up till now."

Our impatience mounted as the minutes passed. We took turns going to the tug to check on our lunch. An hour went by. Jaap and Betti went to the boat and remained there.

"This is shit!" Fernando said to me. "Considering what a cheap breakfast they give us, they don't have the right to delay the lunch. It's cruel."

"I agree. It's much easier to wait for dinner than it is for lunch-
. . . . Well, I'll go see if it's ready."

I went to the tug and entered the hold. Jaap, Betti, and Eloi were
stretched out in their hammocks. I took a deep breath. The aroma of
fish stew permeated the air. It smells great, I thought, starting to
salivate. But the table isn't even set up yet. Guess it's not ready . . . . But
it sure smells ready. I walked over to Eloi.

"Do you know what's going on?" I asked him.

He looked up lazily. "Some problem with one of the machines."

"A serious problem?"

"No, I don't believe so. But the cook had to take a look at
it . . . . Lunch should be ready soon."

Let's hope so, I thought. Man, I've got to get out of here. The smell
of this stew is driving me crazy.

I returned to the flat. Fernando and I spent another long while
complaining about hunger pangs.

"My turn," said Fernando.

"If you want," I said.

He got up and went to the tug. About five minutes later I heard a
voice calling my name. I turned and saw Fernando standing next to the
pilot's cabin. I waved to him.

"Come on in! Come on in!" he yelled.

"Is it ready?" I yelled back.

"Yes. The crew is already eating . . . . Come on in!"

I scrambled to my feet. Strange, I thought. The crew has never
been served before the passengers.

I jogged across the lumber and quickly descended to the flat close
to the tethered pigs. Then, in my haste, as I approached the linkage
between the flat and the tug, I skidded on a glob of pig shit and pitched
forward. The churning water yawned in my face. With a blind desperate effort I threw my arms up and, by luck, grabbed one of the steel
rods in the crook of my left arm. For a moment I dangled over the
foaming water, the steel digging into my bicep. "Fuck!"I reached up
and caught the top of the steel bar with my right hand, then I swung my
legs over the lower bar of the railing and hauled myself aboard.

I stood up and leaned on the railing, staring down at the water.
"You almost did it that time, stupid," I muttered. I took a deep breath
and started for the hold.

Now, my heart pounding from the near miss, adrenalin rushing
through my body, hungry and irritated— I entered the hold and saw

Fernando, Jaap, and Betti huddled in a tight knot with angry looks on their faces.

"What's the problem?" I asked.

"The same shit!" said Fernando. "We're hungry as hell and they still haven't served us . . . . And the sailors are already eating. Man, they haven't even set the table for us."

"It's ridiculous," snapped Jaap. "We are paying customers. We should be served first."

"Very inconsiderate," added Betti.

I glanced at Eloi. He lay in his hammock, stoic, but gazing wistfully at the four sailors strung out along the railing with plates of food in their hands. The sailors seemed well into their meal.

"You see that," said Jaap. "They're eating. Someone should talk to the cook . . . or complain to the captain. Vat nerve! We should be served before the crew. That's how a goot ship is run."

"I don't care who gets served first," I said. "But it's screwed that no one called us to say the food was ready. So what the hell's going on? . . . Where's the cook?"

"We haven't seen him for quite some time," said Betti.

We milled around for about ten minutes, denouncing the cook. Meanwhile, goaded by the delicious aroma of the fresh fish stew, our hunger mounted. There was still no sign of the cook. My irritation began to turn to anger.

"I can't take this anymore," I said. "The smell of the food is driving me crazy. Let's go find the cook and ask him when we're going to eat."

"Yes, that's what we should do," said Fernando. "All of us together."

"Well, what do you say?" I asked, looking at Jaap and Betti. They refused to meet my eyes.

"I don't know," said Jaap. "Maybe we should wait a while longer . . . "

"But you were complaining the most," I said.

Jaap looked at his feet. Aw, forget him, I thought. All talk.

"Shall we go?" I said. Without waiting for a reply I turned and walked toward the galley. Fernando followed on my heels. Jaap and Betti stayed behind. I bypassed the galley and crossed the deck to talk to the sailors. They eyed me cooly as I approached. Their plates were almost empty.

"Excuse me," I said. "Do you know where the cook is? We want to eat, also."

The sailors looked at each other and shrugged, their expressions ranging from indifferent to vaguely contemptuous. No one answered.

"Many thanks," I said, shaking my head at them. What jerks, I thought. They don't give a shit about anyone else as long as they can stuff their own faces. Enough of this bullshit! . . . I spun about and headed for the galley.

"What are you going to do?" Fernando asked me.

"I don't know . . . . Look in the kitchen."

I stood on the threshold of the galley and craned my neck through the narrow entrance. No cook. A lidless cauldron of stew lay simmering on the stove. The steam enveloped my head. The aroma was spicy and delicious. My mouth watered. A pang of hunger shot through me. Damn, it looks good, I thought. Should I? . . . No, I shouldn't. But that smell, ah! . . . Maybe this is self-serve day. Go for it. Why not? No one's here. But . . .

I bent closer to the pot. A fresh spurt of steam blew into my nostrils. It was intoxicating; my head spun and my knees went weak. My thoughts were suspended, as well as my conscience and good judgment. Hunger had taken me over.

Like a man in a trance I selected a plate and a spoon. I filled my plate with rice. Then I took the soup ladle and poured stew over the rice. I was about to dip into the pot a second time when a piercing shriek froze me in place. I twisted about and saw the cook come bounding out of the engine room — like a lion on a hunt.

I dropped the ladle and stepped out of the galley. The cook paused a few strides from me. In his right hand he grasped the long carving knife. For a moment he just stared at me, the pupils of his eyes contracted and the whites immense. He muttered curses and glowered fiercely. Then he gave a shriek, raised the knife to chest level, and stalked toward me. I backed away slowly, holding the plate of food at arm's length as a shield, watching for the bunching of muscles that would signal a spring. A flow of invective issued from the cook's lips. He jabbed the knife in short arcs, just as he had before sending the sow to her death.

Everything moved in slow motion, and I enjoyed startling sensory clarity. From the corner of my eye I saw the sailors watching open-mouthed. I could feel Fernando somewhere behind me. The rush of the river roared in my ears. But the cook's face, set in a hard grimace, loomed before me. He was ready to kill. Watch the knife, I thought. If he lunges, throw the food in his face and try to get it away from him. But talk, man! Say anything!

"*Nao sabía* (I didn't know). *Nao sabía*," I repeated insistently as I backed toward the passenger area, careful to maintain a distance between us. The cook advanced relentlessly, his eyes glazed and his lips curled.

"*Não sabía*," I almost shouted. "*Tudo bem! Tudo bem!*"

The cook halted. "*Tudo bem*," he murmured. He shook his head as though he were awakening from a nightmare. The grimace softened. The glazed mad gleam left his eyes. He lowered the point of the knife.

"No one can enter the galley," he said in a soft, almost apologetic tone. "No one. No one. Only me and the captain. Understand?"

"Yes. I am sorry," I said. "You are right. I am at fault.... My hunger . . . "

"*Tudo bem.*"

To my left I saw the sailors fighting to restrain laughs. It must have been quite a show, I thought. Now how do I end it?

"Take the plate," I said to the cook, thrusting it toward him. "Take it."

The cook accepted the plate. He gave me a confused look. Then he turned around and went to the galley. I breathed a profound sigh of relief and leaned against the railing. My legs were rubbery. The sailors smirked and commented among themselves. The passengers regarded me with shocked faces. I ducked my head. Let those asshole sailors laugh, I thought. What do I care? I was lucky. I got off easy .

I looked up and saw the cook, carrying a plate of food, emerge from the galley. He came over and handed me the plate. "Take it," he said. "*Tudo bem.*" I was astonished. He had added a whopping portion of rice and stew to what I had taken. "What's wrong?" he asked. "Is that enough? Do you want more? More?"

"No, thank you. Thanks."

The cook smiled and walked off. I shook my head. Crazy, I thought. This is by far the most food I've gotten on this boat. Nice way to reinforce bad behavior. . . . I glanced over to the lounging sailors. They looked as confused by the turn of events as I felt. Take that, turkeys, I thought.

I tasted the stew. Boy, I thought, now I know I'm lucky . . . This is delicious. My reward for screwing up and breaking the etiquette of the ship. Of course, I could rationalize and say that the cook overreacted. . . . But, you can't rationalize anything if you're dead. Huh . . .

As I greedily ate my lunch the other passengers stayed away from me. This suited me fine. I continued to speculate on the cook's actions. Still, why would the man give me extra food for trespassing where I didn't belong? . . . It was clearly a stupid move on my part. I've worked in enough restaurants to know how touchy cooks are about their territory. Hell, mothers for that matter. . . . The only thing I can figure is that this guy is a real macho man—in the South American sense of the word. Since a decisive confrontation was averted and he came away with his pride intact, well, no one's the worse for wear. He wants to be friends now. Maybe he admires my audacity for demanding what is rightfully mine, now that he's not pissed off anymore. He probably looks at me in a different light. I'm no longer just a pampered gringo to him. He has to look at me as a human being. . . . Maybe. Aw, what am I talking about? Maybe this is all jive speculation. Who knows what he thinks? . . . I'm just glad I came through it in one piece.

As I was scooping the last crumbs from my plate Fernando came over and squatted beside me. The cook had decided not to use the table. He simply gave the passengers a plate of food and let them eat where they wanted. Fernando was still waiting for his food.

"What happened between you and the cook?" he asked me, a concerned look on his face.

"You saw it, no?"

"Yes. . . . But what happened? What did he say?"

"Not much." I shrugged. "I think we came to an understanding, that's all."

"An understanding?"

"Yes."

"Yes, but . . . " The cook called Fernando to come and pick up his food. Once he got his food he went to eat with Jaap. I finished my lunch alone. Then I took the empty plate to the cook.

"Do you want more food?" he asked.

"No, thanks," I said, rubbing my stomach. "I'm full."

"Tudo bem?"

"Tudo bem."

I went to the lumber pile and sat by myself, trying to maintain a low profile. Late in the afternoon we stopped in another tiny river town. Fernando and I were the only passengers to leave the boat. It was a drab dusty place, much like São Paulo do Olivença. We walked around to stretch our legs. We ran into a store and downed a pair of beers. Nothing noteworthy occurred. We were happy to return to the boat and shove off.

Fernando joined me on the lumber pile. Once again he unfurled his map and traced the progress of our voyage.

"I'm really looking forward to the next place," said Fernando. "It marks the midpoint on the trip to Manaus."

"What's the name of it?"

"Tefé."

"That's right, you told me this morning. . . . But why are you looking forward to it?"

"Because it's a large lumber port. It should be more interesting than these little settlements." Fernando ran his finger along the river. "We're making pretty good time. According to my calculations we're only a little behind schedule . . . maybe half a day."

I laughed. "Why are you so concerned with the time? You have a long way to go."

"That's true, but it gives me something to do. . . . Really, you're right, the time doesn't matter. I have no schedule. I'll get to Paris when I get there."

"That's the attitude, man."

"I'm going to think of right now."

"That's fine. Tomorrow will come quick enough."

"Yes, tomorrow. . . . I hope the captain gives us a few hours in Tefé."

"Why?"

Fernando gave me a sly wink. "It could provide some welcome diversion."

That night, after dinner, Fernando and I returned to the lumber pile. We sat in the circle of light cast by the tug's forward lamps and chatted. The darkness and quiet were soothing. A light breeze ruffled our hair. The sky was crystal clear. We watched shooting stars blaze trails through the other myriad night lights. It was an evening made for romance.

"Yes," said Fernando, pursuing a recurring theme, "I'm convinced that those two Brazilian women are *putas* (whores or easy women). Or if not that, they are the captain's kept women."

"So what? Why are you so obsessed by this subject?"

"Because I am certain they have secured free passage on this boat in exchange for sex."

"That don't sound free to me. And anyway, if that's the case, I wouldn't call them *putas*—I'd call them opportunists."

"You can call it what you want. . . . They are *putas*!"

"All right, so what? What's that got to do with you?"

"It's got to do with . . . ah, well, listen. As you already know, I wanted to go to Manaus without paying, too."

I chuckled. "Yeah, you're not the only one."

"Sure, but I even offered to work as part of the crew. I almost begged the man — but the captain still said no. . . . It just isn't fair!"

"Fair?" I started chuckling again.

"Why are you laughing?"

"Because . . . look at it from the captain's point of view, Fernando . . . those women have nicer asses than you."

"What?"

"Sure. If you wanted free passasge — like them — you should have looked for a homosexual boat captain."

Fernando looked aghast. "Are you serious?"

"Yeah, like in the United States, we have these signs you stick on your car that say, 'Ass, Gas, or Grass. Nobody rides for free.'"

"This is too much of a good joke. Are you calling me a faggot?"

"No, man, of course not. I was just giving you a stupid example. . . . Let's face it, those women have something that the captain wants. You don't."

"Puta!"

"That's the way it is, life is tough, man."

Fernando giggled suddenly. "I have another possibility."

"What?"

"Maybe these are fine ladies who enjoy preferential treatment because the captain is a true gentleman and wants to protect their honor."

Now I giggled. "Having observed the character of the captain, brother, I sincerely doubt that. . . . But if we have nothing better to talk about it's a point to consider."

"They are *putas*."

I threw up my hands. "All right, you win. I surrender to your logic."

A spectacular shooting star caught our attention. We fell silent. The breeze whistled softly through gaps in the lumber stacks.

"You know something," said Fernando.

"What?"

"On my last boat trip from the interior of Peru to Iquitos the captain had a woman with him . . . "

"Yes."

"And he didn't mind sharing her with any of the passengers whom she happened to favor."

"Really?"

"Yes, truthfully. And by luck, I was one of the favored ones." Fernando's voice became soft and wistful. "It would be fabulous if this captain would do the same thing."

"It sure would." I chuckled. "But I think our best bet would be to seduce one of the women without the captain knowing about it. This guy. . . well, he seems to be a businessman. I believe he would charge for anything he could."

Fernando looked up at the star laden sky and answered, "You may be right. . . . But I can dream anyway. There is no charge for that."

I looked at Fernando's exalted countenance and couldn't keep quiet. "Thank God for small children with big dreams, and for big children with small dreams."

Fernando turned and gave me a stern look. "You make fun of many things. Maybe you laugh too much."

"Maybe. I suppose I laugh instead of cry."

Fernando leaned forward and looked me in the eyes. "Well, let me tell you something, brother . . . without my dreams, I would have little reason for living."

"Me either," I replied soberly. "Pleasant dreams."

I got up and went to bed, leaving Fernando with his musings.

CHAPTER IX

HUNG OUT TO DRY

Late at night I was roused from my slumber by a squall that lashed our boat hard. The tug bobbed and rocked, churning my stomach, and rain entered through the sides and ran in rivulets along the deck. The passengers left their hammocks to help the sailors lower the canvas flaps that sealed the open spaces along the sides of the tug. "Hurry! Hurry!" urged one of the sailors. "Don't let the natural rubber get wet — or it stinks like shit." The job was quickly done. After tying down the last canvas flaps, we stepped back to check over our work. We nodded at each other in approval. The boat was virtually watertight; only a few drops of rain seeped through holes in the canvas. Nothing to worry about, I thought. The squall was already beginning to blow over. We congratulated ourselves for handling the minor problem well and drifted back to bed. I had just settled down and begun to doze when I was jarred awake by a sharp banging sound. I sat up and listened. The sound stopped. It came from the engine room, I thought. What was it? . . . The boat seems normal. Ah, probably just some more driftwood hitting against the bottom because of this choppy water. Nothing unusual. . . . I lay back down and closed my eyes, but a vague unease kept me awake.

Later a faint call rose from below. The cook slipped from his hammock and descended to the engine room. Now what? I thought, sitting up. The storm's gone. We're sailing smoothly. The engine's purring. Everything seems fine. . . . Ah, relax, it's probably nothing. Still, I don't like this . . .

A short time later the cook reappeared and came toward me. I put up my hand to catch his attention but he ignored me and walked directly to the ladder and climbed to the upper deck. Now I know something's going on, I thought. . . . Things grew more suspicious by the minute. One by one the sailors left their hammocks or night posts to go down into the engine room. A muffled buzz of conversation rose to my ears. I propped myself on an elbow and tried to overhear them. It was useless. . . . Still, despite the uncertainty, I was more curious than alarmed. The sailors made their rounds stolidly, moving and speaking softly so as not to disturb the passengers. I was the only passenger awake. It must not be too serious, I thought. None of the sailors look that excited, just a little pissed at having their sleep disturbed.

At that moment the captain came, rubbing sleep from his eyes, and went into the engine room to look things over. Now I began to worry.

Soon a sailor was dispatched with instructions for the pilot. I tried to stop him as he came past me. He brushed by without a word. "This is bullshit!" I muttered. Well, I thought, I might as well relax and await developments because they sure don't seem to want me to know anything. . . . I lay down flat on my back and put my head on my hands. Hell, why worry? There'll be plenty of time to get upset later if there really is something the matter.

I lay inert and quieted my thoughts, to better concentrate on the vibrations of the engine and the motion of the boat. Our speed gradually slackened. After a while we swerved radically to the left and slowed to a crawl. We must be heading to shore, I thought. Or to some island. There really is something wrong with the boat. But what? . . . For some reason I became drowsy. My thoughts were hazy and my perception distorted, as though I were submerged under water. The humidity, I thought. Air is heavy. . . . Before long, with the sound of fingernails running over a chalkboard, the bottom of the flat was scraping sand. A shiver ran up my spine. I sat up, alert now. The engine died. We came to a complete stop.

The sailors leaped into action, all around me, raising the storm flaps and carrying thick ropes to use to secure our berth. With the lifting of the canvas, vegetation intruded into the tug. The heavy smell of the jungle was in my nostrils. The darkness was pervasive. . . . This is some dock, I thought. Where the hell are we? . . . Then, as if from afar, a flickering beacon of light broke the darkness. I got up and leaned out over the railing to get a better look. The light came from a lantern held by the cook. In its murky glow I saw two sailors, like phantom hangmen, standing on a wild jungle bank, fastening ropes to the trunk of a gnarled tree. The scene was ghoulish. In that instant I noticed a vine that had twined itself around the post I was leaning against, its clutching tendrils brushing my arm. I started. Then I reached out and tore the vine from the post. "Not so fast there," I said, stepping away from the railing. Settle down, man, I thought. Don't start getting superstitious. It was only a plant. . . . But it sure moved fast.

I took a deep breath. The humidity was leaden. The buzz of mosquitos harsh in the deadness of the night. I slapped at a couple that flew in my face. They're probably malarial, I thought. They're definitely a pain-in-the-ass. It's a good thing I've been taking my malaria pills every day. . . . This place is trouble.

The sailors bustled from one end of the boat to the other, going about their business with professional calm. I made repeated attempts to talk to them. "What is it?" I asked one and all. "What happened?" Some of them rushed past without answering. Others rushed past and said over their shoulder, *"Problemas. Problemas."* I stood in place and fumed, feeling confused and useless. Finally, totally disgusted, I decided to go to the other end of the boat and wake Fernando. I found him already up and pacing the deck.

"What's happening?" we asked, almost in unison. Then we both chuckled and lowered our voices to a whisper, as the other passengers were asleep.

"No one will tell me anything," said Fernando.

"Me either, they must be under orders not to," I said.

"That's possible."

"How have these other people slept through all this?"

"I don't know. But I think it would be better if we go outside so that we don't disturb them."

"Yeah, good idea." I glanced at Jaap's gently snoring form. "Things are confused enough already."

We moved to the prow of the tug to take advantage of a faint breeze blowing off the river. We sat on the deck and discussed the situation in hushed tones, sharing our apprehensions. As we talked I glanced to shore from time to time. The jungle was a black, impenetrable mystery. Strange calls issued from the depths of the forest, seemingly coming closer and closer. After one particularly weird cry, I looked at the pigs to see their reaction. Nothing. They lay with their snouts buried in their trotters, sleeping peacefully. My imagination's getting away from me, I thought.

Later we spotted a pair of sailors with the lantern on the shore. They walked from one end of the boat to the other.

"What do you think they're doing?" I asked Fernando.

"I'm not certain, but it seems that they're inspecting the hull for leaks."

"Yeah, that could be the problem."

When the sailors came aboard we called to them: "Is everything all right? Did you find the problem? What is happening?"

The first sailor walked by silently. The second one glanced at us and

237

said, "I can't talk. We are busy."

I stared at his retreating back for a moment, outraged.

"Man," I said to Fernando, "what is this? This is screwed!"

Fernando shook his head.

"They could at least tell us what they think the problem is . . . . And if they don't know, say so! Hell, it's our necks, too. We're awake. We have the right to know what's going on. I mean . . . shit! All we can do is sit here like . . . like dummies."

"Well," said Fernando, patting my shoulder, "it's probably nothing too serious . . . nothing important. So, they don't want to worry us unnecessarily."

"Oh yeah? . . . Well, if their intention is not to worry me, they are doing one bad job of it. I like to know what I'm dealing with."

"Relax, man, worrying won't help us." Fernando glanced at the sleeping pigs. "Look, the hogs don't seem worried."

"Of course not," I snorted. "Those pigs are fatalists . . . . In their position what else could they be — they know already that they're dead meat. The only question is when."

Fernando chuckled. "Maybe we are in the same position and don't even know it."

"Maybe so . . . . But maybe you're right. Maybe the pigs do have the right idea."

"What do you mean?"

"Since there's nothing we can do about anything right now . . . I'm going back to bed and try to get some sleep."

"Good, let's go."

I returned to my spot and flopped down on the wood. My mind burned with speculation. Is it the engine? No, that sounded fine . . . . The water pump? I heard it going . . . . Could it be a gash in the hull of this tub? Didn't seem like the sailors found anything . . . . Hell, could be any damn thing! What's the difference? . . . I'm only a passenger. Laying here doing *nada* . . . . Maybe it's all part of the tour. Just like the way the cook slaughtered the sow . . . . Ladies and gentlemen, for your added entertainment, a brief jungle stop . . . . Don't be alarmed if an anaconda comes aboard and snacks on one of you. After all, it's only natural, and the show must go on . . . . Huh, now that would make a good cheap Brazilian flick. I can see it now . . . . "The Revenge of the Amazon." Starring—Carmen Miranda and her $Cheeky Booms$ . . . Yeah, yeah . . . . Yeah . . . . Yea . . . . Yea . . . . Ye . . . . Ye . . . . Y . . .

Suddenly all the crew and passengers are assembled on the prow

238

and the captain is addressing us. "We are a bit damaged," he announces, patting Nazaré's rump, "but we should be able to make port without any major problems. Trust me. *Tudo bem.*"

Like hell! I think. Who's he trying to kid? He probably can't fit Milene and Nazaré into that dinky cabin of his at the same time. He can't wait to get both of them into the sack together. What nerve! Risking our lives for a sandwich job in a cheap *pensão.*

We set sail in pitch darkness. Though listing to starboard, we make good headway. Then the storm hits us with full fury. Naturally we're in the middle of the river. We have to ride it out. The boat shakes and rolls, wallows and soars on the bucking river. I'm hurled from one end of the tug to the other. Everyone else is tied securely in their hammocks. I can't latch on to anything, everything slips from my fingers. Fernando reaches out his hand for me as I hurtle past — I miss it by inches. My body is shot like a pinball from one railing to another. My ribs are bruised and sore. It's no use, I think, let yourself go and see where it takes you . . . . Finally, slipping and sliding on the pig shit slick deck, I'm flung overboard into the raging water. My cry for help dies in the whistling wind. I'm tossed like a rag doll. Then I see the runty boar swimming up to me. He seems to be smiling, as though he were merely taking a bath. He stops and dog paddles just in front of me. I try to grab onto him to use him as a float. The torrent sweeps him away. "Now we're really in the same boat," he squeals, as he disappears over a roller . . . . I'm pounded by waves and water gets into my throat. I no longer care. A sense of peace has come over me. I merely try to keep my nose out of the water. As the river sweeps me along I become entangled in a large tree limb. Now I have a canoe. I hang onto a branch with the crook of my left arm and kick blindly. Tiny fish are nibbling at my feet and legs. You little punks, I think, at least wait until I'm dead. Show some respect! . . . To frustrate the fish I climb into the leafy part of the limb. "Now you won't get me at all!" I bellow. "At least not without a fight!" These words echo through my mind. The fish are leaping out of the water to get at me. I break off a branch and swat them away, like a boy hitting pebbles with a stick. The fish keep coming . . .

The engine roared to life. My eyes snapped open. The moon glowed blood red in the first light of dawn. I felt a caressing breeze evaporating the perspiration on my brow. For a moment I was confused, unable to remember where I was and what I was doing there, then I felt the hard wood against my back and the crawling itch of fresh insect bites on my legs and arms. The stink of oil and natural rubber was in my nose. My muscles and ligaments were tight. I sat up and became oriented . . . .

What a bizarre dream, I thought. Weird! . . . Well, I'll figure it out later. Right now I have more important things to think about.

I rose and went to the prow. The tall sailor was there, fiddling with a rope. He saw me coming and turned his face, pointedly. From behind I heard the engine humming, its drone increasing as it warmed up. I walked straight up to the sailor and stood in front of him.

"Good morning," I said.

He looked at me and grunted.

"Are we leaving here now?"

He nodded, his face impassive.

"Is the boat all right? *Tudo bem?*"

He shrugged his shoulders and knelt down to unfasten one of the ropes from its cleat . . . . O.K., sucker, I thought. Be like that. Thanks.

I went astern and gazed at the sweep of the river. The dawn dappled the placid water with golden highlights. A multitude of birds called in the forest. I turned and saw a flock of parrots sweep over the treetops, their brilliant plumage a mosaic against the gray canvas of the sky. All of this had a calming effect on me. When the cook got out of his hammock and went into the galley to make coffee I felt better still. Back to the old routine, I thought. Nothing seems as scary in the light of day. They probably fixed the problem with the boat.

A few minutes later the boat chugged from its mooring, the sand scouring the bottom of the flat, and swung slowly out into the mainstream of the river. All seemed well. But when we reached our channel I noticed that we were moving at a much slower than normal cruising speed. No, I thought, there's still something wrong with the boat. I just can't put my finger on it . . .

The cook came out of the galley, humming softly, and gave me a cup of coffee. I was still the only passenger awake. The cook smiled a good morning and leaned against the sink. He looked tired. He sipped his coffee with half-closed eyes. Maybe he'll tell me something, I thought.

"Listen, man," I said in a low confidential voice, stepping closer to him. "What is the problem with this boat?"

"Problem?" The cook's face went blank. "I don't know . . . . No problem. Nothing. Don't worry."

"But . . . "

The cook turned and entered the galley. Nothing my ass, I thought.

I gulped my coffee and paced the stern. Gradually we drifted to the south side of the river. Once there we hugged the shore. The boat chugged on. I sat down and muttered to myself, "There is something wrong. But why won't the bastards tell me what it is?" I got up and paced some more. We sailed into a low mist, the shore was almost obscured. I asked the cook for another cup of coffee and sat down. A short time later I heard footsteps. It was the captain. His face was haggard, his eyes bleary and bloodshot. I leaped up to speak to him.

"Oh, captain," I said, looming just off his shoulder. "What is the problem with the boat?"

The captain stepped past me as though I were a shadow and stuck his head in the galley. He began a rapid-fire conversation with the cook. I was left standing like a dummy, unable to even understand their talk. I gritted my teeth and fumed silently. Nice fucking captain! . . . Can't even be bothered with a passenger. Damn asshole!

The captain finished his conversation with the cook and accepted an entire thermos of coffee. As he walked past me to return to the helm I held my tongue in check by great effort and stared daggers at him. The captain gave no indication that he noticed me. Chump, I thought. Then as he passed from sight up the ladder my anger faded. Ah, what am I getting so uptight about? The man has a lot of responsibility. It can't be easy guiding a tub like this on this river . . . . He must be tired as hell. Maybe I'm a little too tired . . .

I resumed my seat on the stern. We cruised stolidly for the next hour. The sun burned off most of the morning mist. The passengers stirred in their hammocks and trickled to the stern to receive their morning coffee. Except for Fernando, none of the other passengers seemed aware that anything untoward had occurred. Jaap and Betti were in excellent spirits. Eloi was his usual stoic self. *La Gordita* flirted with the tall sailor. I decided to keep quiet and await developments.

Eventually the boat was directed off the broad Amazon and into a narrow inlet, our speed was reduced even more. Slowly we penetrated inland. To my surprise we were flanked on either side by gently rolling hillocks that were carpeted with cropped grass and shrouded by a swirling mist. The air was fresh and cool. Grazing cattle loomed eerily out of the fog, eyeing the boat, lowing plaintively as we passed.

"They look like sentinels," said Fernando, joining me at the railing. "Strange, no?"

"Yeah, this whole thing looks strange," I said. "This pastoral setting in the heart of the tropics . . . . If I didn't know better I'd think we were somewhere high in the Andes."

"It seems a little like that, yes."

We rounded a bend and the inlet broadened into a lagoon. To our right the terrain leveled out and was covered by typical jungle growth; to our left the hillocks continued, slashed now by a network of footpaths. Several dugout canoes were afloat in the lagoon, manned by dark wiry men with straw hats. With a swirling motion they cast fishing nets into the murky water. As we drew closer one of the fishermen waved and called out to us. The tall sailor came to the railing next to me and waved him on. He paddled his canoe into hearing range and yelled, "What happened? What is the problem?"

"The *motobomba*. The *motobomba* is damaged," yelled the tall sailor.

I nudged Fernando. "What does *motobomba* mean in Spanish," asked him.

"*Motobomba*? . . . Uh, it's a *motobomba*; it's a machine that pumps water."

"Oh, a water pump."

"Why?"

"Because that's what's damaged. I just heard this sailor say that . . . . So that solves the mystery. Now why do you suppose they made such a big deal about keeping it secret?"

"I don't know. Maybe they thought we would panic."

I snorted. "That's crazy. So we have to stop for repairs, big deal. That's fine."

We pushed deep into the lagoon and veered to the left. I turned and looked. Nestled against the hill, at the end of a long pier, stood a supply shed. Beyond that, at the far end of the lagoon, lay another dock and supply shed, with several boats carrying outboard motors already moored there. We pulled in at the closer empty pier. The sound of our engine was just dying out when we heard a tremendous buzz saw noise coming from the inlet. We jerked our heads around and saw a speedboat barrel into the lagoon. The sleak boat banked sharply, kicking up a shower of spray, and headed in our direction at high speed. A collision seemed inevitable. I jumped back from the railing, a thrill going through me. Then, at the last possible moment, the driver cut his engine and swerved the boat. It glided to a stop, neatly parked alongside the tug.

"Good driving," I said to Fernando. "But dangerous."

"Crazy, man," he said. "That man is crazy."

The fishermen were shaking their fists and cussing at the madman behind the wheel; for sure he had driven off all the fish within the lagoon. The driver, a short stocky man with a beard, was laughing uproariously. He ignored the fishermen and vaulted over the railing and onto the tug. He was greeted by our captain. With exclamations of delight they leaped into each other's arms and embraced. After a long moment they pulled apart and looked at each other, grinning from ear to ear, shaking hands, and then, hugging once more.

"Look at that," I said to Fernando. "What's going on here? . . . I haven't seen the captain look so happy since he took my money for the fare."

Fernando laughed. "Yes, they could be brothers."

"Brothers? . . . They don't look like brothers. I'd say companions in crime."

"They definitely know each other."

"Uh huh."

The captain and his friend soon left the ship and climbed the hill to town. The cook called the passengers to the stern for some more coffee and the first crackers of the day. As we munched our snack we were joined in a meal for the first time by Nazaré and Milene.

"Look," said Fernando, nudging me in the ribs. "The two queens are honoring us with their presence this morning. Nothing like a small crisis to bring people together, eh."

"Yeah, I guess. But they sure don't look like queens today," I answered, surveying Nazaré. A scowl distorted her face and matted tufts of hair formed ugly knobs on her head. She really does have a hard face, I thought.

Nazaré thought the cook was a bit slow bringing her coffee and she snapped at him. The cook took it with a mocking smile and served her with exaggerated courtliness. Nazaré glared at the cook and said something else to him in a harsh tone. The cook bowed and entered the galley.

"It would seem that our queen has had a difficult night," whispered Fernando. "Maybe the captain gave her a bad time."

"Or maybe she's upset about this stop here," I said, shrugging. "Who knows?"

Milene went to Nazaré and spoke to her in a soothing voice. The hard lines on Nazaré's face relaxed. For the first time I studied Milene. She was older than Nazaré, late twenties or early thirties, was plain featured, had short straight black hair, a slim, almost boyish figure, and projected a calmness and maturity of manner.

"That's the one the captain seems to be on the most intimate terms with," commented Fernando, nodding his head at Milene. "I see them talking often."

Milene left Nazaré and went to the galley door. She received a cup of coffee from the cook with a word of thanks. Then she came over and found a seat on the edge of the stern right next to me.

"Good morning," I said, smiling at her.

"Good morning," she said, smiling in return. "How are you today?"

"Fine . . . except, I'm a little confused. Maybe you can help me."

"How?"

"Do you know what is going on with the boat? How long we are going to stay here?"

She grinned and gave me a sidelong glance. "Only the captain knows for sure . . . and the captain only answers to the captain."

"Oh, he has no confidant?"

"Not when it concerns the boat."

As I continued talking to Milene, I found her quick and intelligent. She realized immediately that I could understand her if she spoke slowly and enunciated clearly. Also, she understood my quasi-Portuguese better than any of the other Brazilians.

"I like speaking with you," I said. "You seem to understand me better than the others."

"I used to live on the frontier," she said. "I know and speak Spanish . . . . I can piece together what you are trying to say."

"That's good. But I would like to learn as much Portuguese as I can this trip."

She laughed and looked pleased. "Don't worry, we are in *Brasil* . . . . I'm not going to speak Spanish in my country. I will teach you if you want to learn . . . as much as you like."

"*Tudo bem.*"

Fernando leaned over and got Milene's attention. "Is there a town around here?"

"Yes," she said, smiling. "There's a fine little town on top of the hill. I know this place."

"What is there to do here?" asked Fernando.

"Several things . . . . There are bars, billiards . . . even a discotheque. You can fish here in this lagoon, swim, boat, and . . . I hope we don't stay here long but, if we get stuck overnight, I have friends . . . . It's Friday. There could be a party."

"A party, eh," said Fernando. "That would be fantastic!"

"Can you teach me how to dance the *samba*?" I asked.

"Of course," she said, laughing merrily. "I can try."

"I don't expect to be an expert."

"Fine. We'll see what happens."

"Yes, you're right, why make plans? . . . We'll probably leave here in a few hours, no?"

"Maybe . . . . The captain has family here."

Milene finished her coffee and rejoined Nazaré. They soon went back upstairs. As soon as they were gone Eloi came over to visit.

"Well, friend," said Fernando to Eloi, "do you know how long we are going to be here?"

Eloi shook his head. "I don't know anything. I just hope we leave here soon . . . . One of the sailors is working on the *motobomba*."

"Why don't you try talking to him," I suggested. "They won't tell us anything . . . . But, since you're Brazilian, you could have more luck."

Eloi shrugged. "I can try." He walked to the entrance to the engine room and called to the sailor. They held a quick conversation. Eloi turned and gave us the thumbs down sign. He returned to us and sat down with a sigh.

"The only thing he says is, *Vamos embora pronto,* (We are leaving soon)." Eloi spat into the lagoon. "That means nothing."

"*Vamos embora pronto*, eh," I said, rolling the words on my tongue. I laughed sardonically. "That sounds like *mañana por la tarde* (tomorrow afternoon)."

"What exactly do you mean by that?" asked Fernando.

"That's what they tell me in the prison in Colombia whenever I ask for supplies . . . . After a few months there I understood it to mean: tomorrow afternoon, in a few days, weeks, months, years, never, or . . . go fuck yourself, what's the hurry, anyway?"

Fernando laughed. "We say something like that in Peru."

We talked things over among ourselves and, after a lively discussion, defined *pronto* in this instance as a minimum of three hours.

"Let's go explore the village," suggested Fernando.

"Yeah, let's do it," I said. "I'm hungry."

"Hungry?" said Fernando. "We just ate."

"It must be this cool weather."

"I don't want to go right now," said Eloi. "In a while."

"Why not?" asked Fernando. "Let's go, man. Let's check out the town."

"Not now."

"Let's go . . . "

Eloi shook his head.

"It's all right," I said to Fernando. "Leave him alone if he doesn't want to go now. Let's go."

"I'll meet you in town later," said Eloi.

"All right," said Fernando. "Later, then." Eloi left.

We went to the prow of the tug. "Wait a minute," said Fernando. "What about Jaap and Betti?"

245

"What about them? I don't see them around."

"We should invite them."

"Well, I don't want to spend much time looking for them but if we see them . . . "

We walked along one end of the flat without seeing Jaap or Betti. We decided to leave without them. We jumped from the flat to the land and started up the hill. On the trail we met a group of children from the village who were coming down to check out our boat. For a long silent moment they stared at us in bewilderment. We passed them and went on a few steps. Then I paused and looked back. The children were still staring at us. Feeling playful, I waved and stuck my tongue out at them. "How are you doing, kids?" I called in Portuguese.

The children burst into laughter. A couple of them whistled and shouted stuff at us. "See you later," yelled Fernando, as we turned and went on our way.

The slope was grassy and steep. We stepped carefully along a staggered footpath that was booby trapped with mud puddles and steaming mounds of cow shit. Near the summit pockets of swirling mist clung to the hillside. As we climbed higher I heard voices At a bend in the trail I looked up and saw a group of young men lounging by the gate of a barbed wire fence that ran from the head of the trail along the summit of the hill. As our approach was shielded by the mist, we startled the men when we rounded the final bend and appeared before them. We stopped and nodded in greeting. The men recovered from their initial surprise and regarded us with cold and suspicious eyes. A gust of mist-laden air passed and a chill went through my body. "Good morning," said Fernando. The men glanced at each other, their faces tight, and remained silent. "Let's go," I said to Fernando. We approached the gate. The young man standing directly in front of it stood fast. "Excuse me," I said. He moved aside, grudgingly. The loungers resumed their interrupted conversation. We walked past them and stepped over what was left of the bent and twisted gate and down an embankment. We were in the village.

"Not a very friendly welcome," I said to Fernando. "Those guys look tough."

"They think they're tough." Fernando snorted. "This is how some of these dinky river villages are . . . the people are closed and suspicious until they know you."

"That I can understand . . . . But these guys seemed hostile — not at all impressed by the coming of exotic strangers."

Fernando shrugged. "That's how some of these towns are."

My eyes swept the one main street of the town. Cows grazed in the middle of the road and between the houses. A sleepy little village, I thought . . . . Behind us, fronting the town, stood a long low-slung building made of cement blocks, with a corrugated metal roof and steel roll down shutters in lieu of doors and windows. At first I took it for a warehouse; a closer look showed it to be a general store.

"What do you say, Fernando, you want to take a walk around the village? . . . Or see if we can buy some coffee and something to eat here?" I asked, jabbing my thumb toward the general store.

Fernando fidgeted uncomfortably and looked at his feet.

"What do you say, man?"

"We just ate," he muttered.

"Yes, but not much. I'm still hungry . . . . Let's go. I'll treat you."

"I'm not hungry . . . . But if you want to get something—go ahead!"

I regarded him quizzically. He sounds almost angry, I thought. Now what's bugging him?"

"What's the problem, man?" I asked. "What did I do now?"

"Nothing," he replied, smoothing the dirt with his right toe.

"Then?"

"It's that . . . it's that I don't have much money. Especially for spending on unnecessary things . . . . And you have invited me more than enough." He looked up and stared past me to the long row of houses on the main street.

"Oh, so that's it . . . . Listen, Fernando, you're my friend. I wouldn't invite you if I didn't want to, believe me. And besides, I know that if a situation arose where I needed help, you would help me . . . . Right?"

"Yes, but . . . "

"Well, then, don't worry about it. Believe me, I've been in the same situation as you, and someone usually helped me."

"Yes, but . . . you might not have enough money for yourself. You might need the money later."

"Fuck the money! I have enough to get me where I want to go and back. Don't worry, if I run out of money, you'll be the first to know. You might have to help me out someday." I burst into laughter. "This is absurd, man. I'm inviting you to have a cup of coffee—nothing more. If you don't want one it's fine with me."

Fernando's smile returned. "Let's go, then," he said, turning toward the store. "I'll share one with you."

We walked up the embankment and entered the store. It was

divided into two sections; the left side was full of fishing equipment and spare parts for boats; the right side was stocked with foodstuffs. Our captain was standing at the far end of a long counter, on the fishing equipment side, sucking down a beer. He was in animated conversation with a burly store clerk. I looked again. It was the very same man who drove the speedboat. When we walked in the captain acknowledged us with a barely perceptible nod, as though embarrassed to show that he knew us. The clerk gave us a curt, almost contemptuous look and continued talking to the captain.

"Well," I said to Fernando in a low voice, "our captain certainly seems at home here . . . . I don't think he's in a hurry to go anywhere."

"Except maybe to another bar," said Fernando.

We moved up to the counter on the foodstuff side and studied the well-stocked shelves. We saw another clerk in the rear of the store, filling shelves with cans of coffee. He looked up with a distracted air about him and glanced our way. I smiled and nodded to him. A sullen look crossed his face. His lips tightened and he resumed his task as though he hadn't seen us. Huh, I thought, what's this? Is this how it's going to be in this town? Let's see . . .

"Excuse me," I called in a loud voice.

The words hung in the air; both clerks ignored us. Fernando and I exchanged an understanding look. Fine, I thought, if they don't want to wait on us I can take my business elsewhere.

"Shall we go?" said Fernando. "We can find a better place than this."

"Yes, let's go. Why stay where we're not wanted?"

As we turned to leave the captain's friend took note. "Wait!" he called, grinning. "Don't be in such a hurry." He beckoned to the other clerk in the back of the store. "He will take care of you."

The clerk, a blond stocky man running to fat, came forward with a disgusted look on his face. He reached the counter and drummed his fingers on the dull vinyl top.

"What do you want?"

"Two coffees," I answered.

"What? What did you say?"

"I would like two coffees. You know, coffee?"

"We don't serve coffee here. But," he laughed gratingly, "there is plenty of beer."

"No coffee? . . . In a place for fishermen?"

The clerk eyed me hard. He looks like he wants to bust me in the face for no good reason, I thought. Fuck him! . . . But, do I want a beer, this early in the morning? Nah . . . . I looked at the clerk's red puffy face. Especially not now. I don't want anything from this asshole.

"Well?" said the clerk.

"Do you want a beer?" I asked, turning deliberately toward Fernando.

"No, just a coffee."

"We don't want beer," I told the clerk.

The clerk scowled.

From the corner of my eye I had been observing the captain. He watched my exchange with the clerk in silence, but something in his smug face and slouched posture bespoke mockery. I sensed that, for whatever reason, he wanted to see us taken advantage of . . . or humiliated. My eyes narrowed at the thought. I turned to the captain with a smile.

"Excuse me, captain," I said. "Do you want another beer?"

The captain dropped his eyes, the smug expression dissolved into confusion, and shifted his feet. "No, no," he mumbled, and turned to say something to his friend.

I looked at the clerk and shrugged. "What can I do? Nobody wants a beer."

The clerk eyed me darkly and muttered under his breath. Then, as he turned to walk away, the sound of scuffing feet against the cement floor alerted us to the arrival of newcomers. It was Jaap and Eloi.

"Why did you leave without me?" demanded Jaap in English.

"We didn't see you, man. Anyway, we didn't exactly leave secretly."

"Oh." Jaap was looking past me. Suddenly he bounded to the counter and with shining eyes surveyed the long rows of neatly stacked canned goods and boxes. "Wow, they haf everything here!"

"Yeah, everything but what I want—coffee."

Jaap seemed not to hear. The blond clerk returned to the counter. Before we could say a word Jaap addressed him with a torrent of broken phrases and mad gesticulations. The clerk took a step backward, a stunned look on his face. This reaction merely goaded Jaap to greater effort. Pointing insistently to the items he wanted, using his bad Spanish without complex, Jaap ordered sardines, loaves of fresh bread, guava jelly, margarine, and a few other things. I had to admire Jaap's aplomb and effectiveness. Whenever one of his orders was misinterpreted he would eye the clerk with reproach and talk louder — as though the clerk were the foreigner, and what kind of idiot was he to misunderstand such clear instructions. The clerk responded to these reproofs with fawning smiles and hopped to fill Jaap's order. I looked on with a rueful grin, shaking my head.

"I don't understand," I said to Fernando. "I try to be polite and speak their language and this guy treats me like a pest . . . . And here's Jaap, treating this guy like a dog, and he gets excellent service. Why?"

Fernando scratched his head. "Well, he's buying many things . . . . Let's wait and see how much they charge him for this excellent service."

"Yeah, that's true . . . . Otherwise I'll have to chalk up the clerk's change in attitude to Teutonic intimidation."

"What?"

"Nothing, nothing . . ."

The clerk piled the items in a heap and calculated the price in his head. "Only $250 *cruzeiros* for everything," he said to Jaap. "$250, $250 . . ." The clerk looked down the counter to his boss. The bearded man nodded approval.

Jaap gazed at the pile on the counter. After a few moments of thought his face blanched and he muttered something in Dutch. Finally he looked up at the clerk. "It costs that much?"

The clerk's servile smile tightened. "Yes . . . . Only that much."

"Do you think this should be the correct price?" Jaap asked me in English.

"I don't know. It's a little more expensive than the prices in the other towns we've been to, but not too bad . . . . After all, this is a damn isolated place."

"Yes, but they haf to charge the correct price."

I chuckled. "They can charge what they want . . . . Where else can you go?"

"Are you going to buy anything?"

"No! But not because of the prices."

Jaap turned and looked appealingly to the captain. "Captain, the price . . . it is good?"

The captain grinned. "Yes, of course, my friend. It is good and cheap. Quite cheap."

I smothered a snort. Jaap looked at me. "Vat?"

"It might very well be the correct price — but it certainly isn't cheap."

"The captain says it is."

"Look, man, the captain is the owner's buddy . . . . I'm gonna get out of here. The price ain't that bad."

Jaap turned to Eloi. Eloi shrugged his shoulders. Jaap muttered in Dutch and pulled out his money. While he counted out the $250 *cruzeiros* the clerk smiled benevolently and whistled a tune. I decided to take advantage of his good humor.

"Excuse me," I said, catching his attention. "Is there a restaurant or café here that sells coffee?"

The clerk gave me a blank stare. The blood rushed to my face and I spluttered from frustration . . . . Eloi stepped up to the counter and repeated my question word for word.

"Ah, that's what he said," responded the clerk. "These gringos are difficult to understand."

"This one speaks some Portuguese," said Eloi. "You just have to get used to his strange accent."

Or be sharper than this fuckin' moron, I thought.

The clerk looked me up and down, his air of impatience with me suddenly gone. Then he chuckled. "A restaurant? Here?" He turned to his boss and to the captain. "He wants to know if there is a restaurant here." The two men smiled and shook their heads.

"Why is that funny?" I asked.

"Because this town is too small and too poor for a restaurant," said the clerk. "But you can get coffee and fresh bread at the bakery."

"Where is it?"

"Over there," he said, with an expansive sweep of the arm that took in the entire village.

"Where?"

"Over there!" He followed this with a flurry of directions that left me dazed. All right, I thought, I think I got it . . . . In the blue house, over there. Shouldn't be too hard to find in this little place.

"Thanks."

I walked outside to clear my head. Fernando and Eloi soon followed.

"They charge high prices here," Eloi said to me.

"Yeah, gringo prices . . . . But I've seen much worse."

"It's expensive for Brazilians here, too."

"I believe you . . . . Shall we go to the bakery?" I asked, looking at both of them. "I'm inviting."

"O.K.," said Fernando.

"*Tudo bem*," said Eloi.

Jaap stepped out of the store, carrying his groceries in a plastic sack. "Vat you fellas going to do?"

"We're going to the bakery," I said. "You want to come?"

"I already haf bread."

"For coffee."

"I don't know . . . "

"C'mon, Fernando and Eloi are going."

"He doesn't want to go?" asked Fernando.

"He's not sure."

"I would like to . . . but I think I should go back to the ship and see after Betti. To keep her company."

"Why don't you come, Jaap?" asked Fernando.

"We won't be long," I added.

"I don't know . . . "

As we waited for his decision I eyed Jaap. I wondered if leaving Betti alone was his true reason for hesitating to come with us. The day before he had confided to me that he was paranoid about someone stealing from him. Maybe he wants to get back to the boat and stash his loot while we're away, I thought. And, he buys things every time we stop, but he's only shared with us once . . . . Yes, I think our friend here is just a little bit cheap.

"What do you say, man?" I asked. "I'm buying for everyone this time. My treat."

Jaap's eyes lit up. "Well . . . " He glanced at his bag of groceries. "No . . . I should go back to Betti."

"O.K., see ya later."

As Jaap departed the three of us turned to face the village. To our left a rutted dirt path led away from the general store to a rise overlooking the main street. We decided to ignore this for the moment. The main street was broad and muddy, patched in places with mossy grass, and sloped down from the buildings on each side of it, forming a gully to drain away rain and flood waters.

"Let's go find that bakery," I said.

We descended the embankment and found a narrow cobbled path at the center of the street. We followed it. All was tranquil. The sun sprinkled light against the pastel facades of the house, the reflection giving the low-lying mist the look of cotton candy. Various cows wandered untended along the street, cropping at the patches of grass and flicking away flies and mosquitos with their tails. At our approach the cows stopped feeding and looked at us with soft brown eyes. A couple of them were hump-backed cebus. None of them resumed feeding until we walked past. Damn, I thought, even the cattle are suspicious of us here.

"Where are all the people?" asked Fernando, swiveling his head.

"Fishing," said Eloi. "Or in the fields."

As if on cue an old man stepped out of his front door for a breath of fresh air. He looked at us with a startled countenance and went right back inside.

"Soon the whole village will know there are strangers here," said Eloi, shaking his head.

The side of the street fronting the lagoon was strung along its full length with colored light bulbs. Behind the row of houses ran a barbed wire fence, most of it overgrown with bush.

"What's with the colored light bulbs?" I asked Eloi.

"It's Christmas time," he said.

"That's right, I almost forgot . . . . I like the lights."

"Why?"

"Because it makes the village seem like *carnaval* . . . . Is Christmas pretty wild in Brazil? It sure is in Colombia."

Eloi shook his head. "No, it's pretty quiet. Most of the celebration is with your family. *Carnaval* is our wild time."

"What's with the barbed wire fence behind the houses?"

"To keep cows, children, and drunks from falling down the hill."

On the other side of the street we passed a school — the only two-story building in town—with a huge front courtyard containing basketball and volleyball courts.

"Why do they have such a large school in such a small town?" I asked Eloi.

"It's probably a regional school," he said. "Children come from all over the surrounding countryside."

We continued along the cobbled path, saying little, lulled by the morning hush. It's really hard to believe this is still the Amazon, I thought. These brick and stucco homes, the cows, the grassy street . . . . It's like a town from the Andean highlands was magically brought here . . . . Well, except that there are no towering peaks in the background . . . and no real chill in the air . . .

"Wait a moment," said Eloi, stopping and pointing to a nondescript dwelling with faded and chipped blue paint. "I believe that this is the bakery."

"Are you certain?" I asked. "There is no sign."

"They don't need signs in this place; everyone knows everyone . . . . I'm almost sure this is it."

"Almost sure?"

"The man said a blue house."

"But we've already passed five or six blue houses . . . . I think it's farther ahead."

Eloi gave me a puzzled look and shrugged. "O.K., we can walk and see."

We moved on. The street soon terminated at the village *praça*. We saw a tree-lined, cobbled inner square, a high steepled church, a fountain, and a few cottage businesses, but no trace of a bakery. An old man sitting by the fountain watched us with great interest as we walked in circles. Finally Eloi approached him and asked about the bakery.

"You already passed it," he said, his wrinkled and leathery face impassive. He went on to describe the building and its location in detail. I listened closely. When he finished I still had no idea where to find the bakery.

"Thank you, sir," said Eloi, nodding his head. He turned to me with a reproachful look. "I knew all along we passed it."

"Sorry, man . . . . Anyway, where is it?"

"Follow me."

Fernando and I exchanged perplexed looks and fell in behind Eloi. "I was almost positive I understood that guy in the store," I said to Fernando. "This Portuguese is tricky; just when I think I'm capturing it well, it slips away from me . . . . I didn't understand the old man's directions."

"Me either," said Fernando. "Nothing."

"Yeah, it's time for me to shut up and listen to Eloi."

We backtracked and came to the same blue house Eloi had pointed to earlier. Eloi went up to the stout wooden door and knocked tentatively. We waited. No one answered.

"Are you sure that this is the place?" I asked him.

"I think so." For the first time uncertainty was in his eyes. I stepped forward and rapped on the door. After a brief delay the door inched open, squeaking on its hinges, and a pair of bright eyes peeked out at us. It was a young girl, shielding her small body behind the door, gaping at us in wide-eyed astonishment. *"Senhor?"* she asked. Eloi snapped a couple of terse sentences at her. The girl nodded and fled wraith-like into the interior.

"We can enter," said Eloi.

We pushed open the door and stepped into an ill-lit room. The aroma of fresh baked bread was delicious and made my nostrils twitch. For a moment we stood inside by the doorway and blinked our eyes, to more quickly acclimate them to the dim light. A bare wooden table and chairs sat against the near wall in the middle of the long skinny room. The lime-plaster walls were chipped and gashed and smoke stained a grayish-white. Thick intersecting ceiling beams were black from smoke. To the left of the entranceway, through a narrow door, was a sunken living room, furnished with an antique cabinet radio and a battered sofa and easy chair. A checkerboard stone tile floor covered both rooms. A large portrait of the Virgin Mary hung over the wooden table . . . . We took a few more steps into the room and stopped.

"Service!" called Fernando.

A faint reply came from the bowels of the house. Our attention was directed to a dark narrow opening cut into the wall in the rear of the room. Within seconds a slim pleasant-featured woman came bustling through this aperture. She came up to us, smiling shyly, and spoke to us in greeting. We returned her greeting. She motioned us to the table and bade us take seats.

"What would you like?" she asked.

"Bread and coffee," I said.

Unlike the man at the store, she understood my simple order at once, although I got the impression she waited on fewer people than him, especially foreign people. She retreated to the kitchen. Her movements were light and graceful.

The fragrant smell of the baking bread and the warmth and darkness of the room gave me a secure, homey feeling after the trials of the semi-open tug. I tilted my chair back and exhaled a long sigh. For the first time in days I began to feel completely relaxed. The woman returned with three porcelain coffee cups and some plates. Her manner was so solicitous and unaffectedly amiable that I felt as though I were an honored guest rather than a mere customer. Fernando and Eloi seemed similarly affected by her. Her voice was gentle and warm. We basked in her presence. We held her at the table with questions.

"What is the name of this village?" asked Fernando.

"Alvarães," she said. "Do you like it here?"

"We don't know yet," I said. "We just arrived. But I like it here in your house."

"Will you be here a while?" she asked.

The three of us looked at each other and shrugged simultaneously. The woman chuckled, smiled knowingly, and went to get our snack.

"She is very nice, no?" Fernando asked me.

"Yes, she is."

"And pretty."

"Yes."

"Is that all you have to say about her?"

"Yes," I said, discouraging further questions by staring at my plate. That's all I can tell you, I thought. I don't understand this myself . . . why just looking at her gives me a warm feeling. Pretty? . . . Definitely! But not spectacularly beautiful . . . . Lustrous black hair down to her shoulders. Finely chiseled facial features and bright brown eyes.

Slim, graceful figure and bearing . . . but there is more, much more. She exudes a contentment and equanimity with life that I have felt in so few people. She is complete . . . . She knows who she is and what she is about. She already is what I want to be . . .

While Eloi and Fernando chatted, I gazed absently about the room. I spied several small heads peeking at us from the corners of shadowy doorways. I pointed them out to my companions. We played hide-and-seek; whenever one of us caught their eyes, the head would duck from view and muffled giggles would follow. This went on for a few minutes. Then the woman reappeared, apologized for the delay, and set a steaming kettle of coffee and fresh loaves of bread on the table. She excused herself, gently shooed the children to the kitchen, and returned moments later with margarine, marmalade, and a vase of white flowers. A thoughtful touch. We were impressed by her kindness.

"Would you like to sit down and eat with us?" Eloi asked her.

"Yes, please," Fernando and I echoed.

"I'm sorry," she said, "but thank you. I can't."

"Please," said Eloi, patting an open chair with his hand.

"Thank you, but no. I have much work yet." She turned and went back to the kitchen. We tore into the bread. It was light and good and still hot from the oven. The coffee was much better quality than that served on the boat. We ate and drank with gusto. While we ate Fernando brought up the subject of shipwrecks. Both he and Eloi gave accounts of Amazonian shipping catastrophes that claimed hundreds of lives and left sunken treasure to the whims of shifting sands and, said Eloi in a hushed tone, "Supernatural fish and spirits of the river."

"Don't tell me that you believe in those things," said Fernando. "The Amazon is plenty dangerous without any help from spirits or supernatural fish."

"There are many things that no one can explain," said Eloi with a sober face. "Especially in the jungle. It's better to be on good terms with these unexplainable . . . ah . . . forces."

"Yes," I said, "at least if you believe in them."

"Well, I don't know about that," said Fernando, "but we are indeed daring to have risked this voyage on a ship such as ours."

"*Hein*," affirmed Eloi.

"Or we are idiots," I said, chuckling.

"Idiots?" said Eloi. "Maybe . . . . But my father always said that necessity makes idiots out of many people."

"That's a good one, Eloi," I said. "What do you think of this one? . . . Idiots make necessities where there are none."

Fernando chuckled and raised his coffee. "A toast to the club of idiots . . . . And good companions."

We raised our cups and drank. I poured another round. Then, not to be outdone by their disaster stories, I told them that living in San Francisco was like sitting on a time bomb because of the tall buildings and the constant threat of a major earthquake.

"So what," said Fernando. "South America is always getting hit by big quakes — particularly Peru. We had one in 1970 that cost more than 70,000 lives."

"That many?"

"Yes, if not more. That was a rough estimate. An entire city was buried."

"Huh."

"But you don't really worry about quakes that much, do you?" Fernando asked me.

"No, I usually only think about it after a small one shakes things up a little." I shrugged. "You can't do anything about it anyway . . . . Except look for an open area."

"That's true," said Fernando. "Those things are acts of God."

"Yeah, what worried me the most growing up in San Francisco was the traffic, the street crime, and, when I was in school, the racial problems that sometimes became violent. Those were more real and immediate threats."

"Our worst problem in Manaus is with flooding from the Rio Negro," said Eloi. "Especially in the poor *favelas* (shantytown slums) near the docks. Filth is spread by the water and people die like flies. It can be terrible . . . . And violent crime is a problem for us, also — Manaus is a free port with plenty of rough characters. You have to watch yourself . . . . And, of course, the inflation. That kills Brazilians all over the country."

"Well, I suppose every place has its problems," said Fernando. "The trick is knowing how to get along . . . "

"And speaking of problems," I said, turning to Eloi, "did you find out anything more about when we are gong to leave here?"

He gave me one of his characteristic shrugs, as if to say, who do I look like? . . . God?

"Who knows? Everything depends on the famous *motobomba.*" Eloi looked solemn. "If it can't be repaired, the captain will have to go to Tefé to buy a new one."

"Then, we could be here for a while. Maybe days."

Eloi nodded. "And my wife is waiting for me . . . "

We lingered over our snack, enjoying the warmth and security of the home. Our conversation petered out and we were lost in our private thoughts .... Finally, reluctantly, we called the woman.

"How much for everything?" I asked her.

"Well ..." She screwed up her face and tilted her head back as though in deep thought, or as though it pained her to speak of business. "$20 *cruzeiros* for everything. Is that all right?"

"That's fine," I said. Much cheaper than at the store, I thought. Damn cheap! ... I bought a few extra loaves of bread for later. We thanked her for her hospitality and said good-bye. I took a long last look at her face; my eyes thanked her for something I would never tell her about. I walked out of the house and into the sunshine, feeling renewed and vigorous.

"Shall we tour the rest of the village?" I asked.

"Not me," said Eloi. "I'm going back to the boat to check on the *motobomba*."

"All right, man," said Fernando. "We'll see you soon."

Eloi turned and walked off. Fernando and I headed for the *praça*. "He's probably seen many villages like this," I said. "All he wants to do is get home as soon as possible."

"True," said Fernando. "But if he can't, he might as well enjoy himself."

"Whatever. . ." We reached the *praça* and veered left. We ascended a gentle slope, passing scattered dwellings along the way, and after a few hundred paces we were on the edge of town. Beyond a last ramshackle hut lay cultivated fields with rows of fruit trees along the perimeters. Beyond the fields and fruit trees spread rainforest.

"And that's Alvarães," observed Fernando.

"Doesn't seem to be much here."

"Nothing worth seeing .... Why don't we go back to the boat and see what's happening there."

"Fine, let's go." We remained on the slope and followed a grassy trail that lay between a row of shanty houses and the fields. We passed a few more cows. That gave me an idea. As we walked I kept my eyes to the ground, looking for mushrooms. Twice I halted to examine promising clumps, but they were of a variety unknown to me. The second time I stopped, Fernando came back to see what I was up to.

"What are you looking for?" he asked.

"*Hongos* (mushrooms)."

Hongos? ... You mean the kind that you use in omelettes?"

"No .... The ones for your head. The magic ones."

"What?" Fernando's face looked both surprised and disapproving. "Why? Don't tell me you like those things."

"Every once in a while. Not often."

"Do you take a lot of drugs?"

"No, unless you count alcohol . . . . But I like mushrooms once in a while."

"Why? What do they do for you?"

"I believe they give me heightened perception."

Fernando scowled. "I believe they are dangerous . . . . You shouldn't play with those things."

"I don't play with them. I'm aware of what could happen if I were to take too many. It's easy to regulate the quantity."

Fernando shook his head. "I hope you know what you are doing."

"Look, man," I said, a bit impatient now, "don't you worry about me. I'm a big boy and I can take care of myself. I know what I'm doing with these. I'll be sure not to involve you in anything . . . "

"That's not the point."

"Look, it doesn't matter anyway, I don't see any of the kind I'm looking for." I held up a thin stemmed mushroom. "This one could be poisonous. I wouldn't touch it."

Fernando shook his head and, stiff-backed, walked on ahead of me. I was amused. Now he probably thinks I'm a drug addict, I thought.

The grassy trail ended behind the store. We moved around to the front and looked inside. The captain was still there, drinking beer and talking to his buddy.

"It would seem that we're not going anywhere just now," commented Fernando.

"It looks that way. But who knows? Why don't you ask the captain if we are going to leave soon."

"Are we going to be here long?" Fernando called to the captain.

He smiled. "Not too long."

Whatever the hell that means, I thought.

We returned to the tug and were surprised to see Jaap, wearing only bathing trunks, with his hands and arms streaked by viscous grease. Before we could catch his attention — to ask him what was going on — he climbed down into the engine room. We spotted Betti leaning against the railing by the engine room. As we moved toward her she bent over the hatch and peered down. I tapped her on the shoulder. She looked up at me with an expectant smile.

"What is Jaap doing down there?" I asked her.

"Oh, you see," she said, her face beaming with pride, "Jaap knows very much about motors and mechanical things. We own a sailing boat in Holland and he does almost all the work himself. He is very, how do you say . . . "

"Handy."

"Yes, quite."

"That's good to hear! I sure hope he can fix this one."

"If it is at all possible . . . he will do it for sure!"

"Yeah, I like your confidence. Get it on."

Fernando and I squeezed in next to Betti to get a view of the work going on in the engine room. Down in the dark below, at the foot of the ladder, by our partially dismantled water pump, we saw Jaap gesturing and speaking with great earnestness to an attentive pair of grimy sailors. After every couple of fractured or convoluted phrases uttered by Jaap, the sailors would nod and grunt a reply; whether they actually understood him or not was hard to say.

"This reminds me of a cowboy and Indian movie," I said to Fernando.

"Why?"

"It's like when the calvary goes to parlay with the Indian chief."

"Why don't you go down there and interpret for him?"

"What for? . . . That would just confuse things even more." I looked back to the engine room. "Hey, Jaap, you're doing a great job. Get that motor running, man."

Jaap looked up at me. "Do you know anything about engines? We can use some help if you do."

I laughed. "I know how to put oil in a car and water in a battery . . . . That's about it."

Jaap snickered. "Then you are useless."

"If you're talking about mechanics—yep. You got it! But that's all right, we have faith in you. You can handle it."

Jaap grunted and turned back to the sailors. Despite the language barrier, Jaap seemed to get his point across reasonably well to the sailors. He used the water pump as his prop and tried every Spanish, English and Dutch word that might help. The sailors listened and seemed to grasp the essence of his message. He's doing fine, I thought. He certainly doesn't need my help. Let's see what comes of this . . . . I turned and wandered to the other end of the tug.

I picked up Jaap's "Zen and the Art of Motorcycle Maintenance" book and settled into Fernando's hammock. From time to time I heard the staccato report of the *motobomba* coming to life, but for some reason it failed to suction water. Fernando, who was following the operation closely, would come by and give me progress reports. Then came a long period of silence. The book had just slipped from my limp fingers and I had begun to doze when the *motobomba* roared. I heard a brief splatter of water. Then the engine died. An instant of quiet was followed by a clamor of laughter from the engine room. I slipped from the hammock and raced to the engine room hatch. Fernando and Betti arrived a second later. We peered down and saw Jaap, doubled over with laughter, clinging to the ladder for support.

"What is it, Jaap?" asked Betti.

Jaap looked up at us, guffawing and holding his sides. He couldn't stop.

"C'mon, man, what happened?" I asked.

"It . . . it is too funny," said Jaap. "Oh, I am . . . I am laughing so much. I am too veak to climb the ladder . . . . Oh, help me."

Fernando and I reached down and helped pull him up to the deck. Jaap stood and looked at us for a moment. Then he burst into laughter anew. He sat on the roof and continued to belly laugh for what seemed a long time. I peered into the engine room. One of the sailors was wiping his face with a dirty rag. He seemed embarrassed. The other sailor watched him with an ear-to-ear grin.

So what's the big joke? I thought. Jaap looks like he's gonna have a stroke.

Jaap, red-faced and still struggling to gain his composure, was telling Betti what had occurred in Dutch. He paused several times during the explanation when he was shaken by fresh spasms of laughter. Fernando and I could only look on and wonder. Finally, still unable to repress frequent chuckles, Jaap told me that the pump had begun working for a few seconds and splattered filthy bilge water into the face of the sailor who had been holding the hose.

"It serves him right. He never thought it vould vork," said Jaap. "I told him. He never thought it vould vork." Jaap was shaken by a new fit of laughter.

I translated this for Fernando. When I finished he looked at me expectantly, waiting for the punch line.

"That's all," I said.

"That's all? . . . That wasn't so funny."

I shrugged. "Maybe it's one of those jokes that you have to be there when it happens to appreciate."

Jaap was still laughing. Fernando and I looked at him wonderingly. "He's almost hysteric," said Fernando.

"Yeah, maybe he's on the verge of a crack-up . . . . Maybe we all will be if we don't get out of here . . . " I was struck by a thought. "But Jaap," I said, shaking his shoulder, "it worked, right?"

"Vat?" he said, interrupting a series of gasping chuckles. "Vat you say?"

"Didn't you say the pump worked for a moment? Is it fixed? Will it continue to work?"

"Yes," said Jaap, sobering considerably. "It only functioned for a few seconds — but it functioned. I am positive I can get it going goot. With luck, we could leave here soon." With those final words he squared his shoulders and returned to the engine room to wrestle with that damned *motobomba*. His manner was so confident I almost believed he would succeed. I took a seat on the sunbathed stern and waited.

A short while later Jaap climbed out of the engine room with a dejected face and a grime crusted piece of machinery. He came to the stern.

"Well?" I asked him.

"No go. I can do nothing."

"What's the problem?"

"There are several. But the vorst is a burnt . . . ah, how do you say it?" He held up the part.

I shook my head.

"Oh, yes, a cog. A burnt cog. We need some new parts or a new pump." Jaap went to tell Fernando the bad news.

I leaned back against the oil drum with a long sigh. Oh, well, I thought, time to kick back. Looks like we're gonna be here for a while. . . . But what the hell, maybe the village has more to offer than meets the eye.

For lunch we ate leftover pork and, of course, white rice. No one was pleased with the food. Jaap opened a can of sardines and ate them in front of us.

Shortly after the plates were cleared away the captain appeared, resplendent in white yachting togs and a navy blue, gold sashed captain's hat. He brushed aside our questions and spoke briefly to the cook. Then his bearded friend came and they boarded his speed boat and skimmed from the lagoon. As Fernando and I gazed at their foaming wake I commented, "You know, I'm really starting to dislike this captain."

"Why?"

"Because he never tells us a damn thing."

We went to the stern and dangled our feet into the murky water. The afternoon was warm and hazy. We were bored but still too lazy to do anything about it. Then Milene came down for lunch and sat with us.

We perked up.

"Do you know where the captain went?" Fernando asked her.

"Yes," she said, with a disgusted look on her face. "He's gone to Tefé to purchase a new pump."

"That's good!" I said. "But why the sad face? Don't you want to leave here?"

"Of course I want to leave here—soon! . . . That's the point, I know this captain. He will probably get too drunk tonight to return here before tomorrow afternoon." She glared at the lagoon and twitched her lips. "I know him. He only thinks about himself."

Fernando and I exchanged a meaningful glance and shrugged.

"Well," said Fernando to Milene, "your news isn't exactly unexpected . . . . Cheer up, it looks like we're going to have a hot night in old Alvarães."

I chuckled. "Yeah, disco mania."

"I told you that I have friends here," said Milene, brightening. "Maybe they can arrange a party."

"You say there are bars here, right?" I asked. "I didn't see any this morning."

"Of course there are bars," she said. "They're there."

I retrieved my Portuguese book and asked Milene to help me with my pronunciation. She could read fine. The lesson went quite well until I questioned the accent she told me to give certain words.

"But those words sound different on the radio broadcasts I listen to," I said.

"I don't care about your radio broadcasts," she said, flushing. "I am Brazilian . . . . That's how you pronounce the word!"

"*Tudo bem*," I said, not wanting to antagonize her. "Let's stop for now. Later I'll buy you a beer . . . and we can practice better. I always speak better with an oiled tongue . . . and hear better."

"That's fine," she said, laughing. "Tonight, then. I'm going to take a nap."

"Good idea."

She left and I asked Fernando if I could use his hammock. He said fine. I was suddenly very sleepy. I settled into the hammock with a sigh and fell almost instantly into slumber.

I awoke late in the afternoon. The air was sultry and heavy in my lungs. A sour taste clung to the roof of my mouth. I stretched sluggishly, feeling dim-witted . . . . This weather sucks, I thought. I need something cold to drink . . . and some stimulation.

I got up and took a quick look around the boat, seeking company.

Except for the cook, who was busy preparing dinner, it was deserted. They must have gone to the village, I thought. So will I.

I left the boat and sauntered toward the village. I paused on the hillside to watch a group of women wash clothes by beating them against smooth stones. I wondered if they suffered from back problems. . . . Just watching them gives me a twinge in the back, I thought, moving on. I reached the summit and turned into the village. I saw a few cows grazing in the shade of houses but the street was devoid of people. Crazy, I thought. Where is everyone hiding? There seems to be more cattle than people in this damn place . . . . Lost in thought, oppressed by the heat, I watched the rhythmic movement of my feet as I followed the cobbled path. I had almost reached the *praça* when I heard my name called from behind. I spun about and spotted Fernando waving to me from the entrance of a plain, cement brick building. I started toward him.

"What's the matter with you, man?" he called to me. "Are you still asleep?"

I shook my head, feeling sheepish.

"Come over here."

"What are you doing?"

"Come and see."

As I drew closer to the building I saw that it was a bar. Jaap and Betti were inside, drinking beer and shooting pool. Instantly I became alert. Here's something, I thought . . . .I stepped into a cool shady large room and surveyed it with eager eyes. Like the general store, the bar was solid concrete except for the broad metal roll door at the front. The earthen floor with a sand layer was littered with cigarette butts, paper wrappers, and other garbage. Looks like a perfect place to get sloppy drunk in, I thought. Whoever cleans up can just turn the sand over with a shovel . . . .Each corner of the room featured a bamboo table and a set of chairs; another table sat outside the entrance. A bumper pool table dominated the center of the room. A rack of cue sticks hung on the front wall. The bamboo-fronted back wall was virtually papered with soccer posters and advertisements for beer and soft drinks. The bar was on the short right side of the rectangular area—a low bamboo counter with four stools arranged before it. A few dozen polished glasses were stacked on one side of the counter and behind it, against the wall, was a long shelf filled with bottles of clear cane alcohol. A large beer cooler gave the counter a side wall near the entrance and at the opposite end, against the wall, stood a wooden rack filled with assorted liquors and wine. A well-equipped bar, I thought. It's easy to guess what people in this town do in their spare time . . .

264

I finished my inspection of the bar and turned to my companions. Jaap and Fernando were playing bumper pool with great enthusiasm but with little skill. Both of them seemed a bit high. They were bright-eyed, red faced, talking loud, and making less sense than usual. Betti sipped at her glass of beer and moved cooly around the table, calculating the angles, advising Jaap on his shot selection.

"Do you want to play winners?" Fernando asked me, handing me a full glass of beer. I took a swallow of beer; it was warm.

"No, I don't think so."

"Why not?"

"Oh, I just want to relax, drink some beer, and look around."

"As you like," said Fernando, sounding a bit peeved. "Finish the beer in one swallow. That's the Peruvian way." I did. Fernando nodded his approval.

"I'll get a fresh one," I said.

I went to the bar and bought a large bottle from the young stocky bartender. This beer was cold and refreshing. The others were intent on their pool game. With bottle in hand I strolled to the back wall to examine the soccer posters. One of them caught my eye at once—it was a team photo of a club from Rio de Janeiro called "Flamengo." What an exotic name, I thought. Can the city be as exotic as the name of its soccer team? . . . I'll have to go to Rio at the first opportunity and find out . . . . I moved along the wall, drinking from my bottle and scrutinizing the posters as though I were in an art gallery. I ran into a wall calendar featuring the finalists from a Rio beauty pageant. I flipped through the pages. Each month showed a different contestant in colorful skimpy dress. The backdrops were tropical beaches and lush vegetation. The women came in various sizes and colors—all of them were gorgeous. I definitely have to go to Rio one of these days. That's a promise!

I reached the end of the wall and took a seat at the corner table. I sipped my beer and watched the street. The pool game went on and on. As dusk approached more and more people began to pass by the bar. A few stopped to stare at us. Then a group of Brazilian men, a tough and work hardened lot by all appearances, drifted into the bar for a drink. They sat at the table closest to the counter and eyed the pool players. I surreptitiously observed them observing us. Two of the men looked curious, one indifferent, others wary, none friendly. I began to feel uneasy. As Fernando filled the air with Spanish and Jaap and Betti with Dutch, the men grew restive. They muttered among themselves and cast sidelong scowls at the pool players. The hostility was palpable.

Two of the Brazilians tossed down their drinks and got up to leave, giving us dirty looks on their way out. The others drank faster. I looked at the bartender. He was quietly polishing glasses. Well, I thought, at least he doesn't seem to mind our being here . . . even if we are hurting his regular business . . . . But why the dirty looks from these guys? We haven't done anything to deserve this attention . . . . I don't know about this fuckin' town. I wish Eloi were here. There could be some misunderstanding because of language . . . . Ah, I'm being paranoid. They'll get used to us. They just don't know what to make of us.

I surveyed my companions. Betti now looked happily dazed, Jaap the same, but Fernando alternated nervous bursts of laughter with veiled frowns. I don't like this, I thought. Maybe Fernando overheard something from those guys . . . or worse, imagined he heard something . . . . Then, without warning, the remaining Brazilians left the bar. I breathed a sigh of relief.

A few minutes later two young toughs entered the bar. One was tall and wiry, the other short and heavy set. They wore cocky smiles and gave Betti openly lewd looks. They bought bottles of beer and kept close tabs on the pool game, all the while talking in harsh tones and giving Jaap and Fernando hard looks. Fernando now had a set scowl on his face. Jaap's smile was tight and he seemed nervous. The game went on. The two Brazilians grabbed pool cues and tapped them on the ground.

When Jaap and Fernando got down to the final three balls, the two locals told them that they wanted the table when the game was over.

"We're going to play another game after this," said Fernando. Jaap said nothing. The locals gripped their sticks and scowled . . . . The game continued. Soon thereafter, Jaap, needing to sink one last ball, missed his shot and knocked Fernando's final ball in by mistake. Fernando gave an elated yelp and went to the bar to buy another rack of balls. The two locals glowered at Fernando's back and called something to the bartender. Fernando and the bartender exchanged words. I was too far away to hear. The words became loud. I half rose from my chair, my hackles rising in warning. Fernando and the bartender were now shouting and pointing at each other "Fuck!" I muttered. "I knew it."

I moved across the room at a slow walk, keeping a close eye on Fernando and the bartender. Neither one understands the other well, I thought. Both of them probably think that the other is using horrible insults . . . . They're probably right . . . . I stopped a few paces behind Fernando and waited, hoping the argument would die out on its own.

It grew more and more heated. The bartender shook his fist in Fernando's face. I saw Fernando's right hand close . . . . I stepped forward and grabbed Fernando by the arm, pulling him back and turning him around to face me. He tried to shake free. "Wait, man," I said in a quiet voice. "What's the problem?"

Fernando looked at me, his cheeks and neck a flaming red, his eyes glowing like coals. "This guy is trying to charge me $5 *cruzeiros* too much for the pool balls . . . . He is a thief! Nobody is going to rob me like that!" Fernando turned and stared at the bartender. The bartender, who must have understood the thief part (it's almost identical to the Portuguese word), clenched his fists and glared back. Here we go, I thought.

The two locals edged closer, gripping the pool cues. Two other men had wandered into the bar and were watching every move we made. I know whose side they're on, I thought.

I glanced behind me to see where Jaap and Betti were situated. They were gone. Why, the lousy bastards slipped away. But no time to worry about that now . . .

"Hey, Fernando," I said, patting him on the back. "Look at me, man!"

He muttered harshly toward the bartender. I stepped close to him. "Listen, man, calm yourself," I whispered. "We are strangers here. There is no way we can win if it comes to a fight . . . . Let them have the fucking pool table. You can't expect to dominate it all day, anyway. It's nothing . . . "

"Yes, but that's not the point. The bartender . . . "

"That is the point, man! This is their village! Their bar! You can't fight the whole town . . . if something were to happen nobody would ever have to hear about it. It's nothing. Calm yourself, man! Calm yourself!"

Fernando stopped mumbling but he continued to glare at the bartender. I stepped past him and went to the counter. "Excuse me," I said to the bartender. "Give me a beer, please."

The bartender looked past me to Fernando, a glazed expression on his face, waiting for any provocation.

"The beer, please," I repeated, as calmly as possible, my insides seething. "And two glasses. A beer and two glasses."

After a last long look at Fernando the bartender turned and went to get my beer. I noticed the two locals a few steps to my right. They fingered the sticks and eyed me with sneers on their faces. For a second rage coursed through me. Assholes, I thought. How brave would they be by themselves? No, forget them. They're nothing. They don't exist.

The bartender gave me an ice cold beer and two glasses. He no longer looked at Fernando.

"Thanks," I said, slipping him the money for the beer and an extra $5 *cruzeiros*. The bartender accepted the money without a word. The two locals went to the pool table after receiving a nod from the bartender. Everyone seemed mollified. I went to Fernando.

"Let's go outside and drink this beer in the fresh air," I said. "It stinks in here." I moved toward the exit. Fernando followed me, reluctantly, still eyeing the bartender. I placed the bottle and two glasses on the outside table and we sat down in the fading light. I filled a glass and gave it to Fernando. He still glared at the Brazilians, but with less conviction. I sat down opposite him and filled my glass. I took a long drink. We were lucky, I thought. Everyone escaped the situation with their face intact . . . . But it sure can be a pain-in-the-ass to have friends sometimes . . . . And speaking of friends, where the hell did Jaap and Betti run off to? . . . Some friends.

No one molested us — or even looked at us — as we sat and drank our beer. The men who had showed up when the argument was at its height, left; the bartender went back to polishing glasses; the two local toughs were shooting pool and soon became involved in some asinine quarrel of their own. Fernando brooded over his beer for a short time, repeatedly telling me what *huevones* (assholes) the bartender and the two locals were, but after a couple of good belts of beer he was more like his usual cheerful self. Paradoxically, the more I drank the more depressed I felt. I stared at the loud mouth pool players and brooded. "Stupid punks," I muttered.

"What's the matter?" Fernando asked me.

"I don't like this place," I said. "Nothing about it. The people, except for that woman this morning, seem very closed and suspicious."

"What do you expect? I told you, that's how many of these little towns are."

"Not this bad . . . . Sure, they have no reason to welcome us with open arms . . . people thinking about their daughters and sisters and God knows what . . . . But damn! Not even a little frontier hospitality. Man, I've been better treated than this in mafia towns in Colombia."

Fernando chuckled. "I think it would be much better here once the people get to know you."

"Listen to you, Mister Diplomacy himself . . . . Well, hopefully they won't get the time to know us. I want to get out of here by tomorrow. Who needs this shit."

I glanced at the bottle of beer, only foam remained at the bottom. Our glasses were also empty. "Shall I get another bottle?" I asked Fernando.

"Of course, if you want."

I was about to get up and get it when we saw Jaap coming toward us. He had the look of a court herald in bermuda shorts.

"Hey, you guys," he said. "Dinner is served on the ship. If you don't hurry there will be nothing."

I met Jaap's eyes with a searching look. He reddened and shifted his eyes to Fernando. Fernando smiled in greeting and asked, "What are we having for dinner?"

"The same as usual," said Jaap. "But you must hurry."

We rose and followed Jaap. Well, I thought, it seems like Fernando didn't notice that Jaap disappeared just when it looked like trouble . . . or maybe he doesn't care. Maybe Jaap didn't realize what was going on. Maybe he just wanted to get Betti away from possible danger . . . . Maybe. Aw, forget it for now. Nothing happened. But . . .

I left my thoughts and looked around. Total darkness had settled over Alvarães. The colored light bulbs winked on, dashing the village with red, yellow, blue, and green. From the cottages overlooking the lagoon came music, the smell of cooking food, the subdued glow of living room lights, and the hum of conversation. These cheering signs depressed me further. I was reminded that Christmas was upon us.

"You know," I said to Fernando, "this is the second year in a row that I won't see my family at Christmas."

"That's difficult," said Fernando. "It must make you homesick at times, no?"

"Well, it didn't bother me so much last year . . . . I was new to South America and everything was different and exciting . . . . Christmas in Bogotá was a blast. What a party in the streets! . . . But now, what the hell are we doing in this Alvarães?"

Fernando chuckled. "Don't worry, man, we'll be in Manaus for Christmas."

Back on the boat we ate boiled fish with no seasoning, soggy white rice, and some tired old beans the cook must have scraped off the bottom of his pans. I chewed the food mechanically. Got to keep my strength up, I thought. But damn, this food is tasteless . . . . A bottle of cold beer would sure help . . . or a sparkling decanter of wine . . . . Ah, dream on.

Milene noticed that I was feeling blue and tried to draw me out of my shell with a Portuguese lesson. I appreciated her attention but I remained uncommunicative. I feel like wallowing in English for a while, I thought.

Milene turned to Nazaré and began discussing possible plans for the evening. She spoke with great enthusiasm—her enthusiasm was infectious. I perked up. I can wallow later, I thought.

I reached over and tapped Milene on the shoulder. "Are you looking for something to do tonight?" I asked her.

"Yes, of course. I can't sit around and do nothing."

"Do you want to go to the bar in town later? . . . I'll buy you a drink and we can practice *brasiliero*."

"Yes, why not? . . . Fine then, later. Right now I'm going to change my clothes. I'll come by for you when I'm ready to go." With that she arose and went upstairs.

I turned to Nazaré. "And you, do you want to go?"

"Probably," Nazaré shrugged. "I'll go where Milene goes."

"*Tudo bem!*" Great, I thought. Maybe she'll get wasted and happy and I'll have a chance at her . . . . I feel better already.

Nazaré went upstairs to get ready and stayed there. All the other passengers wanted to go to the bar as well. We loafed on the boat for an hour or so, letting the food settle. Fernando wanted to leave immediately. I put him off. Then, after a while, the other passengers grew restless.

"Are you ready to leave yet?" Fernando asked me. "Everyone else is ready to go."

"Not yet, it's still early . . . . Besides, I'm waiting for the ladies."

"The ladies?" Fernando's lips curled. "They've been gone a long time."

"Yeah."

Another ten minutes passed. Fernando paced the deck and gave me funny looks. Jaap, Betti, and Eloi were on their feet and stirring around. Fernando stopped pacing and stood in front of me. "Let's go!" he said. "Why should we wait for them? They can find us if they want later."

"Go ahead, man," I said, irritated by his tone. "You don't need me. And I'm in no rush."

Fernando shook his head. "As you like. We'll see you at the bar, then."

"Yes. I'll be leaving soon."

Eloi came by and gave me an inscrutable look. Then he shook his head and walked away without saying anything.

Fernando, Jaap, Betti, and Eloi left for the bar. I sat and tapped my right foot—waiting and waiting and waiting some more. Damn, why are they taking so long? This isn't fuckin' opening night at the opera. Unless... The ship was too quiet. I got up and walked to the foot of the ladder. They wouldn't leave without me. Or would they?

I climbed the ladder. "Milene... Nazaré..." I called. No answer. Except for the lingering aroma of perfume there was no trace of the women. "Shit! They took off without me," I muttered. The little bitches. That's not cool.

As I climbed the hill throught inky darkness on my way to the village I tried to rationalize getting stood up. Well, I thought, it's certainly not the first time something like this has happened to me... and probably not the last.... But why did they even bother to say they would come by for me? What's the point? If you're not interested—say so. Don't waste my time.... Stupid games...

My disgust ebbed away when I reached the village. A throng of people had come out of their homes and into the street. Many of these were young women. In the winking light of the colored bulbs they looked lithe and sensual. Easy laughter and bright smiles floated past me. Huh, I thought, there certainly are a lot of pretty young ladies strolling around here like they're looking for something to do.... I bet almost any one of them could give me a Portuguese lesson. Why mess around with Nazaré and Milene?...

I quickened my pace and reached the bar. The place was ablaze with light and Brazilian pop music blared from the stereo system. Wow, I thought. What a change from this afternoon.

I stepped inside. The air was filled with smoke and chattering voices. All the tables were filled with drinking patrons who looked happily blasted. Jaap, Betti, Fernando, and Eloi were clustered around the pool table.

"Eh, man," Fernando yelled to me. "Glad you came!"

"Me too. It looks like a party here."

"No, this is nothing. It's not a party until people start dancing....You want to play pool?"

"No, not really.... I'm more interested in a different kind of game tonight."

Fernando laughed. "I understand. Here." He passed me his glass of beer. "Drink up—Peruvian style!" I downed it at a gulp. "That's it. Now get a fresh one." Fernando turned away to take a shot.

I scanned the room. My eyes lit on Nazaré and Milene sitting at the bar. They were sipping wine and batting their eyelids at passing customers. Well, well, don't they look cool, I thought. I think I'll go over there and give them shit . . .

I went over and took an empty stool beside Milene. She and Nazaré had their heads together and were talking in low voices.

"Got here early, eh," I said, nudging Milene with my elbow. She turned her head.

"Ah, it's you," she said, giving me a cheery smile. "How's it going?"

"Fine . . . . But why didn't you come by for me like you said?"

"Because Nazaré was in a hurry. Here, don't worry about it." She passed me the bottle of red wine. "Drink!" Milene's face was flushed and her hair askew, her eyes danced and her lips were slightly parted. No sense spoiling her mood, I thought. I'll just let it slide . . . . But I won't forget.

"What is this?" I asked her, looking at the bottle.

"It's wine."

"I know that. Where is it from?"

"It's Brazilian wine . . . . It's very good!"

"Oh, yeah? I never tried Brazilian wine . . . . In South America only Colombian, Argentinian, and Chilean."

"Try it! Try it!" she said, laughing. "It's good for the head."

"Is it sweet?"

"Yes, very sweet. It's wonderful!"

I grimaced.

"What?"

"I don't like sweet wine."

"Try it! Try it!"

Hesitantly I took a sip, holding the wine in my mouth for a second. I wanted to spit it out. Then I swallowed. I almost gagged. This is horrible, I thought. It's like a combination of "Ripple" and "Mad Dog 20 20."

"It's wonderful, no?" asked Milene.

"How can you drink this?"

"It's delicious!" she responded, grabbing the bottle from my hand and taking a swig. She smacked her lips. "Delicious!"

She won't be saying that tomorrow, I thought. At least if she keeps on chugging like that.

Nazaré had watched us silently, a pouting expression on her face. She sure is a moody one, I thought. Maybe even a real bitch. Maybe Eloi does know something about her . . . . But I can't help myself . . . I'm like a moth that can't keep away from the flame . . .

"How are you Nazaré?" I asked, leaning across the counter to look at her.

"Fine."

"How do like the atmosphere in this bar?"

"What?"

"How do you like the bar?"

"Eh?"

"The bar! The bar! You like it?"

"It's fine," she said, drawing the words out as if with great effort. "It's hard to understand you."

"Milene has no problem."

"Milene is good people."

"What's that got to do with anything?"

For an answer Nazaré got up and wandered to the wall to look at the posters. The hell with her, I thought. She's not going to spoil my evening.

"What's her problem?" I asked Milene. "Why is she so sad?"

Milene shrugged and took another belt of wine. "She's just like that. It's her temperament."

I looked at Nazaré. She was staring at a poster, her back to me, twitching her ass in time to the music. Two Brazilian men at the nearby table leered at her and made comments. That's definitely her best side, I thought.

I turned back to Milene who was talking to a new bartender. I said something to Milene. The bartender stared at me in amazement. He must think I'm a Martian, I thought. I smiled at him.

"How are you tonight?" I asked him. He blinked and gaped at me.

Milene raised the bottle and took a tremendous drink. "Delicious!" she said. "Wonderful!" Her face and eyes were glowing. She started giving my shoulder little pets. I took another sip of wine; it was still nasty.

"Give me a bottle of beer," I said to the bartender.

He just looked at me in befuddlement. Milene giggled and repeated my words. In a moment the bottle was on the counter in front of me. I shook my head.

"Why can you understand me and he can't?" I asked Milene.

"Because I am very intelligent .... Don't you think?"

"Oh, sure .... Or maybe he's an idiot ... or maybe I'm an idiot because I expect him to understand me."

Milene giggled. The bartender was listening to us, he walked away with a scowl on his face. "Oops, he understood that," I said to Milene.

"*Tudo bem.*"

273

I filled my glass with beer and passed it to Milene. She took only a sip or two and left the rest. She's not that loaded, I thought. At least not loaded enough to start mixing drinks.

I turned to look for Nazaré. She was now sitting at the table with the two men, drinking beer. Though she laughed at their comments she still seemed miserable. One of the men pawed at her bare arm . . .

I was distracted by a straw hatted old man. He staggered from a table at the far end of the room, upsetting a few empty bottles on the way, and sat on the stool next to me. He folded his arms on the counter and lay his head on them, his face leering at me. I ignored him and talked to Milene. Soon he started chuckling. I glanced at him. He was smiling at me. I tried to look away before he could say anything to me but it was too late. He leaned over and introduced himself, blubbering in my ear as to how glad he was to welcome me to Alvarães and, he continued, "The occasion calls for a drink . . . . But, and it pains me to tell you, I don't have any money."

"You are joking," I said.

The man grinned, showing a number of missing teeth. His breath was terribly stenchy. He was bowed, grizzled, and wore filthy clothes. But what truly bothered me was his fawning manner. I don't like this guy's style, I thought. I don't even feel sorry for him.

"A drink, sir," he said.

"You come from here, certain?" I asked him.

"Yes, of course. Born and raised in Amazonas."

"Good. Then, you must have credit here, right?"

"Credit?" The man chuckled. "No one has credit here . . . . The inflation, you know. The inflation kills me. Only your money has value. Only dollars."

"Oh, that's too bad. I don't have dollars, only your kind of money." I turned to Milene, happy to swing my nose in another direction. "Who is this man?"

"Him?" She shrugged. "*É um passageiro.*"

"*Passageiro?*" . . . . Wait, I thought. He's a passenger? . . . "You mean to say that he is a vagabond? A bum?"

Milene, the proud teacher, smiled at my flash of insight. "More or less, that's it. He is a *passageiro.* He wants a free ride. A free drink."

"Should I buy him one?"

Milene wrinkled her nose. "I wouldn't."

The *passageiro* patted me on the shoulder. I turned toward him, he was still grinning. "You are American, no? . . . Americans are generous."

"Who tells you that?" Wishful thinking on his part, I thought.

"I was a sailor. You look American."

I smiled crookedly. "I'm not American.... I'm actually a Martian."

The *passageiro* laughed uproariously. "Hah, that's a good one!" He slapped me on the back. "Hah, a Martian! Hah! You don't look green."

"I was sick. The Amazon made me turn white."

"Hah! A Martian! You are fucking with me..." Then he said a rush of things, little of which I understood. Spittle dribbled from one corner of his mouth. When he laughed, frequently, he opened his trap wide and sprayed me with a fine mist. Finally I turned away from him and downed my glass of beer in two great gulps.

"Very good!" yelped the *passageiro*. "You know how to drink. You are a good Martian." He thrust his arms out and tried to embrace me. I fended him off with the crook of my arm. Milene giggled.

"Here," I said, passing the half full bottle of beer along the counter to him. "Hug this."

"Thank you. Thank you. Many thanks," he said, picking up the bottle. He took a long pull and smacked his lips. "This is good. Is the beer on Mars as good as Brazilian beer?"

"Yeah, but it's green. The color bothers earth people."

"It wouldn't bother me," he cackled. He raised his hand dramatically. "You know, you are special.... Your arrival to our humble village is special..."

"Well, thanks."

"Yes, your arrival is special.... The occasion calls for a full bottle of beer." He grinned in my face.

This fucker's too much, I thought. Sorry, pal, that's enough.

"Thanks for the warm greeting to Alvarães, my friend," I said. "Now, if you don't mind, I'm busy with this woman here. Take the bottle and leave me alone."

I turned to Milene. I heard the *passageiro* cackle. He got off the stool, almost falling on his face doing it, and wended his way to the other side of the room.

"I told you," said Milene, "a *passageiro*."

"Now I know exactly what you mean with that word."

A *samba* number suddenly blared from the music box. A far away look came to Milene's eyes. She waved her arms and swayed her torso rhythmically. "*Samba, samba, samba,*" she chanted in exaltation.

"Why don't you get up and dance?" I asked her.

"What?" she said, turning toward me, her eyes glittering like polished ebony.

I leaned against her and spoke into her ear. "You are already dancing in the chair. Why don't you get up and dance?"

"You too?"

"Yes, with you."

"You don't know how to *samba*."

"No, but that's no problem to me. You teach me."

"All right, then. Let's do it." She slipped off the stool. I glanced around the room. The ambiance was good and live. If somebody starts dancing this might really become a party, I thought.

I started to get off the stool. Then I saw Nazaré's somber face approaching us. She went straight to Milene.

"I'm leaving now," said Nazaré.

"Why?" asked Milene, sitting down.

Nazaré took her by the arm and tugged her off the chair and a few steps from my hearing range. She spoke to Milene in a low voice, an earnest expression on her face. Milene shook her head a few times and listened. Finally, a few moments later, Nazaré said loudly, "I'm leaving. . . . Are you coming with me?"

Milene hesistated. She looked at me and shook her head with a frown. I nodded toward Nazaré and waggled my finger near my head. "*Louca* (crazy)," I mouthed silently. Milene smiled.

"Well?" said Nazaré. "Decide."

"Give me a moment to think," said Milene. Nazaré stepped past Milene and headed for the door. "Wait!" Nazaré paused on the threshold, a furious look on her face. Milene walked up to me and patted my arm.

"We'll dance another time," she said. "I'm going with her."

"But why?"

Milene looked past me to Nazaré. "Another time. I'm going."

"But why is she leaving?"

Milene shrugged. "She is like that."

"Like what?"

Nazaré turned and walked outside. Milene followed her. I was disconcerted, for a long moment I gazed at the spot where they disappeared from view. Then I shook my head and tapped the counter with my fingers. Crazy bitches, I thought. What was that all about?

Before I could think things out I was joined by the *passageiro* who, of course, had returned with an empty bottle. He babbled in my ear. The only thing I understood was: "Too bad the lady left without you. But

276

don't worry, I'll keep you company."

To shake the *passageiro*, I rose and joined my companions by the pool table. I leaned against a log support pillar and watched Fernando, Jaap, Eloi, and some Brazilian play pool. Betti sat on a chair nearby, watching the game with sleepy eyes. The pool players laughed and bickered good naturedly over each shot. With Eloi there misunderstandings were quickly smoothed over. Well, at least they're having a good time, I thought. I glanced about the room. Except for one village girl, in intimate conversation with her man of the evening, Betti was the only woman in the bar. Normal for a place like this, I thought. I looked at Betti and our eyes met. To my surprise she sidled over and stood beside me.

"Why did the Brazilian women leave?" she asked me. "Did you scare them away?"

I shrugged. "I have no idea. It was a surprise to me . . . . I think Milene wanted to stay but she left because Nazaré wanted to go."

"Which is which?"

"Nazaré is the curly haired one . . . . The one with the sad sack face."

"Ah, yes. And?"

"Anyway, I was having a good time talking to Milene and then, Nazaré came up to us all hard faced and pulled her aside and gave her a lecture ... as thought she were jealous or something. Then they left with no explanation."

"Quite odd."

"Yes, I think so too." I chuckled mirthlessly. "Maybe they are secretly lovers."

"I do not get that impression."

"No? . . . Well, you're probably right, but . . . " Suddenly a light went on in my head. I looked at the table where Nazaré had sat with the two men. The men were gone. She made an arrangement, I thought. That's it . . .

"What were you saying?" Betti asked me.

"Huh, ah, nothing. Nothing . . . . They must have had something to do . . . . Excuse me, I'll be right back."

I went to the bar and bought two bottles of beer. I handed one of the bottles to Fernando. "Pass it around," I told him.

I returned to the post and took a long drink of beer. The men at the tables looked grotesque. The buzz of drunken conversation and the thick smoke now felt intolerable. I glanced at Betti. She looks bored, I thought.

"Would you like to sit at the table outside and talk?" I asked her.

"Very well."

We went outside. The night was gorgeous, clear and warm. We slouched on the bamboo chairs under a canopy of twinkling stars and flickering Christmas lights. As the minutes passed I found myself looking up at the sky more and more. Our conversation was aimless and desultory. Betti wanted to talk about how clean and advanced and educated and socially aware and humane the northern Europeans are— particularly the Dutch. I wanted to talk about life in the raw, to hear about vital experiences in her life. This would tell me what I wanted to know about Holland. What she was telling me I could get from an encyclopedia. On the other hand, I was wary of what I said to her. I found it difficult to give my honest impressions of things without offending her deeply ingrained middle class sensibilities . . . . Polite talk just isn't my forte, I thought, peeking at Betti over the rim of my glass. Oh well . . .

I drained the beer rapidly. I called for another bottle. I shifted the position of my chair and watched the street. It seemed that every inhabitant of the village was promenading by the bar on their way to the *praça.* Betti and I drew curious looks from the passerbys.

"The people here can be quite rude," commented Betti, after a man with an exceptionally lewd expression on his face strutted past.

"They're just curious," I replied. "Let's face it . . . we're not exactly a common sight here. Especially you."

"It is still rude."

"Yeah, I guess I'm more used to it than you." I chuckled. "Maybe deep down I like the attention. I don't know . . . . But you're right, it can be a pain."

I tossed down another glass of beer. Betti had stopped drinking so there was more for me. I refilled my glass and watched the people . . . . Three young women strolled by our table, giggling, eyeing us as though we were freaks. Sudden resentment flared in me. Betti's right, I thought. What is this? Are we creatures in a fucking zoo? . . . I always wondered how the animals must feel with so many nitwits gawking and making goofy faces and cooing noises at them while they were trying to eat . . . . Now I know. Well, the hell with it. Two can play this game. I'll give them some of their own medicine.

Two pretty girls approached, swinging closer to our table to get a better look. I smiled and winked at them. They averted their eyes and hurried past. "Hey, this works great," I muttered. I continued this play for several minutes. Most of the girls returned my smile and kept walking; the men remained stone faced, or glared, and kept walking. One pretty woman with a gold chain around her neck smiled and stopped. We exchanged a few words. She asked if Betti was my woman. I told her no. Then I invited her to sit down and have a beer. Still smiling, she stepped toward the chair I proffered to her, hesitated, then walked off without a word. For some reason this struck me as funny. I chuckled until Betti gave me a strange look.

"You are drinking quite a lot," she said.

"Not so much."

"You are going to become intoxicated."

"I hope so, that's the idea."

Betti's jaw tightened and she turned to watch the pool game. I surveyed the rest of the bar. A few more men had entered, but not a single woman remained. What a place, I thought. This Alvarães is beginning to look disgustingly upstanding.... At that moment a soused old man slid off his chair, bowling over the stacked bottles on the table, and fell face down onto the sand floor. Well, the women anyway...

Betti tired of watching the pool game and again told me of the wonders of Holland—the dikes, the tulips, the wooden shoes, the boats, the quaint streets of Amsterdam, and so on and so forth.... She sounds like a tour guide, I thought. Enough of this crap.

I downed another glass of beer. Betti's voice and the bar noises grew distant. My head was spinning and thinking, blah, blah, blah. I'm tired of listening to jive. Tired of being alert. Tired of thinking.... Someone look out for me a while—I'm going on automatic...

Suddenly the *passageiro* stood before me, rocking on his feet, that fawning smile on his grizzled face. Aw, why not, I thought.

"Sit down," I told him. "Relax."

The *passageiro* fell into the chair. I pushed the bottle over to him. "Finish it." He did— in one gulp. Betti made a face at my choice of company. She stopped talking about Holland. That's enough to earn him the beer, I thought. He's paid his way. He's no longer a *passageiro*, he's *the passageiro*.

"Why did you allow this horrid man to sit here?" Betti asked me.

"He's the friendliest person I've met in this town .... Except for this amazing woman we met this morning."

"I have no idea of what you are talking about," she said, wrinkling her nose and turning to face the bar.

"And never will," I murmured.

The *passageiro* slid his chair over and babbled in my ear. I understood nil.... Then it started coming in loud and clear, like a dirge, "Americans are generous. Americans are generous. I don't believe you are Martian. You are American. Americans are generous..."

I yawned in his face and answered in English: "Americans giveth, Americans taketh. Americans taketh, Americans loseth."

The *passageiro* grinned stupidly. "Please, don't speak Martian. Let's buy another beer."

"Man, will you fuck off!"

"What? Please, no Martian."

"Maybe later," I said in Portuguese. I twiddled my thumbs and gazed at the sky. The *passageiro* sucked on the empty bottle. Soon he got up and left to hit up on someone in the bar.

Little by little the men were leaving the bar. Jaap came by and led Betti away. A few minutes later Eloi and Fernando came to lead me away.

We shambled down the cobbled path in the middle of the street. Alvarães was now dark and quiet. Stray drunks staggered toward home, keeping to the shadows along the sides of the houses. Small wiry mutts nosed around in the grass for discarded scraps of food. A few young couples necked in the bushes behind the cottages on the lagoon side.

"Are there any *putas* (whores) in this place?" Fernando asked Eloi.

"I doubt it," said Eloi, in a tone that indicated he was uninterested in pursuing the subject.

"What? No *putas?*" I burst out. "That's impossible! There has to be! I've already seen three tonight!"

"Eh, man, not so loud," said Fernando. Eloi glanced at me and quickened his step.

"Eloi doesn't want to hear about *putas,*" I said. "He is a moral man with a wife waiting for him. Right, Eloi?"

"Hah!" said Eloi. "I am a poor man. I already sent most of my money home."

"Then, Eloi is a smart man," said Fernando.

"Hey, Fernando," I said, suddenly remembering, "you don't have any money for that kind of thing anyway."

"That's right.... I was just talking."

"Dreaming again."

We picked our way down the slope in pitch darkness. I stepped in a water puddle and cursed my fate to the heavens. "Life is unfair," I muttered. Fernando and Eloi tittered. We made the boat without further mishap. I stood tipsily on the deck and took stock of the situation. I felt tired, drunk, and very frustrated. I should go to sleep and hope for pleasant dreams, I thought. But wait! Maybe Milene and Nazaré are back and upstairs. They might still want to party . . . . Nah, you must be a glutton for punishment tonight. Ah, why not? Can't hurt to try.

I climbed the ladder. They weren't there. Too bad, they must still be working. Oh well . . .

I returned to the main deck, ready to give my friends an impassioned speech on the quirks of fate that had gone against me this night. But Fernando and Eloi were already asleep. The lightweights. I was left with no recourse but to fall asleep on myself.

CHAPTER X

FROLIC IN A JUNGLE RESORT

The morning dawned foggy. I rolled over and went back to sleep. When I finally got up I felt cranky and hungover. I sat on the stern and stared at the swirling mist. I wondered if the sun were ever going to make a full appearance in this foresaken lagoon. I scratched at a new rash of insect bites picked up in the night. Then I looked at the expanse of the hazy lagoon and to the jungle beyond. I spat into the murky water. This cove is probably a perfect breeding ground for mosquitos, I thought. We're sitting ducks here. No telling what kind of weird disease we could pick up here . . . or have already picked up . . . . I stared at my red-dotted arm.

The cook served breakfast very late—about mid-morning. Fernando joined me on the stern. The other passengers skipped breakfast.

"You know," said Fernando, munching a cracker, "with the captain away, the cook is really taking it easy."

"Yeah, taking advantage," I said. "But where is that damn captain anyway?"

"Probably having a good time in Tefé."

"Yeah, he's an inconsiderate sonuvabitch, isn't he?"

Fernando shrugged. "He's the captain . . . . Do you want to go to Alvarães?"

"No. All I want to do is get out of here as soon as possible."

"Come on, man, it might cheer you up. We could go to the bakery . . . "

"No. I feel dead. I don't want to do anything." I leaned back against the red oil drum. Can't afford to go, either, I thought. I spent more money last night than I should have. If I'm not a little more careful with my funds I'm gonna have problems getting back to Colombia from Manaus . . . . If we ever get to Manaus, that is.

Fernando and I stayed on the stern and talked. The sailors and the other passengers hung around the boat. About noon the captain and his bearded friend finally returned from Tefé. We went to the railing to greet them. The captain was haggard, red-eyed, and disheveled; all the symptoms of a whopping hangover. Still, he smiled at us from the speed boat and tapped his right hand on a spanking new *motobomba*. Everyone let out a cheer. The sailors hauled the shiny machine aboard and we crowded around it.

"It's Japanese," said Fernando, pointing to the manufacturer's label.

"That is goot," said Jaap. "I vouldn't trust a Brazilian engine."

Suddenly we heard an excited yip from the cook. We turned toward the kitchen and saw the captain grabbing the cook's ass. The cook cackled and leaped out of his reach. Then the captain picked up a can of water off the sink and tried to pour it down the cook's shorts. The cook howled and fended the captain off. The battle was on.

The sailors and passengers just looked at each other, astounded by these antics. The captain was laughing and carrying on like an adolescent, for the first time dropping his dignified commander's role before us.

The cook escaped to the galley and came out with a handful of used coffee grounds. The captain turned to flee and was splattered in the back with sopping grounds. The captain came back at the cook with more water. The sailors became infected with their spirit—or feared a similar attack—and enthusiastically cheered on the combatants. After a few more moments of play the captain raised his hand and halted the game. He turned and addressed the sailors, "Let's get this pump installed. We're getting out of here."

We passengers looked at each other and grinned. "Finally," muttered Eloi

The sailors went to work with tremendous energy and zeal. In short shrift the defective *motobomba* was hauled from the engine room and the new one lowered by rope to replace it. "This captain is no fool," commented Jaap. "His show got these lazies to work goot."

"Yeah," I said, "or they're as bored and anxious to leave here as we are."

The *motobomba* was quickly fastened down and hooked to the hose. It ignited with a roar and belched rhythmically. Ugly as the sound was, it was sweet music to my ears.

"Let's see if the pump is dumping the water," Fernando said to me. We hustled to the side of the boat and looked down to the water line, to see if the rubber nozzle was pissing bilge water yet. Though the *motobomba* hummed encouragingly only a few rusty drops of water dripped into the lagoon.

"It's not working," said Fernando. "What's going on?"

"Maybe it has to warm up."

"No, that doesn't make sense. It's not that kind of a machine . . . . It should work immediately."

We continued to eye the hose expectantly, then, as the seconds stretched into minutes, doubtfully. The cook barked at the sailors in the engine room. The pump was shut down. A furious discussion ensued. Soon clanking and banging sounds reached our ears.

"They must be adjusting it," said Fernando.

"Better than the first time . . . I hope."

Finally silence from the engine room. The cook bellowed to the sailors once more. The *motobomba* was switched on. The cook came to stand at the railing near us. He glowered at the rubber hose. The *motobomba* hummed and belched. Nothing from the hose. The cook turned and yelled something to the sailors. The *motobomba* belched louder. The seconds seemed interminable. The tension was oppressive. At last, a few drips of water came from the hose. Then . . . nothing!

I glanced at the cook. He stared down at the water line, his face swollen, the veins popping out on his neck. Uh, oh, I thought. The cook spat explosively into the lagoon. He raised his face toward the river. *"Filho da puta, japones* (son-of-a-bitch, Japanese)!" he shrieked. *"Filho da puta! Desgraçadas! . . . "* In other parts of the ship the same sentiment echoed and resounded in an unholy chorus. Being more reticent than the Brazilians, Fernando and I merely stamped our feet and pounded the railing with our fists.

The cook stomped to the stern. He was soon joined by the entire crew, minus the captain. They gestured violently and cursed the Japanese and the machine. *"Filho da puta, japones.* They sold us a piece of shit!" yelled the tall sailor.

"Son-of-a-bitch, Japanese?" I said to Fernando in a low voice. "More like son-of-a-bitch captain! . . . What kind of fucking idiot buys a brand new water pump without testing it first? . . . Our marvelous captain, that's who!"

"That's true, he should have checked to see if it worked before taking it. Idiot!"

"Yeah, and look at these chumps blaming the Japanese." I laughed. "It's kind of funny . . . . But of course, they have to blame someone, and who's going to blame the captain? One of the sailors?"

"That sailor would get fired in a second," said Fernando.

"For sure . . . . Huh, I'm probably lucky that this machine isn't

284

American . . . or they might make me walk the plank. I hope Eloi didn't tell anyone else that his grandfather was Japanese."

The sailors continued to wave their arms and curse. We watched them blow off steam. Fernando looked sad.

"Do you think they believe in karma?" I asked him.

Fernando shook his head and smiled sardonically. "This is how South America is," he said. "This is why we don't advance. Leaders like this fucking captain . . . "

Fernando looked so melancholy I couldn't restrain a laugh. Then Fernando laughed—a brittle, high-pitched laugh that sometimes precedes hysteria.

"Aw, what are you going to do," I said in a consoling tone. "This could happen anywhere . . . . The damn thing is Japanese."

"I would send it to hell! There was probably a forty percent import tax on it . . . . And it's shit!"

"Maybe they can repair it quickly. It sounds good. It could be a minor problem."

"Yes, they'll repair it." Fernando snorted. "Some year. *Vamos embora pronto,* hah."

"Hell with it. Nothing we can do right now . . . . You know, I had a car once, an American car, a Vega . . . . Anyway, it was total garbage. It seemed to need a new engine every six months. They finally stopped making them they were so bad . . . "

"Yeah, so what?"

"Well, even though it was garbage, it did get me around most of the time . . . . Don't worry, we'll be getting out of here. They'll get this piece of shit running."

Fernando laughed, easily now. "Fucking machines! What a thing to have your life depend on."

"Yeah, almost as bad as having to depend on certain people—like the captain."

"Yeah, where is that guy? He should be here."

"Huh, he's probably in his cabin sleeping off his drunk. He doesn't care."

The sailors separated and went to different stations. The cook went to the galley. I no longer felt angry, just disgusted. The disappointment was numbing. This is like getting novacaine and a dose of laughing gas during a root canal operation, I thought. You don't feel much pain at the time but you know it's going to hurt like hell later.

"Let's get out of here," I suggested to Fernando. "Let's go outside and get a change of air."

We went to the front of the flat. There we found little Jorge, or Jorzinho, standing barefoot on the warm metal, dangling a fishing line into the oily water. He was humming and looked perfectly content. We sat on the flat nearby and watched him.

"Look at him," I said to Fernando. "What right does he have to look so happy when everyone else is feeling so miserable? I've got an urge to belt him one . . . to wise him up."

"What?" said Fernando. "Don't be crazy. Why would you want to do that?"

"I don't. I was just joking . . . . But look at him, he doesn't care how long we stay in this backwater mosquito farm. He already has a group of friends from the village. I saw him with them yesterday. He can run and play, laugh and shout. What does he have to worry about? Nothing! . . . This is summer vacation for him. He can amuse himself watching the adults make fools of themselves."

Fernando laughed. "Yes, I used to do that. It was fun."

"Uh huh, it sure was. Man, I can remember . . . "

Fernando stood up. "Sorry to interrupt you but I'm going for a walk. Do you want to come?"

"No, I'm going to stay here and relax. This little bit of sun feels good."

"All right, then. Later." Fernando went ashore and started up the hill toward the village.

I leaned back against the wood and watched Jorge. "Come on, little fish," he said. "Come to me. Come on, little fish. I have food for you . . . "

A smile flitted to my lips. I started to feel more cheerful. I closed my eyes. The filtered rays of the sun warmed my brow . . . . Seeing him with the drop line reminded me of the many times I went fishing with my friends off the piers in San Francisco. Nothing simpler. We would walk or take a short bus ride to the Embarcadero with a hook, a line, and some lunch. Everything else was provided gratis. We could scrounge some bait off one of the old black men or Filipinos, who were as sure to be there as the sea gulls and pigeons, and drop our lines. The rest of it—the dank fog or bright sunshine, the sharp odors of salt water and fish, the squawking of the gulls and the cooing of the pigeons, the blast of fog horns, the parade of big liners and small tugs, the silent passage or rambling talk of estranged city people, all of this and more—was free for the taking, a wealth of impressions to children hungry for experience. Life around the docks . . . . Sometimes we were content to sit on the pier, basking in the sun, and haul in shiners, bullheads, and rock cod with our lines. Other times, especially when the weather was foggy and mysterious, we would climb under the deteriorating wharves and wend our way among the labyrthine pillars and support beams, staring point blank at the murky green waters of the bay. A shadowy world, with wisps of mist or slashes of sun filtering through cracks in the rotting upper planking, and not without peril. We had to keep a sharp eye for the Coast Guard patrol boats; they didn't like stupid kids playing on the rotted beams, especially when some of those kids could barely swim. Then there were the wharf rats who nested under the piers. Those rats were fearsome—big as cats from eating garbage off the liners and freighters . . . . One time my friend Ted and I were under the docks watching a teenage Filipino boy spear fish. We must have come too close to a mother rat's nest because, without warning, a huge one charged out of the shadows with teeth bared and went for Ted. Ted shouted and leaped to an adjoining beam, a daring and desperate manuever considering that he couldn't swim a stroke. The rat continued on and charged the Filipino. Almost casually he skewered her on his spear and fed the fish a hairy shish-ka-bob. On the adjoining beam Ted and I shivered from the close call. "Boy, mister," said Ted, when he recovered from his fright, "you really took care of that fuckin' rat." The Filipino laughed, showing a gold tooth. "But weren't you scared?" I asked. "It might've bit you and had rabies." The Filipino laughed harder. "Listen, kid, in Manila the rats are twice as big and ten times meaner than that thing was." That was one day we got out of there before the Coast Guard boat ran us off. But what a feeling of exhiliration we carried with us for the rest of the day . . .

"What the . . . " A sudden whoop from Jorzinho shattered my reverie.

"I have something! I have something!" he yelped.

"Don't just scream," I said, jumping up and going to him. "Pull it in! Pull it in!

Jorzinho took in his line hand-over-hand and, when the fish cleared the water, yanked it aboard. A small speckled fish flopped about on the warm metal. Jorzinho grasped the fish and carefully extricated the hook from its gaping mouth.

"Look! Look!" he screamed, thrusting the fish in my face. "Look at this fish!"

"Tudo bem!"

Jorzinho did a war dance, holding the fish aloft and grinning from ear to ear. "I'm going to show my father. My father will like this."

He sprinted away, still holding the fish aloft. I watched him run, smiling, his exuberance completely banishing my earlier glumness. The little man has the right spirit, I thought. Here I am—young myself—acting like a dour old fart waiting for the undertaker to cart me away . . . . Enough of this. I laughed. Hell, I'm supposed to be on vacation.

I looked around me with renewed interest. Toward the mouth of the lagoon, where the sun poked rays through a gap in the overcast, I saw something on the shimmering water. The glare made my eyes smart and I had to turn my head and blink for a moment. When I looked back I saw a man in a dugout canoe rowing toward our boat. He came on steadily and slid past our stern and out of my sight.

I moved to the other side of the flat to see him. He maneuvered the canoe into the thin space between the tug and the supply shed. I started toward the tug. While the man secured his craft to the dock, Jaap mosied over to check him out. I climbed over the railing and onto the tug. Jaap was talking and gesturing to the man in the canoe. He looked at Jaap with a puzzled expression on his face. I moved closer. Jaap kept jabbing his finger toward the bottom of the canoe. The man, a straw hat perched rakishly atop his thick kinky hair, smiled patiently as he tried to divine Jaap's words. I leaned over the railing and saw that the canoe was filled from stem to stern with Brazil nuts. My eyes bulged and my mouth popped open. Look at that, I thought. One of my favorite treats . . .

"I buy those. I buy those. I buy those, please," said Jaap in Spanish, pointing to the nuts.

The man only smiled.

"How much? How much?" persisted Jaap.

"Give me your hat," said the man, his smile widening.

"What?" said Jaap, looking at me. "Vat he say?"

"He said to give him you hat."

"Why? Does he want to trade?"

"You got me . . . . Give it to him and find out."

Jaap placed his hat in the man's callused hand. The man stooped down and filled it to the brim with the brown nuts. He returned the hat to Jaap.

Jaap's face hardened. "How much?"

The man dismissed Jaap's question with a careless wave of the hand. "It is a present," he said in a soft voice. "For free. Welcome to *Brasil.*"

"Thank you! Thank you!" exclaimed Jaap, an incredulous grin on his face. He turned to me. "For free. He give me them for free. It is incredible!"

"Not so incredible, man . . . . Just generous."

Jaap walked off to show Betti, mumbling happily to himself. Well, I thought, I can recognize a good thing when I see it.

"Can I have some of those?" I asked the man.

He smiled agreeably.

"Wait a moment, please. I'll be right back."

I went to fetch my seldom used Panama hat. When I returned and handed it to him he laughingly filled it to overflowing with the precious nuts.

"Thank you," I said, receiving the hat.

"For nothing."

"Where I come from these are very expensive."

"Yes?" He chuckled. "Where I come from there are more than anyone can eat."

"What do you call these?"

"*Castanhas.* Ca-sta-hnas."

"Almost exactly like Spanish . . . . Say, can I invite you for a beer?"

"No, I'm very busy right now. Thank you."

"Well, thank you very much for everything."

We shook hands and the man disappeared into the supply shed. He was certainly a pleasant person, I thought. Things are looking up around here . . . . Then, as though in agreement, the heavens popped a brilliant shaft of light through the haze and bathed the ship in warmth.

Feeling almost lighthearted now, I strolled over to the stern. The cook bustled from the galley to his carving board next to the sink, bellowing at anything that moved. He seemed in an unususaly cheerful mood. Jorzinho had thrown aside his fishing line and was paddling about in the water off the stern like a smooth faced otter . . . . Huh, I thought, he doesn't look the least bit concerned about attacks from piranhas or virulent microbes . . . . The water sure looks tempting. Maybe I'll go swimming after lunch.

The sailors continued working on the *motobomba* without discernable success. Finally they came out of the engine room shaking their heads.

"What's up?" I asked Eloi.

"They need another part . . . . Someone will have to go to Tefé for it."

"Then, at least one more day and night here?"

Eloi nodded grimly.

For lunch we ate boiled fish and boiled rice. No more beans. I supplemented this meager fare with Brazil nuts and papaya. Not a bad lunch, I thought. But the water tastes funny today. I took another sip and swirled it around in my mouth . . . . It tastes brackish.

"Hey, Fernando," I said. "How does the water taste to you?"

"Let's see." He took a long gulp of water. "It tastes a little strange."

"Yeah, I think so, too."

"It must be this lagoon water."

"That . . . or the cook isn't boiling the water like he was before . . . . You're right, he's been getting lazy."

"Yes, that could be it," said Fernando, a serious look on his face. "That is not a very good idea if he's not boiling the water."

"It's a terrible idea."

Fernando smiled. "It's a good thing our systems are used to this Amazon water . . . right?"

"Maybe yours . . . . I'm not so sure about mine."

"You'll be fine, man. I just hope Jaap and Betti will be all right."

"Yeah, me too. As for me, I think I'll only drink beer from now on . . . or mineral water."

"That could get expensive."

"I know . . . . Damn, I should have brought iodine tablets to make the water potable. The nurse told me to . . . . I don't want a bunch of *animalitos* swimming around in my system."

"Don't worry, you'll be all right."

"Maybe. I already drank two glasses of this water . . . . The fish is salty." I took another sip of water.

"What are you doing?" Fernando asked.

"Well," I said, taking another sip, "better sick than dead of thirst. Man, things are really getting loose around here."

"You'll be fine, man."

Milene showed up just as we were mopping the final crumbs from our plates. She had gone to Alvarães and come back in high spirits. She accepted a plate of food from the cook and sat down beside me.

"Hi, stranger, what's happening?" I asked her. "You look happy."

"Good things! If we stay the night . . . there is a party in town."

"Can we go?"

"I believe so."

"Will there be *samba* music?"

"Of course! This is *Brasil*."

"Fine, you owe me a dance."

"Of course, with pleasure . . . " Milene got up and took her food upstairs. All right, I thought. A party with real *samba* music . . . and these beautiful, sultry *brasileiras* becoming high, wild, and passionate.

If the fog goes away, there will be a full moon tonight. And isn't that just made to order for our cast of adventures. I licked my lips in anticipation, imagining my ideal scenario . . .

"I think that Milene is a bullshitter," said Fernando, interrupting my fantasy.

"What? Why do you say that?"

"Well, look what happened last night . . . . She's always talking about parties."

"That's true. I don't call going to a bar and drinking, a party — especially when she leaves with no explanation."

"Yeah, I wouldn't take anything she says too seriously."

"You're probably right. I don't need any mysterious women right now . . . . I'll just relax and take it cool."

We lolled around the boat for a spell. The weather grew increasingly humid. I had almost dozed off when Eloi and Fernando became restless and decided to go to Alvarães.

"Do you want to come with us?" Fernando asked me.

"No, I don't think so."

"Why?"

"I'm resting up for the party."

"Resting for the party?" Fernando shook his head and laughed. "You are crazy."

"No, not crazy . . . . Maybe, after what happened last night, stupid is a better word."

Fernando laughed again. "Rest well. You can use my hammock."

They left and I found myself alone in the hold. I climbed into Fernando's hammock, intending to take a serious nap, but a steady clamor of shouts kept me awake. I muttered and stirred around in the hammock. The noise continued. Finally I got up and sauntered out to the flat to see what all the commotion was about. I had no sooner rounded a corner of the lumber stack when I was hit in the face by a salvo of water. As I spluttered and rubbed water from my stinging eyes I heard a mocking voice from the lagoon. It was Jorzinho.

"You little chump!" I yelled at him in English.

"Come into the water and get me," he laughed. "Come in. It's great!"

As he talked his head bobbed up and down and he swallowed water. He choked and shut his mouth.

I laughed and said, "That's what you deserve."

Jorzinho was nonplussed for a moment. Then he raised his arm and fired another salvo at me. I stepped back and the water splashed harmlessly on the deck.

"I'm going now," I said. "But I'm going to come back and get revenge on you."

Jorzinho giggled and ducked underwater. The next instant I heard a war whoop and a small body plummeted from the top of the lumber stack into the lagoon, just missing Jorzinho as he resurfaced. When the other boy came up for air, Jorzinho, shrieking wildly, went for his throat. Must be one of his friends from the village, I thought.

While the boys tussled I entered the tug and stripped off my shirt and shoes. By the time I came out the two boys were stationed atop the lumber, surveying the landscape with the air of potentates. I chuckled at the thought.

"Come up," Jorzinho called to me. "It's great! We're going to jump. It's great!"

"You're getting redundant, kid," I answered in English.

"What?"

"Forget it. I'm coming up now."

I climbed up the lumber stack to join them. On reaching the top I was surprised to find Jaap and Betti holed up in the niche where the beer and soda cases were stored. At first they didn't see me. They were conversing quietly, their heads almost touching, basking in the flickering rays of the semi-obscured sun like two great lizards.

"You found a comfortable spot, eh," I said.

"Not so bad," said Jaap, looking up.

Jorzinho's friend eyed us curiously and came over to listen to us. He stood with hands on hips and faced us, a yearning expression on his face. Finally he tried to talk to Jaap but soon gave up in frustration—in reponse to the boy's questions, Jaap's only answer was a dumb smile. The boy's face clouded with disappointment. Jaap pointedly ignored him. Go away, he seemed to say.

"These lousy foreigner don't know anything," he said, turning to Jorzinho.

"That depends on the foreigner," I said, stepping toward the boy with a smile.

The boy stepped back and looked me over from head to toe. "This one knows a little," said Jorzinho. "He can speak." Encouraged, the boy directed his questions to me. I answered them as best I could, with whatever came to mind. The boys were soon roaring with laughter—whether at the cleverness of my responses or the ridiculousness of my accent and Portuguese, I really can't say. Probably the latter. These guys look entertained, I thought. It's true—some people are a lot easier to please than others

As I gabbed with the boys, Jaap and Betti stared at me in amazement. I winked at them. They must think I know more Portuguese than I ever let on. And in a way I do. All that I previously learned from the radio broadcasts, the book, and the tapes is beginning to come together. My ears are more attuned to the sounds. I'm beginning to think in Portuguese when I speak it . . .

Jorzinho grew bored and started hopping about like a grasshopper. "Enough talk," he yelled. "Are you going to jump? Are you going to jump?"

"Possibly," I said, moving to the edge of the stack and calculating the distance to the water. "Give me a moment." It was a good fifteen to twenty feet . . . . Small circular oil slicks on the surface made the water look even less palatable. I retreated a step from the edge and turned to look at the boys.

"Are you going?" Jorzinho eyed me accusingly.

"Don't bother me," I said, stepping forward to the edge again. "I'm thinking." For a moment I hesitated, wavering on the brink, my toes gripping the edge of the wood. From behind I heard Jorzinho snort with derision. I turned to give him a dirty look. He gave a short shriek and shot past me and leaped into space. He hit the water, in an awkward splay-legged crash that made me wince, and vanished, ever widening ripples marking his entry point. A dead silence gripped the lagoon. The other boy and I waited anxiously for Jorzinho to surface. The boy and I exchanged looks. Has the little idiot hurt himself? I thought.

Without further thought I dove headfirst. I struck the water with great impact—pain shot through me. I must be out of practice, I thought, heading for the surface. I reached air with my head ringing and red flashes passing before my eyes. After a few seconds my vision cleared and I saw Jorzinho. He was treading water a few feet to the left of me, exaggeratedly applauding my dive.

"Are you all right?" I asked him, swimming closer.

"Of course! And you?"

"I'm fine." I was within arm's length. "But you're not." I grabbed him by the shoulders and dunked him good. Jorzinho resurfaced laughing, unabashed, and spouted water in my face. Furiously I windmilled spray at him, overwhelming him with superior fire power. Jorzinho beat a strategic retreat. From a distance he barked insults at me.

"Come on, boy," I called. "I'm waiting for you."

Jorzinho laughed and swam farther away. I better keep an eye on him, I thought. He's planning something right now . . . . The kid's a royal pain-in-the-ass! But I kind of like his spunk and quickness of mind. He'll probably go far—if somebody doesn't kill him first . . .

The village boy jumped in and swam after Jorzinho. They kept going and disappeared around the tug's stern. I was alone. I took easy stokes and felt the water. The surface was warm, but when I dog-paddled, the water against my feet was almost chilly. I had never felt two such distinct layers in such a short distance. I dove down and swam in the cold layer. Aquatic grass flicked my face. I returned to the warm surface and rolled onto my back. I stared up at the hazy sky and floated. Cotton candy clouds wafted over me, shielding my eyes from the sharp tropical sun. Birds called in the bush. Splashing sounds came from another part of the lagoon. I submerged my ears and all became tranquil. I imagined myself in suspended animation. I felt weightless and relaxed—drifting in time and space. A tremendous sense of well-being flowed through me. No place to go, no clock to obey, no commitment pending — just here and now. All of me . . .

Shock and panic surged through me as water flooded my eyes and mouth. I gasped and came upright, rubbing my stinging eyes, hearing mocking laughter nearby. I spluttered and cursed and thrashed the water. Jorzinho cackled, his voice receding. This time a genuine rage took hold of me. When my sight cleared I struck out after him with determined strokes. The little shit's gonna get it good this time, I thought.

With his headstart he beat me to the stern of the tug and disappeared around the corner. I kept after him, his mocking laughter ringing in my ears, anger fueling my strokes. Then I rounded the stern and pulled up in surprise, thoughts of Jorzinho instantly banished. For there, leaping off the stern of the tug and landing in the lagoon with resounding plops, were Nazaré and La Gordita. They resurfaced, giggling, and splashed about in an ungainly manner. Though La Gordita especially seemed on the verge of sinking, the two of them laughed and capered and enjoyed themselves thoroughly . . . . The cook, soup ladle in hand, grinning like a satyr and making lewd comments, was watching from the stern. I swam to the boat and held on with one hand. The cook winked at me and nodded his head toward the women, all the while chattering at Nazaré. Nazaré swam closer to the boat and flung water at the cook.

"Come in," she yelled at him in a hoarse voice. "Come in and receive your punishment . . . . Are you afraid?"

"You really want me to come in?"

"You won't come in. You are afraid to get wet."

The cook placed the ladle on the sink. Then he turned, cackled lasciviously, and made a wild man leap straight for Nazaré. He crashed in the water within reach of her and tried to pull her under. Nazaré, giggling shrilly, slithered from his initial grab and thrashed at the water in an attempt to escape. The cook clawed at the air and, by luck, snagged the back of her white shorts. He dragged her underwater and the surface foamed and bubbled with their struggle.

After a few moments they surfaced, spouting water and weak from laughter. This looks like great fun, I thought, clambering aboard the tug to get a better view. I chuckled freely as the cook and Nazaré circled each other and bantered insults. Finally they closed and grappled. The cook sought Nazaré's legs, she giggled and hurled water in his face. After a brief but spirited tussle they separated; the cook nursing a small scratch on his shoulder, Nazaré pulling her shorts back in place. The cook climbed aboard and entered the galley, still cackling.

Nazaré swam up to me. "Help me up," she said. I reached down and pulled her aboard. The touch of her damp flushed skin excited me. We stood on the stern and faced each other. She was panting, her breasts heaving against the lacy white top that clung to her skin, the jutting nipples straining to burst through the thin fabric. Her red lips were parted and her face alive and avid. I tingled all over and my knees went weak. I wanted to hug her and kiss those red lips, instead I sat down on the edge of the stern and dangled my legs over the side. I looked up at her. Nazare, beads of moisture dripping from her curly hair, stood and shook herself for a moment to get rid of the excess water. Her bare thigh rubbed against my shoulder. Our eyes met and she smiled at me. She sat down beside me, touching me. Casually she placed the back of her hand on my upper thigh. I looked at her. She smiled again and rubbed against me like a cat . . . . The blood rushed to my face and I felt an erection pushing against my shorts. Nazaré stared right at my groin and laughed.

"Are you going to swim?" she asked me.

"I already have," I said, leaning against her. "I'd prefer to do something else . . . . Are you going back in?"

"Yes!" She punctuated her reply by diving into the lagoon and moving to attack the cook who had slipped back into the water. The cook chattered happily and yelled for me to jump in and attack her. I stood up and watched, waiting for a good opportunity to pull a surprise. My chance came when Nazaré, busy splashing oily water at the cook, turned her back to me. I slipped overboard and made for her like a hunting shark. I hit her underwater, with my head and shoulders, in the tender part of the thighs and, thrusting upward, catapulted her into the air, eliciting a surprised squeal. I came to the surface and waited. All right, I thought. Now what will she do? Is she angry? . . .

The cook swam off to the side and loudly applauded my manuever. Nazaré eyed me blankly for a moment, then she came at me with a delighted grin. I let her close and we engaged in a wrestling match. We thrashed the water and whirled in circles, each of us trying to gain an advantageous hold. The cook shouted encouragement to me. Finally we grappled and became enmeshed in each other's arms. Soon our holds were more like caresses. Nazaré went pliant and yielding in my arms. My hands roamed freely over her body. We sank under the surface. Nazaré took my hand and slid it under the top of her blouse and pressed it against her breast. Her other hand dug into my shoulder. She'll go for it, I thought. Whatever. We only need a place.

We rose to the surface. Suddenly I felt a choking pressure on my windpipe and I was yanked backwards out of Nazaré's arms and dunked. No! Not now! Fuck! . . . A mocking cackle echoed in my ears. Water rushed in through my nose and filtered down my throat. It tasted slimy. I kicked to the surface ready for blood.

I saw Jorzinho holding onto the tug with one hand, his head thrown back, laughing insanely. I looked for Nazaré. She had moved away from me and was straightening her top. She avoided my eyes and looked somewhat embarrassed. The moment of abandoned madness was gone. Damn! The little shit ruined the chemistry, I thought. I'll get him this time . . .

I went after Jorzinho with cold fury. He tried to escape me by going on the tug, but I cornered him near the bathroom and carried him to the stern. I raised him bodily and held him over my head. He kicked and screamed. I looked at his father, the cook. He gave me a thumbs down sign and laughed. I threw Jorzinho as far out into the lagoon as I could. He flew through the air and landed on his back with a sickening splat. That'll teach the little twerp, I thought.

Jorzinho surfaced laughing and swam back to the tug.

"Do it again," he begged me. "Do it again. I like it. I like . . . . Please, one more time."

"Go away," I said. "I don't want to look at you."

"Please, do it one more time." He started to climb aboard. I threw my arms up in the air and dove into the water. He loved flying through the air, I thought. What's the use?

We played in the lagoon a while longer but I had lost my spirit. Nazaré remained at a discreet distance from me and swam with La Gordita. The cook went to the galley to start dinner. Jorzinho was the only person willing to play with me. After I got over my anger I amused him by tossing him out of the water up into the air. He was tireless. He soon wore me out.

I went back to the stern and sat there with my chin in my hands, moping over my lost opportunity with Nazaré. Then the sky clouded completely and it began to rain. Nazaré got out of the water and went to fix her hair. La Gordita followed. Jorzinho begged me to return to the water. I flipped him off and went to change my clothes. That's the first time I saw her genuinely happy, I thought . . .

I returned to the stern and stared at the lagoon. Just as the sun was about to sink behind the hills the clouds dispersed and we were left with the waning sunlight. That figures, I thought. No sun all day until we're about to lose it.

Fernando returned from Alvarães and joined me on the stern. We discussed our activities during the afternoon.

"Yeah," I said, "you missed an opportunity at La Gordita. She was swimming around here most of the afternoon. Too bad."

"Really?" Fernando shook his head. "Well, we had a good time shooting pool . . . . But it would have been nice to take a shot at La Gordita instead."

"Maybe tomorrow."

The dinner hour arrived and, to our surprise, Nazaré came to eat with us on the stern. She was still in good humor.

"Did you see Milene in the town?" she asked Fernando.

"No, but I saw her at lunch."

"I saw her then," said Nazaré. "Later she went back to town for some reason and she hasn't returned yet."

"Did she tell you anything about a party tonight?" I asked her.

"Yes, that's why I want to talk to her . . . to see what's happening with that."

"Are you that anxious to go?" I asked.

"Of course, what do you think? I am *brasileira*." Nazaré smiled. "I want to dance and be happy." She shimmied her upper body and clicked out the sound, "Chi, chi, chi . . . chi chi . . . chi, chi, chi," between closed teeth.

I laughed, delighted. Her brown eyes swam dreamily. She looked very attractive at that moment. "Will you teach me how to dance the *samba?*" I asked her.

"Yes!" She nodded emphatically. "If you want."

"Nothing would please me more." I gloated to myself. Lovely . . . . Maybe she'll lose control like she started to when we were wrestling. Maybe I will, too. That's what I'm looking for . . .

"Where are you from?" Fernando asked Nazaré.

"I am from Manaus." Nazaré's expression saddened. "From one of the poorer favelas . . . . I travel frequently to get away from there."

A city girl, eh, I thought. From a slum. That figures. She has that hard exterior . . . . Yet, from time to time, she shows a crack in that mask. She seems like a very lonely person . . . . Maybe she perceives herself as tragic. I gazed into her eyes. For a moment I thought I saw something of my own personality there and it scared me.

"Was it very difficult growing up in Manaus?" Fernando asked.

"Yes, where I grew up. There was, and is, much violence and drugs and poverty . . . . But other parts of the city are marvelous. You will see. There is nothing like it in the rest of Brazil."

"I can understand what you're talking about," I said. "The city I come from is something like that."

Nazaré fixed me with a hard stare. "Don't tell me that! How can you understand? You are American. You can have whatever you want."

"What? . . . That is shit! Where do you read these fairy tales?"

"I know what I see from the gringos who come to Manaus. They throw their money around and think they can buy whoever they want." Nazaré stood up. "That's what they think!" She turned and stalked off.

Fernando and I looked at each other and shook our heads. "What a freak!" I said. "I'd like to take her to the South Bronx and leave her there overnight."

"Yes, what a temperament she has—like a match . . . . But what is this South Bronx?"

"It's a neighborhood in New York that's like a combat zone. It's, uh, forget it. What's the difference?"

After dinner I stretched out under Fernando's hammock and read while we waited for Milene to show up and tell us where the party was. Fernando paced the deck nearby, anxious to leave. The time passed. I read three chapters. Fernando stopped pacing and stood before me.

"Why don't we leave. This Milene is too unpredictable. She seems to have trouble distinguishing fact from fiction . . . . I don't believe in her party."

"Yeah, you're probably right. But why don't we give her a few more minutes?"

"All right, a few more minutes."

I read another chapter. Then I set the book down and looked at Fernando. "Shall we go?"

"Yeah, forget the *puta!* Let's go already."

Eloi was laying in his hammock staring up at the ceiling. "Do you want to go with us to town?" I asked him.

He shook his head. "No, not tonight. I'm not in the mood."

Fernando and I left the boat and carefully picked our way up the hill. A full moon, veiled by luminescent clouds, cast eerie shadows along the trail. An animal scurried past, rustling the bushes, startling us. We paused for a moment. I thought I saw a crouched figure laying in wait for us on the side of the trail, but it was only a moss covered boulder.

We reached the summit and ran into Milene and La Gordita at the tumbled gate. By the light of the moon and the Christmas bulbs we saw Milene's face in stark relief. She was flushed, bright eyed, and grinning dopily.

"Going to the party already?" she asked in a slurred voice.

"Already?" I said. "You already been drinking woman. Where have you been?"

"I already went to the party."

"That's cool. The party already started and you forgot about us."

She gave us a cynical laugh. "Lies, lies . . . . The party is later . . . or, possibly, there is no party. But no matter, I have friends here."

"That's what you keep saying . . . "

Milene snickered, stepped past us, and began sliding down the trail. "Try the other bar," she called back over her shoulder. "There could be something there."

"She's crazy," commented Fernando. "Let's see what we can find on our own."

As we walked along the brightly illuminated street I wondered what Milene meant by the "other bar." We had seen no other bar in town. Well, we'll see, I thought.

The street was jammed with villagers enjoying the evening air. Lively talk and hearty laughter surrounded us. Most of the people seemed in a festive mood. I swiveled my head and drank it all in.

"You notice anything different about the people tonight?" I asked Fernando.

"Yes, they seem livelier . . . . Why not, it's Saturday night."

"Yeah, but besides that, they don't seem to be staring at us as much."

Fernando glanced around. "That's true. Now that you mention it."

"The novelty is wearing off . . . . Now we'll have to earn attention with our own merits or idiocies."

We reached the familiar bar with the bumper pool table. "Do you want to go in for a quick beer?" I asked.

"If you want, it's all right . . . . But I wouldn't mind going on to the plaza to check out the *coquetas* (promenading girls) first."

"All right."

As we continued on I saw two men ahead of us sharing a bottle in front of a well-lit entranceway. We detoured to investigate the bright light. "Maybe this is the other bar Milene mentioned," I said.

"Yes," said one of the drinking men, eyeing us as we approached, "it's a shame to think that Brazil has fallen to the point that the inflation is so high that an honest working man finds it almost impossible to buy a good stiff drink from time to time."

"You are right," said his friend. "It's a sad commentary on the state of our country when a man can't even afford to lessen the pain of living."

"I blame it on the international banks," said the first man, passing his friend an almost empty bottle.

"Good evening," I said to them, nodding my head and stepping past them to the door without making eye contact. I can sympathize with them, I thought. But I can't afford any *passageiros* tonight. My money is evaporating like spilled beer in this tropic heat. Fernando, trailing me, caught the brunt of their reproachful eyes.

We pushed throught swinging doors and entered an old fashioned tavern. It featured a long, polished-wood counter with bolted down swivel stools running along its length. Bottles of liquor were rowed before an immense mirror behind the counter. Shaded red lights were set in niches along the wall and a large neon *Cerveja Antarctica* sign hung above the mirror. Hugging the wall opposite the bar counter were assorted round-seated red stools and a line of small tables extending to the back of the room where the space broadened into a tiled dance floor with a jukebox. Beside the jukebox, in the center of the rear wall, was a narrow doorway with a purple, gilt lined curtain and a multi-colored hand painted sign above it reading "Discoteque." On the wall opposite the bar were a series of team and action soccer posters

We went to take a look at the Discoteque. We were met at the door by a polite, bearded young man who prevented us from entering. He informed us that there would be a dance party later and that we were welcome for a small cover charge.

We returned to the bar, took stools, and ordered beers. Fernando treated me. We tried to talk to the bartender but he was disinclined to make an effort to understand us beyond taking our order. He pointed to a lone man sitting a few stools away from me and said, "You can talk to him. He is Colombian. He speaks Spanish."

The Colombian had been talking to the bartender in Portuguese, but after this off-hand introduction he turned to us with a grin and spoke to us with the Colombian accent I was so familiar with . . . . I was overjoyed. He used all the slang expressions I had fallen into the habit of using in Colombia. True, I constantly spoke Spanish with Fernando, but it wasn't the same. With him, I eliminated much of the slang I knew and tried to speak straight Spanish. I realized all of this with a shock. Has Colombia really taken such roots in me? Do I actually miss the place?

As we talked we finished our beers. I ordered another round.

"What do you think of Brazil?" I asked the Colombian.

"I like Brazil very much. It is my home now. There are very good people here and they have accepted me."

"How long have you been here?"

"Two years . . . living here. I passed through on business before that."

"How was it when you first arrived here to live?"

The man chuckled and gave me a bemused look. "In what sense?"

"Oh, did you have trouble with the language?"

"Yes, when I first came to this town it was very difficult. I couldn't understand anyone well and they could barely understand me. I was very lonely and wished to return to Colombia . . . . But, I remained, and I'm content with my decision. Although I still enjoy visiting Leticia, when I go there for business."

"Well, sir, it's a pleasure to talk to you."

"Why do you say that?"

"Because you seem like an honest man . . . . Most of the Colombians I've previously spoken to, tell me that Portuguese would present no problem for them if they ever went to Brazil."

The man laughed. "That's because they don't know any better . . . . And probably never will go to Brazil. I used to think like that myself."

We waded through another round of beers. The man asked me

questions about the United States. Fernando felt neglected and wandered off to look at the soccer posters. As we talked, a number of young women, teenage girls, and a few matronly older women filtered into the bar and congregated in the rear near the Discoteque. Except for the older women, who looked to be chaperones, the average age of the group was somewhere around fourteen.

"Ah, look at all the hot blooded young fillies entering the corral," said the Colombian. "Aren't they lovely?"

"Yes. But what about the old ones?"

"Those are the mother hens watching the brood. Don't they look properly severe? . . . But believe me, a few of them have probably come here to do more than watch . . . "

"Why are most of them so young, no more than girls?"

"Young?" The Colombian looked startled. "They aren't so young. They are just about the right age." His face took on a far away expression. "The coming of age. The age of innocence and sweetness and romance. Isn't their laughter and eagerness beautiful?"

"Yes, it is . . . but in my country they would be considered jail bait. You can get in big trouble for playing around with girls this young."

The man laughed. "Really, what a thing! Of course, you could get in big trouble here, too—especially if some father or brother doesn't like what's going on . . . . But listen, you have little choice in the matter, most of the women in this town over sixteen are already married and have children. These ones here will soon be taken."

"Yeah, why not, that used to be the custom in my country not too many years back . . . . One of my grandmothers was married at fourteen. But still . . . "

He clapped me on the back. "Don't worry about it, friend, let nature take its course . . . . Youth is fleeting and should be taken advantage of to the maximum. Besides, here on the edge of the jungle, you can't truly call them girls. They are given much responsibility when they are very young and they mature rapidly. Here you catch them in full flower . . . . Of course, there is much to be said for the mature woman, but sometimes their cynicism is depressing and saps my vitality. The young woman, unskilled as she might be, gives me a feeling of strength and newness."

I just looked at the man. He was about forty. He soon turned from me to talk to a friend. I picked up my beer and joined Fernando. He was studying a team photo of the Argentine National Selection, World Cup Champions of 1978.

"Knowing what rivals Brazil and Argentina are in soccer, I'm surprised to see this picture here," I commented to Fernando.

"Why? We South Americans are always happy when a South American team wins, no matter the country."

At this moment Milene and Nazaré stepped through the swinging doors and paused on the threshold. Milene spied us and came over, all smiles. "How intelligent you are," she said to me. "How did you know the party was in this bar?"

"I didn't know." I smiled back. "I just followed the drunks."

Milene guffawed. She weaved ever so slightly and her face was alight and frisky. She seemed to have drunk exactly the right amount of whatever it was they were drinking. Nazaré, on the other hand, looked unsteady. She stared at the poster of the Argentine Selection for a long moment. When she finally recognized the team she began to scowl.

"What's going on, Nazaré?" I asked. "How are you?"

She swiped at the poster with the back of her hand and replied, "This picture is shit! Champions of the World? . . . *Brasil* should be Champions of the World, not Argentina! *Brasil* didn't lose a single game in the competition of the World Cup. Argentina lost to Italy. *Brasil* was the better team! We didn't deserve to lose!" She was almost screaming now. Then her eyes lit on Fernando and she fixed him with a stare. "You! You Peruvians are to blame! *Brasil* didn't win because the Peruvian team sold out and let Argentina beat them by, 6-0."

For a moment Fernando was taken aback by her vehemence. "There is no proof that they sold out. I don't think that they did . . . . Argentina played very well and they were playing at home with the fans behind them. Maybe the Peruvian team was intimidated. I don't know . . . . They might have been attacked by the crowd if they had played better."

"Shit!" snapped Nazaré. "The Peruvians sold out! They wanted another Spanish speaking country to win . . . . It's certain! Even the Peruvian goalie was a nationalized *argentino*. They sold out, the fucks!"

Fernando was reddening with anger. Nazaré balled up her fist and looked ready to strike him. The five drinking men at the bar turned to watch. Once again Fernando and I were the center of hostile looks.

"Listen, Nazaré," I said in a soothing tone. "Why don't you leave him alone. He had nothing to do with the game. He's not a player. It's not that important to him . . . . And Argentina did play inspired against Peru."

"Shit! Don't stick your nose in this discussion! What do you know? You are a gringo!"

I flamed with anger. This bitch is asking for it, I thought. I never

303

wanted to hit a woman so bad in my life .... My mind snapped cold and clear.

"Let's forget where I come from for a moment. Let's forget about Argentina and Peru .... For your information, I follow soccer. I saw many of the last World Cup games on a big screen at a sports arena with many Brazilians in the audience. I saw Brazil's great championship team of 1970 bomb Italy. This 1978 team was a shadow of that ... "

"The Peruvians sold out!"

"They tied three games with low scores. They were conservative and boring in their style ... "

"The Peruvians sold out!"

"They barely qualified for the second round. They had a chance to beat Argentina *mano a mano* .... They tied ... "

"The Peruvians sold out!"

"You are right, Nazaré, maybe Brazil didn't deserve to lose .... But they didn't deserve to win, either. They didn't play Brazilian soccer!"

"The Peruvians sold out!"

The listening men at the bar gravely nodded their heads. One of them raised his beer glass and toasted me. "The gringo has a good point," he said. "The Peruvians did sell out. But our coach was an idiot! Because of him we were in a bad position."

"Yes," said one of the men, "even Pelé said that."

Nazaré heard the commentary. Her face was bloated and purple with rage. She trembled and spluttered wordlessly. Milene took her by the arm and literally dragged her to the Discoteque. "Enjoy the party," called Milene from the door. "We'll see you later."

"Yeah, get her away from here," I said to Fernando. "She can't handle her liquor. That's one of her problems."

"What are some of the others?"

"She's probably on the ... on the ... " How do you say rag in Spanish, I wondered. "On her menstrual cycle."

"Ah, yes. That could be a problem."

"I wanted to tell you in English, man. It sounds better. We have an expression .... I wish you knew more. English is a great language for insulting people."

Fernando laughed. "You teach me. I'll be sure to learn more .... But that still doesn't explain to me why she did that. Of course, soccer is a very emotional thing here, especially the World Cup, but that was over a year ago." Fernando shook his head in perplexion. "I haven't done anything bad to her."

"Forget it. She's a freak . . . . I'm just glad that these guys at the bar are reasonable soccer fans or we might have been attacked. Come on, I'll buy you a beer."

We took seats next to the Colombian man. "Well done," he said, shaking my hand. "Though half of what you said was in Spanish, you got your point across in Portuguese. It wasn't bad . . . . Of course, she's a typical woman. She knows nothing about soccer."

"Well, she knows something," I said. "I just didn't like her jumping on my friend for no reason. Not to mention me. She could have got us in trouble . . . . Bring us two beers," I said to the barman.

He brought them over in a moment and placed them before us. "On the house," he said with a smile.

"Are you going to the party?" I asked the Colombian.

"What party?"

"Over there," I said, pointing to the back of the room.

"Oh, the Discoteque . . . . No, my wife and children are waiting on me for dinner. Not tonight."

"I see." So much for his speech about young women, I thought. Or maybe he's out of money . . .

The Colombian downed the rest of his beer and stood up. "Take care. Good luck on the rest of your journey." He disappeared through the door.

With the Colombian gone I became pensive. I stared into my beer glass and drew water circles on the polished counter.

"What are you thinking about?" Fernando asked.

"Oh, that our little incident over there has probably ruined any chance I might have had at Nazaré . . . . Huh, it's hard to believe that just this afternoon I was getting along with her pretty well."

"Forget about her, man. She is crazy. She's nothing but problems . . . . You don't need that. Anyway, she's a *puta.*"

"Well, maybe you're right, but . . . Huh, the Peruvians sold themselves. She's a fine one to talk. I suppose that some forms of selling yourself are more acceptable than others . . . . *Viva Brasil!*"

"What are you talking about?"

"Nothing. I'm just babbling to myself."

As we talked, more and more girls streamed into the bar and milled around near the entrance to the Discoteque. They wore a rainbow of bright, vividly colored dresses and pants suits, with red, black, and canary yellow predominant. The girls exuded energy and vibrancy, reminding me of racehorses waiting for the starting bell. Not a single one paused at the long bar for a drink.

"What do you think these girls drink?" I asked Fernando. "They sure have plenty of energy."

"Sodas."

"Kool-Aide spiked with coca leaves?"

"No. That's a Peruvian specialty." Fernando laughed. "They say this *Guaraná* soda has some exotic tropical formula. In its powdered form it's supposed to give vigor and stimulate the sexual appetite."

"That sounds like what they used to claim for Coca Cola when it really had cocaine in it .... Now they claim that all the sugar and caffeine is refreshing."

"*Guaraná* has much sugar, too."

"For sure. But I don't think these girls need any artificial stimulants to get going anyway."

The bearded man came out of the Discoteque and raised the curtain. He allowed most of the girls to enter without paying. He charged a handful of young men. Must be a private birthday party or something, I thought.

Soon we heard the sound system start up, sputter scratchily, blare for a moment, and fall silent.

"This place must be jinxed," said Fernando. "More mechanical difficulties. And their stereo sounds like trash."

"Yeah, I'd rather see a native pound on a bongo drum than deal with this constant mechanical failure .... Their system does sound bad. Do you still want to go in? I don't care one way or the other."

"Of course! Let's go and dance and see what the *brasileiras* have to offer. At the very least we can drink some more beer. The night is young .... And maybe the stereo will sound better inside the Discoteque."

"All right." We moved to the curtained entrance. Before paying the cover charge we peeked inside. The room was dark and cavernous, the only illumination provided by a pair of strobe lights that cast purplish shadows on the dance floor and activated the silvery threads of numerous black light posters with jungle themes. Small rectangular tables were flush against the walls to provide maximum space for dancing. A crowd of about twenty people was on hand, most of them teenaged girls and boys, with a smattering of pre-adolescents. For the moment the chaperones remained outside near the jukebox. Nazaré and Milene were nowhere in sight.

"*Tudo bem?*" inquired the bearded man, with open palm.

"What do you think, Fernando? It looks like we'll be the senior citizens in this group."

"Let's go in. I want to dance tonight."

We paid the cover and went inside. We took a table on the left side of the room and ordered a beer from a tentative teenage boy. The price of the beer was five *cruzeiros* higher in the Discoteque than in the bar.

"What a difference a curtain makes," I commented.

"Thiefs," said Fernando.

While someone tinkered with the defective sound system most of the girls roamed about the room and gossiped. They pawed at the hardwood floor and quivered with anticipation, anxious for the music that would send them into motion. There were a few false starts. Then, without fanfare, the scratchy speakers blared sound and, after a moment of hesitation, while everyone waited for someone else to begin dancing, the entire group was on its feet and gyrating about the floor with frenetic movements. Because of the lack of males, many of the girls danced with each other or with their own shadows silhouetted against the wall.

I sat and watched, glued to my chair, stunned. The music was "Staying Alive," pure unadulterated "Disco" from the "Saturday Night Fever" long play. These Brazilians, living in the heart of the Amazon, were trying to imitate the moves of John Travolta . . . . Man, I thought, what is this? Where is the *samba* or one of the other traditional Brazilian rhythms? Where is this rich Brazilian culture that I read about and am so avid to experience? Where am I? Am I hallucinating? . . . Is this Alvarães on the edge of the jungle? Cows cropping grass on the main thoroughfare and the "Bee Gees" on the record player . . . . *Ordem é Progresso.* One small step for man, one giant leap for American record sales and Japanese electronic products. Leaping into the space age without any intermediate steps . . . . No wonder everyone is so damned confused. Well, at least I am . . . . But these girls don't look confused . . .

Their eyes glazed with ecstacy, though their movements were somewhat jerky as they sought to catch the proper rhythm, the *brasileiras* were having a fine time. One Disco number succeeded another. "Boy," I muttered, "in the small towns in Colombia they usually play their own music—*cumbias, vallenatos, bambucos,* whatever . . . not this much American music."

"What?" asked Fernando, leaning across the table to hear over the music. "What did you say?"

"Nothing. Just babbling to myself again."

"Why don't you get out there and *boogie?* This is your music."

"My music?" I snorted. "I don't like Disco that much."

307

"What do you like, then?"

"I like Jazz and Rock and Blues and . . . lots of stuff. I'd like to hear some Brazilian music right now."

"Don't worry about it. This music is great for dancing . . . . Come on, let's go *boogie*."

"You go *boogie*, man. Set the example; I'll watch you."

"All right." Fernando got up and walked over to one of the girls who was dancing with her shadow. In seconds he was whirling around her as though he were a courting peacock. I chuckled. He caught my eye and gave me a mocking grin. He motioned for me to get up. I smiled and gave him the finger.

I saw Nazaré and Milene enter the room through a back entrance. They took a table on the opposite side of the dance floor and ordered a tall bottle of beer. I watched them for a while. They put their heads together and talked, not once getting up to dance. They're maintaining a low profile, I thought. Maybe they feel as self-conscious as I do among so many kiddie corps people . . . . And I know they saw us, but they don't want to show it . . .

After the "Saturday Night Fever" album finished they finally put on a *samba* number. The dancers yelped with glee and flooded the floor. They looked much more rhythmic and natural than they did dancing to the Disco music. They chanted along with the song. It was obvious that this was the music that was imprinted on their souls from infancy. I watched mesmerized as the girls shook, swayed, bounced, and whirled, their faces lifted in exaltation . . . . Some of these girls are incredibly pretty, I thought. Such exotic features—they're a racial amalgamation of Europeans, African blacks, Orientals, and native Indians. You can't pigeon hole them into a classification. They are melding into a handsome "new race."

Milene glanced at me from across the room and I caught her eye. What the hell, I thought, as the *samba* number ended. Why not?.

The disc jockey put on some hybrid samba-pop-disco music. I got up and made my way to their table. Milene saw me approaching and regarded me with a cool smile. Nazaré eyed me with blank indifference. She was now in control of herself.

"How are you two doing?" I asked with a bland smile.

"Tudo bem," replied Milene. Nazaré looked at the dancers.

"Which one of you two is going to teach me to *samba* — like you promised."

"This isn't really *samba*," said Milene. "It's Brazilian pop."

"That's all right. It's close enough."

"Not right now," said Milene, "we're talking. Maybe later."

"Am I bothering you?"

"Yes. Come back later."

"Fine, I just want to say one thing . . . . Do me a favor, don't make me any more promises, and I promise not to bother you two . . . . If you want to play games with me, I can play games with you. But life is too short to waste time bullshitting . . . "

Nazaré looked at me with a startled expression on her face. Hit close to home, eh, I thought.

"I'll show you how to dance the *samba* if you show me how to dance to American music," said Nazaré.

"Fine. It would be a pleasure." I offered my hand.

Nazaré turned from it with disdain. "Later," she said. "We'll see how I feel. Right now I feel tired."

She bent and lit a cigarette. I stood and waited for her to turn in my direction again. She blew smoke toward me.

"I haven't seen you dance yet," I said. "I'm beginning to think you were born tired."

Nazaré blanched and began talking to Milene in rapid Portuguese so that I couldn't understand. I laughed. "Your game is weak," I said. "I quit."

I turned on my heel and went to my table. I downed the rest of my beer at a gulp. I'm just going after her because of my ego, I thought. Enough is enough. There's nothing to be gained from this. The only way she'll have me is if I give her money—and I'm not prepared to do that. So . . .

I got up and danced with the young Brazilian girls. Their energy and enthusiasm was a refreshing counterbalance to the negative thoughts rushing through my head. They flung themselves into the music, body and soul. I flung myself after them. I pirouetted about the dance floor, trying to lose myself in the music, smiling and clapping my hands. The D.J. put "Staying Alive" on again, loud and scratchy. I stayed on the floor and danced. Then a girl, must have been all of twelve years old, approached me and asked, "You are American, certain?"

"Well, actually I'm a Mar . . . Yes, I am American."

"That's great!" She grinned. "Teach me to dance Travolta."

I almost collapsed from laughter. "What's wrong?"

"Nothing. It's just that I don't like . . . *Tudo bem!* I'll show you how to dance Travolta." I went into my act. I must not have been overly impressive because no one left the dance floor to let me do my bit solo. By the end of the song I felt winded. Too much inactivity aboard the boat, I thought.

I staggered through a few more numbers before returning to the table, sweat soaked and panting. Fernando joined me. He wasn't having any luck picking up on a girl but he enjoyed the dancing. I ordered a tall beer for us to split. I looked across the room. Milene and Nazaré were gone. Whatever, I thought. I lifted my glass and drained the beer. The rush went to my head. I poured another glass. Fernando sipped his. We were quiet.

The Disco music started to hammer at my head. It was repetitive and terribly squeaky from the bad speakers. My thoughts were in a turmoil. I tossed down my beer in a gulp. I felt an overpowering urge to get out and move around in open air.

"I'm going outside and walk around," I said to Fernando. "Do you want to come with me?"

"No, not really. I want to finish my beer and relax. I danced too much."

"All right, man. I'll see you later."

"Are you coming back here?"

"I'm not sure . . . . But don't wait for me."

"Fine. Don't get lost."

As I was walking out the door a gorgeous young woman asked me to dance. We danced. During the song — it was a long one — she never looked at me. She was in a world of her own. Without a word I turned and left before the song finished. She was left alone in the middle of the dance floor with a startled look on her face. I was surprised she noticed. That's definitely enough, I thought. It's just not my night . . .

I left the bar and walked, inhaling the balmy air. The street had thinned out, only a few stragglers moved about. My mind was empty. The moon, incredibly huge and bright in the equatorial night, was my beacon. For a crazy abandoned moment I was tempted to bay at it like a solitary coyote and rid myself of all the repressed longings threatening to explode within me. I gazed up at it and opened my mouth. Nothing came out. "Too many complexes," I murmured. "Just walk."

I headed toward the lagoon. A young black woman came out of a house just ahead of me and walked a parallel course. With my longer strides I soon drew abreast of her. She looked at me. Her countenance was open and sympathetic. I tried to talk to her. Unfortunately she didn't know how to take me. I watched with trepidation as her expression changed from surprise, to amazement, to puzzlement, and finally, to fear.

"Don't be afraid," I said. "I won't do anything."

310

Her expression reverted to puzzlement.

"I'm sorry. Good-bye." I strode quickly away, headed for the boat. Time for bed, I thought. Then I chuckled, struck by a sudden image. I'm behaving just like some of those burn-outs on Powell and Market street back in the City . . . . Now what's the difference between them and me? A narrow thread. It could happen to anyone.

I walked unerringly down the hill. On regaining the boat I fell into a deep and dreamless sleep.

CHAPTER XI

THE CAPTAIN'S PARTY

The morning dawned brilliantly. As I sat on the stern and drank my coffee, I had to cover my eyes to protect them from the strong glare reflecting off the placid lagoon. I felt calm and relaxed, lethargic but without ill-effects from the drinking of the night before. Two of the sailors were working on the *motobomba* and seemed to have matters in hand. The new part had arrived at some pre-dawn hour. The tall sailor left the engine room and came to the stern for coffee.

"What do you say?" I asked him. "Can we leave today?"

"Yes. Today for certain. The pump will work."

"Let's see."

Around mid-morning they hooked it up and gave it a try. Hallelujah! The *motobomba* kicked over and pumped brackish water into the lagoon.

"Perserverance wins out over inertia," said Fernando, patting me on the shoulder. "We can finally get out of here."

"Well, the pump works . . . . But where's the captain? I haven't seen him since yesterday morning."

"He might be up in his cabin hungover."

"Or in town drinking with his friends."

"Say, that's right! Today is Sunday. He might not want to work. Maybe we won't leave until . . . "

"I don't care anymore. It's a beautiful day. We can have a good time playing in the lagoon."

Fernando chuckled. "You're beginning to think like a South American."

"I don't want an ulcer, man. When we leave is out of our control right now. I'm going to enjoy what's available."

I put on my shorts, grabbed a towel, and climbed to the top of the lumber stack. I spread my towel and stretched out under the bright melting sunshine. Birds called in the bush. Straw hatted fishermen trawled the lagoon in their dugout canoes. Whenever the sun became too hot for my skin, I would simply dive into the water and explore the cool soundless bottom. Plants, little fish, and who knows what else tickled my flanks as I rolled and shimmied in the refreshing water.

After a while Jorzinho climbed the lumber to join me. He stopped a few paces from me and regarded me owlishly.

"What do you want?" I asked him.

"Are you still angry with me?"

"I should be . . . . But no, I'm not." I chuckled. "Maybe you did me a favor yesterday."

"Why?"

"Forget it. Your not old enough to understand . . . . I don't think." I can't hold a grudge against him anyway, I thought. He's like an impish little brother. He's brought me out of more than one bad mood on this trip.

"Let's do some more dives," he suggested.

"All right. You go first." We took turns making twisting leaps from the top of the stack, applauding or snorting derisively after each effort by the other. Imagination and the amount of bizarre contortion put into each jump, not smoothness, was the criteria for gaining applause . . . . I suppose we were a little fortunate that no one was injured. But it was fun.

After a dozen or more leaps, my head began to throb from some nasty landings. It was time for a break. I rolled onto my back and leisurely kicked across the lagoon to the marshy shore opposite the boat dock. Jorzinho yelled at me to return. I ignored him. I left the water and started to explore the fringes of the bush, but the ground was slimy against my feet and bristly scrub clawed at my ankles. I need shoes and pants for this, I thought.

I quickly returned to the water. Fernando stuck his head out of the tug and called me in for lunch. I reached the boat and climbed over the railing, feeling agreeably tired.

Lunch, or brunch, (there had been no breakfast save for coffee) was the same monotonous fare as the day before. Boiled fish and plain white rice.

"Eating is becoming like a chore," I confided to Fernando. "This tasteless stuff doesn't give me any pleasure. I'm only eating it to keep up my strength."

"Well, remember, whatever you don't want, I'll take . . . . But I understand you. For what we paid, and for this stupid delay, they should give us something better."

For dessert we filled up on Brazil nuts. After eating, all the passengers climbed into their hammocks for a nap. The cloudless day was taking its toll on everyone. I tried to nap but I was too restless.

I left the tug and strolled around the perimeter of the cargo flat. I was just about to return to the tug when a glint of metal from a nook formed by two stacks of lumber caught my eye. I reached into the crevice and came out with an orange. Further groping netted me two tins of sardines, marmalade, a piece of stale bread, and more fruit. Ah hah! I thought. So this is Jaap's secret cache of food. He's been holding out on us . . . . I should raid it to teach him a lesson. He hasn't been sharing like almost everyone else . . . . Nah, that'll only make him more paranoid. We don't need the extra food.

I restashed the food in the nook, keeping only an orange to quench my thirst. I settled down on the front of the flat and kicked up little waves with my bare feet. I wondered what had become of Milene and Nazaré. They haven't made an appearance all day—not even for meals. They must have found a good party after they left the Discoteque . . . or maybe the captain had them working overtime.

One of Jorzinho's friends from the village came by and chatted with me for a while. But with the sun beating on my bare back, I soon excused myself and returned to the cover of the hold.

The passengers had abandoned their hammocks and were swimming in the water off the stern. Before I could join them one of the sailors came forward and beckoned to me. He was taking long sips from a bottle of red wine.

"A gift from the captain," he said, passing me the bottle. I accepted the bottle without enthusiasm. It was the same rotgut Milene had let me taste in the bar Friday night. I studied the label for a moment. It showed a charging black bull with banderillas stuck in its back. It should have a skull and cross-bones, I thought. But what the hell, it is Sunday. I raised the bottle to my lips and took a deep draught.

"That's it, man!" The sailor beamed his approval. "Take another. It's Sunday, let's party!"

"*Tudo bem*! Why not?" I took another hit and returned the bottle to the sailor. "Sunday is as good a reason to party as any."

The sailor smiled and took a drink. "Do you like the wine?"

"Well, my grandfather always told me that red wine is good for the blood . . . . Of course, he never mentioned the liver. But he lived to be 84 . . ."

The sailor laughed and passed me the bottle. "Take another drink and tell me if you like it."

I took a long drink. The wine rushed to my head. "It does the job.

Tudo bem."

The sailor chuckled. "You speak more than a little Portuguese, eh."

"Very little. I believe it's more Spanish."

"Spanish is very similar." He nodded sagely. "Truthfully, it's Portuguese badly spoken."

I giggled.

"Why do you laugh?"

"Because that's what some Colombians have told me—but in reverse."

We talked for about five minutes, passing the bottle back and forth. It was the first time I had spoken with one of the sailors at any length. Before they had always been too busy or too taciturn. The wine loosened this man's tongue. He struck me as a good, earnest person.

"You Brazilians like to party, eh," I said.

"I like to . . . but not always." His face turned serious for a moment. "Most of us have to work very hard just to have enough to eat. A bottle of wine once in a while is special for me . . . . You have to be someone like the captain to be able to party a lot."

"Yeah, or be a bum."

We shared a few more swallows, emptying the bottle, and went our separate ways.

My head buzzing, I went to the stern and joined Jaap and Betti. Fernando, Nazaré, Jorzinho, La Gordita, and the cook were splashing around in the lagoon. "Come in the water," Jorzinho called to me. "Come in and make me fly."

"Later," I answered. I turned to Jaap and Betti. "Why aren't you two in the water?"

"Not in that water!" said Betti, wrinkling her nose. "It is dirty! And I have read that the Amazon water is dangerous to swim in."

"Yeah, I read that, too . . . . But the Brazilians don't seem worried about it. Maybe this lagoon is all right."

Betti shrugged. "How 'bout you, Jaap?" I asked.

"I want to get one of those canoes," he said, pointing to the fishermen on the other side of the lagoon. "It vould be fun to go boating . . . and I could take Betti."

"That's an idea," I said, watching the fishermen trawl the lagoon. The fishermen paddled rapidly to gain a coast, dropped the paddle, stood up in the canoe, and cast their nets with a graceful swirling motion. When the canoe coasted to a stop, they yanked the net out of the water and sized up their catch. The entire process took seconds. Doesn't look too hard, I thought. But it must take practice to balance themselves so easily.

I sat on the stern and watched the swimmers play. Soon I was joined by Milene. Her eyes were puffy and bloodshot and every movement she made seemed to hurt her. She was somber and subdued.

I gave her a sympathetic smile. "How was the party last night?"

"Party?" Her forehead wrinkled. "Ah, yes, it was nothing special. It wasn't really a party. After we left the Discoteque we just went to the house of a friend of mine and drank some more. It was a long night."

"I believe you. You look like you have a bad hangover."

"That's not all I have," she snapped. "I'm angry with the captain."

"Oh yeah, why?"

"Because I want to get out of here and on to Manaus . . . . The *motobomba* is fixed. We're not leaving yet because the captain has relatives here and he wants to party with them even more. He is very selfish!"

I shrugged. "What can I say, I don't know him that well. Except that he never tells us anything, he doesn't seem like such a bad guy . . . "

"I know him! I know him well! He is a bad man! A very bad man! He's a selfish . . . "

"Milene!" Nazaré climbed onto the stern, dripping water, and grabbed a quarter-full bottle of wine that was on the sink. "Milene, have a drink."

Milene turned the wine down with curled lip. Nazaré shrugged and chugged the rest of the wine. She ignored me. This early in the afternoon she already looked thoroughly ripped, but no happier than usual. She tossed the empty bottle into the lagoon and began gabbing with Milene.

"See you later," I said. I dove off the stern and into the lagoon. I want no part of her head trips today, I thought.

I splashed around with Jorzinho and watched with amusement as Fernando unsuccessfully tried to score with La Gordita. After a while he gave up and went to the stern to talk to Jaap and Betti. A short time later they called me out of the water. I climbed onto the tug to see what they wanted.

"Look there," said Jaap, pointing across the lagoon to the marshy shore. The fishermen had gone for an excursion in the bush and had left one of their canoes beached in the muck. "Now we haf a chance to go boating."

"Oh yeah? Did you already ask them if it was all right to take the canoe?"

"No, we don't want to take it. We just want to borrow it. Since you speak the most Portuguese, we decided you should be the one to go ask."

"Nice of you to decide that for me . . . . Maybe I don't want to. What's wrong with you guys? You're not crippled."

"Come on. Don't you want to go boating? If complications arise you are the one who can best explain to the Brazilians."

"Sure, I'd like to go boating, but not that bad. These complications you mentioned . . . I'm not that anxious to get another knife or machete stuck in my face. I'm no John Wayne, man."

"You are, ah . . . how do you say . . . exaggerating. Come on."

"There are plenty of little boats and canoes tied up around the dock here. Why don't you ask someone in the supply shed if you can rent one?"

"Vat? And pay for it? No way!"

I shrugged my shoulders.

"Then you won't do it?" Jaap stared at me reproachfully. My temper flared.

"You want the canoe so bad — go get it yourself!"

Jaap's face reddened. "You don't think I vill?"

"I could care less . . . . You might, if you want it. I'm not going to do it for you."

Jaap finally realized I was serious. But he wanted that canoe. He leaned on the railing, wrung his hands, and gazed across the lagoon with intense concentration, as though sheer will power could bring the canoe to him. He turned and glanced at Betti. She smiled and patted his shoulder. Jaap straddled the railing. "I go."

"Go for it. Good luck." I gave him the thumbs up sign.

Jaap slipped into the water. He swam slowly, pausing indecisively several times, but finally made it across to the canoe. Once there he moved quickly. He seized the canoe and fumbled around with it, trying to drag it into the shallows. The sticky mud made his feet slip and sucked at the canoe. Then, as though materializing out of thin air, two Brazilians stepped out of the covering bush and yelled at Jaap. Jaap, already knee deep in the lagoon, let go of the canoe and frantically waved his arms. The two men, both carrying machetes as they had been cutting wood, moved forward to accost Jaap.

"Oh, do something," said Betti, grabbing by arm. "Jaap could be in trouble."

"Aw, shit!" I dove into the lagoon and started for the opposite shore, keeping my eyes on the men as I went. Jaap was still waving his arms and explaining to the men. They put their machetes in their leather sheaths and listened. Finally I saw one of the men smile and he motioned for Jaap to take the canoe. Jaap shook their hands and took possession of the craft.

"Well, what do you know," I murmured, dog-paddling in the middle of the lagoon. "He did it."

Jaap lay down in the canoe and hand paddled toward the tug. I waited for him in the middle of the lagoon. As Jaap drew close he grinned triumphantly, proud captain of his boat. "Yah! I did it! Yah! I told you!"

"Good job," I said. "Don't you feel good now that you did it all by yourself."

He paddled faster, making slow progress. "Do you want me to tow you?" I asked, swimming easily beside the canoe.

"No, I can handle it. I know you. You just want to get your hands on the boat. But I got it. It's mine!"

I laughed. "You can have it. You earned it."

I swam to the tug and climbed aboard. When Jaap arrived, Fernando and Betti congratulated him. Jorzinho, chattering away, opened a utility chest and brought out a pair of plastic paddles. He tossed them to Jaap. With our help, Betti stepped daintily down from the tug and into Jaap's arms in the canoe. She tousled his hair and whispered terms of endearment in Dutch. Then they settled down and shoved off.

They had gone about twenty yards from the tug, when a speed boat roared from its mooring at the other dock and raced crazily across the lagoon, swerving at the last possible instant to avoid the canoe and creating a wave that almost capsized poor Jaap and Betti.

"Those fucking idiots!" I said. Jaap waved his fist. The occupants of the speed boat were the captain and, presumably, his relatives; four men in all. For the next ten minutes or so they skittered about the lagoon in break-neck fashion, passing a bottle of wine around and laughing like lunatics as they played chicken with various canoes. Damn jerks! I thought. They deserve to have an accident . . . . I just hope that fool captain doesn't kill himself. We need someone to pilot our boat.

Finally their outboard motor killed and they couldn't get it restarted. They coasted it back to the dock.

All of this whetted my appetite to go boating. I watched impatiently as Jaap and Betti paddled aimlessly for what seemed hours. Then, as they were finally making their way back to the tug, Betti grew arm weary from paddling and put her oar down. Jaap continued paddling. The canoe spun in slow circles without the counterbalance of another paddler. The canoe went dead in the water. Jaap put his oar down and said something to Betti. She flushed and answered back. Jaap tried paddling by himself. This was difficult. With no one to align the prow the canoe inched toward the tug at a haphazard snail's pace. What is this crap? I thought.

I dove into the lagoon and towed them to the tug.

"Are you done with the canoe?" I asked Jaap.

"Yah! Take it!" He was red in the face and glared at Betti as he spoke.

As the couple left the canoe and climbed onto the tug they began arguing in Dutch. I was just happy to get a hold of the canoe. In my eagerness to climb aboard I capsized the damn thing. I resurfaced, blowing water out of my nose and choking it out of my throat. Chagrined, I righted the canoe and hoisted myself aboard, carefully. This time I succeeded. I grabbed a paddle and began stroking as fast as I could, alternating sides. I was a fair distance away when I heard a yelp from the tug. Turning, I saw Fernando at the railing, frantically waving at me to come back and pick him up.

"Swim," I yelled, pointing to the water. "My arms hurt."

"What?"

I mimicked a diver. Then I winked and grinned devilishly.

"What an asshole!" he yelped.

"For sure!"

He dove in and quickly made it to the canoe. I helped him aboard and handed him a paddle. "It was easier for you to swim than for me to paddle, man."

"No problem."

We spent the next few minutes in a ludicrous attempt to synchronize our paddling. We kept drifting from one side to the other, never achieving even the semblance of a straight line. Finally we settled on a manageable system—while one of us paddled the other used his oar as a rudder. This enabled us to move, more or less, where we wanted. We were ready. First we circuited the lagoon. Then we headed for an extreme edge of the lagoon where vegetation from the bush trailed into the water.

"There may be a stream over there," said Fernando. "We can paddle into the jungle if there is."

"That sounds like a good idea. Let's find out."

After pushing aside a thin curtain of overgrown foliage, we did find a creek running into the lagoon — a very narrow creek. We halted the canoe.

"Shall we explore it?" I asked.

"Of course, let's go."

We paddled forward. The creek was choked with enormous water lillies and other such green flotsam. Huge gnarled trees with algae-crusted trunks loomed over us and blocked out the sun. The dank odor of decaying vegetation pervaded the air. Water bugs skittered out of our path. A green water snake dove for cover.

The farther in we penetrated, the narrower grew the stream and the dimmer the light. It was almost spooky. It was definitely claustrophobic. The water became even more brackish and stagnant. Death was everywhere — a death from which sprang riotous life. The vegetation brushed our faces. I yearned for space and sunlight. Still, we pushed on, until finally, the canoe barely moving, I jammed my paddle into the water and felt it sink into marshy ground. When I tugged the paddle free there was a strange sucking noise, as though some giant living creature were smacking its lips. A chill ran through me.

"Let's turn back," I said to Fernando. "We're going to run aground like this."

Fernando stared at the surrounding jungle, mesmerized by it. "Let's go on a bit more."

"I don't think that's a good idea. My paddle is hitting soil. I have a bad feeling about this place."

"All right." Fernando nodded his head. "Maybe you're right. There could be quicksand."

We turned about with great difficulty. The lillies had twined about the boat and had to be forcibly ripped away. Once started we ploughed through the clinging lillies and plants. I paddled with a strength bordering on desperation. When we broke into open water and the sun shone in our faces, I felt tremendous relief. I don't want to go back there again, I thought.

We headed for the opposite end of the lagoon, toward the inlet that led to the Amazon. Suddenly we were halted by a shout from the tug. It was Nazaré, sitting on the lower deck railing. She flailed her arms and screamed at us to come and pick her up.

"What do you say?" I asked Fernando. "Shall we get her? She's been nothing but a pain-in-the-ass lately."

"I don't care. If you want . . . . Who knows, it might be fun to take her for a ride and dump her somewhere."

"That's an idea," I laughed.

We cruised toward the tug, slowing our speed the more Nazaré yelled at us to hurry up. Then La Gordita came to the railing and Fernando paddled faster. We came alongside the tug. Both Nazaré and

La Gordita climbed down the railing and got into the canoe. For a moment the prow sank dangerously; the waterline rushed up and sloshed into the canoe. I grabbed Nazaré and pulled her to the back. The canoe bobbed uneasily on the surface before reaching a tentative equilibrium. "Try to be more careful," I said to Nazaré. "You almost sank us."

"What do I care?" Her eyes were drunkenly bright. She pointed to the other boat dock and said in a loud preemptory voice, "Take us to my friends over there! Or abandon the canoe!"

Fernando and I looked at each other for a moment. Then we burst into laughter. Nazaré stamped her foot and fumed.

"Right away, my princess," I said. "Calm down."

Nazaré sat down and spoke to La Gordita in such fast and harsh sounding Portuguese we couldn't understand her. Fernando and I retaliated by speaking in fast and slangy Spanish. Nazaré's face seethed. We ignored her order and headed for the center of the lagoon.

"If she wants a lift somewhere she had better learn to ask in a nicer way," said Fernando. I saw him gazing hungrily at La Gordita.

"Where do you want to go?" I asked him.

"Let's take them to the shore and see if we can convince them to go into the jungle with us."

"I don't know . . . I think that would be a waste of time. But it's an interesting idea." I glanced at Nazaré's smooth thighs.

"Why do you say it would be a waste of time?"

"Because you know who is very bad humoured and can't seem to enjoy herself doing anything . . . . She wouldn't go for it, I'm sure. And I think La Gordita will do what Nazaré tells her to do."

"She's a hell cat, that one, a bitch. She would probably enjoy a good fight."

"Nah, she's not worth the trouble."

Nazaré stood up in the canoe and screamed, "Take us to dock! Now! Take us! Where are you going? Take us now!" She rocked the canoe by shaking her hips. "I'll sink this canoe! Take us now! . . ." Water sloshed into the canoe. Her rough, high-pitched voice rasped on me like sandpaper.

"Shut up!" I bellowed. "Swim if you want to go there. You don't order me to do anything!"

The effect was magical. Nazaré looked at me as though I had slapped her. She quietly subsided into her seat. La Gordita bit her lip and stared straight ahead. "That's telling her," said Fernando.

We advanced steadily, staying to the center of the lagoon. Soon the other dock came into view, about fifty yards astern. The captain and a small group of men were pounding wine in the shade of the storage shed. A portable radio blared *samba*. They seemed to be enjoying themselves.

"Looks like a real party over there," I said to Fernando. "Shall we try to join them?"

"Of course! Why not?"

"All right."

I pointed the prow of the canoe toward the dock. At that moment the men caught sight of us and let out a yell. Most of them got up and shouted, "Bring the girls! Bring the girls!"

Nazaré reacted as though she had been touched by an electric cattle prod. She leaped to her feet, almost tipping the canoe over, and screamed, "Take us! Take us now! Take us now you son-of-a-bitch!"

"I'm the captain of this boat," I said. "Remember that! You don't give me orders. You can ask."

"You take us now or . . . I'll . . . I'll jump."

"Tudo bem."

Nazaré turned from me and yelled to the men on the dock. "I'm coming! I'm coming." Her fine ass leered in my face. I couldn't resist. I reached over and pinched one of her inviting buns. She let out a squawk of surprise and flew into the water.

When she surfaced she called for La Gordita to follow her. La Gordita remained in her seat, looking uncertainly toward the boat dock. The drunken men bellowed at Nazaré to hurry. "Come!" urged Nazaré. "Come! They are having a good party. *Tudo bem!"*

Still uncertain, La Gordita half rose, then Fernando grabbed her by the seat of her cut-offs and hurled her into the lagoon. We watched as La Gordita followed Nazaré, hesitating all the way.

"Masters of the boat again," said Fernando. "What a bitch that Nazaré is . . . . Good-bye."

"Yeah, but it's not going to be as interesting without them here. Just a lot quieter."

"Shall we join the party anyway?"

"I don't know." Some of the men on the dock were staring at us, warning us away with their eyes. "Nah, I don't think we'd be too welcome over there."

We sat and watched as the two women swam easily over to the dock. Each of them latched onto a support pillar and waited for the men to come and help them onto the dock. The captain was the first to arrive, but instead of giving Nazaré his hand he passed her a full bottle of wine. Nazaré accepted the bottle with one hand, while holding onto the pillar with the other, and chugged half the bottle. The men on the dock whooped and applauded. Man, I thought, she is hard-core.

The captain grinned approvingly and helped her onto the dock. The men rubbed their hands together and licked their lips. I shook my head. They're probably thinking of pulling a train on her, I thought. Who knows? Maybe it's already arranged. Bile surged up into my throat. I swallowed thickly.

"Well, let's move on," said Fernando. "Too bad we can't join the party . . . it looks like pure craziness."

"You take the boat if you want," I said, seeing Nazaré disappear into the storage shed. "I've had enough of this for today."

"Do you want a ride to the boat?"

"No, I'll swim." Without another word I dove into the water. I swam back to the tug with furious strokes. No sooner had I climbed aboard than I spotted Betti pacing the deck, with a decidedly ugly scowl on her pretty face. She walked right up to me.

"What's the matter with you?" I asked.

"Nothing! Just nothing!" Her face took on a pouting expression. She half turned and stared morosely across the lagoon to the marshy shore. I shrugged my shoulders and started to walk away. "Oh!" She turned to me with an appealing look. "I'm upset because Jaap went into the jungle to gather fruit with some Brazilian men."

"So? Why are you upset about that?"

"Because he left without telling me. He probably did not want to take me . . . . I am furious with him!"

"I still don't see the problem. So what if he left without telling you?" I winked at her. "Now's your chance to do something you want without him."

"Oh? . . . For example?" Betti stepped toward me. I backed away, surprised. This ain't for real, I thought. She just wants to make Jaap jealous . . .

"What do you think I should do?"

"Whatever you want. That's for you to decide."

I turned and strode off. I took a glance behind me and saw her gazing after me with a puzzled look on her face. I bet she's wondering what I meant by that crack, I thought. Nothing! I meant just exactly what I said. It's time to grow up, baby.

I picked up my Portuguese handbook and sat down on the bench by the fold down table. For a time I stared blankly at Portuguese verb conjugations, too preoccupied to concentrate. My thoughts were on the other boat dock. Suddenly I heard the roar of an outboard motor. I looked up and saw a motor powered, aluminum row boat skimming across the lagoon with Nazaré, La Gordita, and two teenage boys riding in it. They took it to the opposite shore and coasted to a halt. Everyone got out. The boys dragged the prow free of the water and beached it. The four of them settled on a fallen trunk in plain view of the tug and shared a bottle of wine. I glared across the shimmering lagoon, stabbing Nazaré with my eyes. My face burned and I felt sick. I shook my head, hard. This is crazy, I thought. What is the matter with me? How can I be jealous? . . . I know what this woman is about. But it hurts. She's going to go with these two teenaged boys.

I spat over the railing and into the oil fouled water. Suddenly I heard a harsh cackle from behind me. I turned. It was the cook. He stood before me with his arms folded, looking me in the eye, then he glanced past me to the opposite shore. He cackled again. It rang cruelly.

"You want to fuck her, eh?"

"Who? Me?" I sneered at him. "You are crazy. I don't!" He chuckled amusedly this time. His red-rimmed eyes were suprisingly sympathetic. I shrugged my shoulders and let out a deep breath. "All right, yes. Of course! I want to screw her. If I could . . . "

"You can. You already know what it would take . . . . On this boat people have fucked her," he finished in a teasing voice.

"I know that. The captain, certain? And who else? You?"

"Me—no! Not with that hell cat." For a moment he regarded me as though I were Jorzinho. "If you want her, all you have to do is play by her rules. Don't be a fool over this." He cackled again and turned away, headed for the galley.

"Eh, cook!" I called. He pivoted about. "Fuck off! But thanks."

He made no reply. His laughing refrain was the final word.

As soon as he was gone from sight I chuckled, thinking of the irony of the situation. He's absolutely right. I'm being a stubborn fool. It's simple—either pay or don't play. And to think I was running away from women in Leticia.

Feeling more impersonal about matters, I returned my sight to the opposite shore to watch the unfolding drama of the young boys in pursuit of the more experienced older women. The younger of the two boys was trying to put his arm around La Gordita's shoulders but she kept shrugging him off. The other boy, a bit older and much bolder than his companion, was clumsily fondling Nazaré's breasts. After a while the younger boy appealed to Nazaré for help with La Gordita, who had moved away from him to the far end of the trunk. Nazaré went over to La Gordita and urged her to drink more wine. La Gordita complied.

Then Nazaré put her face close to La Gordita and seemed to lecture her. From their excited gestures I could tell there was an argument. The two boys stood off to the side with arms folded, seemingly unconcerned with the negotiations, letting Nazaré handle everything. Finally, La Gordita rose and walked to the water's edge. Nazaré followed her, talking and waving her arms as she went. La Gordita cast a long look at the tug. Then she turned and resumed her seat on the felled trunk. When the younger boy sat next to her, she allowed him to hold her hand and slobber on her cheek. The other boy attacked Nazaré's breasts with renewed ardor.

After about ten minutes of this groping foreplay, Nazaré stood up, drained the bottle of wine, tossed it in the bushes, and beckoned to the group to follow her. She led them onto a narrow footpath that disappeared into the bush. La Gordita hung back, casting more looks toward the tug. Nazaré came back, got behind La Gordita, and urged her on, giving her littles shoves from time to time. They vanished into the trees. There was a leaden feeling in the pit of my stomach. Nazaré orchestrated La Gordita into something she didn't want to do, I thought. Eloi is right about her.

I buried my nose in the Portuguese handbook. A short time later Fernando came along with a big smile on his face. "What's happening?" he asked.

"Nothing. Unfortunately, absolutely nothing here."

"The same for me .... Do you want to go to the village and see what's happening there?"

"Sure, why not. Let's get away from here for a while." I tossed the book into my bag and got ready to leave.

We were on our way out when we heard a shout from the lagoon. Jaap and two unknown men were paddling to the tug, in a canoe loaded to the gills with tropical fruit.

"I have to give that Jaap credit," I said to Fernando. "He's a damn good forager. He finds food everywhere."

"That he is .... He's very resourceful."

Betti spotted Jaap about the same time we did. She moved away from the railing, where she had been anxiously waiting, and came over to stand by us. As Jaap hauled himself over the railing, an ear to ear grin on his face, Betti turned her back on him and assumed an attitude of righteous indignation. Still wearing a happy smile, unaware of Betti's anger, Jaap reached out and tapped her on the shoulder. Betti spun about like a tigress at bay. Her steely gray eyes glinting fire, she snapped something off in Dutch.

"Vas? Vas?" muttered Jaap, his face a picture of utter consternation.

Betti was telling him "vas." Unfortunately we couldn't understand — or maybe fortunately. Jaap's sunburned skin turned crimson. He looked to us for support, or an explanation, or something. I looked at Jaap compassionately, pointed an index finger to my head, and twirled it, to indicate that he was dealing with a nut. Betti stood with hands on hips and glared at Jaap. When she finally stopped scolding, Jaap spread his arms and went into an explanation.

"Shall we go?" I asked Fernando. "I don't know about you . . . but I'm no marriage counselor. Let's get out of here and let them settle things alone."

"All right," said Fernando, his face troubled. He remained silent until we started up the hill. "I don't like to see them fight," he said. "They are good people . . . . What's the problem with them? do you know anything about this?"

"It shouldn't be anything serious," I said, shrugging. "Earlier, Jaap became angry with Betti because she stopped paddling the canoe and he had to do all the work. Later, Betti became angry with Jaap because he went to gather fruit and didn't ask her if she wanted to go along . . . . Outside of that, I think the pressure of the trip is starting to get to them, especially to Betti . . . . She always wants Jaap by her side. She's clinging too hard. Jaap is more adventurous than she is — He needs a chance to get away once in a while and rough it. She has to be patient. She'll have her opportunity to do more cultural things when they get to the big cities. But for now, aw . . . they shouldn't stay mad long. On this trip they are everything to each other." I stepped around a mound of cattle dung. "Yeah, it would seem the party is turning sour for some people. Did you see Nazaré and La Gordita go off with those two boys?"

"Yes," he replied in a flat tone. "It's nothing. I told you she was a whore."

"I never doubted that, Fernando. But what about La Gordita?"

"You obviously saw what happened . . . Nazaré pushed her into it. She's not a whore! She's just a normal healthy girl with strong appetites. The sun and the wine must have got to her. I just wish it had happened with me . . . . Anyway, who cares? What's your obsession with this Nazaré? If you want her so bad — just pay her and be done with it."

"I can't do that with her."

"Why?"

"Because this has become something personal between us. I could never be satisfied going to bed with her on a straight business arrangement . . . . I need to know that she's doing it because she wants to—and for no other reason. There are plenty of other men around to pay her. I think that's part of the reason she's so damn cynical. Worse than me . . . "

Fernando shook his head. "Who cares? She's a *puta!*"

I burst into laughter. "Who isn't?"

Fernando's face flamed. "My mother isn't!"

"No, relax, man." I giggled. "I don't mean it that way . . . "

"What do you mean?"

"What I mean is . . . well, ah, do you know anybody who hasn't had to sell themselves at one time or another? Whether for money, or love, or status, or whatever. It's all the same to me. No sense feeling superior to someone because they sell themselves one way and you or me does it another way. Sometimes people have to do things just to survive . . . . Right now, Nazaré doesn't have to go to bed with me in order to survive. She can afford to do it just because she wants to. And if she doesn't . . . well, I still wanted to find out how flexible her price was."

Fernando shook his head and gave me a sidelong owlish glance. "You know, when you talk like this . . . sometimes I think you're crazy — and sometimes I think you're a crazy liar."

"All right, well . . . maybe I am crazy, but not a liar. At least not usually."

"O.K., o.k., man, don't be so serious."

We crossed the tumbled gate and walked in silence down the embankment and onto the cobbled path. I was gathering my thoughts.

"I'm sorry if I got too heavy for you," I said. "But I can't help myself sometimes. Thanks for listening to my babble . . . . You know, I really did want to make love to her."

"And now?"

"No, the price is too high. Sometimes free is the highest price of all."

Fernando thumped me on the back. "Forget about her! There will be many others in your life — women much better than her."

"Ah, yes. Of course! There are always others. But that doesn't help me here and now. I wanted her."

"I can't believe this! You almost sound like you're in love with her! A whore!"

"No one's talking about love." I snorted. "I'm not even certain I know what that word means . . . . I feel empathy for her. She strikes me

327

as a tormented person . . . . And I'm attracted to her physically. That's all."

We dropped the discussion when excited yelps and whistles came to our ears. We reached the schoolyard. A volleyball game was in progress. We turned off the street to watch. There were eighteen players on the court, mostly high school students with a smattering of young adults, and scores of people along the sidelines watching. The teams were mixed. A real community event, I thought. What better to do on a lazy Sunday afternoon in Alvarães.

Fernando and I moved forward and wormed our way into the crowd along the school building wall that bordered one side of the court. This time no one paid much attention to our presence. We watched the game. I grew itchy.

"Do you want me to ask if we can play?" I queried Fernando. "Some exercise might do us some good."

"Sure, fine. I like volley."

After a moment of indecision I turned to a girl standing next to me. "Can we play?"

Her face showed astonishment. "You two want to play with us?"

"Sure! Why not?"

"*Tudo bem.* Wait a moment, I'll see what I can do." She moved off to talk to some of her friends. She returned shortly. "*Tudo bem.* You two can play on our team next game." She eyed me boldly. "At least you are tall. Are you any good?"

I laughed. "Let's wait and see. I haven't played this in a long time."

Within ten minutes we were on the court and batting the ball around. It felt strange. I even had a few butterflies in my stomach. Though in general I was a good athlete, good enough to compete in intercollegiate sports and jump up and catch a basketball rim with two hands on a good day, I had played very little volleyball. Baseball, track, basketball, and football were my favorite sports to play, in that order. Still, thanks to my height, at a shade under six feet I towered over most of the other players, and leaping ability, I was an imposing figure in pre-game warm-ups. Then, once the match started, I was paired in the front line against a short bearded stiff who was completely intimidated. My teammates set me up with lobs, and though I mishit the bulk of them, the guy on the other side of the net was unable to return my patty cake smashes. We won the game with ease. My teammates came over and shook my hand or patted me on the back. Fernando came over and I slapped palms with him.

"Man, this is a joke," I said. "I'm like a superstar here. Maybe the

328

mayor will give me a key to the city."

Fernando just looked at me; he thought I was serious. A new team took the court to challenge us. They had been watching closely from the sidelines and they knew exactly how limited my game really was. Now things were totally different. I became just another player. My teammates stopped feeding me lobs because I wasn't putting away enough of them. I settled in and adjusted my game to complement my teammates. Ah, I thought, fame is so fleeting sometimes. This game was well-played and hotly contested. A number of the Brazilians, both men and women, were talented natural athletes with fluid moves and an excellent grasp of the game. Though the teamwork was good, there was also a high regard for slick and flashy play, individuality and creative expression within the framework of the team. These people sure aren't robots, I thought. I really dig their style. They play all their sports like this. They're as flashy as the Colombians but with a better team concept.

As the game went on, close and hard fought, everyone was laughing and jiving around, enjoying themselves immensely. I felt most of my tension and disappointment seep away — like air from a punctured balloon. I became loose and relaxed. In the end we edged them by a couple of points. It didn't seem that important. Then, as the next contest was about to begin, two new players raced onto the court from the street.

I blinked in amazement. They were the very same boys who had gone into the bush with Nazaré and La Gordita. As they took their places on the opposite side of the net, I saw that both of them had flushed faces, wide smiles, and glistening eyes. The bold one, who had gone with Nazaré, strutted about the court like a bantam rooster. He was a handsome, olive skinned boy, about fourteen, well-built, and wearing a green striped soccer jersey. Most of the young girls on the court followed him with their eyes. The other, shyer boy, took a position directly in front of me. He was slighter and less developed than his friend but would probably fill out to become a good-looking man. I gave him a crooked, insinuating smile. He blushed and lowered his eyes. They must have got their rocks off, I thought, no longer feeling envious. Maybe they were virgins. Maybe I misjudged Nazaré — she might be a true humanitarian, teaching these youngsters the rudiments of lovemaking before they practice on someone less experienced and get into trouble . . . . I feel the fine hand of the captain behind this entire business. He must be these kids' uncle or something. Nice of him to take such an active role in their sex education. A real practical guy . . . . Hell, I could have used an uncle like that — might have saved me some complexes if I had had an understanding, experienced older woman . . . . Of course, the captain would probably take a machete to a guy who would dare to screw a niece or daughter without a wedding ring, assuming he ever found out. These hot blooded women here have their ways of getting around anything. Nature won't be denied . . .

We played another three games, until the sun started to dip below the horizon. Cheerful and sweating, Fernando and I returned to the tug.

The cook served dinner early. Sitting through the meal was an ordeal. Jaap and Betti were still at odds. For the most part, Jaap stared at his plate, chewing mechanically, his face sullen and confused. When she looked at Jaap at all, Betti thrust recriminating glances at him. They passed the meal in a tense silence that made us all uncomfortable. Eloi, Fernando, and I gulped down our food and got away from the table.

Then we just sat around and waited. The word from Eloi was that we might leave at any moment. Fine with me, I thought. I've had enough of those bars for a while.

After the table was cleared and Jaap and Betti retired to their hammocks, I grabbed my book and sat at the table near the light to read. I was soon distracted. From the corner of my eye I watched as Jaap, his face rosy and tight with agitation, sued for peace with Betti. He spoke to her in a pleading tone of voice, palms out in a gesture of supplication. For a long while Betti listened to him stone faced, her arms folded, hard and unyielding. I grew disgusted with her. She wants him to crawl, I thought. I don't know if Jaap deserves this or not, but she's carrying things a long way. What does she want? For him to turn into a worm? Ah, it's none of my business . . .

Eventually Betti relented. She allowed Jaap to put his arm around her, but maintained a pouting face. Jaap whispered in her ear. A short time later they were cocooned in the same hammock, swaying to and fro, Jaap bellowing Dutch folk songs in a not unpleasant baritone, and Betti listening with starry eyes and a complacent smile. Milene and Nazaré came down to see what the singing was about. When they saw Jaap and Betti they almost melted on the spot. Nazaré was particularly affected. Her eyes glowed with a soft light and her lips parted. *"Namorados,"* she declared in a vibrant voice. *"Namarados namorado (lovers in love)!"* As her sentimental side came to the fore her hard mask dissolved. Again I was taken by how pretty she could look. In that instant, I wanted to forget all the trouble between us and take her in my arms. But it's just not to be, I thought, a bittersweet taste in my mouth.

Nazaré approached me at the table. She was composed and distant, showing absolutely no ill effects from the wine she had guzzled.

"Do you want to play cards?" she asked.

"All right."

She went up the ladder to get the cards. When she returned, Fernando joined us. We played a Brazilian version of "Hearts." Then after a few hands of that, she taught us some other card games. The time slipped along. It was evident that we were staying another night in Alvarães. We played cards and chatted about vague superficial future plans. The guards were definitely up. Nazaré, reponding to a query from Fernando, told us that she was going to look for a steady job when she arrived in Manaus. She never mentioned what line of work she was interested in. She played cards with great concentration. Fernando and I soon grew bored with it and stopped playing. We remained at the table and talked. Nazaré spread out a hand of Solitaire and withdrew into herself. Just like I do sometimes when I want to think about something, I thought. What could be going through that mind of hers? . . . "

A short while later, to our great surprise, the captain came down and joined us at the table. He spoke familiarly to Nazaré, even cracked a few jokes, but he seemed very uncomfortable with us and had almost nothing to say. He must have some sort of stupid rule about fraternizing with passengers, I thought. Nazaré was deferential with the captain, almost timid. This surprised me. She accepted playful jibes from him without retort or complaint. Nazaré finished her game of Solitaire and scooped up the cards.

"Luis, do you want to play cards?" she asked.

So that's his name, I thought. Luis! Seven days aboard and I've only heard him referred to as *O Capitão* and *Filho da Puta*.

Luis accepted and they began playing. Fernando excused himself and went to bed. They played two hands of cards. The captain won both and gloated over it shamelessly. Nazaré merely smiled and won the next two games.

"You are getting lucky," the captain told her.

"This next game decides things," said Nazaré, quite serious. "If I win, you have to buy me something I want."

"*Tudo bem.* Let's go!"

The match began. The captain fell behind and stayed behind. Nazaré was well on her way to an easy victory. As the game progressed, the captain's expression changed from confident, to puzzled, to worried, to frustrated, to angry. Nazaré played poker-faced. Finally the captain glowered at Nazaré, stood up, slammed his cards down on the table, and barked, "You are cheating me! The deal is off! This is shit!"

Nazaré accepted his outburst in silence, a disconcerted look on her face. When he finished, she spoke in a quiet matter-of-fact tone: "I don't cheat in cards."

The captain snorted a reply, turned on his heel, and stomped up the ladder to his cabin.

With the captain gone, Nazaré lost her disconcerted expression and chuckled quietly. The whole thing seemed like a put on by the captain, I thought. He just didn't want Nazaré coming out on top in front of someone else.

"He acted like a little child," I said to her.

She cocked her head toward me and replied softly, "He is." She spread a new Solitaire hand on the table and gazed at the cards. I watched in silence as she played out her lonely hand, the naked bulb on the wall above us glaring into my eyes, until I was overcome with weariness and dozed where I sat.

CHAPTER XII

MUTINY IN TEFE

I jerked awake as the engines roared to life. The sailors scuttled about the boat in preparation of departure. I rolled on my side and looked out to the sky. It was a soft grey — the pre-dawn color of mourning following the passage of the night and preceding the brilliant flash of sun signaling the birth of a new day. The grayness was also in my mind. I shook my head to and fro to lose it. As it slowly dissipated I became aware of a vague unease in the pit of my stomach. I closed my eyes and withdrew deep within my body. I felt steady warning signals, light to be sure, but gradually increasing in intensity. I tried to stand; it was an effort. I trudged to the stern. My head spun and cold chills rippled through me. Damn, I thought, something is wrong with me.

Fernando was already sitting on the stern, waiting for his coffee. He turned to me with a big smile. "We're finally going to get out of here. Great, no? . . . Say, what's wrong with you?"

"I don't know, man. I must be coming down with something."

"Well, you don't look too bad. It's probably just a cold that will pass amid the gentle breezes of the Amazon."

"Huh, I don't know about that. But thanks for the poetry."

The motor chugged harder and we slipped from our mooring and headed for the inlet. I squinted toward the small mesa, where Alvarães sat. Only a few breakfasting cows and the tumbled gate came to view. A fitting last sight of Alvarães, I thought. A place I could imagine living in for a while but not one I'd want to return to for another vacation spasm.

We cruised through the inlet and were soon on the broad Amazon. The cook brought us our coffee. The hot sweet liquid dispelled some of my chill and gave me a pop of sugary energy, but the improvement was shortlived. I had no appetite for the tasteless crackers. Fernando talked to me but I was unable to concentrate well enough to understand him. Finally I excused myself and returned to my pallet. I lay still, trying to conserve my strength.

As the morning slipped along, unable to sleep, I rolled onto my side

333

and gazed dreamily at the passing shore. Strange, I thought, we're travelling closer to the shore than we ever did before the *motobomba* was damaged. Are we simply sailing in a safe river channel, or is there still something wrong with that damn machine? Our speed is only fair . . .

The sky became heavily overcast and a light drizzle, almost a mist, covered our vessel with a silvery sheen. The dense monotonous forest dripped and steamed. I started counting individual trees. I had almost lulled myself to sleep when the landscape began to change. My interest perked up. Thatched huts on stilts appeared, and each lot included a plot of corn, wide-fronded banana trees, and a small variety of other agricultural and animal produce. At first, these enclaves in the jungle were scattered, but soon they began to abut and form a continuous line of development. Some of the larger properties were fenced. We must be nearing Tefé, I thought. This is weird. It reminds me of driving down a main highway in the western U.S. and seeing the string of coffee shops and gas stations in the middle of nowhere.

Fernando came to me with map in hand. He opened it up and traced the river until he came to Tefé. "Well," he said, "three days behind schedule, but it looks like we're finally going to reach Tefé. We're halfway to Manaus now . . . . A little more than halfway."

"Yeah, you told me before. I just hope we go right on by it and head straight for Manaus. I feel terrible."

"I hope we do stop. It would be a shame if we didn't. This place is pretty large. The map indicates a population of around 20,000 inhabitants. But if the captain wants to make up for lost time . . . "

No sooner had he uttered these words than we swung hard to the right and made for a channel created by a large island. We stopped talking and watched. The channel led us to a bay seething with a variety of vessels, ranging from tiny fishing skiffs to monster freighters. Looking to shore, a bustling wharf fronted a ragamuffin sprawl of buildings that ran helter skelter from the edge of a moon shaped beach, up a steep incline, and to the top of a small plain. More houses ran serpentine to either side, on the hills adjoining the central plateau.

"Not very pretty, is it?" said Fernando.

"No, it looks like this place just grew without any plan . . . . But look at all the lumber."

"Yes, from what little I read about this place, almost everything is geared to the assembling and distribution of lumber . . . . They should have everything one might want here." Fernando winked.

As we drew closer to shore, the air was replete with the sweet sappy aroma of fresh hewn lumber. I breathed the air with delight. Fernando and I moved to the prow of the tug. The captain was at the helm. He maneuvered us agilely through the thick river traffic and docked our vessel with admirable skill, squeezing the flat between two massive lumber barges, with no more than four feet of clearance on either side.

"Well done!" I exclaimed. "This captain can really do the job when he wants to."

"He's a good sailor," said Fernando.

Our engine sputtered to a halt. Fernando and I looked at each other.

"Now what?" I asked. "How long will we be here?"

"He can't take too long. We're way behind schedule."

"Huh, who knows what this guy's schedule is — it certainly has nothing to do with the passengers. This guy has been consistently unpredictable. You never know, he might have family or some mistress here, too."

"Maybe, but he must have some deadline to deliver his goods. He can't delay here, I don't think . . . "

"Well, let's go see what we can find out. Maybe Eloi will know something . . . . And if it seems we might delay here too long . . . well, this might be our chance to look for another ship. I'm getting sick of this bullshit!"

We entered the hold and found Eloi talking to the sailor who had given me the wine the day before.

"Do you know how long we are going to be here?" I asked.

He regarded me impassively for a moment, then answered in a fatalistic tone, "Who knows? The captain might have relatives here, too." Eloi shrugged. "But the captain told the crew one hour."

The listening sailor confirmed this with a nod.

"Do you believe him?" I asked.

"The only thing I believe is that he will do what he wants. That's the way it is."

At this moment the captain descended the ladder and swaggered past us to the stern, a self-satisfied smirk on his face, acknowledging no one, his fat gut and dissolute countenance now magnified to my eyes and taking on grotesque qualities. He directed a pair of sailors to the engine room. They proceeded to haul the *motoboma* onto the stern deck. "It's still not working right," said the sailor.

Eloi and I walked to the stern and stared at the gleaming machine with impotent fury. "I'd like to take a sledgehammer to it," I muttered in English. Unpainted spots of shining stainless steel seemed to mock me with a smile.

"What did you say?" Eloi asked me.

"Nothing . . . . That I'd like to destroy this machine."

"That probably wouldn't help any — the problem is with the people working on it."

"Yeah, you're right."

I glanced at the captain. He was at the galley door, chatting with the cook. His cool aloofness infuriated my feverish brain. I'd like to wring his neck to wake him up, I thought. But that coolness is also his greatest protection. He knows how to deal with crisis. He knows how to manipulate situations. I have to keep cool myself and look at some other options. This Tefé looks like the place to do it . . . . Now where's Fernando?

I found Fernando amidship in earnest conversation with Jaap. They were nodding and pointing toward another boat, docked about a quarter mile from us. Jaap saw me approaching and said, "Look! You see that boat?"

"Yes." It was a tub-like three decker, resting low in the water.

"I think it is one of the Recreios for Manaus. Vat do you think?"

"I don't know. It sure could be—it looks like the pictures I've seen of it."

"We go and see about that boat. I don't trust this one anymore." A worried wrinkle creased Jaap's forehead. Fernando looked at me expectantly.

"Jaap wants to change boats," I said to him. A sudden wave of nausea swept through me. My legs were weak. "I think he has a good idea. As sick as I feel right now a cabin with a bed could be just what I need but . . . on the other hand, I don't feel like making the effort if we really are going to leave soon. What do you think?"

Fernando stared glumly at his toes. "I wouldn't mind changing boats if you three are — but I don't have the money for that."

Jaap understood him and looked disappointed. "Vat do you say? Shall we go see?"

"Why not give the captain one more hour. We could go to town and get something to eat and see if he keeps his word when we get back."

"No!" Jaap shook his head and grimaced. "I go to see right now!" He walked away with his jaw tilted up and a set expression on his bearded face.

"I'm going to talk to him," said Fernando, following Jaap.

"Go! I don't care anymore what he does." He's just going to look out for himself and his woman anyway, I thought. I got to get away from

336

this boat and move among strange people. I need to clear my head.

I slunk off the tug and onto the cargo flat. Then Fernando came from the other side and caught up to me. This was fine.

"So?" I asked him.

"He says that he will wait for a while."

"Whatever."

We crossed from our cargo flat to another, much larger one, by tightroping over a sagging plank. Once across I paused for a moment. My head spun crazily. I blinked my eyes and looked around. We were standing on an enormous pile of lumber. A gang of stevedores rushed to and fro with long planks draped over their shoulders. They worked like ants, stacking the lumber in high neat piles. Most of the men were squat and muscular, with hard eyes and faces.

Fernando and I shuffled along the pile toward the beach. We were alert to avoid the rushing men, some of whom saw us and, with mocking looks, made no effort to avoid us. Jerks, I thought, too sick and weak to really feel angry. I shivered as we walked. The weather was cool and overcast. A drizzle fell, the moisture clammy against my skin.

We reached the end of the lumber and surveyed the beach. The sand was soot colored and gravelly, striped in places with spilled oil, littered with garbage and broken glass, and bore the weight of enormous packing crates loaded with machinery.

We leaped down to the beach. My hands struck the sand and came away encrusted with filth. As we picked our way through the debris, we spotted Nazaré and Milene ahead of us. Fernando called out to them. The two women turned, startled, as though we had caught them doing something wrong, and rushed off toward a stand of horrible looking shanties on the edge of the beach. Fernando and I looked at each other and exchanged wry grins.

"Probably off for a quickie with some recently paid sailors," I surmised.

We reached the street and were confronted by a shantytown. The houses were made of wood, brick, sheets of aluminum, scrap metal, cardboard, and anything else the owner could use that might hold the mess together. The streets were unpaved, open sewers with garbage for stepping stones over the muck. As we stood on the edge of the beach, trying to figure out which way to go, three girls in worn clothes came down the street and walked past us. Cheap jewelry flashed. Their eyes were bold and speculative. No shy village girls here, I thought. Only the cynical tough survivors of a rowdy squalid river port. They have the lean hungry demeanor of famished wolves . . . and they checked us out like we were doddering old mooses ready to fall. And that's about how I feel right now.

"Did you check out those girls?" Fernando asked.

"Yeah, now I understand why they call prostitutes piranhas in Amazonas."

"Who told you that?"

"Eloi. . . . We better watch ourselves here. This looks like a very rough place. Don't stare at anybody."

We detoured to the right, around the worst of the makeshift houses, and found a paved street that led us to the shopping district. As we strolled between lines of food stands and shops, stepping over cracked and broken pavement that sometimes improved to smooth dirt, ignoring the hawkers who tried to lure us into their stands, I felt danger on all sides. Teenage girls with the faces of old women watched us. Hard faced men with knife scars watched us. Little street urchins watched us. All the eyes were alert and gleamed with anticipation — some were hooded like birds of prey. Many of the stores were surprisingly well-stocked with expensive imported goods. The faces of the owners were from Middle Eastern bazaars.

"Plenty of Arabs here," I commented to Fernando. "Just like Colombia. Probably Lebanese and Syrians."

"Yes, wherever there is commerce in South America, you will find them. In Peru we call all the people from the Middle East, *judios (Jews)*."

"Really? . . . Shit, you call an Arab a Jew in my country, you better be prepared to die—and vice versa." I shook my head. "That's really strange. You know, in Colombia they call all the Arabs, *turcos (Turks)*."

"Why?"

"Because many of them came to Colombia while most of the Arab countries were under Ottoman rule . . . . So they had Turkish passports. But they don't like being called Turks."

It began to rain a bit harder. We ducked into the first sit down restaurant we encountered. It was a combination cafe-discoteque, very similar to the one I had gone to with Sandra the week before in Leticia. Wow, I thought, was it a week? Seems more like a year . . .

The place was empty, save for two gentlemen dressed in business suits sitting in the back of the room and facing the entrance. They looked up and scrutinized us for a moment, before deciding that we must be tourists, or otherwise harmless, and resuming their conversation. We sat down a few tables away from them and were immediately waited on by a pretty young lady — who looked as though her services might include more than merely serving men food.

"How can I serve you?" she asked.

A flip answer leaped to my tongue; I stifled it. "Bring us coffee and milk . . . . Fresh milk if you have it. And bread and butter and . . . ah . . . marmalade."

She wrinkled her nose at my accent but seemed to understand me well enough. Still, she walked away muttering, twitching her ass as she went. As I gazed after her I was rocked by another spasm of chills. I touched my forehead. It was hot. Deep inside my body I could feel whatever it was I had gnawing away at my reserve of strength. This could be bad, I thought. I need to get to Manaus as fast as possible if it is.

I put my face in my hands and leaned my elbows on the table. Behind me I overheard the two men discussing a narcotics transaction. After hearing my accent, they must have assumed I couldn't understand them, or they didn't care. They used plenty of slang. Eloi's training was paying off. I laughed to myself. It's great when you can understand when people don't think you can.

"How do you feel?" Fernando asked me.

"Not very well. Worse than I did early this morning . . . . So, what do you think, Fernando, should we look for another boat or stay with the Magalhães?"

Fernando scratched his mop of black hair. "As I said before, it would be fine with me if we can change to another boat — but I don't have the funds to do it."

"Well, we could check around and see what it would cost . . . . If it's cheap enough we might be able to arrange something. Who knows?"

"Of course, we can look . . . . But we've already paid our passage with the Magalhães. Why not stay with what we know?"

"What you say makes sense. I'd be perfectly willing to stay with our boat if I knew that we would go directly to Manaus without anymore delays. But the way things have been going . . . And the captain's attitude is beginning to bother me. He's an arrogant fuck. Since he got our money he could give a damn about us. Five or six days to Manaus he said. Well, we already passed that limit . . . . Of course, accidents can happen, but he's been treating us like he's been treating those pigs—eat, shut up, and wait to see what happens. I'm tired of that!"

"All right, man, I understand you. It's true that the captain is a *huevon* . . . . But he pilots the boat well. I feel certain that he will get us to Manaus safely — eventually."

"That's my problem. When will we get to Manaus? . . . This delay will already make it difficult for me to return to Colombia by boat. And I don't think I will have enough money to fly back the way things are going. Man, I don't want to give up my beer. And I don't want my visit to Manaus to last only a few days. I want more than a week."

Fernando chuckled. "Go on, man, I only have a few pennies to my name and I fully expect to reach Paris. Don't worry, I'm sure you can make it back to Bogotá. The thing will work itself out."

"Maybe so . . . . But I'd prefer to do something instead of depending on fate."

The waitress interrupted us by bringing a porcelain kettle of coffee and, delightfully, a cup of fresh milk. The first non-condensed milk I had seen since arriving in Amazonas. I drank the hot liquid eagerly. Though it revived my spirit, it did little for my stomach. The toasted bread, with butter and marmalade, seemed to stick in my throat. I forced it down.

We ate and discussed the lighter side of the past few days. It felt good to get away from the tension and uncertainty of the boat and relax with my friend. He had become my confidant in an amazingly short time. I ordered another kettle of coffee and we drank it leisurely. My mind drifted into a pleasant fog. The time slipped past.

"We better get moving," Fernando urged me.

"Ah, what's the hurry? They're not going anywhere."

"Perhaps, but we can't take the risk. All our gear is aboard the boat. We must go!"

"All right," I said with a sigh, reluctantly rising from my comfortable chair. I chuckled. "Look who's acting like a gringo now."

Fernando was still laughing as we went out the door. Once on the street he went at a fast walk. I was unable to keep up with him. I felt dizzy. I had a strong desire to lay down somewhere—anywhere. "Can't you go faster?" Fernando asked. "We can't miss the boat!"

"No, I can't. You go ahead and hold the boat for me if you want."

Fernando glanced around at the mean street. "No, that's all right. But try to hurry."

We reached the beach without incident. Our boat was still there, as were a very excited Jaap and Betti. Jaap rushed forward to meet us. "Vhere haf you been? Ve haf been vaiting . . . . The Recreio is . . . is . . . ah . . . "

"It is the Recreio," said Betti. "It is going to Manaus and they have room aboard. We can go on it."

I looked at Fernando. He had understood the gist of Betti's words and looked pretty unhappy over it.

"Well, shall we go see about this?" I asked him.

"Of course, we can go see. But I don't believe I'll be transferring boats."

"When does the Recreio leave?" I asked, turning to Jaap. "And how much does it cost?"

"I'm not sure when it leaves," said Jaap, in a calmer manner. "But we should hurry!"

"I believe it costs $2000 *cruzeiros* for a cabin and $1000 to use a hammock," said Betti.

"Can you wait a few minutes longer? . . . Just let us go to the Magalhães and check on the situation there. Anyway, if we do decide to go on the Recreio, we need our baggage. All right?"

"A few minutes," said Jaap. "But hurry. We don't wait too long and lose the boat."

"Let's go," I said to Fernando, the adrenalin surging through my body.

We ran to the Magalhães and entered the hold. The first thing we saw was the *motobomba* still sitting on the deck with an unknown mechanic working on it with a wrench. The second thing we saw was Eloi reclined in his hammock. We went over to him.

"What's going on?" I asked him. "How much time until we leave?"

Eloi stretched his arms over his head and yawned. "Oh . . . not until noon at the earliest. They finally got an expert to work on the *motobomba*."

"What? Noon? This is too much! . . . Two more hours here minimum?"

Eloi shrugged.

"We're tired of these delays," I said to Eloi. "We might go on the Recreio. You want to come with us and see about it?"

Eloi gave me a sharp look. "The Recreio is no bargain . . . . Anyway, I've already paid here. I can't change boats. Don't worry, this one will be all right. *Tudo bem*."

"All right, Eloi. But maybe we'll check anyway." I turned to Fernando. "Shall we check on the other boat?"

Fernando nodded.

We quickly gathered our gear and hurried back to the beach. Jaap and Betti were gone. We looked down the beach and spotted them in the distance, trudging toward the Recreio, weighed down by their enormous backpacks.

"They sure didn't wait any few minutes for us," I commented. "They must have taken off as soon as we left."

"Let's go," said Fernando. We ran after them and caught up with ease. Together we covered the remaining distance to the docked Recreio. We traversed a steel gangplank and stepped through an aperture into a dark reeking hold.

I stopped for a moment to look things over while Jaap, Betti, and Fernando went on ahead to an elevated platform, where a cigar chomping man sat behind a desk and checked off items on a list. The hold was a bustle of activity. People and cargo were being crammed into all corners, pushing and shoving, piling up like ants on a piece of candy. Hammocks hung everywhere. The space was also occupied by huge bunches of bananas, crates of all sizes, live and dead domestic animals, oil drums, blobs of natural rubber, and so many other things that my eyes rolled. Many of the passengers were straw hatted country folks, wearing ragged and unwashed clothes, the faces of the old, seamed and weary, the faces of the young, stolid but wary. Scattered among the crowd were brightly dressed hipsters, their faces lean and predatory, their bright eyes roving, professional confidence men and women, ready to prey on the untutored. A cute woman in a bright red dress caught my eye and smiled with false invitation. I twisted my lips wryly. Her face scowled and she turned to talk to a hip young man nearby . . . . So this is it, I thought. Just like I've read about. The great Latin American migration of country people to the big cities. Looking for a better life, most of them ending up with something no better than the hold of this ship. Filling up the slums, losing their personal dignity and integrity for an equally poor life. But a few of them get lucky— enough to keep the others coming . . .

"Come on," said Fernando, coming back for me. "What are you doing? We need you to talk to this guy."

We pushed our way through the milling crowd to the desk. The man saw us coming and seemed to smirk. Jaap and Betti joined us and we went to the desk together. The man looked down at his papers and made us wait. He gave us a glance, chewed his cigar, and finally looked at us with a sarcastic smile on his avaricious face. I don't like this guy, I thought. He looks at us like we're fresh meat.

"What you want?" he asked in English, openly leering at Betti.

"We want to see your prices . . . of passage," answered Jaap in Spanish.

The man frowned and showed us a typed sheet of paper with a list of prices on it. They were as Betti said.

"But it is very dirty here," said Jaap. "For that money, you have more better?"

The man laughed. "Down here, with the low lifes," he said in Portuguese, "it costs $500 *cruzeiros*. These prices," he tapped the paper with his finger, "are for upstairs. Where the meesters stay."

"Where?" asked Jaap.

"Upstairs." The man pointed a nicotine stained finger to a nearby ladder. "Your *paisanos* travel there."

Though Jaap was perspiring, he smiled. "We can use hammock there?"

"Yes, of course," said the man. "Whatever you want."

Jaap spoke to Betti. They headed for the ladder. The man looked down at his papers. I tried to talk to him, to get more information, but he ignored me. I was just about to turn and leave when a sailor, standing five paces behind the desk, said, "Listen to him. He is speaking Portuguese. You can understand him if you listen."

The man at the desk looked up at me with a hostile squint. Good, I thought, he's as suspicious of me as I am of him. Maybe my impression of him is right.

I asked him how long it would take us to get to Manaus and at what time would he be leaving. Then I asked him about the meals and other accommodations. He gave me curt vague answers. Here we go again, I thought. Pay your money and shut your mouth.

"Let's get out of here," I said to Fernando. "I don't like this."

"Well, we're here. We might as well take a look."

"Yeah, you're right."

We ascended the ladder to the second deck and ran into Jaap and Betti just as they were about to leave. Their faces were elated.

"It is very good!" said Betti. "It is so clean!"

"Yah, I like it," said Jaap. "I think we take it. You going to come with us?"

"I don't know," I said. "I want to take a look around for myself first. We'll see you in a little while."

"Yah, o.k. But I tell you now, it is goot. Better than the other boat."

They disappeared through the hatch and down the ladder. Fernando and I made a quick inspection of the second deck. The floor was indeed immaculately swabbed. A string of hammocks hung in a straight row. There was a bar. The deck was airy and spacious. I looked at one of the cabins. For $2000 *cruzeiros* it was a stuffy closet with a bed much too short for my sprawled length; a deluxe double cabin would cost more. There was no fan. Sick as I feel I need air, I thought. Not a broom closet. This don't make it . . . . And outside, sure, everything is nice and neat and, for sure, expensive, with extra charges if you want decent food and other sundries. The man downstairs didn't want to talk about that.

"What do you think?" I asked Fernando.

"I like it fine. It's much more clean and spacious than our boat . . . . But, as you know, money is my primary consideration. Paying an extra $1000 *cruzeiros* for the privilege of hanging my hammock would be stupidity for me . . . . And you?"

"Man, I don't know yet. There are many things to consider. Let's go back to the other boat and see what's going on there."

Jaap was waiting for us at the foot of the ladder. "Vat do you say? It is goot, no? You buy the passage?"

"Not yet, man . . . . It's all right here, but if the Magalhães is ready to sail I'll probably stay with her. Anyway, Fernando doesn't have the money to change boats."

"Well, we haf decided. We are going with this one." Without another word they went to the desk and purchased tickets.

Fernando and I took a last long look at the hold. More and more cargo wheeled in as we watched. The barnyard conditions were worsening. The Magalhães isn't nearly as bad as this, I thought. Jaap and Betti may be sleeping above in the penthouse but they still have to eat the same food as everyone else or pay extra. And there are a lot more people here to distrust. Lots of hustlers. Right now I trust just about everyone on our boat.

While Jaap and Betti ironed out some details and stowed their gear, Fernando and I took off. We walked at a brisk pace, crunching the pebbly sand underfoot.

"Well, have you decided?" Fernando asked.

"No, but right now I'm leaning toward staying with our boat. I know what to expect there and, except for the captain, I have no big complaint. And the only thing I have against the captain is his indifference toward us. The guy we talked to on the Recreio seems like a total asshole. I wouldn't trust that guy for anything."

"I'm glad to hear you say that. I'm sorry that Jaap and Betti are leaving but it will be good to have you with us. There are Europeans and Americans on the Recreio, it will be better for Betti."

"Yeah, and that's another reason I prefer our boat. I don't like travelling with large groups of gringos. It's like being a walking target here. You attract too much attention. The only real bad problems I've had in South America have come when I've been with groups of foreigners."

We reached the lumber stack and headed for the tug. Eloi was waiting for us on the prow. "So, what's happening here?" Fernando asked him.

The *motobomba* is completely repaired and ready to go—But, we still aren't going to leave for a while, and the captain won't say why or when—the dirty son-of-a-bitch!"

"Why that dirty dog!" I exclaimed, walking away and entering the hold to think things over, the emotional pendulum swinging me toward the Recreio. Now what do I do? Looks like the same old bullshit here. I could afford a cabin on the Recreio—if I cut back on other things . . . . But who do I want to travel with? Jaap and Betti, or Fernando and Eloi? Huh, no question, Fernando and Eloi. But either way I have problems.

While I pondered my dilemma, Jaap and Fernando entered the hold and stood by the railing overlooking the Recreio. Soon they fell into animated conversation. I got up and went over to join them.

"What are you talking about?" I asked them.

"I was just saying that we should ask the captain for a reimbursement of $500 *cruzeiros* since we only completed half the trip to Manaus," said Jaap.

"That makes sense," I said. "But only for you. Why do you assume that we want to leave this boat? I'm still not sure what I'm going to do."

"Well, you had better decide fast . . . or it is too late. The Recreio leaves soon."

"Huh," I said, thinking aloud, "getting $500 *cruzeiros* back could make my decision a little easier." I turned to Fernando. "Would you change boats and come with us if we can get $500 *cruzeiros* back from the captain?"

"Maybe," he replied, his face extremely agitated. "I would certainly like to continue the trip with you, and Jaap, and Betti. . . . But I truly doubt that the captain would give any money back."

"Yeah, I agree with you. Why should he? He has us in the palms of his hands. . . . Sure, we can switch boats, but that would be from our choice. He hasn't told us to leave. He's under no obligation to refund anything."

"Why don't you try speaking to him, Craig," said Fernando. "It can't hurt. And you know the most Portuguese."

"Yah, he is right!" said Jaap. "I will go, with or without the money, but it would be nice to haf some back."

I looked at them, shook my head, and walked away. No way! I thought. We're in an untenable situation. Plus, I don't like the way they tried to lay the responsibility on me — especially Jaap. He's got the most to gain from this and he doesn't want to do anything for himself . . . . Why should I ask for the money back — and maybe get myself in trouble with the captain — when I don't even know if I want to leave yet? And what's with Fernando? He blows hot and cold. This is crazy!

I sat down on my pallet and kept my eyes on Jaap and Fernando. The captain was standing by the bathroom talking to the cook. He seemed to be in a good mood. He laughed frequently as he told the cook a story. Well, I thought, if Jaap's going to do something, now's his chance. He better hurry . . .

Minutes slipped past. Then, to my consternation, Fernando approached the captain with flushed face. "Captain, may I have a word with you?" Fernando spoke in slow, perfectly enunciated Spanish. Jaap moved in behind him to lend moral support. I sat and watched, in perfect position to see and hear everything.

"Yes," said the captain, a quizzical yet guarded expression on his face. "Speak."

"We want to leave your boat and go on the Recreio . . . . We would very much appreciate it if you would please return half of our fare. . . . Since Tefé marks only the halfway point of what we paid for . . . "

The captain listened to Fernando with the same look on his face throughout. He's trying to play like he's stumped, I thought. But he has to understand exactly what Fernando is saying—I know he does.

"What do you say, captain?" Fernando asked after a long pause.

The captain passed a hand over his balding forehead and clucked sympathetically. "I'm sorry that you feel it necessary to leave my boat. I want to wish you all the best of luck . . . . You were good passengers . . . "

"What does he say?" broke in Jaap, tugging at Fernando's arm. "Tell me! What about the money?"

"He hasn't said anything about the money yet," said Fernando excitedly. "Give me a chance to ask him again."

Jaap's face stared blankly. He understood nothing. Fernando switched to French. Jaap's face became totally confused. "Vas? Vas? . . . "

I would have burst out laughing if everyone hadn't looked so serious. Yeah, Jaap, I thought, I remember you bragging about what excellent French you speak. . . . Just like your excellent Spanish that enables you to get by in Portuguese with no problem.

As Jaap and Fernando struggled to communicate, the captain looked from one to the other with incredulity. He had an inkling that something extraordinary was afoot, and wanted nothing to do with it. He took advantage of their confusion to slip away and up the ladder to his cabin. Once he was gone, Fernando and Jaap exchanged recriminating looks. But the damage was done. Neither had the heart to pursue the issue. Jaap walked off muttering in Dutch. I got up and went over to Fernando.

"It's all right," I said, thumping him on the back. "We already knew the captain wasn't going to return any money. Don't worry about it."

"Well, at least I tried," he said wearily, fixing me with his eyes.

Jaap and Betti were gathering the remainder of their gear. I strolled to the bow and reviewed the incident with the captain in my mind. It was kind of funny....But I didn't enjoy seeing the captain humiliate Fernando by walking away from him as though he were a statue. He really is an arrogant turkey. And I could have done something — at least have gotten a real answer from the man. But I stood by and watched it happen without lifting a finger. He's done this same thing to us so many times on this trip.

I paced to the other end of the boat. My stomach was churning and my head burned from fever, the symptoms of my illness aggravated by my anger. I paced back to the bow. Maybe I'm a chickenshit. Maybe this captain has me intimidated. You're afraid of him, man! It's obvious!...I became more and more excited, adrenalin pumped through me.... How many times has he failed to communicate with us when we might have been in danger? How many times has he ignored our legitimate questions? Too damn many!... Remember how he lured Nazaré and La Gordita away from our boat with bottles of wine and who knows what else.... And now, this final indignity, walking away from Fernando and Jaap without even bothering to answer them. Who the fuck does he think he is?... God?... Captain of the ship, the same thing. Well, we're docked now. We don't have to go along with this bullshit.

My pacing brought me to the foot of the ladder. I placed my hand on one of the rungs and leaned against it. Fernando watched me from his hammock. I took a deep breath and placed my right foot on the first step.... Remember how the baby walked away from the card game with Nazaré when he was on the verge of losing to her.

That did it—my mind shut off, the fever cooled. I was possessed by a cold determination. Quickly I mounted the ladder.

I paused for a moment outside his cabin, composing what I would say, then I knocked firmly on the door and said in my best Portuguese, *"O capitão!* I want to speak with you."

347

"One moment." He emerged warily, like a gopher poking its head from the top of its burrow. We stood midway between his cabin door and the ladder. At this moment, Jaap and Fernando climbed the ladder and looked on with anxious faces, providing welcome support. My confidence soared.

"What can I offer you?" asked the captain.

I looked the captain in the eye and tried to keep my tone calm and business-like. "We want you to return to us $500 *cruzeiros* . . . because we've only come half the distance to Manaus. . . . And this trip is delaying too much. Much more time than you said."

The captain was silent for a moment. He looked from one serious face to another. He knew we meant business. Consternation was reflected in his dissipated countenance. Two of the stevedores, working on the neighboring flat, paused to watch our confrontation. Their faces were intent.

"It's not my fault that the trip has been delayed," said the captain in a slow firm voice. "I had no control over the *motobomba*. It's not my fault."

Fernando and Jaap craned their necks toward me, wanting a translation. My mind was sharp and focused. I translated rapidly, almost unconsciously, in both English and Spanish.

I turned back to the captain. He was waiting patiently this time.

"You're right," I said. "It wasn't you fault about the *motobomba*—but it didn't seem like you wanted to leave that town, either. And the *motobomba* wasn't our fault . . . "

"Why leave? . . . We're going to be away from here within one hour. We will be in Manaus in less than three days. We're no longer going to make as many stops."

I shook my head. "We always seem to be leaving . . . but we never get anywhere."

He considered this briefly. Then he spread his palms toward me in a gesture of helplessness and said, "I can't give the money back . . . . You all signed contracts for $1000 *cruzeiros* and I have to answer for them to my boss. Because of the papers I can't give you the money back. Not even half . . . "

"But it's not fair! The Peruvian . . . " I indicated Fernando with a sweep of my arm, "is very poor. And doesn't have money in order to continue on another boat."

The captain scratched his receding hairline with nervous jerks. His eyes were lost in thought. To his credit he was considering the circumstances. He doesn't want to be an asshole, I thought. If he can help it . . . . What he says about the contracts is probably right. I can't blame him if he refuses us. I did what I could. At least I got him to listen.

"Well," he said, "this is what I can do . . . . I can give each one of you $200 *cruzeiros* for each passage paid. But no more! $200 *cruzeiros*, no more!"

He looked on expectantly as I translated his offer to the others.

"200 *cruzeiros*?" said Jaap. "That is goot! Very goot! I'll take it." He grinned thankfully.

Fernando frowned. "Well . . . yeah, I suppose . . . "

"They say *tudo bem*," I said to the captain.

He nodded and retired to his cabin. He returned in a moment and thrust $200 worth of worn bills into my hand and $400 into Jaap's hand. He started to pass a couple of grimy notes to Fernando, but, after a moment's hesitation, Fernando shook his head, refusing the money. I was stunned. I stared at my friend askance. The captain shrugged and returned to his cabin with obvious relief.

Jaap let out a joyous yelp. "This is super! I expected nothing." Jaap fingered the money. "I haf to tell Betti the goot news." He almost toppled down the ladder in his haste. I waited to have a word with Fernando.

"Why didn't you take the money?" I inquired heatedly. "I force a showdown with the captain because of you guys, and then you don't take the money! Why?"

Fernando shrugged resignedly and said, "$200 *cruzeiros* still leaves me short of passage by $800. I have only $400 *cruzeiros* to my name. My passage and food is already paid for here . . . . So, why leave?"

"You're right, of course. But why . . . ah, it doesn't matter now. Look, what if we lend you the money so that you can continue on the other boat? Give me a moment to speak with Jaap. Maybe we can fix this problem."

"You can if you want," said Fernando, raising his head pridefully. "But I don't want to be a burden on you. I'm fine here."

I hustled downstairs and found Jaap rolling up some more of his gear. He whistled as he worked.

"Jaap!" He looked up.

"That was goot," he said. "I really did not expect anything. So, $400 *cruzeiros* is very goot! No?"

"Yes, very good. And speaking of that, I need to ask you something serious . . . "

"Vat is it?"

"Why don't we lend Fernando $400 *cruzeiros* apiece so that he can go on the Recreio with us . . . . He doesn't have enough to make it without help."

The smile that had remained pasted on Jaap's face since he received the money from the captain vanished. He eyed me doubtfully. "I . . . I . . . I . . . "

"Come on, man, he's your friend. It's not much money."

"Yah, but . . . I . . . I . . . "

That was his answer. I turned away from him with disgust and strode off, wanting to strike him. Yah, yah, I thought, but friendship is one thing and money another. The words are stuck in your heart. Fernando has been your friend, more than I have . . . . He's shared beers and food with you out of the little money he had and this is the pay back. I know they're not hurting for money. Betti said they are going to buy precious stones in Brazil later. And as Jaap said, he expected nothing from the captain, and we got him something! To deny a friend the equivalent of $10 lousy dollars when he truly needs it . . . Yah, Jaap, you're a nice guy—but you're also a cheap chickenshit motherfucker! I wouldn't go on the same boat with you people now if it were the last one for the next week . . .

After I walked off some of my anger, I went to give Fernando the bad news.

"Yes, that's all right," he said. "I wouldn't expect him to give me anything. He has Betti to think of."

"Yeah, but, I know some things that . . . "

Fernando held up his hand. "They're good people. It doesn't matter, I feel good on this boat . . . . So, what are you going to do?"

"I'm staying here. I prefer the company. I know my things won't be molested here."

"That's great, man!" exclaimed Fernando, sticking out his hand. We shook on it.

"The only thing that bothers me is how I'm going to give the captain his money back. I'll feel like an idiot."

"Don't worry, he'll be happy to receive the money."

"Yeah . . . . I'll see you later. I'm going to lay down for a while."

I went down the ladder and stretched out on my pallet. Fever coursed through me, along with mortification, as I thought of returning the money to the captain. Well, no sense worrying about it—it's done! I did what I thought was right at the time . . . . Unfortunately I got caught in Jaap's and Fernando's hysteria against my better judgement. Now Jaap reaps the reward and I pay for it. Shit! . . . Anyway, I smiled at the memory, it was nice to see the captain squirm a bit after the way he's been treating us. Might do him some good to give people a little more respect. It did me some good . . .

As I calmed down a creeping exhaustion invaded my body. The weather was overcast and warm, making me apprehensive when a new series of chills knifed through me. Whatever this is, it's getting worse, I thought. I better take things easy for a while.

Suddenly Jaap let out a tremendous yelp and bounded to the railing near me. I followed his gaze. The Recreio had slipped from its berth and was chopping across the bay to an unknown destination. Jaap held onto the railing and hopped up and down, squawking at the Recreio in Dutch. The boat kept moving along. Then Jaap made a mad dash about the hold, his face red and his eyes popped. I was beside myself with laughter. My side hurt. Then I was hit by a coughing fit. Jaap made another wild rush. I laughed harder. Then he stopped and glared down at me.

"Vat are you laughing at? This isn't funny. The Recreio is leaving with some of our stuff."

"I'm laughing at you, man. What goes around comes around . . . . You understand that?"

"Ach!" Jaap continued his interrupted dash. Finally the tall sailor, his nap disturbed by Jaap's noise, got up and told him to quiet down. Jaap subsided and listened.

"The Recreio has gone to take on fuel," said the sailor. "It will return to the passenger zone shortly. Understand?"

Jaap nodded and retreated to the comfort of Betti's soothing voice and comforting arms. I looked at him and shook my head. It would serve him right if the Recreio took off without him, I thought. Nah, I wouldn't want them to lose the ship. What the hell, he's suffering enough right now from his own imagination. He probably thinks the sailor only told him that to shut him up. Look at him . . . . Jaap sat cross legged on the deck, his face a picture of misery, as he spoke in anxious tones to Betti. She gently massaged his neck and murmured in his ear. Her face was stoic and serene. Her tone of voice and every mannerism was pure reassurance. Jaap began to settle down. He's lucky to have someone like her along, I thought. At least in times like this. They complement each other.

Eventually — fortunately for all concerned — the Recreio returned to the passenger dock. Jaap and Betti stood up and hefted their bindles with audible sighs of relief. Fernando came over and grabbed me by the arm. "Let's accompany them to the other cargo flat and wish them luck."

"Leave me alone, man. I feel horrible."

"Come on. Just for a minute."

"All right."

We went with them to the adjoining lumber flat and shook hands all the way around. I wanted them to hurry up and leave, hot and cold chills wracked me, but Fernando became emotional over their departure.

"Do you have a possible hotel lined up in Manaus?" he asked Jaap. "It would be nice to get together there over a good meal and compare notes."

Jaap gave him the name of some hotel, but didn't assure him that they would be there. I stood near Betti and waited. She looked nervous. Jaap was bluff and hearty. We helped them onto the adjoining cargo flat and passed them their bindles. "Good luck," said Fernando. "Have a good trip. See you in Manaus."

"Yah, yah," said Jaap.

"Good-bye," said Betti. "The best for you."

"Good luck," I called, meaning it. "Don't buy any glass beads in Minas."

We watched them until they disappeared from sight. Then we turned and headed for the tug. "I'm really going to miss them," said Fernando. "They are good people . . . . And you?"

"Well, I'm not going to cry over their departure . . . but yeah, I'll miss some things about them."

"We'll probably be seeing them again."

"Maybe . . . ." I'll definitely miss Jaap's innate sense for the ridiculous. His wild up and down temperament. His honest naivete . . . . This quality will serve him well in his travels, as will Betti's delicate looking body and sensitive face. They stir compassion in people. I chuckled. That Betti . . . I lay down on my pallet and drifted into a fog, still thinking about Jaap and Betti. I admired certain qualities of this obstinate couple. They were adventurous and hungry for a strong taste of life. They had endured the hardships of the trip with a minimum of complaint. And of all the travellers on the Magalhães, they were the least equipped, in terms of cultural experience, to deal with the strange environment . . . . Yet they're doing pretty damn well. Yeah, I wish them well.

Soon after our companions departure, the engines were ignited. I sat up and looked for the captain. He was standing near the galley. What do you know, I thought. He was telling the truth for a change. The captain gave some final instructions to the cook and came toward me on his way to the pilot's cabin.

"Captain!" I said, reaching into my pocket to draw out his money. He looked at me impassively. "Here is your money. I decided to remain with this boat." I could feel my face flushing.

"You are going to remain?"

"Yes. I'm going to remain . . . if I can."

Tentatively he accepted the proffered bills. His face tightened and he crumpled them in his hand. *"Tudo bem,"* he said coldly, and strode away.

Tudo bem my ass, I thought. But since we've both been jerks . . . what the hell. That's that . . . . Beautiful, I can't think of anything else I have to worry about right now. I put my head in my cupped hands and settled back on the wood, trying to space the world out. I felt terrible. During my tête à tête with the captain, and thanks to my ensuing anger with Jaap, my body had sustained itself on nervous energy and adrenalin. But now, with the pressure off, I sagged like a flag on a windless day. I began to shiver spasmodically. I touched my forehead. It burned. I got up and put on my thickest jeans, two pair of socks, and a sweater. I lay back down. The engine revved loud and we backed from the dock and set sail. The breeze from the motion of the boat cut through me. I wrapped myself in the mosquito netting and held it tight against my chest. Fernando came by to see how I was doing.

"Man, you definitely look sick now. What's wrong?"

"I don't know. But I have hot and cold chills."

"You can lay in my hammock if that will help you."

"Thanks, I think I will." I got up and staggered to his hammock. With difficulty I flopped and rolled my way on. My muscles felt like jelly. Once I finally settled into the hammock I shook worse than ever, my teeth chattered. Fernando saw this and placed his wool ruana over me.

"You can rest here for as long as you need," he said, his face clouded with concern. "Is there anything else I can do for you? Do you want some water?"

"No, thanks. You've already done plenty. I just need to rest and I should be fine. Thanks again."

"For nothing. Get some sleep." He turned and went to the stern.

Boy, I thought, I'm glad he's my friend. I sure need one right now. Now if I can sleep . . . . My thoughts raced a mile a minute, giving me no peace, denying my body the rest it needed. Damn! Why did I have to get sick? I can't stand being sick! And right now I can't afford to be sick . . . . You're a traitor, body. Of course, I've been abusing myself for

353

the past month now—both here and in Cali. It's finally catching up to me. I wish I could crawl away into a cave somewhere and get away from the world until this goes away . . .

And the worst of this is that I have no idea what's wrong with me. It could be almost anything . . . . A common flu bug. Internal parasites going wild from the unboiled water we've been drinking lately. Just a general breakdown from lack of sleep and too much drinking and activity. Or—I shuddered involuntarily—malaria. Yes, it could be that. True, I've been taking my Arylin pills daily—but the nurse warned me that that's no guarantee against catching it. The drug will just control the symptoms so that the person can more or less function and stay alive. Then, with continued use of the drug, a month or so, the disease will go away . . . . I sure hope she's right. I sure hope I don't have malaria . . . . But who knows? The whole time we were in Alvarães I had a bad feeling. All those mosquitos buzzing in my ears . . . feeling them land . . . feeling that cursed itch a few moments later . . . slapping away but knowing you'll never get all of them . . . falling asleep and being completely at their mercy . . . . One of the most helpless feelings I've ever had—knowing that such a tiny creature can effectively end your existence with a little scratch—like a knit sweater that unravels because of one loose thread. The fabric of life is so tenuous—never know when that loose thread will slip out. Makes me realize that I can't waste my time—it reminds me.

As the afternoon wore on I alternately stewed in my own clammy sweat or shivered at the intrusion of any vagrant breeze. The Magalhães forged ahead at fast cruising speed. The captain seemed intent on making up for lost time. At intervals, I would drift into uneasy dozes, these interludes of unconsciousness relieving my suffering, but on awakening, I felt no better than before. I tossed and turned and muttered to myself. Everyone left me alone.

Late in the afternoon we stopped at yet another backwater river port. All of the passengers and most of the sailors left the boat. I lay in the hammock and sweltered in the air of the breezeless shore. I started to feel as though I were suffocating. My throat was parched. I rolled out of the hammock and climbed shakily to the second deck to get water from the cooler. I drank water and leaned against the railing, catching the faint breeze off the river. Suddenly my legs gave out, I flopped against the railing and held on, my head spun crazily and chills swept through me. After a few seconds I recovered enough to take a couple of steps and fall into one of the nearby low hanging hammocks. It was made of heavy cloth. I'll just rest here for a little while, I thought. I rolled up in the hammock and grew warm. It was very comfortable. I closed my eyes and my head stopped spinning.

"What are you doing in my hammock?" said a sharp voice.

I opened my eyes and looked up. It was Milene, with hands on hips, a disgusted look on her face. I started to rise. "I just wanted to rest for a moment . . . "

"Hey, you look sick."

"I am."

She raised her hand. "You can stay there for a while. I don't need the hammock right now."

"Thanks." I settled back against the cloth. Milene went into the captain's cabin.

A short while later Nazaré showed up. I feigned sleep and watched her through half closed eyes. She stood and regarded me curiously for a moment, almost wistfully, or so it seemed to my foggy brain. Then she climbed into the adjacent hammock to take a nap. Save for the soft whooshing of our respiration, we lay in silence. I felt more peaceful. The mere presence of another person was a comfort. I began to doze off . . .

The boat cast off and we resumed our fast pace. With the boat in motion the second deck was much draftier than the hold. The chills pulsed through me. I began to quiver and twist uncomfortably, causing the hammock to sway and bump into Nazaré's. After a few minutes of this, she stirred and gave a low groan. I leaned on an elbow and peeked over the rim of the cloth to see if I had awakened her. She lay with her back to me. I gazed at her for a long moment. Then, having sensed me, she rolled over and gave me an irritated scowl.

"What are you looking at?" she demanded.

"Nothing. Everything . . . . I don't know. I feel ill."

"Ill?" She eyed me dubiously. "What's wrong with you?"

"Good question. I don't know . . . . It could be the flu . . . . Maybe malaria . . . . Maybe I'm dying . . . "

"I doubt it!"

"Yeah, me too. But I still feel bad."

Her scowl returned. "Listen, I'm very tired and want to sleep. Besides, you shouldn't be in Milene's hammock."

"She already knows. She saw me a little while ago. *Tudo bem* . . . . But, maybe I'll go downstairs."

"Well, if she said you can be in her hammock. I don't care. Whatever. Just don't move around so much!" She rolled back onto her face and belly.

I grinned and settled back into the hammock. My head felt better but the breeze continued to knife into me. It was impossible for me to sleep. Finally I gave it up and returned to Fernando's hammock. There, inexplicably, I fell immediately to sleep.

The next thing I knew, Fernando was shaking my shoulder and telling me it was time to eat. I got up, feeling extremely weak and groggy, and sat at the table. A plate of boiled pork and white rice was set before me. I had no appetite. I picked at the food. Finally I gave the pork to Fernando and ate about half the rice. Eloi gave me a pair of oranges; these I ate. Then I sat at the table with my head in my hands, my brain numb. Fernando and Eloi tried to converse with me, but I could barely understand what they were saying, let alone respond. The only thing I wanted to do was sleep.

Shortly after the plates were cleared from the table I tried to stir myself. I need a bed, I thought. I can't expect Fernando to let me sleep in his hammock tonight. Let's see . . . .

Two new passengers had come aboard on our last stop. One of them, a shady looking character with a long knife scar down the side of his cheek, was also without a hammock, and had taken over my spot on top of the engine room roof. I went over there to gather up my stray clothes. The man watched me suspiciously, giving me evil looks from time to time. When I finished gathering up my clothes, he placed his sea bag directly on the spot where I had been sleeping. I grinned at him.

"I'm going to sleep here," he said.

I laughed. "You're welcome to it . . . . But if I were you, knowing what I know now, I'd look for a different spot. It's noisy here."

He regarded me skeptically. I chuckled and walked away. He'll find out, I thought. Mr. Hard Guy. He looks tough enough to handle it— stupid enough, too. No more fucking banshee for me. I have a better place.

With Jaap and Betti gone, and their ridiculous outsized backpacks, there was plenty of space to make a bed on the low platform under Fernando's hammock. I cleared an area away from the aisle and piled shirts, dirty pants, socks, and whatever else I could use onto the spot. Then I wrapped the whole mess in my mosquito netting. Not a bad mattress, I thought, testing it with my hands. About time the mosquito netting came in handy for something . . . . I lay down on it. Just slightly lumpy. But the best bed I've had since Leticia.

Fernando came over and threw his ruana over me. "You can use this tonight," he said. "I don't need it. I have a warm sweater I can sleep in . . . . How do you feel?"

"Weak and dizzy. But I should be all right. This doesn't feel like anything fatal."

"Yeah, I doubt you have anything to worry about." He vaulted into his hammock. "You should be fine by tomorrow."

I lay with my eyes open and stared at the ceiling beams. Suddenly the cook stood over me, with those red-rimmed eyes that had flashed malevolently at me on more than one occasion, but this time they were filled with concern. "You are truly sick, eh?"

I nodded silently.

"Can I do anything for you? Can I get you something?"

"Well . . ." I considered briefly. "Yes, I could use a cup of hot water and a lemon."

"Lemon? Lemons?"

"Yes! Lemons."

"One or two? They are small."

"Two, then."

He nodded and went to the galley. A short time later he returned with a steaming mug of water and two green lemons. I borrowed Fernando's pen knife. The cook watched attentively as I split one of the lemons and squeezed the juice into the water. Then I cut the other one, squeezed one half into the water, and rubbed the other one against a small cut on my foot that was showing signs of infection. The cook nodded his approval.

"What?" I asked him.

"My mother used to do that to me when I was sick. Lemon juice for infections and colds."

"Did it work?"

The cook thumped his chest. He was a rock of a man. Either it worked or he has wonderful genes, I thought.

The cook wandered off and I sat up and drank my aromatic water. It would have been better with some tea, I thought, finishing it. Then I lay down and buried my head under my arms to block out the light. The hot water was making me sweat, my forehead burned. Man, I wish I had a nurse to put cold towels on my forehead . . . or anyone for that matter. It would be nice.

I must have dozed off because when I next became aware, it was to the pattering of bare feet against the deck. The sounds approached my head. I opened my eyes and looked up, dully, and there were Milene and Nazaré, looking down at me with sympathetic faces. I must be dreaming, I thought.

"You really are sick, *hein*?" asked Milene.

"A little bit."

"Can I do anything for you? There is a box of medicine upstairs . . . . Should I bring it?"

"No, thank you. I don't think you have medicine to help what I have . . . . You are very kind, but I just need to rest. Anyway, I already drank some lemon water."

"Lemon water? What does that do?"

I smiled. "Maybe nothing. But as long as I believe it does something, it has value."

"Can I help you with something?" offered Nazaré.

"Are you serious?"

"Yes, of course."

I studied her face. She seemed sincere enough. I know what she can do, I thought.

"Yes, Nazaré, you can help me."

"How?"

"Give me a kiss." I smiled.

"A kiss?" exclaimed Nazaré.

"Yes! A kiss. Nothing more."

"But why?"

"I need some kind of inspiration to fight this illness."

Milene guffawed. "It would seem that he isn't as sick as he looks."

"I'm probably sicker than I look . . . "

Nazaré took advantage of the diversion to back away toward the ladder. She looked genuinely nervous. I was surprised by this.

"Come on, Nazaré. What's wrong?"

"I can't do that. I don't want to do that."

"Why not? It's a very small thing to do."

"Yes, do it," said Milene. "It's not anything."

Nazaré crept toward me while speaking to Milene in a fast low voice. I understood almost nothing, but her face was visibly shaken. Maybe the joke has gone a little too far, I thought. She might be imagining that I have some exotic contagious disease or something.

Nazaré got down on her knees by my head.

"Listen," I said, "you don't have to do this. I was just joking."

"No! I said I would do something for you."

"*Tudo bem.*" I puckered my lips.

She leaned over me and, ignoring my lips, gave me a peck on the forehead.

"Thank you. I feel better already from that."

Nazaré replied by turning around and fleeing up the ladder.

Milene laughed uproariously. "That was good," she said, finally controlling herself. "Just what she needed."

"What do you mean by that?"

"Nothing . . . . Good night."

Milene followed Nazaré to the upper deck. I rolled over and thought about it. Why did Nazaré make such a big deal out of that? . . . In her profession she's risking disease almost every time out. That was weird. But I feel better now. It was somehow entertaining . . . . Nice of them to come down and see how I was feeling. In fact, almost everyone on this boat is being nice to me. It almost makes the suffering worthwhile . . . . Nah, I wouldn't go that far. But I'm glad I stayed with this boat.

As the evening wore on a few of the sailors came by to check on me. They all offered words of encouragement. Though my fever continued to rage, I was comforted by the concern of my companions. A peacefulness of mind and spirit came over me. Before too long I drifted into easy slumber.

Later, with the hold in darkness and all still, I awoke with a start. I felt more alert than at any time since my confrontation with the captain. The shirt I was using for a pillow was soaked with perspiration. I swiped at my forehead with the back of my hand. It came away damp. Then I rubbed my forehead with the tips of my fingers. A surge of elation went through me. "All right!" I murmured. This isn't that thick greasy sweat I've had all day—this is the light watery coolant preceding the breaking of a fever.

CHAPTER XIII

SAILING ON CALM WATERS

When I rose for breakfast I felt much improved. I took a few steps to test my legs. Though they trembled slightly, I was able to move about without the queasiness of the day before. I bent at the waist and took a deep breath. Something deep inside of me felt amiss. There's still some kind of organism lingering around in there, I thought. Just biding its time—like a dormant volcano. I can feel it. It's going to erupt on me in the future and waste my guts again . . . . Well, can't worry about that now. Might as well enjoy the respite.

"Good morning," I said, going to the stern and greeting the cook and three sailors.

"Good morning," they echoed.

"How are you today?" asked the cook.

"Much better . . . . I'm hungry."

The cook chuckled and went to get my coffee and crackers. The three sailors inquired after my health. I was gratified, but embarrassed by the attention.

"I'm much better, thank you. Don't worry yourselves over my condition. I'll be fine."

The sailors nodded and fell silent. As we drank our coffee we speculated on the amount of time to Manaus. Our boat was slicing through the water at a steady fast clip.

"At this velocity we should reach Manaus tomorrow afternoon . . . or early in the evening," said the tall sailor. Then he leaned close to me and said in a low voice, "If that *filho da puta* (son-of-a bitch), captain doesn't screw us again."

"Or have another convenient accident."

"Hein!"

As soon as the sun burned through the light mist I headed for the lumber pile. On the way I passed the scar faced man who had taken my spot on the roof of the engine room. He sat on his haunches and rubbed his eyes. His face was haggard and his muscles seemed stiff. I nodded to him. He grunted and put his right hand on his back. I know how you feel, I thought. But I warned you, turkey.

I went to the front of the flat and found Fernando and Eloi embroiled in a discussion. They paused for a moment, to greet me and allow me to find a seat, then resumed without skipping a beat. Eloi was doing most of the talking. His customary stoicism had deserted him. With his face screwed into tight lines he waved his arms and berated some one or some thing. I felt as though I had walked into a movie at intermission.

"What's the problem?" I asked him. "Who are you talking about?"

"Who? Who else! That *filho da puta,* captain! *Filho da puta!*" He pounded the plank he was sitting on with his fist. "You know, I have a child that I have never seen yet—and because of that captain . . . well, I should be seeing him today. And my wife, too! I haven't seen her for such a long time . . . . *Filho da puta,* captain!"

"Take it easy, man," said Fernando. "We'll soon be there and the wait will be over."

"Yeah, one of the sailors told me that we'll be in Manaus, by tomorrow . . . . You just have to wait a little longer. But you're right— he is a son-of-a-bitch," I said.

Eloi laughed. "Everyone on the boat knows what happened yesterday between you and the captain . . . . That was good. I wish I had been there to see it."

"It was nothing."

"No, it was something . . . . Something than *filho da puta* deserved!" Though his dark eyes continued to smolder Eloi's face relaxed and he assumed his usual calm demeanor. I looked at him thoughtfully. Eloi seems like a man who can hold a serious grudge . . . . I wouldn't want to be in the captain's shoes if he ever has the misfortune to run into him in some dark alley in Manaus, and all this bottled fury comes uncorked. Man . . .

We chatted of other things for a while. Then, lulled by the river, we fell silent. The morning slipped along. The sun shone hot and bright. Finally Eloi lifted his face to the sky and, in a throaty vibrant voice, began to sing. Fernando and I exchanged looks. Eloi paused and looked at us. "Go on!" we both said. Eloi smiled and continued. His voice was strong and pleasant. We listened to him appreciatively, speaking only to encourage him to sing more. I listened to the lyrics. I could actually understand him easier in song than when he spoke. He enunciated the words clearly and completely. He sang songs of travel and pain and love. He was telling us his story with these songs, baring his soul to the glare of our thoughts. I was moved, tingles went through me. I sat with glazed eyes, looking out over the river.

Eloi's voice rose as he began another love song—it was a strident joyful song of passionate love. Eloi was calling out across the water to his wife and children. His voice rose one octave higher on a final word and he was done, as abruptly as he had begun. Fernando and I clapped. "Bravo! Bravo!" said Fernando. "That was beautiful!" Eloi lowered his head for a moment, embarrassed. When he raised it he wore a contented smile on his bronzed face and his oval eyes gazed peacefelly out over the river. I shook my head in wonder. That's one way to get rid of a bad mood, I thought. It was nice to see . . .

A short while later we stopped at a tiny village. It was similar to the one where I traded the magazine for the papayas. As I walked up a gentle incline, accompanied by Eloi and Fernando, I began to stagger and my head whirled. I stopped for a moment. The heat felt intense, sapping my already weakened body even more. I was jelly-kneed and my breath came in short gasps. Man, I thought, what is this? Normally I could take a slope like this with ease. That bug did a job on me . . .

I moved on, following in Fernando's dusty wake, and made it to the top in time to see the captain and two sailors calling to a bare-chested man who had the bearing and countenance of the village honcho.

"How goes it?" called the honcho, raising his arm in a salute between equals.

"Tudo bem," said the captain, saluting back. They met and clasped hands. Then the negotiations began in earnest, with gesticulations and hearty laughter. We moved in for a closer look. But even Eloi had no idea what they were discussing. Then the captain pointed to a mud crusted pig who was roaming freely about the village compound. The honcho nodded and offered a few comments, some kind of sale's pitch no doubt.

"Tudo bem," said the captain.

"Very good," said the honcho.

He beckoned to a teenage boy, perhaps his son, and gave him some instructions. The boy retrieved a rope and made a slip noose of it. Meanwhile, another man dumped some green bananas and rotten oranges near the pig. The boy finished preparing the rope and crept toward the pig, who was munching unconcernedly on the bananas. The boy drew within range and set himself. The pig, warned by some sixth sense, turned and saw him. The boy cast. The pig skittered aside at the last possible instant and the rope deflected harmlessly off one of his sinewy haunches. A few of the bystanders snickered. The boy muttered a curse. The pig moved a few paces away. He still wanted the food.

The boy would have a chance to redeem himself. Now the entire village gathered to watch the show. The boy retrieved his lasso, a look of grim determination on his face. He moved with the cold purpose of the serious hunter. If he failed this time, he would be shamed in front of the entire village. The boy placed the noose on the ground, set some oranges within range of it, and hid himself along the side of a palm thatched cottage. The villagers and their guests from the Magalhães strung themselves in a ragged semi-circle encompassing the cottage and the noose. The crowd clucked eagerly as the pig minced toward the oranges and the waiting trap. The pig stopped several times and sniffed the air. He was wary and alert. He reached the first orange and gobbled it down. Then he snuffed about the rope with his active snout. The boy remained immobile. The pig ate another orange. There was one left, on the other side of the noose. The pig stretched his snout over the noose. For a moment he stood poised, then he started forward and one of his trotters strayed within the noose. The boy gave a shout and yanked the rope. He came up with air. The pig made a lightning hop and bolted away.

The boy was furious. He threw the rope aside and chased after the pig. The villagers shouted encouragement. Two young men joined in the chase. After a minute or so of frantic bolts and dizzy cuts, they managed to corner the pig against a stack of firewood. The men circled him. The pig stood at bay, its chest heaving. "Leave him for me," said the boy. The other men halted. The boy smiled and moved in on him. His arms gaped open. The pig stood poised on his front trotters and watched . . . . The boy made a quick off-balance lunge. The pig bolted between his legs and left the boy plowing a furrow in the dust with his chin. The other men were caught flat-footed. A man in the crowd tried a flying tackle and knocked the pig into a roll, but he scrambled to his feet and escaped into the surrounding bush.

For a few seconds everyone was stunned to silence. Then, like a swelling wave breaking onto the beach, the laughter grew and there were exclamations over the pig's resourcefulness. The boy picked himself from the dust, a distraught look on his face. The only injury was to his pride. As I watched him pat the dust from his body I thought, they'll never let him forget this one. Three strikes and you are out—at least until you get up again.

The crowd started to break up. The captain, the honcho, and a pair of villagers huddled together and decided not to pursue the pig into the jungle. The captain bought a case of fruit.

"We don't need that pig anyway," commented Fernando. "We still have two more aboard the boat and that goat that we picked up in the other town yesterday. I don't understand why he wanted this one . . . "

"Who knows?" I said. "Maybe he wants to sell livestock in Manaus . . . or make another extended stop somewhere."

"He better not," said Eloi.

We turned and headed for the boat.

"That was a strange spectacle," I said. "Like a bloodless bullfight."

"No, it was more sporting than a bullfight," said Fernando. "The pig wasn't penned in and therefore had a chance to escape."

"Escape?" exclaimed Eloi. "Escape to where? To the jungle? . . . Forget it, he has no chance there. The jungle is a cruel place of refuge . . . .The pig is domestic. He will return to the village when he loses his fear."

"Maybe the people here will let him live a while more in honor of his great struggle," I said.

Eloi shrugged and looked at me. "Maybe—if they don't have to sell him or eat him right away. He could be good breeding stock."

We reached the boat and Eloi retired to his hammock. Fernando and I returned to the wood pile, alone there for the first time in days. Fernando probed me with questions concerning my life in Colombia. Then, out of the blue, he asked, "You've been away from your country for a year, right?"

"A little more than a year."

"That's a long time. I wouldn't want to be away from my home and family for such a long period."

"What do you mean? . . . You will be if your plan succeeds."

"Yes, but . . . well, how is it for you? Don't you get homesick? Don't you miss certain things from the good life in the United States?"

I laughed. We've been all through this before, I thought. His good life and mine just aren't the same. . . . Fernando regarded me seriously, waiting for an answer. Maybe I can tell him a little more.

"Well, that's a good question you ask me. . . . Do I miss the United States? You know, after the first few months of adjusting to Colombia that's a question I rarely ask myself anymore. My life in Colombia is far from perfect—but I've made a home for myself there. In fact, except for watching much less sports on television, my style of life is almost the same. And besides, there are still many places in South America I want to see before I return to the United States. . . . So, I suppose the answer is no, I don't miss the United States that much."

"But you must miss something. . . . Come on."

"Well, I miss my family—my parents, my brothers and sisters. Some good friends and familiar places. What else? . . . I miss the diversity of San Francisco. It's a cosmopolitan city with almost every culture in the world represented in one way or another. In that city, you can almost imagine yourself travelling around the world without ever leaving. It's like a great experiment trying to assimilate so many different races and cultures . . . . Yeah, I miss that variety. And also, I miss some of my sports . . . "

"Yes, but," interjected Fernando, "what about the way of life? The luxuries and the facility for education and work?"

"I told you, man, my style of life is almost exactly the same here as it is there. . . . Look, Fernando, right now, as a Peace Corps volunteer, I have a higher standard of living than I ever had in my country. Before, I either lived with my family or I was a student. I almost never had extra spending money. Now here, on what I make, I can eat out every day if I feel like it."

"Really?" He stared at me incredulously. "It's difficult for me to believe that you live better in Colombia than in the United States."

"It's true, in my case." I shrugged. "I have no reason to lie to you . . . . Yes, even working part time in the U.S., I made more dollars than I do now—but what I make here goes a lot farther. What I make now wouldn't even pay the rent in my country."

"Yes, because the dollar is strong compared to our currencies. . . . But you can certainly make a lot of money in your country if you have a good profession. And you have the facility for education. The cost of that is prohibitive for most people in my country."

"I went to the university with a full scholarship; I still graduated deep in debt. It's not free—at least not at the prestige places. Those are like private clubs. . . . Anyway, I've learned much more on my own, by reading and travelling around, than I ever did in the university. All they do there is certify your knowledge . . . . And for what I want to do, I don't need certification."

"I'm puzzled by you . . . . What exactly do you want to do?"

I took a deep breath. "That's something I tell very few people . . . "

"Why? What's the secret?"

"Because most people either scoff or they get the wrong idea about my motivation. In neither case do the take me seriously . . . . So, it's better not to talk. I'll just let my actions speak."

"You can tell me. I take you very seriously from what I've seen of you on this trip."

"Yeah, I think you would." I smiled. "I want to write."

"Ah, so that's it," smiled Fernando. "You want to be a writer. That explains many things to me."

"Maybe not everything. . . . I said I want to write—not be a writer."

"What is the difference?"

"The difference is that I don't look on my writing as a profession—but rather as a vocation!"

Fernando's forehead was wrinkled.

"You see, man, I have to write. Whether I ever make a cent at it or not is besides the point. . . . It's something that I do for its own sake. When I really sit down to write—I am passionate about it. It gives me a feeling of power and absolute freedom of expression that liberates me. I recreate my world . . . . When I have that feeling I am free of everything else."

"How long have you felt this way?"

"For as long as I can remember. I simply couldn't articulate the feeling. Before I even knew how to write I loved to create things in my mind. This is the same thing. Writing is merely my tool of expression. It could be something else for someone else."

"But why writing?"

"I don't know . . . . When I was a child I used to see my father read everything he could get his hands on. We never talked about it, but as soon as I learned to read, I became the same way. I read everything. Writing was a natural progression. I wanted to make known my own impressions of life—if to no one else, then to myself."

"So, have you begun a book yet?"

"Of course, hundreds, but right now they're all in my head."

"When are they going to come out?"

"I don't know, yet. . . . But soon. Right now I'm not ready. I'm still playing around with things . . . "

"Playing around? Why?"

"Well, it's even hard for me to explain to myself. It's not clear, it's trying to form, it has something to do with me feeling so strongly about something that I have to put it down and share it with other people. But before I can do this, there are certain things within me that I have to kill and bury. Then I can write for publication."

"Things inside? Like what? Are you speaking of amoebas?"

I laughed drily. Maybe this is getting too serious, I thought.

"No, Fernando, not amoebas. More like illusions."

"Illusions of what?"

"Illusions of how I thought the world should be."

"Illusions," said Fernando in a dreamy voice. "They can be important, also."

"Yes, of course! They can keep you going even when you don't know why. . . . But if they become so real that you can't even tell the truth to yourself for fear that it will destroy you . . . well, then maybe they do more harm than good."

"Fine. But what is real for you may not be real for me. We live in different worlds with different realities."

"That's true. But you still have to know your own before you can ever hope to know someone else's."

"All right then, speaking of illusions. . . . How do you propose to live while you wait for these stories to come out of you? What do you plan to do when you leave Colombia?"

I laughed. "The same thing I'm doing now — living! Keeping my eyes open and learning what I can. My curiousity is still sharp."

"That's fine. That's fine. But how will you make a living? Learning doesn't pay the bills."

"I don't know. I'll do what I have to. . . . Get some job in recreation . . . counsel juvenile delinquents . . . maybe work as a translator . . . get a job with some international organization . . . deliver telephone books . . . whatever! That's all secondary to me. I just need enough money to do what I want—write! I don't need a lot of excess things cluttering up my life."

"You mean to say that you don't like nice things?"

I shook my head. "On the contrary, I do like nice things. But I don't need them. There's not a thing in the world that can give me the pleasure that writing does. . . . Now if I have to do something else to get a nice car and house—at the expense of my writing . . . well, forget it! I don't want to be weighed down by a lot of possessions. I don't want my actions dominated by them."

"Yes, of course, not to dominate your life . . . but to make life more comfortable—more secure. Don't tell me that you couldn't write better if you were financially secure."

"Who knows? If I were financially secure I might lose my edge and fire." I chuckled. "Anyway, if there's one thing that I've learned in the course of my life, it's that nothing is more fragile than life. I want to live! Not live to accumulate possessions. That's fine for other people— but not for me!" I giggled. "Now wait a moment, who are you to be speaking of the value of security? If you're so security oriented, what are you doing making this trip?"

"Well, as I told you before, this is something special in my life. . . . But someday I expect to be a lawyer and I will live very well."

"Living well . . . I'm still not sure we agree on what that means."

"To me it means having what I need."

"Then, we agree, in a relative sense."

"Relative? How relative?"

"Well, for example, when I was growing up we lived in a neighborhood that, by the standards of the United States, was poor. But I never felt poor until I went to high school and started meeting poeple from other parts of the city. I mean, growing up, I had plenty of food, a home, a family, friends, activities, a community. I picked my own friends. We roamed around the city together and saw things on our own. I never felt deprived. . . . On the other hand, my father was a gardener, he had some wealthy clients, and he used to take me to work with him once in a while. . . . Anyway, one day when I was about eight or nine years old, he took me with him on a job. Man, this house he was working at was a mansion. The lady who owned the place showed me around; it was clean enough to eat off the floor and was filled with antiques. 'How would you like to live in a place like this?' my dad asked me. 'I don't know,' I said. 'It seems more like a museum than a home.' Then later, I was playing around in the backyard with one of her children. He was dressed in very nice clothes. Really too nice for the rough game of tag we were playing. . . . Anyway, we were having a good time, when all of a sudden this black maid comes out of the house and yells at him not to get his clothes dirty and to act like a little gentleman. Man, you should have seen the embarrassment on that boy's face. A few minutes later she called him into the house for good. Maybe his mother didn't want him playing with me—but he wanted to. So, I saw that he was no happier than I was. I perceived that his wealth also put restrictions on him. He had to watch what he said, be careful of who he played with, in general abide by more structured rules than me. That struck me as way too restrictive and all together boring. I thought, if all rich people live like that, I want no part of it . . . "

"Yes," said Fernando excitedly, "but money can also give a person great freedom! The freedom to travel, to be educated, to buy things . . . "

"To be bought and never do what you really want! . . . All of what you say is true, if the person with the money doesn't become obsessed by it. But if they do . . . they can carry it on their back until it sinks them. . . . Man, Fernando, I saw how the rich people in Bogotá live . . . behind high walls with broken glass atop it. It astounded me.

Armed guards patrolling openly with machine guns. The children having to be guarded wherever they went for fear of kidnapping. Man, if that's the security wealth brings you—than you can have it! You might as well be living in a comfortable prison. Sorry, I feel absolutely no envy for people living like that. Really, I see them as stupid. Rather than share just a little of what they have—they want to force people who have nothing to take it away from them . . . . Inevitably that will happen—anywhere."

"Yes, well, that's an extreme example. I'm not talking about that kind of money . . . . I'm talking about being comfortable."

"All right, let's take you for an example . . . . Do you think you would have taken a trip like this to get to Paris if you had enough money to fly?"

Fernando tugged at his hairless chin for a moment. "Who knows?" Then he grinned. "I probably would have flown."

"There it is! And you would have missed out on this adventure. Now I wonder if a 16-hour plane ride, or whatever it is, would have been as memorable as the experience you've already had—and who knows what's to come for you on the rest of the trip. Man, this is intensity! It's you out in the world taking your chances without insulation. You're probably gaining more experience from this trip than most people get in a lifetime . . . . Money couldn't do that for you. You had to do it for yourself."

"This is true . . . with more money I would have had a different kind of adventure. But, don't tell me that you're defending the virtues of poverty . . . . You should go to some of the *pueblos jovenes* (slums) of Lima and see what it does to people."

"I know what it does to people. It did it to some of the best friends of my childhood. And they weren't really that poor compared to other people—they just thought they were and that was enough. So, poverty or necessity can either drive you so deep inside yourself that you shrivel up and die, or it can drive you out of yourself to scale the heights . . . "

Fernando was eyeing me with wrinkled brow. I fell silent, thinking of the past.

"Whatever made you think like this?" he said, breaking the silence.

"Everything I've been telling you . . . . Plus, high school is when it really started; the heavy symbols. If you don't have these clothes, and this car, and this ring, and this friend, and this piss, and this shit—than you're not a man. Or, better said, a man of substance, as though a car or clothes can give a person character . . . . And what really got me—

most of the people giving me this advice on how to become a man, well, a number of them had personal lives that were disasters. I listened, but I also thought, who are you to be giving advice on how to live to anybody? You better take a look at your own life and get your own act together first . . . "

Fernando laughed. "I know what you mean. . . . Misery loves company. It seems that sometimes the people who are least sure of what to do give the most advice—especially when they don't have the conviction to follow their own advice. . . . But they usually mean well."

"Yeah, so did Hitler — for Germany."

"Man, you are brutal. I would like to hear the kind of advice you give to the delinquents in that prison you work at."

"Really, the only thing I tell them is to learn how to think for themselves—to take responsiblity for their own lives. If I, or anyone, gives them advice, and it's wrong for them, the person who gave the advice doesn't suffer the consequences—the person who took the advice does. Now I might say, if you do this or that, this will likely be the consequence. . . . I might not agree with what they want to do, but I can't tell them not to do it. I just say be prepared for the consequences. And don't make excuses and don't have regrets. And don't say you did it because someone told you to—be aware that you made the decision from your choice . . . "

Fernando laughed again. "Now I've got you figured out . . . . You are a non-conformist existentialist."

"Whatever that is . . . hate categorizations. Let's just say that I've never tried to fit in anywhere, as a consequence, I think I can fit in everywhere . . . "

"What?"

"I just want to be myself . . . . A person can like me, or they can dislike me, as long as they do it because of the person I am and not for some artificial reason. That's all I ask. My individuality is the one thing I never want to compromise."

"I like you!" said Fernando.

"I like you, too! When I meet someone like you it makes all the unpleasant meetings with other people worthwhile."

We were silent for a moment, both of us somewhat embarrassed.

"A non-conformist existentialist," I laughed. "That's a good one . . . . In high school my nicknames were Martian and Caarazy. The one you gave me is certainly an improvement—I think . . . . So, now that you know what I am, what do you think you are?"

Fernando looked out over the river. "I'm not sure, yet . . . "

We watched the wash kick over the prow of the flat and spray our legs and feet. The wind gusted hard, seeming to sift through my ears and into my head, swirling my thoughts into a confused jumble. I felt drained.

"There's one other thing I wanted to ask you," said Fernando.

"Ask."

"Don't you want to make money from writing?"

"Of course, then I wouldn't have to do anything else . . . . But I'm prepared not to make money. That won't stop me."

"That would be very difficult."

"Definitely! Just like making this trip is difficult . . . . But if you're truly not certain that you want to do something, you can always find reasons not to . . . . And if you're truly certain that you do want to do something—you just do it! Exactly like you making this trip."

"Then you're absolutely certain?"

"Yes! I already did all my soul searching. I'm compelled."

"Good luck."

"Thanks. I'll need it."

Shortly afterwards there was a shout to our rear. We turned and saw the first mate in the pilot's cabin waving us in to lunch. We got up and headed for the tug. One of the sailors was swabbing the deck near the tethered animals. Another pig was gone; only the boar remained, along with the newly acquired goat. The boar looked pathetic. He had buried his head between his trotters and was trembling violently. How excruciating, I thought. Watching the other pigs go down one by one. Now he only has the goat for company—and he looks as terrified as the boar. What a life!

We ate lunch with Eloi. Our conversation was light. Without Jaap and Betti, things had really calmed down.

After lunch Fernando and Eloi climbed into their hammocks for a nap. I headed for the lumber. On my way out of the tug I spied La Gordita and the tall sailor making out in a dark corner. Their embrace was impassioned. La Gordita saw me and pulled out of his arms. I kept walking and gave them the thumbs up sign. *"Tudo bem."* I'm glad someone found romance on this tug, I thought.

I went to the sunken niche atop the lumber stack and lay down to nap. The sun was high and hot. I awoke after a short while with my face burning. I draped an extra shirt over my head and face and tried to nap again. It's such a beautiful afternoon, I thought drowsily. Why haven't the girls come out to sunbathe? . . . They haven't come down for meals, either . . . . Maybe they're avoiding us . . . . If they are, they're doing a

371

good job of it.

As the afternoon progressed, I dozed off and on. Eventually the sun was partially obscured by vagrant clouds. Then a thick overcast set in. Our speed decreased. Eloi and Fernando came and joined me.

"We're approaching another fairly large port," said Fernando. "We're going to stop for a while."

"This is Coari," said Eloi. "I know it. I used to work here. It's not a bad place."

"We're now three/fourths of the way to Manaus," said Fernando. "At this speed we should reach it by tomorrow."

I crossed my fingers and shook them in the air.

"If God and the *filho da puta* so desire," added Eloi.

We chugged into the harbor; though active, it was less frenetic than Tefé's. We were soon docked. The town of Coari lay before us.

We went ashore and crossed a wide, fairly clean, pebbly beach. We hit the town. Immediately we entered a market area with considerable commercial bustle, but it was tempered with an air of easy familiarity. The majority of the shoppers stared at us with more curiosity than hunger. As we strolled along streets of alternating pavement and dirt, we felt at ease. We browsed among fruit stalls and ambulatory vegetable vendors. The vendors were helpful without being pushy.

"This place is all right," I said to Fernando. "It seems to have a character somewhere in between the extremes of Alvarães and Tefé."

"Yes, it's boring."

I laughed. "We can probably use a little boredom before we reach Manaus . . . . From what I've heard and read, that's one wild city."

"We'll see."

"How long will we be here?" I asked.

"The first mate said about an hour," said Eloi. "We still have time."

We headed for the center of town. It began drizzling. We ducked into an open-ended market with a corrugated steel pavillion. There were lines of fruit and vegetable stalls. I decided to buy some fruit. I went down the line, picking and rejecting as the prices dictated, everything negotiable, playing one vendor off against another. Fernando got on me some; he didn't think I haggled enough.

"Ah, what for?" I said. "If I think the price is reasonable I take it. Everyone has to make a living . . . . Besides, I'd rather eat than talk right now."

"You could still get a better price, man. This can be fun."

"Yeah, yeah. But I hate shopping."

"Do you have anything like this in the United States?"

"Nothing exactly like this . . . . But we have flea markets."

"Flea markets?"

"Yeah, strange name, eh?"

I quickly bought small bags of oranges, lemons, and mangos for us to suck on while we made the rounds and looked at the leather goods on the other side of the market. We saw nothing special. We chatted with some of the vendors. We were listless, marking time, anxious to cast off and get on to Manaus. The adventure was definitely losing its zest. I felt like a commuter going to work. The big city—Manaus—was calling to me.

"We better get back to the boat," said Eloi.

Silently we filed onto the street. We walked fast through the drizzle. My legs were leaden and my breath short. I lagged behind. Fortunately Fernando stopped at a *barraca* (bamboo stall) near the beach. These things are everwhere, I thought, catching up to them. Just what you need for light refreshments.

Fernando ordered a glass of ice water, and totally butchered the Portuguese pronunciation of *gelada* (ice).

The old woman behind the counter flinched at the sound. Eloi and I giggled behind our hands.

"*Espanhol?*" asked the woman, looking at Eloi. He nodded.

Fernando flushed all the way to his chest. "Well, what do you want?" he said in Spanish, his tone irritated. "I've only been speaking this tongue for a month."

"There's no problem, man," I said. "Relax. It sounded funny but it's all right. Like this you learn . . . . Shit, I can't count the times I've been laughed at in Colombia because of my accent. What are you going to do? Take it and learn. When I know I sound funny I want them to tell me how to say it correctly . . . . And the only way I know is if they laugh or something to tell me."

Fernando's face was still red and upset. "No, that's not the way. That is rude and tactless!"

I shrugged. "I think it's much more rude and tactless to let someone go on making a fool of themselves. That's what I do if I want to get back at someone—I let them make fools of themselves."

"Well, that's you! I don't like being laughed at."

"Who does? . . . But do you want to get laughed at one time or ten times?"

"Zero times!"

"All right, man . . . . But the lady didn't laugh at you, she felt insulted because you mispronounced her language. Eloi and I laughed—be mad at us, we're your friends."

Fernando was finally appeased when the woman handed him a glass of water with ice and said, "This is how you pronounce it . . . . Ge-la-da. *Gelada.*"

Fernando took a drink and repeated the word. The woman nodded in approval.

"I bet you never mispronounce that word again," I said.

Fernando smiled. "No, I suppose not."

We returned to the tug and lounged in the hold. We resumed our passage at dusk. A short time later dinner was served. I picked at my food. Since the onset of my illness, my appetite for solid food had deserted me. The insipid pork and white rice before me did nothing to reawaken it. Still, I ate.

Our table conversation was desultory. There was an air of tension and impatience gripping the hold. Almost everyone had retreated into private shells, as though we were loath to say the wrong thing, because it might upset our luck and cause a catastrophe. A superstitious lot, I thought, and I must be one of them. The sailors are walking around as though they're about to enter a battle. I used to feel like this before football games in high school. . . . Anxious to get out on the field and begin the game but . . . this hold is relatively cozy and secure now, like a familiar locker room. But we'll soon have to take the field in Manaus—a strange, unknown, and perhaps, hostile place. What awaits me there?

I dove deep into the lake of introspection. I walked out to the prow. The night had turned warm and clear. I climbed across to the flat and went to the niche atop the lumber. I sat and thought, mesmerized by the forward lights of the tug as they winked like bulbous fire flies. Just how expensive will this Manaus be? I've spent much more money than I anticipated so far . . . . Can't imagine things getting any cheaper in a big tourist city. But away from the tourist zone, it shouldn't be too bad. Ah, why worry, I'll find out when I get there.

Fernando emerged from the tug and climbed up to join me. He had a preoccupied air. We sat in silence for a while.

"What do you think Manaus will be like?" he asked.

"I don't know. But it's a city. I know how to take care of myself better in cities than I do in towns. . . . Coming from Lima, I suppose you do, too."

"Yes, probably, Lima is an immense city. Much bigger than Manaus. . . . But it's my city and they speak my language there. This is something else."

"Yeah, well, it's something else but it shouldn't be all that different . . . . When I arrived in Bogotá, I spoke very little Spanish, and it's a city of around six million people, but I got around all right on my own when I had to. . . . Sometimes better on my own."

"Do you know where you are going to stay in Manaus?"

"No, I don't have the faintest idea. Unless someone on this boat gives me a tip . . . I'll just grab a bus or taxi and go downtown to some cheap place."

"Maybe we can look for a place together . . . "

"Sure, if you want. . . . But what about your friends?"

"It may take me a day or so to locate them. I don't have an exact address."

"No problem, man. It'll be good to have your company." We shook on it. "But I warn you now, we're talking about a very cheap place. I'm running low on money. I can see right now that I'm going to have a hell of a time to get back to Colombia. Everything is more expensive than I expected."

"Yes, I understand," said Fernando, nodding his head rapidly. "Once I find my friends, they might be able to put you up for free, or for next to nothing . . . . They might even be able to get you some work."

I laughed. "If there's one thing that I don't want to do in Manaus—it's work. I want my vacation, man. But thanks for the thought."

"What if you run out of money?"

"Oh, I'll think of something. . . . I can always call the Peace Corps—if I have to—to advance me some of my money. But I don't want to do that. . . . Anyway, let's forget about the possible problems for a while. From what I've read, Manaus should be an exciting city."

"Yes, the fabulous capital of the rubber barons. The rococo opera house constructed from materials brought from different European cities. The floating market. The colonial architecture. The first South American city to have street cars. Incredible, all of this in the middle of the mostly unexplored rainforest . . . "

"Yes, and aside from that tourist stuff, I read that it's a *zona franca* (duty free port). That usually attracts all sorts of adventurous and strange people. It has to be a wide open city."

"For sure, with much temptation—expensive hotels, elegant clubs, good restaurants, tour packages, beautiful women, gambling, musical shows . . . "

"Uh huh." I listened with my eyes closed, imagining some of the temptations, especially the restaurants.

"And another thing," gushed Fernando, "maybe the grandest of all—the fabulous 'Wedding of the Waters.' "

I opened my eyes and looked at him. "I've heard of that. But what exactly is it?"

"It's where the muddy brown waters of the Amazon meet the blue-black waters of the Rio Negro outside Manaus. The force of the two great rivers are such, that when they meet, their currents flow side by side for many kilometers without intermingling—like a wedding procession, the two colors clearly delineated, moving together toward an eventual union. Then the Amazon, the great mother of all rivers, dominates in the end with its café au lait. . . . It's a phenomenal natural display."

"Yeah, the way you describe it to me."

Fernando laughed. "Thank you, but it must be beyond mere description. I can't wait to see it."

"Yes."

Fernando covered his mouth with his hand and yawned. "Well, I'm sleepy now. I'm going to my hammock and rest up for tomorrow. . . . Are you coming in now?"

"No, it's pleasant here tonight. I think I'll stay out a while longer."

"All right, later." He was gone.

I looked at the stars. Then I folded my arms over my knees and rocked myself. I grew drowsy. A breeze kicked up and fanned me uncomfortably. I lay down flat on the bottom of the niche and the breeze became a gentle caress on my upturned face. The engine noise and water pump were distant hums. The whooshing of the flat through the water was akin to the reassuring patter of a spring shower against a bedroom window. I dozed off, woke, and dozed again. I woke again and struggled up on my elbow. Ah, the hell with it, I thought. It's comfortable enough to sleep right here. Why not?

I lay down and slipped into dreamland. . . . I was in bed with that dark haired, light complected, fiery girl from Medellin, just as I had been a month before in Cali. We were in the same sleazy *pensión* room near downtown. We were having a wonderful time. But how did I get back here? I thought . . . .The room and the girl vanished. Suddenly I was a small boy again, in bed, at my parent's home on Folsom Street. I was sound asleep, a silly grin on my face, dreaming of a voyage I was making with Jack London. Then I felt something wet cascading over my face and into my mouth. I spluttered and opened my eyes. It was my older brother, dumping a glass of cold water over me and laughing like a fiend. A typical raunchy joke of his. Incensed, I leaped to my feet on the bed, ready to brawl. My brother disappeared. His laughter rang in my ears.

No! I was back on the lumber pile. A shower dribbled from the sky, each drop clear and individual, plastering my hair to my scalp and my shirt to my skin. "Fuck!" I exclaimed. "Can't I have even one night of complete peace!" Well, this isn't too bad, I thought. Maybe I can wait it out.

I made a partial roof from some loose short boards. Then the rain began coming down in buckets. I shivered as the wind gusted. That's enough, I thought, getting to my feet. I can't fight nature—especially one as fickle as this. Time to go into the tug and bury my nose in a smelly old shirt. Damn!

With caution I climbed down from the lumber and onto the metal flat, my worn tennis shoes slipping as I went. I'll have to buy some new ones, I thought. More money I can't afford to spend.

I was distracted from my thoughts by the plaintive whimpering of the animals. I looked to the right. There, their shadows silhouetted against the lumber wall be a feeble glow from the tug, were the boar and the goat, huddled against each other and pushing against the unyielding wood, desperate to escape the rain. I was touched by their plight. I stepped toward them. They pushed harder and looked at me with fearful eyes. I knew it was foolish, but I was unable to repress a feeling of sadness.

I turned away and climbed into the tug, haunted by their eyes. How stupid I was to be angry at the rain, I thought. What do I have to complain about? At least I have a choice right now . . .

CHAPTER IVX

THE WEDDING OF THE WATERS

All of the sailors and the male passengers were up and on the stern at the crack of dawn. We ate the tired crackers and slurped the sweet coffee with new enthusiasm. There was one consuming question on the minds of all of us . . . . Would we reach Manaus before nightfall? The sailors predicted that we would, barring an accident or an act of the captain.

"After all," said the tall sailor, "we've already had more than our share of bad luck on this trip. The wind must shift in our favor."

"But can't anyone here calculate exactly when we will arrive?" asked Fernando.

"Early evening or late afternoon," said the tall sailor. The others nodded in agreement. "I hope for the sake of you passengers it's the afternoon—it would be a shame not to see the *'Casamento das Aguas'* (Wedding of the Waters)."

"But you could always go on a tour and see it later," said another sailor. "An expensive tour."

"It would never be the same for me if that happened," I said. "Not after this trip."

"Don't worry. We should arrive before dark."

"Now, when we arrive and dock, is it easy to get to downtown? Is it close?"

"No," said the tall sailor. "It's not close. But you can take a taxi without much problem."

"Yes," said another, "but be very careful and alert. Where we dock is near one of the worst *favelas* of Manaus. A very bad place . . . . Where the shadows can jump at you."

All right, I thought, I'll keep that in mind. But for now . . . we have the sweet coffee and an invigorating breeze. There'll be time to worry later.

We broke up and went our separate ways. Fernando and Eloi went to the lumber. I stayed behind to take my second shower of the trip in the tug's bathroom, this time careful to keep my hair dry and free of sand. Then I went out to join Fernando and Eloi.

Eloi was singing again, with even more joy than he had displayed the day before. The word *você* kept resounding in the clear morning air. Eloi raised his voice each time he sang it, as though he were trying to talk to someone far away through sheer sentiment. When he finished the song he paused to catch his breath.

"Who were you singing to?" I asked him.

For a moment he regarded me as though I were a moron for asking such a question. His face told me that some things are just understood without explanation. I bowed my head.

"I'm thinking and singing of my wife and home," he said. "With luck, and if God wills it, I will soon be there."

"I suppose you can hardly wait, eh," said Fernando, giving him a broad wink.

Eloi ducked his head shyly. "The wait is killing me."

Fernando and I exchanged furtive glances. It was understood—no one would be waiting for us in Manaus. We looked at Eloi and smiled wistfully.

"Eloi," I said. "When you say *você* (you), is that your most familiar form to address a loved one?"

"Well, as you know, we have three ways to say you in Portuguese. . . . Some people use *Tu* as the familiar form. . . . But for me, *você* is the most intimate word. When I think of my wife, I think of her as *você*, even more than her name."

"So, if I want to get intimate with a girl in Manaus, I should use *você*?"

Eloi chuckled. "Yes, and you can get away with it right away because you are a foreigner—whereas for a Brazilian, who should know better, it might be considered very rude."

"Listen, Eloi," said Fernando. "What are my chances of catching a boat from Manaus to Belém?"

"That's no problem. . . . It just depends on how much you want to pay."

"I don't want to pay anything. I would like to work my way there."

"Of course, that can be done, if you find a boat that needs a common laborer. But many people are looking for work like that—and a Brazilian will normally get first preference—or they will try to take advantage of you."

Fernando listened to this with furrowed brow. The closer we drew to Manaus the deeper grew the furrow and the more often it appeared.

It's going to be a wrench for him to leave this boat, I thought. Back to a life of total uncertainty. . . . As for me, I'm anxious to get off. I'm ready to throw myself into the seething anonymity of the city. I need space to move and think, lose myself in the mob before I return to the little town . . .

Fernando was still questioning Eloi concerning transportation. He had little concrete information to share.

"You just have to go to the docks and go from boat to boat, asking questions," said Eloi. "Patience is the key. All is possible with patience."

Huh, I thought, how many times have I heard this cliché in South America? Ten times a day.

"That's it," said Fernando. "You're right, patience and luck."

"A little desperation probably wouldn't hurt, either," I added. "A feeling of urgency—it works miracles. . . . Especially when you're basically lazy like I am."

"Changing the subject," said Fernando, turning to Eloi, "what does 'The Wedding of the Waters' mean to you?"

"O Casamento das Aguas?" Eloi placed his chin in a work-callused palm and pondered for a moment. "Well, it is something very special. It is . . . It is . . . It is beautiful!" He smiled. "It is very difficult for me to express. I think for you, it would be better to wait and see it without another person's feelings intruding. . . . I say only this, for me it represents home. The gateway to Manaus."

Fernando and I looked at each other and chuckled.

"Why do you laugh?" asked Eloi.

"Because you sound so mysterious," said Fernando.

"Yes, almost mystical," I added. "Now you really have me curious."

"That's very good," said Eloi. "It will increase your pleasure at seeing it. . . . Let's not speak of it anymore."

We nodded in agreement and fell silent for a while. We sailed fast, our course was near the center of the river. After a time, a tug, similar to our own but without a cargo flat, appeared off to our left, traveling in the opposite direction and hugging the shore. I watched it approach. The tug seemed to make no headway. It was moving at a crawl, floundering against the current. Look at that, I thought. The power of this river is absolutely staggering.

"How long does it take a boat like that to make the trip from Manaus to Benjamin Constant?" I asked Eloi, pointing to the huffing and puffing tug.

"Depends on the amount of cargo and stops. . . . Normally it would take between eight to ten days—without problems," he finished sardonically.

"Without problems?" I chuckled. "And with problems?"

"Two weeks."

"Well, if that's the case, that doesn't leave me much time to see Manaus. In order to return to Colombia in time to begin work I'd need to leave within two days."

"Can't you fly back?" asked Eloi.

"Maybe I'll have to . . . . Well, I'll worry about it when the necessity arrives."

"Yes." Eloi smiled. "You will certainly arrange something. You are a strong person."

"Strong? What do you mean? . . . Stubborn?"

"Yes, but also, I've watched you—you have a strong will to accomplish your mission."

"My mission?"

"Yes, you know what I'm speaking of . . . "

I left it at that. Eloi saw something that I was still working out for myself.

The morning dragged interminably.

"It seems that there will be no stops until we arrive at Manaus," said Fernando.

"Tudo bem," said Eloi. "It's about time the *filho da puta* turned serious."

"It's kind of boring without any stop," I said.

A short time later the first mate yelled at us to come in for lunch. We walked over the top of the lumber and encountered Nazaré and La Gordita in the niche, sunbathing in their bathing suits.

"Why so exlusive?" I said playfully. "You could get better sun where we were. Don't you like us anymore?"

La Gordita chuckled goodnaturedly. Nazaré gave a derisive snort. "The sun is fine here," she said.

"What is one to do with you?" I said, laughing. I followed Fernando and Eloi who hadn't bothered to stop.

Lunch was more of the same. Soggy white rice and leftover pork. I served myself a small portion and ate it.

"Is that all you want?" Fernando asked me. "There is more for you."

"No, you guys eat it. . . . I was just thinking of the big chicken dinner I'm going to eat at some restaurant in Manaus tonight. . . . Accompanied by a cold beer or two. . . . And a mixed salad." I licked my chops. "I can hardly wait."

Fernando laughed. "But that's later. What about now?"

"I don't want to spoil my appettite."

After lunch we returned to the top of the lumber stack, settling down in the niche to cut the edge off a brisk wind that had driven Nazaré and La Gordita to cover. Fernando unfurled his map and spread it on a plank, determined to pinpoint where we were and when we could expect to arrive at Manaus. He traced the river with his index finger to where it converged with the Rio Negro. Then he squinted up at the already descending sun. He shook his head and sighed. "It would be a tragedy, after all that has happened, if there's not enough light to see the coming together of the waters."

"It's out of our hands," said Eloi.

Fernando and Eloi chatted. I remained quiet and watched the shore. Little by little signs of a large population center appeared along both banks. The jungle was retreating from the shore, ebbing back as though from a beach at low tide, the wild vegetation replaced by sizeable cultivations of grains, vegetables, and neatly rowed fruit trees. Interspersed among the plantings were the now familiar thatched homes of the Brazilian farmer and his retinue of domestic animals. Corrals with horses began to appear. Then, glaring whitely at us from a field of green, came a mammoth plantation mansion, enclosed by wrought iron gates and flanked by carefully groomed lawns with dashes of bright flower beds. Its graceful arches and columns soared artfully over the river.

"By God!" exclaimed Fernando. "Look at that! That must be one of the colonial mansions of the rubber barons. It looks as though it were dropped here from outer space."

"Yeah, it's beautiful," I said.

"A beautiful mausoleum," said Eloi. "My grandfather told my father stories of the butchery and blood letting that went into the building of these mens' fortunes."

"It must have been like the Gold Rush in California," I mused aloud. Rubber barons, robber barons, same old shit, I thought.

Other mansions now appeared at regular intervals. The plots of tilled land lengthened and thickened. We twiddled our thumbs as we watched the procession. The sun dropped steadily.

"Do you think we'll get there before the darkness comes?" I asked Eloi.

He shrugged. "I believe so. . . . But if not, you can get a launch and see it later. There are some cheap ones. But that would be a shame."

"A shame? . . . It would be the shits!" said Fernándo.

I looked at the sun and chewed on a fingernail. Then I stood up and stretched my arms. The sailor at the wheel in the pilot's cabin, the darkest and most muscular of the crew, saluted me. I returned his salute and smiled. A few minutes later he was relieved and, to our surprise, came to join us. "Can I sit with you guys?" he asked.

"Sit," we said.

He glanced apprehensively behind him before flopping down in the niche, keeping his head low and out of sight of the pilot's cabin. "I don't want that *filho da puta* to see me," he explained without being asked.

"Who? The captain?" I asked.

"Who else?"

I laughed. "I'm beginning to wonder if his real name is Luis—or *filho da puta?*"

The sailor regarded Fernando and I inquisitively. "Are you two going to stay in Manaus for a long time?"

"Only as long as it takes me to find passage to Belém," answered Fernando.

"Belém!" said the sailor. "That's where I come from. It is a great city! . . . And you?"

"I don't know yet. . . . A week or two. I can't stay any longer because I work in Colombia and I have to be back at my job by January 5."

"You work in Colombia?" The sailor looked startled. "I thought you were a student . . . or something like that."

"Why?"

"Because we noted your interest in learning Portuguese. . . . And you already knew some. That's unusual for us to see from a normal tourist."

"Well, I suppose I am a student of sorts. . . . Just not a conventional one."

"What kind of work do you do?"

"I work in a prison for juvenile delinquents . . . " Eloi stepped in and explained to him in rapid Portuguese more or less what my job entailed.

"But why would a, pardon the word, gringo want to work in a Colombian prison? I don't understand." The sailor stared at me.

I laughed and said, "I can't understand why anyone would want to do such a thing. . . . Maybe because of . . . " I suddenly recalled that cab driver in Leticia. "Because of the circumstances of life."

"How is that?"

I related the anecdote of the cab driver. When I finished the sailor laughed. "Now I understand you . . . . That more or less explains why I am working on this boat. This is not the kind of work I want to do."

"What do you want to do?"

"What I really want to do, well, not what I want to do, but what would be better than this . . . is to gain employment at some nice hotel in Manaus . . . or some other city. Where I can earn some decent money and not have to work so damn hard. Working on these boats can make you old in a hurry and, unless you're involved in running contraband, the pay is bad."

"So, where do you think you can get a job?" Eloi asked.

"Maybe the Hotel Amazonas in Manaus. . . . Or if I have no luck at a good hotel in Manaus—I could go back to Belém. There are many good hotels there, and you can get good tips from the tourists."

"Is there any other kind of work you can do?" I asked.

"Nothing I can make much money at. . . . I've thought of going to Venezuela. They pay common laborers much better there than here. But the trip is expensive . . . . What do unskilled poor people do in your country?"

"Well, most of them get a shit job, go to jail, or join the army."

The sailor laughed. "That sounds like here. But they must pay better in your country."

"Yeah, for unskilled work the pay is better than here. But so is the cost of living higher . . . "

"It must be tough anywhere when you are poor."

"Amen," said Eloi.

"What time will we arrive in Manaus," Fernando asked the sailor.

"Around 7:00 or 8:00 at night." He shrugged, his face impassive. "I can't say for sure."

"Then, we won't reach where the waters meet before dark?" I asked.

"I can't tell you for sure. That happens outside Manaus. . . . I think we should get there before dusk. But, who knows? If the captain . . . "

"Who knows!" I interjected, smiling. "That's all I hear on this boat. The only thing anyone knows is who knows."

"You are right." The sailor grinned. "It's better like that. . . . If we really knew what was going to happen we might all go crazy. We know better than to build up unrealistic expectations concerning things outside of our control."

"Maybe you are right . . . when you put it like that. At least you can admit you don't really know what's happening. That's better than thinking you know everything absolutely."

We talked with the sailor a while longer. Then the tall sailor signalled to us from the pilot's cabin and he left us and went back to the wheel.

We returned our attention to the shoreline. Dusk was fast approaching. As the sun hovered over the trees, shadowy spears slanted from the land and invaded the river. An ominous prelude. Ahead, but still distant, we could discern where the Amazon seemed to hook in its course and merge with the sky.

"Perhaps that is the confluence of the two rivers," said Fernando. "Now, if we can only reach it before it is blanketed with darkness . . . "

I crossed my fingers and stared at the flaming sun, silently willing it to slow its descent. The shadows on the river lengthened. The sun ignored my wishes.

There were ships and boats plying the river on all sides of us now, both coming and going. Several of them, with light loads and souped up engines, roared by us as though we were standing still. I wish I was on one of those, I thought. They'll definitely beat the darkness.

Eloi left us and returned to the tug. A few minutes later the wind picked up and whipped very hard. Drops of water flew into the air and reached us atop the lumber pile.

"We might as well go inside the boat now," Fernando said. "I want to start packing my gear. And we can see almost as well from the prow of the tug as from here."

"All right. Let's go."

We reached the hold and found almost everyone gathered by the fold-down table, talking in hushed tones. Eloi, Milene, Nazaré, La Gordita, Jorzinho, and the cook all stood in a compact group, casting anxious eyes toward the creeping shadows that were fast approaching the tug. I shook my head. They look like they're at a wake, I thought. What is this? . . . I can't believe that seeing the "Wedding of the Waters" is such a big deal for them . . . . Ah, maybe it is. I wonder how I'll feel when I see the Golden Gate Bridge again? . . . Or are they just being superstitious again?

"How is it going?" Fernando asked them.

They mumbled reponses. Fernando and I looked at each other and shook our heads in perplexion. Then we started packing our gear. I checked my money belt, which I had left unattended in the tug for most of the trip, not a single bill had been touched. I remembered Jaap's paranoia with a smile. But maybe they would have stolen from him, I thought. But I doubt it. I wonder how he's doing on the Recreio

I spied my Panama hat lying a few feet away from my bag. I picked it up, repaired a pushed in spot near the crown, emptied some Brazil nut shavings from the inside, and put it on. I know I look ridiculous with this thing on, I thought. I took it off and spun the crown on my finger as though it were a white basketball. Now, do I really want to wear this crazy topping in the streets of Manaus? . . . I already attract enough of the wrong kind of attention as it is.

I noticed Nazaré, her back to me, lolling on the bench in quiet conversation with Milene. It would definitely look much better on her. She has the right kind of head for it.

Sneaking up from behind, I jammed the hat onto her fluffy mane of hair and down over her eyes. She squealed with shock. I stepped back a pace. She ripped the hat from her head and whirled to confront me, her eyes glinting murderously.

"It is yours," I said, cutting off her explosion.

"For me?" Her mouth dropped open. "You want to give me a remembrance of this trip?"

"Yes."

"But why?"

"Because you gave me some things to remember. . . . Besides, it looks much better on you than it does on me."

She put the hat on and tilted it rakishly; it looked cute on her.

"Much better on you," I said.

"He is right," added Milene.

"All right, thank you," she said, trying to smile but managing only a smirk. She resumed her conversation with Milene. Good, I thought, now I don't have to drag that damn thing around with me.

I returned to my travel bag and idly played with the straps and zippers. The seconds stretched into minutes. I looked outside. The sun was barely peeking over the treetops. The shadowy spears had united and were coming toward the boat in a solid block, advancing like an incoming tide, threatening to engulf us in darkness. Silently I cursed. I looked again. In our favor, we were catching all of the waning light as there were no clouds in the direct path of the sun. The water near the boat glimmered with golden streaks, giving me hope. Maybe another half hour of good light, I thought.

I left my travel bag and leaned over the railing. Eloi joined me.

"See that hill over there?" he asked. I nodded. "I recognize that, it means that we are close to the confluence of the rivers."

"Then, we will arrive before dark?"

"We should. . . . Barring some freak accident."

The sun dipped a trifle more, seeming to set the treetops aflame. I tapped my fingers on the railing and strained my eyes. A speedboat shot past us . . .

Then came a shriek from the prow of the tug. Jorzinho popped into the hold, screaming incoherently. He hopped from one foot to another as though he were treading on hot coals. Then he turned and pointed with urgency to something in the distance out of our line of sight.

Fernando, Eloi, and I bounded to the prow railing as one. We leaned our torsos out over the water and craned our heads away from the glare of the dying sun, our eyes on the purplish horizon.

"Do you see anything?" asked Fernando.

"Not yet," I said.

All I could make out was a vegetation covered headland, a low plateau. It diverted the course of the river into a different channel. I scanned the horizon to the left of the headland. The water in that direction appeared much darker, but it was veiled by shadows. We steamed closer."There it is," said Eloi in a calm voice.

The panorama lay before us, a feast for our eyes. A wide blue-black river, careening straight for the muddy brown of the Amazon, colliding, making no headway, and then, caught in a vortex, funneling into a new united course, the rivers flowing side by side, their colors distinct.

"You are right," I said, addressing Eloi. "It is better to see this for yourself."

"Hein."

We were about to enter the waters of the Rio Negro, when the captain altered our course and we paralleled the flow of the two rivers so that we could observe the phenomenon at our leisure. The Amazon thrust cafe-au-lait fists into the opposing flow, the Rio Negro sent blue-black fingers of its own. Neither made much penetration into the other. I looked into the distance. The rivers maintained their separate identities for as far as the eye could see. I returned my sight to close range. Along the seams, where the waters overlapped and undercut, eddies and whirlpools formed prisms of color—one particularly fascinated me. It's not really a color, I thought. It's more of a pale transluscence. . . . It's bizarre.

I gazed spellbound at the waters. Soon we changed course and bisected the confluence of the rivers. We were sailing on black water. The color amazed me. I wondered if it were dirty. What causes this color?

I knelt on the deck, stuck my arms through the gap in the railing, and dipped my hands into the water. It felt like any other water. I cupped my hands and drew some of the liquid out of the river and looked at it in the red-orange glow of the setting sun. It looked like ordinary clear water. I tasted it. Except for a faint tang of oil, it was fine. Nothing unusual about this stuff, I thought. It's water like any other . . .

"Dinner is ready," called the cook from the hold. I stood my ground on the prow. Dinner was the last thing on my mind. Then Fernando came over and took me by the arm and almost dragged me toward the table.

"That was fantastic!" he said. "An incredible phenomenon! It was . . . " As Fernando continued to exclaim over the "Wedding of the Waters" I guarded silence, lost in my thoughts. I felt strange, unsettled, as though a squirrel were racing around in my guts looking for an escape hatch. Ideas swirled in my mind.

In this condition I sat down to dinner. The food was an unwelcome distraction. I glanced disdainfully at the pork and rice set before me and pushed it away.

"What's the matter with you?" Fernando asked me.

"Nothing. . . . I'm not hungry. You guys can have my food."

"Don't be crazy! You need to eat."

"Nah, not right now. I'll eat in Manaus."

"All right, whatever you want." Fernando split the food with Eloi. I concentrated on the thoughts surging through my mind, trying to organize them.

While Fernando and Eloi ate, darkness overtook us. As soon as Fernando finished eating, we climbed to the second deck to see the skyline of Manaus. We stood along the side of the pilot's cabin and leaned on the railing.

"See those lights that project over the water?" asked Fernando.

"Yes."

"That should be the floating market . . . said to be the largest of its kind in the world."

"Well, all I see from here are a bunch of lights. . . . Maybe we can visit it tomorrow in the day." I looked upriver. Low hills rose above the shore. Thousands of pulsing lights winked at us, beckoning us to enter the city. This is it, I thought. We've finally arrived.

"Maybe we should start saying our good-byes," I suggested.

"Good idea. Some people may rush away as soon as we dock."

Fernando and I turned and went in opposite directions. I walked around the pilot's cabin and ran smack into the captain. He looked weary. Then his expression went blank and he started to step by me.

"Wait, captain," I said. He stopped. "Thank you for getting us here safely." I held out my hand.

He grunted something under his breath before he shook my hand. His grip was limp, like overcooked pasta. I let go quickly. He entered the pilot's cabin. Well, fuck you, I thought, chuckling aloud.

I turned to go down the ladder, but before I reached it, Jorzinho pranced around the pilot's cabin and called my name. He came up to me with a big grin on his face. I smiled. I stuck out my right hand and he shook it with his left hand. I stuck out my left hand and he shook it with his right hand. He laughed.

"Make me fly one more time," he said.

"*Tudo bem*. But only one time."

I grabbed him around the rib cage and tossed him into the air. He laughed hysterically. I caught him on the way down and held him aloft. "One more time. One more time."

"No more.... I can't right now." I set him gently on his feet.

"Later?"

"Who knows?"

He laughed and scampered off. Now him I may miss, I thought. Maybe.

I descended the ladder. Milene, Nazaré, and La Gordita were standing nearby, leaning against the railing. They were staring at the city lights and making plans. I walked up to them. "Excuse me.... I just want to say good-bye."

Milene gave me a hug and a kiss on both cheeks. "This is Brazilian style," she said. "Your education is complete. Now you need a more advanced teacher."

"Maybe in Manaus," I said, looking at Nazaré. Her face was cool and indifferent.

Milene laughed. "It's possible. Not many gringos who spend much time in Manaus can escape single."

"I'll be certain not to spend too much time here, then. Good-bye."

Nazaré gave me a hug and the two kisses. La Gordita followed suit.

"Until later," I said.

I walked around the hold and shook hands with every sailor I saw. Then I went to the galley to say good-bye to the cook who was washing dishes.

I held my hands up. "I'm clean, man. No knives, please."

He gave me that cackle. Then he gave my hand a firm shake. "Good luck," he said. "Just watch yourself and you'll be fine."

"Yeah, *tudo bem*."

I found Eloi in his hammock. "What do you say, man?" I asked. "Fernando tells me that you are going to catch a cab with us downtown."

"I didn't tell him that. It's possible   But I think it would be better if I sleep on the boat tonight. It's a long way to my neighborhood from the dock. . . . A taxi would cost too much money. Tomorrow I can get a bus cheap."

"Well, all right. We'll check with you before we leave."

"Fine. But I'm pretty sure I'll stay here tonight."

I left Eloi and climbed the ladder to the second deck for the last time. I found Fernando and Milene standing by the railing on the side of the pilot's cabin. I walked over and stood beside them. Soon Milene excused herself and went to join Nazaré.

Without a word Fernando and I walked around to the front of the pilot's cabin. The Magalhães swung around and headed for the dock. We faced the city and gazed into the darkness that made the river virtually invisible—but magnified the brilliant crown of lights of Manaus.

"Mission accomplished," murmured Fernando.

"Yes, for now."

"You know, you never gave me your impression of the "Wedding of the Waters."

"It was pretty. . . . I . . . I don't know. It was pretty."

Fernando chuckled. "This is the first time on this trip that I've found you at a loss for words."

"Sometimes it takes me a while to find the correct ones. . . . So, if I don't have them, better to say nothing."

"Do you have anything like that in your country?"

"Nothing exactly like that . . . . The only thing I could compare it to would be this place in California called 'Big Sur'."

"What's that?"

"It's a piece along the coast where the ocean meets wooded rocky cliffs."

"What's special about that?"

"It's beautiful."

"Ah, all right." Fernando fell silent.

The lights grew larger and brighter. A warm feeling suffused me, as though the lights had penetrated by body. I glowed with satisfaction, listening to the water rush below us. Certainly there were nagging doubts in the back of my mind concerning what lay ahead of us in Manaus, but for the moment, I was content to savor, along with my good companion of the voyage, a remembrance of shared trials and adventures. . . . It suddenly struck me that the entire voyage had been a

"Wedding of the Waters." Though every person on the boat had been separated by some shade of language, culture, nationality, color, or background, we had all been moving on a parallel course and, in the end, had achieved a certain unity—a lapping and merging of the waters. All of us were different in some aspect of our make-up, yet, like water, so similar as to make the differences minor.

I recalled the sight of the Rio Negro and the Amazon achieving a harmonious wedding after their initial violent encounter. I smiled. Then another memory entered my mind and my smile faded. It was "Big Sur" on a stormy day. After a time the result is inevitable—the rocks crash into the sea and are buried by the raging surf . . . . Which is it to be for us, I thought. Who knows?

END

EPILOGUE

Though my memory of this time is blurred, I know I spent a tumultuous two weeks in Manaus. The illness that overtook me on the boat trip came back to plague me for the next six weeks. It was an insidious sickness. For a day or two I would feel relatively well, then for a couple of days fever would engulf me and my body would turn to jelly. On my bad days I could do little more than crawl out of bed to take care of my necessities; on my good days I would go out and roam the streets.

Manaus proved a cosmopolitan city with an active bar and café life. I met students from all parts of Brazil and travelers from assorted European and Latin American countries. I made friends and packed as many activities into each day as time and my health would permit. Twice I went to night clubs with friends I met at a café near the Teatro Amazonas; on both occasions brawls broke out and the police were called in to restore order. One of the rows was caused by a wild beautiful woman who became angry with her boy friend and hurled a shot glass at his head. He ducked just in time. Though I was seated close by, I managed to stay clear of the disturbance — fortunately. Hot humid weather and hot tempers made for a number of violent incidents.

As for my companions on the Magalhães... Fernando and I shared a cheap hotel room near downtown while he looked for his Peruvian friends. It took him several days to find them. In the meantime, we took an afternoon to look for Eloi at the address he had given us, in a poor outlying neighborhood, but were unable to locate him. Fernando went several times to the hotel where Jaap and Betti were supposed to lodge but they never arrived there.... I ran into Milene and Nazaré in the financial district one sunny morning. They were well dressed and seemed in a hurry. We exchanged pleasantries and quickly went our separate ways. Business as usual. *Tudo bem.*

When Fernando located his friends they gave him a free place to stay and helped him find a job. As he packed his bag in the hotel room, I bought his hammock from him for a souvenir of the trip. We saw each other one more time on Christmas night and that was the last I heard of him for a long while.

After Christmas I spent another week in Manaus. By this time my money was running dangerously low; it was time to face an unpleasant reality. I still had enough money to return to Colombia by boat—but not enough to return by plane. I was worried. I had neither the time nor the physical stamina to make the return trip up the Amazon against the current. I needed help.

I went to the U.S. Consul agent in Manaus and told him my story. Fortunately he was a kind and sympathetic man who took his job seriously. We called the Peace Corps office in Bogotá and arranged to have the air fare taken from my readjustment allowance. The Consul agent fronted me the money for the ticket and was reimbursed later.

Two days later, after enjoying the gracious hospitality of the consul and his wife, for which I am forever grateful, I returned by plane to Bogotá. A few days after that I returned to work in Piedecuesta to finish my final year of Peace Corps service.

Six months later I received a postcard from Paris, France:

How are you? Mission accomplished . . . . Fernando!